THE LONDON
DMS

THE LONDON
DMS

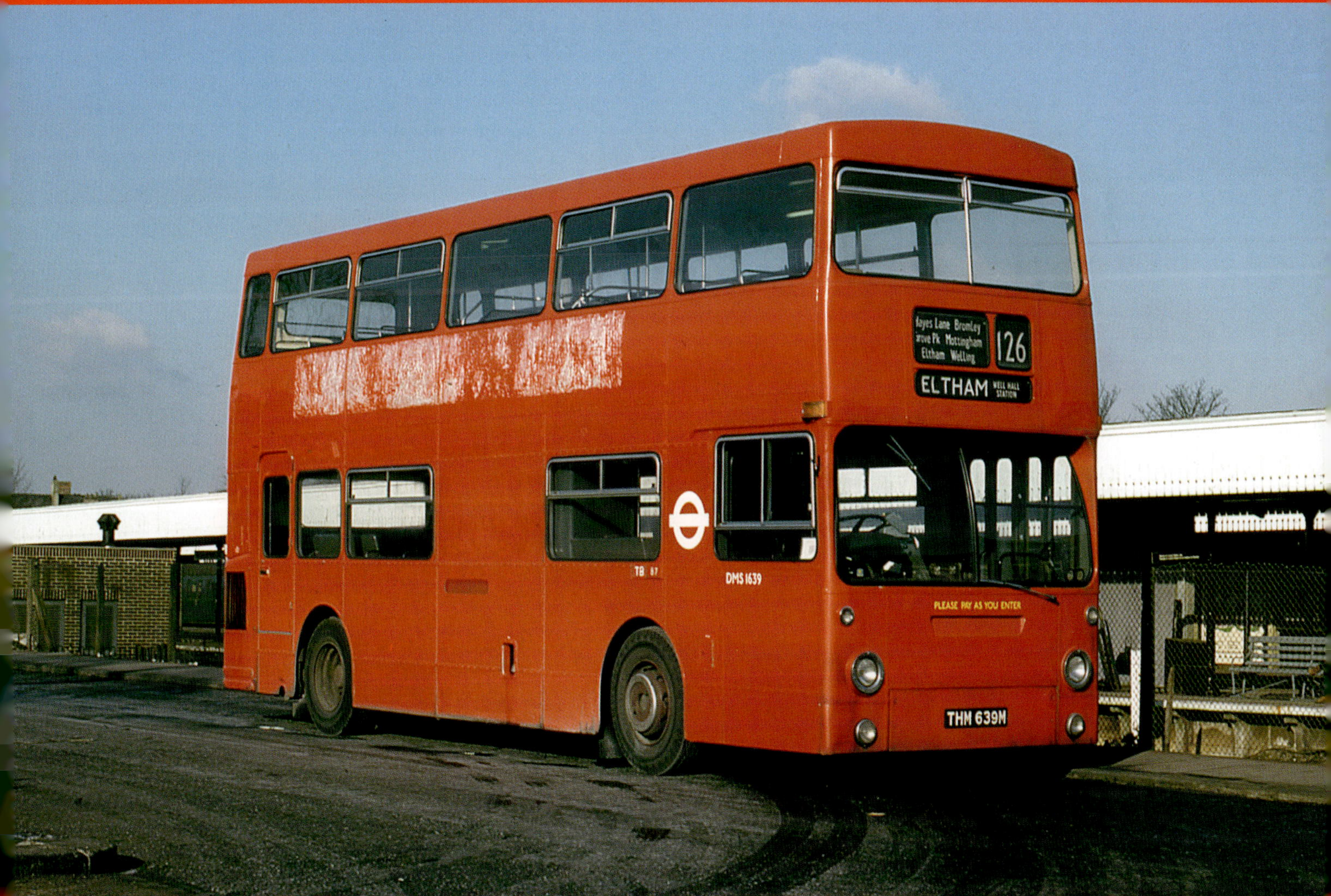

MATTHEW WHARMBY

Cover: **The DMS family of Daimler (or Leyland) Fleetline racked up 22 years in London service. If the goal of this book is the rehabilitation of one of London's least popular bus types, then the choice of a B20, the most unhappy variant of all, as cover picture may serve as a fitting example. Merton was one of two garages to complete two decades with DMSs, and on 22 April 1985 outside Brixton garage (the other such garage qualifying for this achievement) is MCW-bodied DMS 2327 (THX 327S), new in January 1978 and lasting in London until May 1991.** *R. C. Riley*

Rear cover, top: **Thornton Heath took its first DMSs on 4 December 1971 for the 64 and was still running them on that route up till 21 July 1990. To address criticism of the initial all-red livery, a white band was added on the 1971 order, exemplified by DMS 213 (JGF 213K) at West Croydon on 18 February 1975. This bus lasted only the seven years given it by its initial Certificate of Fitness (CoF), and was sold in 1979.** *R. C. Riley*

Rear cover, middle: **The remit of the DMS was to extinguish conductors, but in fact a fifth of the fleet was specified for dedicated crew operation as the DM class, exemplified by Holloway's DM 1086 (GHV 86N, right). Further new DMSs replaced the equally troubled Merlin and Swift single-deckers, as Camberwell's DMS 2110 (KJD 110P, left) has done when caught at Waterloo on 12 August 1977. This too is in an attractive variation on all-red, but one that was also not to last. Much later, it donned a new livery altogether when it spent two years as part of the notorious Bexleybus.** *R. C. Riley*

Rear cover, bottom: **As London Transport was forced to accept competition from 1985, the fledgling new operators invariably bought second-hand. Ensign parlayed its expertise in selling on the DMSs it acquired from LT into becoming a successful operator in its own right. Seen at Romford on 16 June 1990 is 215 (GHV 118N), formerly DM 1118, which had been sold in 1983 after the standard seven years.** *Malc McDonald*

Title page: **The vast majority of the 'middle order' of DMSs, i.e. those not overhauled, would see out a single seven-year CoF), usually with an intermediate repaint. Metro-Cammell-bodied DMS 1639 (THM 639M) entered service at Barking in May 1974 but in August 1975 was transferred to Bromley; while there, it was repainted in October 1977 and it is at a sunny Beckenham Junction on 11 February 1978 that we see the full benefit of the new coat of paint. Its final garage was Leyton and it was withdrawn from there in January 1981.** *R. C. Riley*

DEDICATION

To Claire

with all my love.

ISBN 978 1 78383 173 9

Published in 2016 by Pen & Sword Transport
an imprint of
Pen & Sword Books Ltd
47 Church Street, Barnsley, South Yorkshire, S70 2AS

Copyright © Matthew Wharmby, 2016

The right of Matthew Wharmby to be identified as the Author of this Work has been asserted by him in accordance with the Copyright, Designs and Patents Act 1988. A CIP catalogue record for this book is available from the British Library

All rights reserved. No part of this book may be reproduced or transmitted in any form or by any means, electronic or mechanical including photocopying, recording or by any information storage and retrieval system, without permission from the Publisher in writing.

Typeset by Matthew Wharmby
Printed and bound by Replika Press Pvt. Ltd

Pen & Sword Books Ltd incorporates the imprints of Pen & Sword Archaeology, Atlas, Aviation, Battleground, Discovery, Family History, History, Maritime, Military, Naval, Politics, Railways, Select, Transport, True Crime, and Fiction, Frontline Books, Leo Cooper, Praetorian Press, Seaforth Publishing and Wharncliffe.

For a complete list of Pen & Sword titles please contact
PEN & SWORD BOOKS LIMITED
47 Church Street, Barnsley, South Yorkshire, S70 2AS, England
E-mail: enquiries@pen-and-sword.co.uk
Website: www.pen-and-sword.co.uk

CONTENTS

Foreword 6
1. XA versus XF 8
2. Enter the Londoner 16
3. Concerns and Crews 52
4. The B20 74
5. Withdrawals and Overhauls 98
6. B20 Reprieve 138
7. Declining Years 182
8. Afterwards 238
   Conclusion 248

Appendices
1a: London Transport Fleetnumbers, Registrations, Engines, Chassis and Body Codes 250
1b: Park Royal Body Numbers 251
1c: Bexleybus Fleetnumbers, 1988-1990 251
2: Re-Registrations in London Transport Ownership 251
3a: Date of Delivery 252
3b: Date of Entry into Service and Initial Allocation 255
4: Sales by London Transport 258
5a: London Transport Garages and Routes Allocated DMSs 262
5b: Independent Companies' Garages Allocated DMSs, 1985-1996 264
6: Independent Companies' DMS Acquisitions for LRT Tendered Routes, 1986-1988 265
7a: DMSs Overhauled by Aldenham Works, 1977-1982 268
7b: Outshopping Dates of DMSs Overhauled by Aldenham Works 269
7c: DMSs Overhauled by Contractors, 1985 271
7d: DMSs Recertified at Aldenham, 1979 271
7e: DMSs Recertified at Aldenham, April 1980-February 1981 271
7f: DMSs Recertified at Wandle garages, May 1985-February 1986 271
8: DM to D conversions and reversions 271
9: B20 DMSs converted to Iveco engines, 1987-1989 271

Bibliography 272

FOREWORD

I depended on DMSs to get me from home in Putney to school in Wimbledon and back – journeys that usually ended up being far more interesting than the seven hours of school that separated them. Although the Daimler Fleetline was roundly vilified both by enthusiasts and London Transport as being difficult to love and impossible to tame, I can testify that in over 800 journeys made between 1983 and 1992, none ever broke down on me – and this was the particularly troublesome B20 variant!

Politics runs through the story of the DMS from beginning to end; forced by changing laws to take a vehicle it didn't want and couldn't handle, London Transport later aroused criticism by disposing of the type prematurely, only for the sold buses to be used by its nascent competitors to steadily undercut it out of existence. Unloved by passengers and enthusiasts in London, the DMS could find valediction only in its success everywhere but the city it was intended to serve; finally, forty-five years after entry into service, this is that story.

In contrast to popular perception that the buses all looked the same and indeed were intended to be as standard as possible, there is surprising variety within such a large fleet and this book attempts to cover as many aspects as it can, but it is inevitable that the gruelling process of selection has obliged the omission of some combinations of routes, liveries, garages and locations; nonetheless, the pictures have been chosen as examples that best combine several needs in one. The opportunity has also been taken to immortalise in colour for the first time popular views known until now only in black and white when production costs for colour publications were prohibitive. To this end, my thanks are due to my regular band of photographic contributors, who endured my requests for ludicrously obscure workings or ephemera but came up with exactly what I wanted; to my editor and proofreaders for consolidating it into a form which will hopefully become the definitive text on the subject, and to the publishers for taking a chance on it to begin with.

Matthew Wharmby
Walton-on-Thames, Surrey
September 2016

A Note on the Text:

Until the Pay and Productivity agreement struck with the union in June 1980, DMSs were specified for OMO only and DMs for crew operation; after this date most DMs were fitted with powered baseplates for Almex E ticket machines and thus became capable of both crew and OMO. London Transport progressively reclassified these vehicles D, and correspondingly restored their DM classification upon withdrawal. The 18 was the last officially DM-operated route, but subsequent OMO conversions phased in Fleetlines in the months prior, thus including both DMSs and Ds; this account shall use the collective term 'DMSs'.

Additionally, OMO (one-man operation) is referred to until about 1984, when the preferred acronym became OPO (one-*person* operation), reflecting the increasingly female proportion of London's bus-operating workforce.

Above: As all bus books are essentially a celebration by the author of the favourite types of his childhood, so does the B20 DMS take that role in this one's. Never thought particularly highly of, the humble B20 nonetheless achieved 14-15 years in front-line service and not one ever broke down for the author. The great migration of the 400-strong B20 subclassification to Wandle District was carried out in 1982-83 and DMS 2339 (THX 339S) was one of the affected buses, coming out of overhaul to Sutton in September 1982. In August 1984 it is seen setting off from Putney Bridge Station on the 93, the author's route to and from school between 1983 and 1984. *Haydn Davies*

Left: History hasn't been as sympathetic to the DMSs as this account endeavours to be; in fact, scenes like this at the former AEC works on 23 December 1983, showing large numbers of withdrawn DMSs (and MDs) underscored the waste for which the old London Transport was known during the 1970s; a consequence of (according to where your sympathies lie), the failure of the Fleetline and its associated one-man operation, or the body's refusal to adopt modern off-the-peg buses rather than its expensive bespoke preferences of years past. However, the coda of LT's withering away altogether reprieved the type; DMS 2109 (KJD 109P) closest to camera was returned to service in 1988 as a Bexleybus. *John Laker*

CHAPTER ONE

XA VERSUS XF

1965-1970

After a shortlived postwar peak, custom for public transport in London and nationwide began a steady decline. Increasing living standards prompted the purchase of cars in growing numbers, not to mention changing leisure patterns which saw people tend to stay at home in the evenings to watch television rather than go out to the pictures or other forms of evening entertainment hitherto reached by buses. While custom fell and car traffic grew sufficient to impede buses' reliability, staff and management in both London Transport and provincial concerns continued to wrestle over what remuneration would be paid as inflation endured. Competing work at better wages and at more sociable hours lured away busworkers to produce nagging staff shortages, and gradually it became clear that one way of restoring the cost of operations to an even keel with revenue was not necessarily to drive up crew wages to compete with such work, but to delete the role of the conductor and alter the physical layout of the buses to permit one-man operation (OMO), which in other Western countries was the norm by now.

London Transport, of course, had its own way of doing things, and although its purpose-designed vehicles remained at the pinnacle of quality and longevity, the organisation was slow to grasp the fact that its practices weren't doing it any favours either in terms of revenue or reliability. Not permitted to make a loss, but also prohibited from setting its own fares, LT was stifled in either direction and reliability was drifting downwards, because traffic conditions in the capital had become helpless almost as soon as the motor car replaced horse-drawn transport at the turn of the century. As more and more people wanted cars and gained the financial standing to purchase them, that made one fewer person who would be using the bus.

The Daimler Fleetline story predates that of the London DMS by over a decade, when the model was introduced in 1960 as a competitor to Leyland's innovative Atlantean, which had addressed the likelihood in the future of one-man operation (OMO) by moving the engine to the rear and the entrance to the front. It was as highly thought of as the Atlantean and became just as popular.

In June 1964 the London Transport Board amended its 1965 order to include fifty Leyland Atlanteans (XA 1-50) and 8 Daimler Fleetlines (XF 1-8), all with single-door Park Royal bodywork to H41/31F capacity. The XAs were delivered between 14 June 1965 and December and the XFs arrived in August, the latter class all painted in Lincoln green and powered by

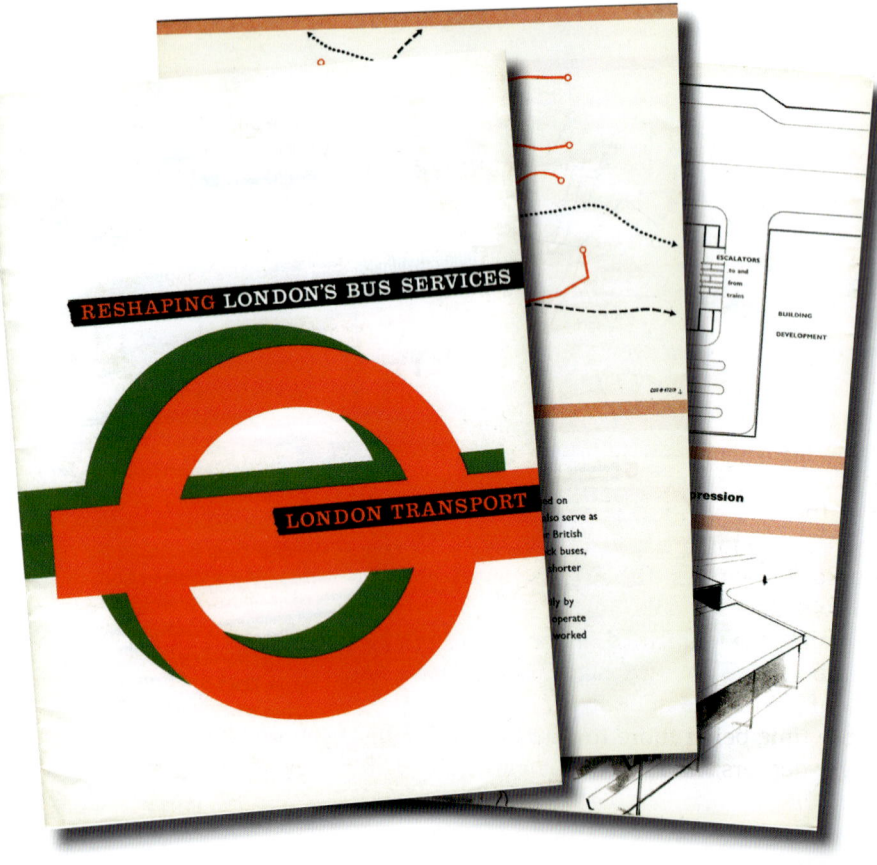

Below: **The Reshaping Plan of 1966 was an 18-page publication laying out London Transport's plans to sectionalise crew-operated trunk routes and turn their outer portions over to flat-fare standee operation. The career of the DMS actually came about owing to the plan's failure and the need subsequently to maintain the capacity afforded by double-deckers, helped by the legalisation of one-man operation (OMO) on such buses.** Author's collection

Above: **The Fleetline was not a new design by any means, and the Atlantean with which it competed for a spell with London Transport was even older, only ingrained tradition and the desire to maintain full employment having kept the rear-engined double-decker from becoming predominant in British bus operations. The eight XF-class Fleetlines were found superior after trials alongside the fifty Atlanteans of XA class, and LT plunged into vast orders, hoping to 'reshape' its operations wholesale. Wearing the Country Area's green, XF 3 (CUV 53C) is seen at Tottenham in May 1968. Ironically, the subsequent hived-off London Country company was destined to prefer Atlanteans and take them in large numbers. XF 3 is preserved, alongside XF 1.**
Tony Wilson collection

the first Gardner engines since the mid-war austerity B and G classes. The XFs' debut on 15 September on Country Area route 424 from East Grinstead had to be as crew buses due to the lack of permission given for LT's intention to close off the upper deck and effectively operate the buses as OMO single-deckers. Each of XA and XF classes, along with RMLs for comparison, spent short periods at one or all of Highgate (route 271), Chalk Farm (24), Stamford Hill (67) and Tottenham (76) over 1966 as well as the 424, which offered a very different set of conditions from the Central Area routes.

In September 1966 the groundbreaking Reshaping Plan was published. Its tenets included the universal adoption of OMO by 1978, following the broadly successful conversion of a handful of RF-operated services on the fringes of the red-bus area. To make this possible would require a new generation of rear-engined, front-entrance buses (at the moment single-deckers by virtue of double-deck OMO not yet being legal) similar to the AEC Merlins that had inaugurated new short-hop commuter route 500 from 18 April 1966. These would be fitted with automatic machinery to take the workload of fare collection away from the driver, who would have enough to do once shorn of his conductor (but be placated with an increase in his wages). Longer trunk routes would be pruned, their outer ends to be taken over by flat-fare services anchored predominantly on railway stations or purpose-built bus interchanges.

Fuel consumption figures published later in 1966 did throw up a winner of sorts, the XF, whose 10.8mpg in Country Area conditions and 7.4mpg in town comfortably beat the XA (10.3mpg and 6.6mpg) while falling short of the overall standards of the RML (9.8mpg and 7.8mpg). Even so, a third competitor was about to enter service, AEC's and London Transport's own FRM 1. This rear-engined Routemaster was to prove successful and well-liked by the staff and mechanics who got to know it, and it outperformed the XA and XF alike, but its prospects following Leyland's takeover of AEC would be tenuous; the new parent wished to consolidate its stable and was indifferent to pursuing a one-off for London in the manner of the past. The FRM had come too late for manufacturer and operator alike, LT's thinking at the time being more towards crush-loading single-deckers, and its debut and indeed, its

XA VERSUS XF

Below: **Single-deck crush-loading was an increasing aspect of the urban British bus scene, given that one-man-operation was not legal on double-deckers. Several municipalities, still losing money, chose the compromise of single-deck OMO. Nonetheless, it came as a rude shock to Londoners, who had become used to their expensive but prestigious model of at-seat service conferred by crew operation and failed utterly to cope with the automatic machinery that was trying to replace it. It helped not a bit that the Merlins and Swifts specified for this work and delivered in large numbers proved unreliable in the extreme. Here turning at Alexandra Park on 9 September 1968 is Merlin MBS 68 (VLW 68G), whose otherwise attractive Metro-Cammell bodywork offered an indicator of how future double-deck bus design could proceed; as it happened, DMSs were to sweep away Wood Green's Merlins en bloc after only five years.** *Paul A. Bateson*

whole service career, was more subdued than the attractive and reliable design deserved. Conjecture as to how much LT regretted that turn of events continues to bedevil historians' minds – certainly this one's; it definitely signed AEC's death warrant. Yet who's to say in hindsight whether LT might not have wasted the fleet of 2,492 FRMs it once envisaged in the same manner as it did the DMSs?

Government intervention in the country's bus operations was by the second half of the 1960s at greater levels than at any time in history, spurred by the Labour administration's transport secretary, Barbara Castle, and her far-reaching ideas on the complete reformation of Britain's bus services. In order to fix problems in recruitment stemming from full employment, the Ministry of Transport proposed to speed up OMO with New Bus Grant, by which the government paid 25% of the cost of new buses conforming to a rigidly-defined standard OMO specification applicable from 1 September 1968. One critical piece of legislation at the tail end of 1966 was the document that legalised double-deck OMO; until then the half-measure of sealing off the XFs' upper decks when operating without a conductor was permitted in time for such a mode to begin on the 424 on 2 October 1966. Not overly successful, it lasted for only six months. To keep the flow of deliveries going, LT ordered large numbers of AEC Merlin single-deckers for delivery in 1968 and 1969; while the spirit of Reshaping principally envisaged single-deckers, the major trunk routes (albeit with the intention to be shortened) would still need to be treated using double-deckers to replace the still-enormous stocks of RTs and their Routemaster successors, and all in less than ten years!

Thus it was to be the Fleetline that would carry forward double-deck OMO, its superior fuel economy by comparison with the Atlantean helped in engineering eyes by the fact that the engine and gearbox were separately mounted, easing cooling, but LT could not start placing orders until protracted wrangles with the unions were undertaken involving compensation. While the delicate negotiations were progressing, an order was proposed for delivery in 1969, included in which would be 46 OMO-specified double-deckers (17 for the Central Area and 29 for the Country Area). Having finally secured a deal with the union on 15 July 1968 which would enable the large number of Merlins stacking up to enter service with compensatory pay worked out, the Board noted the likelihood that deliveries would not be able to be fulfilled in 1969, and reduced the order, the double-deck component shrinking in turn to seventeen. In view of the performance of the XF over the XA, this was firmed up as 17 Fleetlines with Park Royal bodywork. The need

THE LONDON DMS

to place orders for 1970 forced LT to increase this number by 100 in March 1969, and by another 250 (for 1971 delivery) before the end of the year, despite hopes of evaluating a small number first before taking the plunge with volume orders. In a move designed as much to prepare for decimalisation (to be implemented on 15 February 1971) as it was due to the unreliability of the Setright equipment, all existing flat-fare routes were altered on 13 December 1970 and 16 January 1971 to farebox operation, by which boarders dropped the exact fare into a chute supervised by the driver. No Almex E ticket machines were carried in this mode.

The design of the new Daimler Fleetlines was to be to London in terms of fashion as the angular yet attractive Mancunian was to Selnec PTE in Greater Manchester. Between the operation of the XAs and the XFs and the placing of the order for their successors, policies were defined over what manner of operation would be standard; after a handful of experiments using a mock-up which determined the best position on the bus for automatic fare-collection (AFC) machinery, this was settled on as front entrance, with boarders paying either the driver (who was equipped with a powered Almex E ticket machine mounted at an angle on the cab door edge) or the AFC machine over the nearside wheelarch opposite him. To gently herd passengers towards the machinery, the entrance doors opened against a centrally-placed pillar, discouraging anyone from changing their minds once on the first step. Exit would be by centre doors (which, however, folded to the outside without the central pillar), opposite which was a forward-ascending spiral staircase carried in the third bay of this six-section bus. The blue-green (Straub) moquette introduced on three late-model RMLs and subsequently spread to Swifts and London Underground Victoria Line stock, would be standard, even though its combination with stamped metal panels inside made for a slightly more cold-feeling ambience than hitherto.

The first 17 Fleetlines were to be delivered in 1969, but the likelihood of late deliveries due to the run on bus manufacturers following the introduction of New Bus Grant prolonged beyond possibility both this and the delivery of the next orders for 100 and 250. The Fleetline was a popular choice for provincial operators as it was, so LT did not have the luxury any more of dictating the delivery times of its own preferred chassis whilst not having to worry whether other organisations were in the queue for them. Thus it was not until April 1970 that DMS 1's chassis was completed at Coventry and driven to Park Royal for bodying. The first complete DMSs finally started to arrive in September 1970 in the form of DMSs 1 and 2, which were shown off at the International Commercial Motor Transport Exhibition at Earl's Court between 18-26 September (DMS 1 on Park Royal's stand and DMS 2 on Daimler's). London Transport used the show to undertake a colossal gamble by placing a further order for another 1,600 of the type for delivery in 1972-74, it being envisaged that 600 new buses a year would be needed to fulfil the Reshaping Plan's goal of 100% OMO by 1978. There were now 1,967 DMSs on order without a single vehicle in service and without any evaluation

Below: **The 1970 iteration of the Commercial Motor Show was held between 18-26 September and featured DMSs 1 and 2, on the stands of Park Royal Vehicles and Daimler respectively. Each vehicle has a British Leyland roundel on the front, tellingly, underscoring Leyland's control of Daimler, and thereby the vast majority of British double-deck bus manufacturing. The histories of these first two DMSs would be particularly divergent; DMS 1 would complete eleven years in service including an overhaul, and as doyen of the class, go on to official preservation which continues today. DMS 2 (EGP 2J), identical in every respect, would be one of the first withdrawn, departing for scrap in February 1979.** *C. Carter / Online Transport Archive*

XA VERSUS XF

Above: If only the FRM hadn't fallen foul of Leyland's megalomania, is the accepted wistful line from enthusiasts who shook their heads at the problems the DMS family would suffer ten years after it came out. But who's to say that London Transport wouldn't have mistreated production FRMs in the same way? In any case the sole front-engined Routemaster, FRM 1 (KGY 4D) became a legend and one of the great what-ifs. It is seen at Roundshaw after it was sent in 1969 to Croydon's 233, sleepy but significant in its own way for introducing double-deck OMO. *David Wilkinson collection*

Right: The décor of the DMS took a new direction, as befitting an entirely new London Transport generation. This time the colour theme was blue, but unlike the cosy interiors of the RT and Routemaster families, ended up feeling rather cold, especially when teamed with stamped metal side surfaces. DMS 1 (EGP 1J), in official LT museum preservation since 1983, demonstrates when displayed at Walworth garage's open day on 19 July 2014. Although the garage is now part of Abellio, it fits in perfectly with the narrative as DMS 1 served from there in London Transport days. *Author*

having been undertaken whatsoever. The only example of double-deck OMO at all in the fleet was that of the 233 at Croydon, converted on 22 November 1969 with just the one bus, single-doored conventional-OMO Atlantean XA 22, followed a little later by FRM 1.

Attempting to continue the process that had given the world its most recognisable bus, the Routemaster, London Transport declined to refer to the Fleetlines by their proper Daimler title, for fear of confusion with its own upcoming Fleet Line then under construction. Instead a small ceremony was held on 31 December 1970 at Victoria garage starring DMS 38, which was emblazoned with posters introducing 'The Londoner Bus' to the press and public alike; Sir Richard Way, Chairman of LTE, broke a bottle of champagne across it. The Londoner name did not catch on, the Underground line in progress was eventually dubbed the Jubilee Line to tie in with a later occasion and the vehicles themselves soon became known as just DMSs. As for the code itself, the same level of confusion has lingered as over the RT family's coding thirty years earlier. Standing for either **D**aimler **M**ono-**S**tandee, **D**aimler **M**ulti-**S**tandee or even **D**ouble-Deck **M**erlin **S**tandee (in a nod to SMSs!), perhaps the only thing one can be certain on is that the code signified Daimlers that were configured for standee operation. As the final S letter was omitted for conventional-OMO Merlins and Swifts, it made sense some years later to adopt DM for crew-operated Fleetlines, though at this stage that was about the last thing officialdom would have envisaged for the class that was intended to sweep London to full OMO within eight years under the tenets of the Reshaping Plan.

Aesthetically, the DMSs would prove a shock to aficionados of the curvaceous RT and RM families; basically an upright rectangular box with sharp edges, the look of the DMS was not helped by the failure to relieve its all-red livery in any way. The blind boxes were identical to those on the RM save for the number panel being switched back to the nearside; provision

for side and rear blinds was starker, with just a route number able to be carried on the side (to RT/RM canopy-size) and a KK-sized route number box at the rear. Either side of the rather unbecoming flat front, with its centrally-positioned, widely-spaced headlights, were placed symbolic 'coin-in-the-slot' logos as on Merlins and Swifts, plus a black-on-yellow 'PAY AS YOU ENTER/exact fare please' notice reinforced by an illuminated 'NO ENTRY' light next to the rear doors. The dual-door configuration precluded the application of a full-width gold LONDON TRANSPORT logo, even in the non-underlined style then coming into vogue, so a new outline bullseye in white (as had been carried experimentally by XA 10 since late 1969) was placed on the panel just behind the exit doors; on the offside it took up position on the staircase panel. The generally anonymous look was perpetuated by there being no logo on the front other than on DMSs 1 and 2, which wore one when on display at the Commercial Motor Show. Tellingly, that on DMS 2 was a British Leyland roundel rather than the traditional Daimler scroll, worn alone by DMS 1. If either managed to retain them into service, they didn't last long and no identification on the front was ever carried thereafter. At the rear, to counter the likelihood that car drivers following immediately behind would not be able to see the simple red/orange light clusters and single offside-carried reversing lamp, an

Above left: **DMS driver's cab.** *TfL from the London Transport Museum collection*

Above: **AFC cabinet with turnstile.** *TfL from the London Transport Museum collection*

Far left: **The driver's periscope and mirror, enabling him to see the upper deck.** *TfL from the London Transport Museum collection*

Left: **The rear doorway on the DMS lined up neatly with the foot of the central staircase, underneath which was a recess for folded pushchairs and umbrellas.** *TfL from the London Transport Museum collection*

Above: **Upper deck, looking to the front. Capacity upstairs was 44, four more than the comparable RML.** *TfL from the London Transport Museum collection*

Above right: **Upper deck, looking to the rear. The inward-facing single seat made the most of the space.** *TfL from the London Transport Museum collection*

Below: **Lower deck, looking towards the front.** *TfL from the London Transport Museum collection*

Below right: **Lower deck, looking towards the rear.** *TfL from the London Transport Museum collection*

illuminated 'REVERSING' light was installed under the rear lower-deck window closer to eyesight level.

For the driver there was a fully-automatic gearbox and a raised driving position (countering criticism of the low position on the earliest Merlins) plus a periscope and a public address system (both external, the loudspeakers located in the leftmost corners of the windows either side of the doors, and internal) if he chose to use it, which proved to be rare; capacity was H44/24D plus 21 standees downstairs. Illuminated throughout by fluorescent strip lighting, the surprisingly spacious saloon offered the passenger that chose to go upstairs four rows of seats ahead of the staircase, while one quirky feature for each deck was a single inward-facing seat directly behind the staircase upstairs and a similar one (albeit with its own handrail) shoehorned in behind the AFC cabinet. The powerplant chosen was Gardner's 6LXB 10.45-litre engine displacing 170bhp at 1850rpm – more powerful than anything London Transport had used in the past – and it was driven by fully automatic transmission with manual override and power-

assisted steering. Air brakes and leaf springs made their return with the DMS, together with body-on-chassis construction. Significant deviations from the standard were London Transport's own design of cab, incorporating the characteristic minimalist instrumentation binnacle, looking out through a barrel-shaped windscreen adapted from that used on the Merlin and Swift. There was a clear family resemblance between those single-deckers and the DMS.

Overall dimensions of the DMS were 14ft 6in tall, 8ft 2½in wide and 30ft 10in long, with an unladen weight of 9t 15cwt. LT's codes for the DMS began at 1D1, the first number denoting body and the second chassis; a myriad of subsequent classifications would ensue, which are captured in Appendix 1. Body codes, specified with the full expectation that bodies would be separated upon overhaul in the conventional manner, were displayed in the cab and started at D1. Unit cost for each DMS was a whopping £13,000, but a quarter of this high price was, of course, paid by the Government under New Bus Grant.

As legislation advanced with the highest-minded of intentions regarding safety, no innovations were more bold than those designed seemingly to protect the passengers from themselves. The door interlocking system was designed that the driver could not put the bus in gear until the doors were fully closed, lest careless passengers tumble out, and only after that could neutral be disengaged. The effect on a bus of having to wait till this process was complete every three or four minutes the bus took to get between stops was never imagined, nor were the further precious seconds that were added to timetable maintenance when the comparable RT or RM would load up in a trice and be on its way, the passengers expected to have taken the responsibility of getting themselves sat down before preparing their fares for the arrival of the conductor.

Having been criticised over the past decade for ordering the effectively obsolete bespoke Routemaster, LT was now bowing to that opinion by taking an ostensibly standard product, gritting its teeth and hoping for the best. Hobbled by not being able to design its own vehicles and thus having to press reluctant manufacturers to include its own features, LT was at the same time sparring interminably with the union and the workforce as to what extent they needed to be reimbursed for learning how to use them. Still, specifying modification after modification, while par for the course in any bus-operating organisation, took the Fleetline considerably away from its manufacturer's standard product, which was adequate to start with, and in terms of mechanical simplicity and ease of repair, considered excellent. Many of these modifications were to the electrical systems, particularly the grafting on of LT's proprietary ignition system activated by a start button, while the batteries could not be isolated mechanically as on the standard product.

By compiling its own maintenance manuals for the class and allegedly denying garages access to those issued by the manufacturer, LT was in effect treating the DMS as if it was its own product, ignoring those who designed it, and thus got bitten on the behind when failures became commonplace. Hindsight continues to wonder whether the unaltered version of the Fleetline, which had been successful both mechanically and in sales terms for over a decade and would continue to be so for another one in a variety of operating environments, some as extreme or even more so than London, might have served better.

Modern detractors, especially those of provincial background and justifiably envious of the finance lavished, then and now, on the amenities of the capital, like to punish London Transport for cultivating a 'not invented here' attitude that rendered them seemingly unwilling, and certainly unable, to come to terms with the demands of modern vehicles, but it's pointless assigning blame in retrospect. After all, if you worked for LT as a conductor in those days, would you be in support of a system that threatened to make you redundant? Whatever one's opinion of London Transport, it seemed that either way, it couldn't win, and the passengers, as always, were the first ones to suffer. And how they were about to suffer...

Above: **It wasn't as if London Transport wasn't working as hard as it could to re-educate its bus passengers after a lifetime of established customs of boarding and paying and indeed, following the experience of the flat-fare Merlins, a simplified setup was worked out whereby just one turnstile-operated automatic ticket machine would be in evidence, mounted over the nearside wheelarch. For those without the correct fare (and who among us was conscientious enough to be sorting and separating change beforehand when we didn't necessarily know in our heads what the fare would be, when that had hitherto been the conductor's worry), the driver would issue change. Prior to the entry into service of the first DMSs, London Transport photographed a montage of typical passenger types boarding an early delivery set aside at Aldenham, and they don't look particularly confused or harried; out in service, with timetables to keep up to and impatient fellow passengers shuffling behind them in all weathers, it would be a different story.** *Colin Tait / TfL from the London Transport Museum collection*

XA VERSUS XF

CHAPTER TWO

ENTER THE LONDONER

1971

For some time, there had been plans to commence DMS OMO on the 4A from Highgate, using the first seventeen Fleetlines on a trial basis, but the time lag and resulting volume order made this redundant and three other services were selected for permanent conversion, routes 8A, 24 and 74. Scheduling problems saw the 95 (Brixton) and 220 (Shepherd's Bush) substituted for implementation on 2 January 1971, by which point several dozen DMSs had been delivered and stored or used to train drivers; interestingly, it would not be until 1985 (the 4, successor to the 4A), 1986 (the 8A and 24) and 1987 (the 74) that these intended pilot routes were one-manned! Neither 95 nor 220, both RM-operated, were any lightweights; the former brought commuters into the City from the south and the 220 was the direct descendant of the former trolleybus 630, though for its conversion to DMS another section was pruned, that beyond Tooting to Mitcham (the 630 had gone even further south, to Croydon) to warrant a PVR of 26 DMSs against 31 RMs, it being determined at the time that the DMSs' increased capacity (of four seats and 14 standees per bus) would make up for the reduction. At 00:47 on Saturday 2 January 1971 DMS 1 took over from an RM the 00:35 College

Below: **Shepherd's Bush's DMSs 9 (EGP 9J) and 27 (EGP 27J) have found themselves bunched up during the first summer of DMS operation in 1971, necessitating a short turn for the leader.**
Bob Greenaway / Online Transport Archive

Park–Tooting Mitre journey at Shepherd's Bush Green, returning as the 01:30 to Shepherd's Bush garage, after which the scheduled Saturday service commenced at 04:11. DMSs 1-5, 7-10, 16, 20-22, 24-28, 32, 33, 36-39, 41-43, 45 and 51 formed Shepherd's Bush's complement, with Brixton taking DMSs 17-19, 23, 29-31, 34, 35, 40, 44, 46-49 and 52 for the 95; DMS 31 set off from its home garage on the 04:10 Telford Avenue–Cannon Street journey, albeit two minutes late after a first-day ceremony at the garage. DMS 6 was kept behind for use at Chiswick Works, as was traditional with early examples of incoming new classes (it entered service at Shepherd's Bush in December after a period of gearbox and chassis testing for engineers' familiarisation). Key portions of London's infrastructure, however, were not yet up to the increased weight of the new buses; plans to include the Sunday-only 95A (which ran across London Bridge to Aldgate) in the DMSs' debut fell foul of a weight restriction on the approach road to the route's terminus (outside market hours) at London Bridge Station and had to be altered to introduce a Sunday service on the 95, going via Southwark Bridge to Aldgate and no farther north than the Elephant before and after market hours.

On 16 January DMSs 53-56 and 58-67 entered service on the 271 at Highgate; XFs had briefly been a staple of this formerly RML-operated ex-trolleybus route. Two weeks later came the fourth DMS conversion, Merton's 189 (ex-RT) on 30 January. Its projections beyond Raynes Park to Worcester Park were not entrusted to OMO vehicles and were instead appended to the still RT-operated 77A.

Decimalisation was implemented on 15 February 1971, LT and London Country receiving dispensation to wait six days until enough 'new pence' were in circulation, and this was as good an opportunity as any to review the performance of the Bell Punch AFC machinery, which was proving unreliable due to its method

Above: **Route 95 had been better known as the final host of the RTW class, but less than five years after the exit of these venerable vehicles, the RMs that replaced them were in turn swept away as the route became joint first to receive the new DMS class. Brixton took sixteen, one of which was DMS 35 (EGP 35J) seen at a misty Elephant & Castle on the first day, 2 January 1971. It can be seen straightaway that in terms of blinds, little provision was made for the passenger approaching from the side, only a route number being deemed sufficient.** Bob Greenaway / Online Transport Archive

Left: **The rear of the DMS was neat, even if the side shrouds were purely cosmetic and could be removed easily enough. This is DMS 21 (EGP 21J), allocated to Shepherd's Bush for the 220 and seen at that route's Tooting stand on a chilly 8 January 1971.** Paul A. Bateson

ENTER THE LONDONER

Left: Holloway's 271, descending only a decade earlier from trolleybus route 611, was the third route to receive DMSs, and on 19 January 1971 DMS 63 (EGP 63J) is seen on the familiar hilltop stand at Highgate Village. *Paul A. Bateson*

Below left: The 189 was a more important route than it subsequently became, most of it being covered well enough by the 152 and the section into Surrey subject to withering away as cross-border co-operation hardened. Its first spell of DMS operation from 30 January 1971 spanned eleven years, and on 19 February is seen in the person of Merton-allocated DMS 70 (EGP 70J) at Clapham Common, Old Town. *Paul A. Bateson*

of issuing tickets from a folded concertina pack; natural road juddering meted out to the buses was jamming the machinery, which relied upon sensitive levers to detect the correct coins. DMS 72 was therefore experimentally fitted with a Setright system, which issued its tickets from a roll.

It wasn't long before the gloominess of the DMS's all-red livery attracted opprobrium, and in March DMS 76 had a white band added within the side mouldings prior to joining Shepherd's Bush's fleet. It was decided to adopt this livery from the first of the '1970' order, DMS 118.

On 13 March the fifth route to assume DMS OMO was Cricklewood's 32, itself only nine months old since having been separated from the 142. This took the place of the 96, which was treated a little later in the year. On 17 April a particularly ambitious target was executed; that of the 5, which once constituted trolleybus 665 and which was now set going anew with seven DMSs each from Poplar (including white-banded DMS 76 on transfer) and West Ham. After this conversion the 'coin-in-the-slot' symbols were no longer applied, LT feeling that OMO was familiar to enough of its passengers not to need continued distinction. One further attempt at imprinting the 'Londoner' name on the public involved the treatment of DMS 114 to posters proclaiming the same and sending it to represent LT at the Bus of Yesteryear Rally on 23 May and again at the Festival of London Stores parade a week later. While the GLC, Conservative-controlled at this point in time, was aware of a creeping unpopularity with OMO ever since the Reshaping Plan had kicked into gear nearly three years earlier, its green paper 'Future of London Transport' released on 6 July recommended that conversions continue regardless of complaints, and moreover, as

Left: Seen at Aldgate long enough after entering service for the bus wash at Poplar to have scoured off some of the paint on its sharper corners, DMS 103 (EGP 103J) spent its first seven years at Poplar. *Haydn Davies*

Above: **Cricklewood's DMS 81 (EGP 81J) has picked up a little winter slush but otherwise looks smart in this January 1973 photo taken in Colindale. This was one of the 22 DMSs deployed for the conversion of the 32 on 13 March 1971, and demonstrates an intermediate application of the front-mounted payment instruction before the introduction of the more visible yellow sticker as seen in the picture below.** *Haydn Davies*

quickly as possible. Figures showing that only 10% of passengers were using the AFC equipment were particularly disheartening, though the disappearance of the sixpence from circulation was cited as a reason in this case; on 1 and 8 August relevant fares were rounded up or down by ½p to reflect this change. It was recognised that fare simplification was necessary to assist progress in OMO conversions, though quite how to do it without jeopardising revenue remained frustratingly unclear.

The '1970' order commencing at DMS 118 finally commenced delivery from 14 May; as well as the white band, modifications included the deletion of the PA system and revisions to the air pressure system. DMS 132 was experimentally fitted on 9 July with a Leyland O.680 engine (11.1-litre rated at 170bhp at 1850rpm), occasioning its reclassification to 1/2DM1, and spent six months under test. Two routes were converted to DMS OMO on 24 July; Brixton received a second batch of Fleetlines to replace the 50's RTs and shift the route southwards to take over the 133's Streatham-Croydon section, while the 170 at Wandsworth was also converted to accompany a curtailment that saw the Westminster-Shoreditch section withdrawn and the route pointed to Aldwych (or Euston at peaks) instead.

Above: **Wandsworth's DMS 125 (EGP 125J) enters Nine Elms Lane from Vauxhall on 26 July 1971, two days after the 170's OMO conversion, but it's an early instance of having a side blind in the front number box; maybe a similarly-sized side aperture should have been thought about at design stage.** *Haydn Davies*

ENTER THE LONDONER

Above: **Leaving West Croydon on 29 July 1971 is Brixton's DMS 134 (EGP 134J) on the 50, the garage's second DMS route. While the white band certainly livens up the all-red of the DMS, it wouldn't fit round the entire bus for fear of crashing into the rear ads and front blind boxes, and was soon discontinued and forgotten about.** *Paul A. Bateson*

4 September saw Highgate (HT) renamed Holloway after the closure of the bus garage of that name that had used the code J. Two weeks later the 267 was one-manned, Fulwell needing twelve DMSs and Turnham Green four. Part of this deployment included DMSs from DMS 168 with a major modification that widened the front headlamp spacing to comply with new legislation; it was feared that under night-time conditions the centrally-carried headlights confused oncoming traffic as to the buses' width. The sidelights moved up to the corners, directly underneath the windscreen. Similar modifications covered the last 100 Swifts, though to less impact aesthetically. It was never seen fit to amend DMSs 1-167, other than DMS 83, which was done uniquely. Also deleted at this time was the vertical 'NO ENTRY' light next to the exit doors.

Walworth's route 184 was one-manned on 16 October, the first conversion to specify Setright AFC equipment throughout. In November LT announced its intention to phase out the unreliable Bell Punch AFC equipment with its concertina-ticket mechanism and refit the DMSs affected with Setright machinery as pioneered on DMS 72. Bell Punch-fitted examples comprised DMSs 1-71, 73-157 and, since sufficient Setright machines could not be made available in time, DMSs 285-367. All Bell Punch machines had been replaced by Setright units by the end of 1972.

The 96 was duly converted to DMS operation from 6 November, these being Bexleyheath's first examples. For the first time, OMO conversions were carried out with the same number of buses as in crew-operated days, plans to employ fewer OMO buses due to their greater total capacity being stymied by the fact that passengers were shunning the AFC equipment and thus taking longer to board by each paying the driver. The shortcomings of OMO were becoming well known, and soon the reliability of the intended vehicles would take a turn for the worse.

The short-lived white-band livery definitely made a difference, and although it was deleted after the batch of 250, it made enough of an impact that future forms of relief were seriously thought about. DMS 140 (JGF 140K) was one of fourteen into Fulwell for the 267 in concert with Turnham Green (which used five) on 4 September 1971, and is seen at the southwestern end of the route on the 18th. *John Laker*

20   THE LONDON DMS

Left: London Transport dignitaries look on as DMS 162 (JGF 162K) undergoes the tilt test at Aldenham prior to entering service, which would be at Walworth on 16 October 1971. *David Wilkinson collection*

DMS 6 now entered service after its period of use by Chiswick, as did DMS 88, which had been held back for experiments by Ricardo Ltd of Shoreham that attempted to address the increased noise levels put out by the class; part of these trials included moving the radiators to baffles within the cosmetic shrouds at the rear, which unlike the rest were fixed to the bonnet rather than bolted to the sides of the bus. As OMO conversions were now in full swing, the Government accelerated the timetable by increasing the percentage it paid operators for each new compliant bus under New Bus Grant from 25% to a mouth-watering 50% from 1 December, to apply in theory till 31 August 1975 (but in the effect lasting several years

Below: During July 1973 DMS 189 (JGF 189K) from Bexleyheath garage heads into Woolwich on the 96, converted on 6 November 1971. *Haydn Davies*

Left: **The longest unbroken spell of DMS operation fell to the unremarkable 64, operated by Thornton Heath for most of its tenure with Fleetlines and then with those of Croydon able to step in right at the end. The conversion from RM was executed on 4 December 1971, and at West Croydon on 14 June 1972 we see DMS 238 (JGF 238K).** *Paul A. Bateson*

Below left: **More important than its creep round the back of the more populated areas of inner north London would suggest, the 67 was early in the queue for DMSs and went over on 4 December 1971. The anticipated sea change to passengers' time-honoured boarding and paying customs was considered so great as to prompt the display by LT of one of the new buses, DMS 205 (JGF 205K), at Stamford Hill two days prior to the conversion.** *Paul A. Bateson*

longer). To gain the maximum effect of this, two upcoming OMO conversions were postponed from 20 November to 4 December; these were Thornton Heath's 64 and Stamford Hill's 67. One particularly unhappy effect of OMO was the increased exposure of drivers working alone to assault and robbery; Brixton, with two DMS routes so far, went on strike on 4 December in protest at this.

As no single bodybuilder could possibly body all 1,600 of the DMSs on order within the two years expected for their delivery, the work was divided. Park Royal was assigned DMSs 368-1247 (880 bodies) and Metro-Cammell Weymann the remaining 720 (DMSs 1248-1967), with the orders to run concurrently. The appearance of stock numbers in the 1200s thus nonplussed observers unaware of the number split. Similarly, a second power option was explored with the order of 850 Leyland O.680 engines, following the trials undertaken on DMS 132.

Right: **DMS 239 (JGF 239K) was the lowest numbered of 22 allocated to Catford for the conversion of route 124 and its Sunday offshoot 124A on 8 January 1972. These were the first DMSs at Catford, which would go on to field large numbers of them in the next twelve years, and on 16 February 1975 this particular one was still there when captured in its garage yard. It would never work from anywhere else, seeing out all seven years of its Certificate of Fitness there.** *R. C. Riley*

22   THE LONDON DMS

Left: **Single-deck OMO had been a gamble ahead of its time and one that was now acknowledged to have failed. When attitudes towards increasing OMO faltered at the same time, new DMS deliveries were turned to replacing Merlins and Swifts on particularly hard-pressed routes operated by these single-deckers, and one such was the 297, converted to DMS on 5 February 1972 with DMS 310 (JGF 310K) and seven others. The operating Alperton garage is the location of this sunny 25 March shot.** *John Laker*

1972

No time was wasted getting more DMSs into service as 1972 opened; 8 January saw OMO conversion of routes 124/A from Catford (ex-RM) and 177 (ex-RT), shared between New Cross and Abbey Wood. Even by now it was proving difficult to sell the travelling public on split-stream OMO, so DMS 240, the latest guinea pig of the experimental shop at Chiswick since November 1971, had its entrance doors painted yellow in the manner of the MBs used in this role at Hounslow. DMS 240 was experimented upon further in May through the fitting of two-piece doors, the entrance versions of which folded over each other to the front. While this bus had standard doors refitted before entering service in October 1973 (incidentally without a white band), the idea would not be forgotten.

On 5 February the 85 at Putney and 297 at Alperton were converted from single-deckers (SMSs on the 85 and MBs on the 297) to DMS, representing the first reversions to double-deck of routes that had been one-manned with single-deckers; more would follow as it was realised what little popularity or success was being enjoyed by standee single-deckers. This particular pair of double-deckings only came about because the new DMSs' intended deployment to the 106 and 295 were postponed at a late stage owing to the decision to replace Bell Punch AFC equipment with Setright, which was considered to be more reliable due

Below: **Getting ready for their first day out on the 85, Putney's DMSs 148 (JGF 148K), 303 (JGF 303K), 301 (JGF 301K) and 304 (JGF 304K) repose at their inaugural home garage on 4 February 1972, the night before the conversion of the 85 from SMS. Putney took in fifteen DMSs for this route.** *David Wilkinson collection*

Above: **What as a whole was then called Thamesmead was futuristic in a way that lent itself unfortunately to a more dystopian outlook, the pedestrian walkways of Abbey Wood and the town centre having already been featured notoriously in** *A Clockwork Orange* **(1971). Still, London Transport was near-obsessed with linking this growing but isolated area to central London in whatever form could be driven through, whether by the proposed Fleet Line of the time or by humble bus; the latter mode is personified in July 1973 by Abbey Wood's DMS 247 (JGF 247K) on the 177, OMO DMS since 8 January 1972. Points off for the lack of a via blind, but the interestingly-dressed passengers who have just disembarked don't seem to mind too much.** *Haydn Davies*

to the manner in which it issued tickets from a roll rather than a folded concertina pack, which tended to jam. It made little difference, as AFC use had increased from 8% to no more than 30%.

Four of New Cross's DMSs used since February on the 177 (DMSs 328-331) were put to work on a service linking Waterloo with the Ideal Home Exhibition at Olympia between 29 February and 25 March, charging a flat fare of 24p. March also saw the first MCW-bodied DMSs appear, headed on the 30th by DMS 1250, numerically the third of the batch. It was intended to maintain some standardisation by engining the MCW-bodied DMSs with Leyland engines; however, problems ensued when the Leyland engines fitted to them failed noise regulations and completed buses had to be stockpiled engineless at Chiswick, pushing back plans to one-man more routes. A batch of 124 Gardner engines was diverted to Metro-Cammell and fitted to DMSs 1248-1371 from June 1972, allowing their dispatch to service. Delivery delays by the autumn soon led to the appearance of Leyland engines in Park Royal bodies and pretty soon we could see combinations of Leyland or Gardner engines in both Park Royal and MCW bodies, breaking up any idea of neatly segregating batches. Early plans to deploy specific configurations to routes thus had to be superseded by events, and eventually all varieties became thoroughly mixed, as was only sensible for an ostensibly standard bus. In the event the original order for 850 Leyland engines and 750 Gardners was adjusted substantially in Leyland's favour following production delays suffered by Gardner, and the vast majority of the main 1,600-strong order was Leyland-engined. Even so, continuing noise and reliability problems with Leyland engines necessitated a further Gardner component to the 679-strong order that came after; it seemed that you could either have reliability or punctual delivery but not both, and usually neither!

MCW bodies were virtually identical to their Park Royal counterparts but for some minor differences in construction, most notably the continuation of the aluminium bracing above the upper-deck windows around each roof dome, the somewhat smaller upper-deck rear window and the lack of strapping between window pans. Additional beading on the rear by comparison with Park Royal necessitated the wider placement of rear corner adverts. The rainwater channels above the cab were

Right: **On 23 May 1972, ten days after the 78's OMO conversion, Peckham's DMS 325 (JGF 325K) passes through Aldgate.** *C. Carter / Online Transport Archive*

more curved on the MCW body, with a slope. MCW's design of offside emergency-exit doors was also rather taller, with rounded corners, while the drain holes at foot level on the upper deck were round rather than rectangular. At the rear, the registration number was carried in a distinctly squarer typescript reminiscent of that used on the trolleybuses. There was a slight increase in overall weight by comparison with Park Royals. Whether it was intended to swap different manufacturers' bodies between chassis upon overhaul is not known but surely intended, given LT's reliance on the Aldenham system, but that would have been six years away if current CoF standards were adhered to, and it was not LT's habit to look that far ahead.

Additionally, from Park Royal DMS 368 and all of the MCWs, laminates replaced rexine on seat backs and walls, though this change rather reinforced the cold-seeming interior of the DMS with its blue fabrics and metal surfaces. Accordingly, after the brief, 250-bus interlude with white relief, all-red livery was resumed from this batch onwards, on the inevitable cost grounds.

Peckham's 78 was converted from RT (or RM at weekends) to DMS on 13 May; interestingly, the garage's night routes N85 and N86 followed suit, making them the first to go OMO and controversially so, operating through an area with social problems that were beginning to suffer some bad press. On 17 June the 44 at Wandsworth lost its RTs for new DMSs, heralding the entry into service of the first Park Royal-bodied DMSs of the main 1,600-strong order; the 44's reduced PVR on Saturdays prompted the introduction of Saturday-only 168B to use six of the new Fleetlines in place of the 168 on that day of the week. It was not, therefore, a very good time, for a 14-ton weight limit to be introduced on London Bridge, which meant that from 18 June the 44 was not permitted to carry standing passengers

Below: **For the first few DMS conversions, LT attempted to soften the blow of such an extreme change by displaying in advance one of the new vehicles. On 15 June 1972, two days before the conversion of the 44 from RT, DMS 378 (JGF 378K) is doing just that at London Bridge Station while an unconvinced RT 1978 (LUC 67) pulls past.** *R. C. Riley*

Left: Barking received its first DMSs on 17 June 1972 when new route 199 was created out of the southern end of the 179. DMS 353 (JGF 353K) is seen deep within the Thames View Estate during October. *Malcolm K. Allan*

Below: Although it travelled deep into the West End, the 39 was an early choice for OMO DMSs. On Saturdays they ran as 39A and on Sundays were kept in use through a sectioning off of the 19 as 19A; Tooting Bec is where Battersea's DMS 407 (JGF 407K) is seen on 19 July 1974. *David Wilkinson collection*

across it! Wandsworth also figured in the one-manning of the 295, which was transferred from Shepherd's Bush on 17 June. Across the river, Chalk Farm's 46 was converted from RM to DMS and allotted a Sunday service to replace the extension northwest of the 63 over its roads. And further east, the southernmost portion of the 179 at Barking was snipped off to produce new DMS-operated 199 serving the Thames View Estate; as this route did not run on Sundays, its DMSs were put to use on the 179 on that day of the week in replacement of its SMSs.

OMO marched on. On 15 July the 61 at Bromley introduced the first MCW-bodied DMSs into service now that their powerplant problems had been ironed out (by fitting them with Gardner engines); the simultaneous deployment there of Park Royal-bodied variants meant that there was not yet felt to be a need to segregate them, at least not in bodywork types. At Battersea the 39 and its Saturday-only counterpart 39A replaced their RTs with DMSs; another backdoor partial one-manning involved the curtailment of the 19 on Sundays at Clapham Junction and its replacement to points south by new Sunday-only 19A. Finally for 15 July, the 263 was converted to OMO; Finchley was in charge alone during weekdays, but on Saturdays and Sundays the route swelled

Left: **DMS 1248 (JGU 248K), the first of the Metro-Cammell-bodied DMSs, peeps out of Sutton garage on 19 April 1973. The 213 and partner 213A had been one-manned on 5 August 1972 and both were shared with Norbiton. This was not the only 'first' for which DMS 1248 would become known, as it became the first to be written off from the fleet altogether due to its consumption by fire on 17 August 1978.** *R. C. Riley*

beyond Archway to operate into town, adding a Holloway element on those days.

From this time it was decided to keep MCW and Park Royal bodies separate upon allocation after all, though this proved impossible to stick to if delivery timetables were to be met; the last joint conversion for the moment involved the 213 and 213A pair from 5 August (after a three-week postponement), Sutton and Norbiton sharing the former and Norbiton only featuring on the 213A on Sundays; the Belmont bifurcation during the peaks was switched from the 213 to the 213A. Norbiton took Park Royal-bodied DMSs and Sutton had MCWs, though the latter undertook some swapping with Bromley a little later to get solid blocks of fleetnumbers in one place. The one-manning of the 106, postponed since earlier in the year, now took place on 12 August, Tottenham needing nine DMSs and Hackney ten, all MCW-bodied. The route's passengers ought to have known what they were in for, as DMS 1250 had been displayed outside Hackney Town Hall just prior to conversion date; perhaps in view of what would befall this route in particular, the practice of demonstrating a future driver-only bus to its intended clientele ceased thereafter! Perhaps a greater vision saw Park Royal-bodied DMS 451 form LT's contribution to the Commercial Motor Show at the end of September.

Left: **The unfortunate 106 was a shining symbol of the failure of the DMS to perform as it was supposed to. Still, the route, purely inner-city after the gradual removal of its legs out into Essex, was slow-moving enough to tax the DMSs allocated to Hackney and Tottenham. The first day of the new order, 12 August 1972, sees Tottenham's DMS 1249 (JGU 249K) looking shiny without any adverts as yet; even though it's just turned from Blackstock Road into Brownswood Road, already this duty has been curtailed to Mile End Station.** *Malcolm K. Allan*

ENTER THE LONDONER

Right: **Theatreland remains the major draw for West End bus custom, and a concerted effort to make economic use of the local area's new DMSs once their normal routes had tailed off after the evening peak saw the advent of Starbus, a branded service callng in DMSs from four garages within reach of its Edgware Road-Aldwych route. The main effort invariably fell to Victoria, whose DMSs like DMS 1302 (MLH 302L) split the 10 in half on 28 October 1972; the resulting 10A is demonstrated at Victoria shortly after.**
Haydn Davies

Enfield garage received its first DMSs on 9 September when the 107 was upgraded from SMS operation, this route being extended to epic length by virtue of swallowing up the 107A. When not needed once the evening peak had died down, DMSs from four garages within reach of central London were put to an innovative use from 14 October operating the new 'Starbus' service linking Aldwych and Edgware Road so as to speed theatregoers to their venues in association with Westminster City Council. Seven of Victoria's DMSs (1297-1303), taking up this role two weeks before their official deployment on new route 10A, had white stars applied between decks. Of their support,

DMSs 169, 175 and 176 from Walworth and DMSs 285-287 from Putney had white bands so the stars were blue. Wandsworth's DMSs 385-387 were all-red so received white stars. The 28th of this month was when Victoria's star-daubed Fleetlines came into their own; their new 10A was commissioned to sectionalise the 10 in town. This lengthy trunk route, which fell back to London Bridge Station, was also one-manned, Bow receiving its first DMSs. Not far away a piece of the 22 was rerouted at Dalston southwards to Liverpool Street and christened 22A (in a change from plans to call it 128), using BESI-fitted Clapton DMSs (although its intended projection past Homerton to Clapton

Right: **There were two kinds of Starbus branding, as the white band on Putney's participating DMSs necessitated blue stars for the proper colour contrast. Otherwise allocated to the 85 since its double-decking from SMS operation on 5 Feburary 1972, DMS 287 (JGF 287K) makes ready for the off at Kingston.**
Haydn Davies

28 THE LONDON DMS

Left: **On 28 October 1972 new route 22A was created with Clapton DMSs, allowing City-bound passengers from the Dalston area an alternative route than via the Hackney Road. On 9 August 1973 DMS 1304 (MLH 304L) is seen heading off from Liverpool Street. Not long after their introduction, Clapton swapped most of its MCW-bodied DMSs for an equivalent number of similarly-aged Park Royals, but DMS 1304 managed to stay put and indeed never worked from anywhere else. Forty years later it survives and can still be seen in town from time to time in the ownership of Red Route Buses.** *R. C. Riley*

Park was not implemented until 18 December due to the roads in the Clapton Park Estate needing to be cleared for one-way operation), and on much the same roads Leyton's 55 was converted from RT to DMS OMO. Further to the south-east West Ham took DMSs (including DMSs 463-467 with two-leaf doors) to replace the RMs on route 278, the Sunday shortfall being used to one-man the 262 on that day of the week. Among West Ham's allocation were DMSs 463-467 fitted experimentally with two-piece glider doors like DMS 240 but painted red. After two weeks with four garages operating the Starbus, all but Victoria's participation was taken off.

Leyland engines resumed from DMS 495 (Park Royal) and DMS 1372 (MCW) in November, the noise issues having been resolved by Leyland tuning the engines down. DMS 132 entered service at Thornton Heath on the 18th, but on 15 January 1973 soon moved to Croydon to join other Leyland-engined examples introduced there.

During 1972, London Transport had been conducting an in-depth study into its operations known as BOSS (Bus Operations Special Study), and its publication on 9 November revealed little but criticism for its enforced headlong rush towards OMO. Aside from terrible unreliability problems now beginning to make themselves

Left: **The 107 was at one point the longest bus route in London, but the sheer length of it, which included dipping out of London altogether before re-entering the GLC area, made it troublesome to handle and it was divided again not long after DMSs came along. DMS 423 (MLK 423L) was one of the buses allocated new to Enfield for the conversion from SMS and is seen when new plying the route in Brockley Hill, north of Edgware.** *Tony Wilson*

ENTER THE LONDONER

felt on the purpose-built vehicles (10-15% of them reported as being off the road at any one time), revenue had dropped due to passengers being put off using AFC-equipped buses, which required up to 10% longer dwell time at stops just to get everyone on and issued with tickets. Far from saving money by being able to use fewer buses at a lower frequency on OMO-converted routes due to having additional overall capacity (seated plus standees) over RTs or RMs, the reduced number of DMSs on the road simply could not keep to time, and beginning with the treatment of the 96 to DMS on 30 October 1971, conversions had to be accomplished on a one-for-one replacement basis. Even this couldn't help them, and from late 1972 the number of DMSs on a one-manned route actually had to be increased! If they could see one coming on roads with more than one route, passengers would wait for an RT or Routemaster, knowing it would invariably catch up to and overtake the slow and weighty DMS.

It wasn't just excess weight that was hampering the DMSs' speed to the detriment of timetable maintenance, though the extra two tons over an RM, plus another ton's worth of passengers, did its part to wear out brake linings and gearboxes that much faster. In quite the reverse of what LT drivers were used to, DMS gearboxes were designed for gear changes with the foot off the throttle, not while at full pelt. The engineers, meanwhile, were perhaps spoiled by the sheer simplicity of RT and RM maintenance where engines and drivetrains could be swapped out as quickly as between shifts, and therefore numbered fewer than at comparable bus companies nationwide. They were not used to having to change the oil and filters more often than was necessary on front-engined precedessors, and quickly became overwhelmed by what was, to the rest of the country, an acceptable rate of failure. Recruitment to fitter roles thus suffered along the same lines as that of platform staff.

Like the Merlins and Swifts before them, the DMSs were structurally compromised by the presence of what was effectively a hole in the centre of the bodywork where the centre doorway was. While they didn't quite crack in the middle as was common to those unfortunate single-deckers, stress flexing problems were created under load which prevented the door interlocks from operating as they were supposed to, even if there was nothing visually amiss to the passenger, and thus locking the doors open or shut to his or her detriment. Horror stories exist of DMS

Below: **The 55 was one-manned on 28 October 1972, requiring 22 DMSs. On 24 November Leyton's DMS 449 (MLK 449L) picks up at Clapton Pond; other than one reported loan to Stamford Hill, this bus would work only out of Leyton, lasting just the one Certificate of Fitness ticket.**
Bob Greenaway / Online Transport Archive

Left: **All the way out at the very eastern edge of London Transport bus operations, North Street replaced the 247A's RTs with DMSs on 18 November 1972. Here pulling away from the compulsory stop on Collier Row Road in May 1973 is DMS 485 (MLK 485L).** *Malcolm K. Allan*

windscreens popping out of their mountings for the same reason, not to mention roofs leaking and the inevitable corner damage which was more obvious on a sharp-edged design like the DMS than on predecessors, whose smooth curves laughed off attention by tree branches. The slightly lower general carriage prompted bumps and bashes to the panels closest to the roadway, while steering problems and fuel leaks were just some of the mechanical mishaps that cropped up with increasing regularity as the buses racked up high mileages in stop-start conditions up to twenty hours a day without rest. Gearboxes and engines alike overheated in slow traffic, sealed as they were in isolation at the rear with restricted airflow by comparison with buses cooled by front-mounted radiators, sometimes with fiery consequences. Perhaps the only advantage the DMSs had was that they were shorter than the Merlins and Swifts, seated more people and took up less physical space in garages and on the road alike.

And there was no going back; only compromises could be executed, given the havoc being played on London Transport's orderly plans by the DMSs' poor performance and the refusal of their passengers to accept the changes to their travelling patterns and payment methods that had been thrust upon them. While suburban OMO was forecast by the BOSS study to continue broadly on schedule with the 1,967 DMSs currently on order, the application of the concept to central London just could not be made feasible at the moment with the existing fare structure. The BOSS report was followed on 12 December by the publication of a GLC document which agreed with LT's decision effectively to call a moratorium on central-area OMO conversions while also recommending the deferment of further flat-fare introduction in the interests of eventually introducing a zonal fare system. The fare structure at present was considered complicated, but off-bus pre-purchased tickets had brought some improvements; even so, flat fares were not only problematic to subsidise but difficult to increase without passenger resentment and the resulting reduction in numbers. The GLC agreed to make an annual grant to LT to fill in for cash requirements not met by central government, though there was the old chestnut of still being required to break even.

On 18 November two RT-operated services in the furthest eastern corner of town, Hornchurch's 246 and North Street's 247A, were one-manned. A change to Wandsworth's 295 took it out of the East Acton theatre and pointed it northwards to Ladbroke Grove instead; a Saturday service was added. Another theatreland service to employ Victoria's starred DMSs was the 'Wells Bus' from 11 December, linking Waterloo and Sadlers Wells.

Problems with DMSs at New Cross, Putney and Fulwell by December 1972 necessitated the diversion of new deliveries to these garages to stand in for them; all that aside, 370 DMSs had been delivered during the year (DMSs 296-537 from Park Royal and DMSs 1248-1372, 1378, 1379 and 1382 from MCW.

ENTER THE LONDONER

1973

Although changing PSV regulations now dictated that black-on-white reflective numberplates would be mandatory on all vehicles delivered after 1 January 1973, not a single London Transport Fleetline was delivered with one, and barring a small minority of the later M and T classes, LT's attractive traditional plates endured all the way to 1986. Virtually none – certainly fewer than five – DMS-family vehicles in the service of LT or its unit-based successors went on to be retrofitted with reflective plates other than some of the Ensign-resurrected examples for Bexleybus in 1988.

1973 began with very large numbers deployed to south London garages for SMS replacement on busy routes that would have received DMSs upon their original OMO conversions had they been available; on 6 January five Croydon routes (166, 166A, 197B, 233 and 233A) were converted thus, plus straight one-mannings of the 194 (Elmers End) and 222 (Uxbridge). Croydon's intake became the first DMSs to be used on rail replacement work when on the 14th they covered for the West Croydon–Crystal Palace leg not far from their base. Also occurring on 6 January was the one-manning of Fulwell's 90B (ex-RM), with a shuttle service added to Kew but lasting only until 20 April. On the 20th Croydon received further numbers to eject its XAs from the 234 and 234B, which conversion also made the FRM redundant for the time being. Another double-decking was at Cricklewood, where DMS replaced SMSs on the 245 – but not on the Sunday-only 245A, which remained SMS-operated due to an industrial dispute at Cricklewood.

Between 17 February and 29 March Croydon's remaining XAs were replaced by new DMSs through the conversion of routes C1-C4 using the first DMSs to be fitted with fareboxes (DMSs 1373, 1376-1397); on 17 February new route C5 was added to serve the southernmost portions of the New Addington estate. Unlike Croydon's initial Park Royal DMSs, its new MCW-bodied entrants were blinded for the garage's graduated-fare DMS routes as well so could be used if necessary with just a ticket machine and the AFC roped off. 3 March saw Starbus withdrawn, its operation having failed to carry the number of passengers expected, while the Saturday-only DMS-operated 168B lost its

Below: **On 6 January 1973, the first day of OMO DMSs on the 90B, Fulwell's DMS 1371 (MLH 371L) shares ground at Yeading with Southall's RT 2037 (LUC 279).** *John Laker*

Right: **Uxbridge's 222 also received DMSs on 6 January 1973, and on 29 July 1973 DMS 1360 (MLH 360L) and partner are seen at their home garage. This would be a one-garage bus, coming off after a single seven-year CoF, whereas DMS 1371 above, withdrawn at the same age, at least got eight months at a second garage (in its case, Sutton).** *John Laker*

THE LONDON DMS

Above: **DMS 132 (EGP 132J)** became famous as the testbed for Leyland engines; having begun its career at Thornton Heath, it was transferred to Croydon on 6 January 1973 to replace SMSs on five routes, including the 166 and its Sunday offshoot 166A. The presence of a 119A across the road from this shot outside East Croydon station in mid-1973 marks it as a Saturday. Although DMS 132 lasted no further than October 1979, all of it now at Croydon, it has gained some repute today as one of the longest-preserved DMSs around, having regained its original livery after a long spell in Brighton. *Haydn Davies*

Left: **The opportunity to sell the XA class in its entirety to Hong Kong proved too good to pass up, and DMSs from ongoing deliveries were adapted with fareboxes to take over. during the late winter of 1973. Distinguished from run-of-the-mill graduated-fare routes through its attractive white-on-blue blinds, Croydon's DMS 1387 (MLH 387L) passes through central New Addington during March.** *Haydn Davies*

33

Right: **In the days when Sunday schedules were substantially different from those on Mondays to Fridays and on Saturdays, it was made sure that new vehicles were never left to sit unused when their routes' Sunday PVR was otherwise far lower than during the week. The 259 hadn't had a Sunday service since 1966 and it didn't regain one upon one-manning, so the route's new DMSs were put to work on an adjunct to the 279. The 279A covered the in-town portion, a strategy which would be reversed later as Sunday car traffic swelled to parity with weekday levels. DMS 806 (TGX 806M) actually came at the end of 1973, as a crew bus for the 149, and it wasn't until after it had been converted to OMO specification (staying put at Edmonton) a year further on still, that it was captured for these pages, now carrying the latest 'PLEASE PAY AS YOU ENTER' transfers on the front.**
David Wilkinson collection

suffix. On 10 March the 259, shared between Tottenham and Edmonton, was converted from RM to DMS. To give the new Fleetlines work on Sundays the 279 was pulled back to Finsbury Park on Sundays and new DMS-operated 279A introduced between Lower Edmonton and Liverpool Street, diverting away from the usual direction to offer passengers the option of attending the Sunday markets. At Putney the 85A was converted from RM to DMS, while at Barking DMSs replaced RTs from the 156 and RFs from the 291; the 156 was extended over the withdrawn 23C to Creekmouth.

Having struggled somewhat with how to show off the DMS to its best advantage when the bodystyle simply didn't allow for such embellishments as relief bands, LT phased in a new set of livery standards altogether from March 1973, to be applied to all vehicles save RTs. These controversially deleted the traditional black-outlined gold leaf fleetnumbers for stark solid-white transfers of a slightly smaller size, combined with a solid white roundel with no writing thereon. The roundel was printed on self-adhesive clear plastic and applied on top of the coat of varnish rather than wet transfers

Right: **Two Barking-operated routes took DMSs on 10 March 1973; neither the 156 nor the 291 were major-league, but the more ambitious trunk routes in the sector, like the 5, were already struggling. DMS 298 (JGF 298K) is seen in Ripple Road on the southwestern fringe of Barking town centre, having spent a full year as a trainer at Barking before being put into service. It lasted the seven years and a repaint customary to this batch, but was not one of those redeemed through overhaul, and after a period with Muswell Hill was sold for scrap.** *Haydn Davies*

34 THE LONDON DMS

Left: **Out went the white cantrail band, but thoughts towards modernisation brought in white filled roundels and fleetnumbers instead. With proper upkeep, it didn't look as harsh as did some fashionable contemporaries (the insipid pair of NBC colours come to mind), and probably suited the era in which the DMS existed. The 221 was shared between Finchley and Wood Green when it was one-manned on 24 March 1973, and the 31st in New Southgate we get a chance to see the two liveries (and bodyworks, and garages) side by side in the form of Wood Green's DMS 1419 (MLH 419L) and Finchley's DMS 570 (MLK 570L).**
Malcolm K. Allan

between paint and varnish stage as hitherto. On the offside of DMSs, these were carried, as before, on the staircase panel, and on the nearside above the entrance door. Instead of the yellow label offset to the nearside to inform passengers whom to pay and with what, yellow 'PLEASE PAY AS YOU ENTER' transfers occupied a central position underneath the windscreen. DMS 580 was the first thus from Park Royal, and DMS 1416 from MCW, DMS 1418 continuing. Yellow entrance doors were now specified, DMSs 563-565 having them upon delivery but losing them soon after. It will be noted that not a single DMS was chosen to carry any form of all-over advertising livery of the kind enjoyed by a large number of RMs and RMLs since 1969; readers can make up their own minds as to why this should have proven to be the case.

Common to both Park Royal and MCW bodywork from the '1973' deliveries was the specification of front upper-deck opening window panels manufactured by Beclawat, by which the passenger pulled them inwards to open, rather than pushed outwards with a central handle, as on the previous versions supplied by HSC or Weathershield. DMSs 540 onwards (less 545-554), DMS 1346 and DMS 1348 onwards would have them from new, and earlier buses that survived to overhaul would have pull-in units retrofitted. Another innovation, implemented with effect from March and April 1973, was the addition of a nearside destination blind box alongside the 14in-wide 'PP' number panel from DMSs 586-594 and 597 onwards (Park Royal, DMSs 595 and 596 being delivered with '1972' bodies) and DMS 1428 onwards (MCW). Coded YY, this carried a blind of 36in width. Getting staff to turn the displays correctly was to prove an uphill struggle, use of the side destinations eventually proving erratic and, before long, liable to union objection without the appropriate compensation, but it was a touch that passengers had been asking for, action finally being taken following a request by the London Passengers Transport Committee in 1972. While LT promised to investigate retrofitting earlier DMSs with side destination blinds, this never came to pass. Regarding engine fitment, Gardner engines were interspersed amid the Leylands, comprising DMSs 608-611, 617-619, 637-639, 659 and 660 of the Park Royal deliveries and DMSs 1452-1467 of the MCWs.

Finchley and Wood Green shared new DMSs, some of them in the new livery, for the one-manning (ex-RM) of the 221 on 24 March, which date also saw Battersea's DMSs working the 39 and 39A pushed through from Southfields via hitherto unserved roads to Putney Bridge Station; three new examples entered service to this end. 20 April saw the 83's Sunday OMO service at Alperton lose its MBs for a unique mix of three SMSs and seven DMSs, which had to be the case until enough DMSs were made available for the whole route by converting the 92 later in the year. During April Clapton and Cricklewood exchanged their most recent DMS intake, Clapton taking the Park Royals and Cricklewood the MCWs.

Elections to the Greater London Council on 12 April 1973 installed a Labour administration,

ENTER THE LONDONER

Right: **Catford's DMS 1437 (MLH 437L)** looks smart on 18 June 1973 as it picks up passengers at Victoria. The 185, one-manned on 12 May, was the second DMS route each for both Catford and Walworth.
R. C. Riley

Right: **DMS 629 (MLK 629L)** was one of eighteen put into Merton for the 131 and 157, and on 13 May 1973, the second day of such operation, is seen at the Sunday Clapham Common terminus of the route, added to replace the 155's projection westward.
C. Carter / Online Transport Archive

Right: Its heritage from trolleybus route 657 still not dead in locals' minds, the 157 was converted to DMS OMO on 12 May 1973. Seen at the foot of the difficult ascent of Anerley Hill on the 19th is Merton's DMS 635 (MLK 635L).
R. C. Riley

36

which would have much to say in the life of the DMS. Its first intention was to demand an operating grant for London Transport rather than its request to raise fares to stop it from falling into a deficit; as time went on it was clear that this would be unavoidable, and the lag in time meant that increases would have to be more severe than if carried out gradually.

A round of one-manning hit south London on 12 May, the routes affected being 131 (Norbiton and Merton), 154 (Sutton and Thornton Heath), 157 (Merton), 185 (Catford and Walworth) and 197A (Thornton Heath). The 131's OMO conversion incorporated an extension on Sundays over the 155 to Clapham Common or Victoria Embankment, allowing that RM-operated service to be withdrawn on this day of the week. These conversions introduced the new livery to a growing audience, and it went without saying that repaints (when commenced in October 1973 on Shepherd's Bush DMSs 1, 2, 24 and 25) would retroactively introduce it to earlier examples.

Hornchurch became the first 100%-OMO garage when its route 165 was converted from RML to DMS on 16 June, which date also saw the splitting of the lengthy 175 into three sections; at this stage only the western end (as new Upton Park-operated route 173 from Becontree Heath (or Dagenham Fords) to Canning Town with peak journeys to the Blackwall Tunnel) was with DMSs. The Romford-Ongar end (renumbered 175A) was also intended for OMO, but DMSs could not be accommodated along these roads so a North Street RT stood in. At West Ham the 241 replaced its weekday RMs and Sunday SMSs with DMSs daily, additionally losing its entire service north of Stratford to new RM-worked route 230, while the 278 was cut between Leyton and Walthamstow Central. On 2 July the 85's Alton Estate journeys were rerouted via Bessborough Road.

14 April 1973 saw DMSs commence work on the Round London Sightseeing Tour, restoring a London Transport participation on this rather forgotten but increasingly important operation that just seemed to cry out for augmentation. DMSs 586-594, 597, 598 and 614, lacking AFC equipment (a luggage area being fitted instead) and with the route, destination and side blind boxes painted over in black, were allocated to Stockwell, the intention being to substitute new ones every six months so that the incumbents could go on to bus work and thereby qualify for New Bus Grant, which only applied if 50% of the first year's work was on stage service.

Realising from the BOSS study that OMO conversions had not been a qualified success in London, to say the very least, but with DMSs still in the process of delivery, LT announced its intention in March to suspend OMO conversions in central London and alter the ongoing order of DMSs to include a crew-operated variant known as the DM class. 460 of these would enable enough Routemasters to be cascaded to replace RTs with CoF expiries and boost number of this still supremely-reliable vehicle in the face of a shortage affecting the entire London Transport network. To be numbered in the same ongoing series as the existing DMS order, the new DMs would be 71-seaters (H44/27D) by virtue of the replacement of the AFC cabinet with a three-bench seat (affording, for the interested observer sat there, a perfect lesson in how to drive a bus) and the deletion of the circuitry connecting the Almex E baseplate to the driver's cab edge. In advance of this, 105 DMSs in the process of delivery would be taken with empty AFC cabinets, cordoned off for the moment but ready to have the inner workings fitted for reallocation once DMs had come on stream. At the time it was not intended to replace RTs directly with DMs, this being considered too much of a technological leap, while garages like Seven Kings were actually undergoing reconstruction so that they could accept RMs. So much for DMSs replacing RTs and then Routemasters, though; already the remit of the DMS was diverging sharply, and expensively, away from its original intent. In August the GLC authorised the withdrawal of the entire Merlin fleet upon the expiry of their initial seven-year CoFs, citing the excessive cost of their upcoming overhaul as much as their general unreliability. New DMSs would now be replacing the MBs and MBSs rather than the RM family, which would take the Merlins' place in the queue for Aldenham overhauls. It was envisaged at this point that the Red Arrow MBAs would also be replaced in this way, at

Below: **The first of the Round London Sightseeing Tour Fleetlines comprised twelve taken from the ongoing Park Royal batches and allocated to Stockwell with rudimentary advertising and two of their three frontal blind boxes blacked out, but at least the AFC equipment was removed. Entering Trafalgar Square on 21 April 1973 is DMS 591 (MLK 591L). Five months later it would find itself replaced by a newer bus from the DMS 696-710 range and transferred to Catford.**
Bob Greenaway / Online Transport Archive

ENTER THE LONDONER

Above: **DMS 614 (MLK 614L) is carrying a full load round Trafalgar Square on 21 April 1973 despite bearing no RLST signwriting. It spent until September at Stockwell for this and then moved to Stamford Hill.** *Bob Greenaway / Online Transport Archive*

Below: **The two-leaf doors on DMS 464 (MLK 464L) would soon become the norm. Turning at Tooting on 29 September 1973, it would spend four years at Brixton.** *C. Carter / Online Transport Archive*

mechanical unfitness. The spare-parts shortage endemic at this time had resulted in over 200 vehicles being off the road, a situation with no signs of improvement in the near future.

The regular intake of RLST DMSs into Stockwell now put examples into service from the 600s and 700s block of fleetnumbers during August; this time their AFC cabinets were retained but not used. Their predecessors were released and dispersed around the current ranks of DMS operators. In time to be put into service at Turnham Green in August, DMS 1332 was fitted with a hydraulic braking system manufactured by Clayton Dewandre and similar to one in use on a batch of Routemasters; the hydraulic concept was also tested out on the throttle and doors while in service. Speaking of doors, the glider doors-fitted DMSs 463-467 were transferred from West Ham to Brixton in July in exchange for five K-registered examples.

British Leyland was now embarking on a programme of consolidating its manufacturing, by which the facilities of acquisitions would be folded into that of the parent; to this end Fleetline production started moving from Coventry to Farington during 1973, DMS 742 of September delivery being the first completed here despite remaining badged and coded as a Daimler. The move was protracted and would impact delivery dates, but this wasn't the last imposition by any means.

At Barking, 1 September was the date of the 169's one-manning, enough new DMSs being in stock not to need to use any M-registered examples. This route's new Fleetlines broke new ground down Fullwell Avenue in Barkingside to Claybury, while Saturday-only route 169C also got the DMS treatment with an extension to the Gascoigne Estate. On 20 October the Merton DMSs operating the 189 saw their route extended from Raynes Park along the 152 to Esher, to allow that route to divert to Hampton Court in part-replacement of the 72 in that direction; four new DMSs (1505 and 1507-1509) were delivered to Merton for this task, though only these had the correct blinds for the moment. 27 October saw the 92 at Southall and Alperton take on DMSs, enough of which were now spare at the latter to fully man the 83 on Sundays, and a similar SMS-to-DMS upgrade fell to Turnham Green's 91 on 10 November.

Abbey Wood garage commenced new route 198 on 17 November, taking two new DMSs (1535 and 1536) to link Woolwich and Thamesmead East via Nathan Way, served hitherto by the 54; the 177 was pushed eastwards to Alsike Road in support. The last OMO conversion of the year was to Elmers End's 194B on 1 December, ex-RT (the Sunday shortfall of DMSs being used to one-man the 54 on that day of the week),

least on routes 503 and 507, to which end DMS 1601 was treated to a prospective Red Arrow livery of red and white and special blinds were run up, with a proposed implementation date of December 1975. Payment would be via two streams of flat-fare fareboxes.

Edgware received its first DMSs on 14 July for the OMO conversion of the 292, which was introduced on Saturdays and Sundays to replace the 292A and make the garage 100% OMO. The 1 August year letter change was implemented from DMS 696 (TGX 696M) for Park Royal and DMS 1500 (THM 500M) for MCW. Many of the last L-registered MCWs had to enter service at various garages to fill in for earlier examples of the class falling out through

Left: **Southall's DMS 734 (TGX 734M) was one of the 92's new complement from 27 October 1973 and is seen at Greenford station on 3 November. Southall fielded nine DMSs to Alperton's six.** *John Laker*

Left: **Alperton's 83 was busy enough for its daily OMO conversion to be held back all the way till April 1983, but the Sunday service was one-manned on 15 May 1971 with Merlins, which nonetheless came up against Wembley market traffic. The unsatisfactory half-measure of running three MBs and seven DMSs on it from 20 April 1973 was ameliorated by the 92's double-decking, which furnished enough new DMSs to complete the entire Sunday runout. On such a working DMS 718 (TGX 718M) is seen coming up to Wembley Park the following April.** *Haydn Davies*

Left: **DMS 548 (MLK 548L) had come to Barking for the 156 and 291 in March 1973, but from 1 October added the 169 and 169C to their duties. By this time the combination of outlined white roundel and gold transfers was coming to an end, and this bus, seen at Barking, was one of the last to carry it.** *David Wilkinson collection*

39

Below: **Turnham Green's DMS 1511 (THM 511M) has had a mishap going round the swirling maelstrom of Hammersmith Broadway on 19 August 1974, nine months after entering service on the 91. The damage doesn't look too bad, but it took the bus off the road for a recorded two months.** *Bob Greenaway / Online Transport Archive*

and the year was rounded off with an unusual deployment of DMSs to the 16 at Cricklewood (replacing initial intentions to use them on Holloway's 214) and 134 at Muswell Hill – but in crew mode with AFC cabinets not fitted. This was in preparation for these services' receipt of purpose-built DMs as soon as they became available and was implemented due to the need to get RMs from these routes to replace RTs on the 77 group. Unfortunately, despite the ability of the crew DMSs to be converted to OMO buses when the time came, their spell on central London work was none too efficient from the outset; the layout of the DMSs counted against itself when a conductor was on board. With passenger ingress and egress hampered by the opening and closing of the doors when the interlocks allowed, the saloon itself was effectively divided into four sections by the central staircase, precluding truly efficient coverage by the conductor, who had nowhere to stand out of the way of circulating passengers, even though a limit of five standees was imposed. As much time was thus added to boarding with a conductor as was the case without one, but nothing more could be done for the time being.

The replacement of the Conservative GLC administration by Labour after 12 April 1973 saw the abandonment for the moment of plans to close Aldenham and transfer its work to Chiswick in reflection of the labour situation, but it was still felt that future London Transport buses (perhaps B15s) could be built at Aldenham, and indeed a report by *The Sunday Times* of 9 September 1973 revealed that LT and British Leyland were investigating the possibility of establishing a joint manufacturing concern in which up to 600 buses a year would be built at Aldenham. This was under consideration due to LT's dissatisfaction with the off-the-peg purchases of the last five years, which might be ameliorated if LT were to build its own vehicles again. Until that possibility could be made reality, LT announced in August plans to order 938 new buses subject to GLC approval. 843 of them would be double-deckers and, it was speculated, would include a number of Scania's BR111DH chassis that was representing an unwelcome but frankly necessary aspect of foreign competition into an industry riven almost to despair by industrial action and the unsuitability, perceived or actual, of current domestic models. The Merlins having been sent packing, these buses, it was envisaged, would take care of the remaining RTs and RFs. The combination of the Scania chassis with MCW bodywork was christened Metropolitan, and NVP 533M, a yellow-painted demonstrator, paid a visit to Victoria in December 1973.

Operational ideas were also in the forefront, particularly the Speedbus concept of a route whose roads would be controlled by universal bus lanes and kerbside parking bans. This idea, having been kicked around since the start of 1973, was first made public in June, ten routes being envisaged for operation with crew-operated double-deckers to 'quiet bus' specification, but it was realised that a great deal of time would be needed to implement changes to road infrastructure before this could be seriously considered. Already in 1972-73 the final series of one-way systems had been put into place in town centres where it was practicable to divert traffic without massive rebuilding, while bus lanes continues to be marked out and activated and plans were laid in October to fit transponders to 500 buses to allow them to trip selected traffic lights to green. Aboard buses themselves, OMO was given a push by the announcement in October (following GLC approval) of plans to sell bulk tickets on flat-fare routes H1, M1, P1-3, S1-3, W1-4, W7, W8 and W21, with the accompanying withdrawal of change-giving.

1973 had seen DMSs 538-806 and 1381-1602 added to the fleet from Park Royal and Metro-Cammell respectively; together with the Merlins and Swifts, they operated the 37% of the London Transport network that was OMO.

Above: **The only indication that what was otherwise a DMS was actually crew-operated was the lack of 'PLEASE PAY AS YOU ENTER' on the front. DMS 761 (TGX 761M) was allocated to Cricklewood for the 16 in December 1973 and on 22 February 1974 is waiting at Victoria.** *John Laker*

Left: **The 134 was also very busy and penetrated deep into the West End, though its most advanced penetration to Victoria and Pimlico had been snipped off when the Victoria Line came along. On 19 October 1974 Potters Bar's DMS 1562 (THM 562M) gets ready for the off outside its home garage, geographically almost another world away from distant central London.** *David Wilkinson collection*

ENTER THE LONDONER

1974

Just four days of 1974 passed before another big round of one-manning. The 144, shared between Wood Green and Walthamstow, succumbed to DMSs on 5 January, as did the 197 at Croydon (additionally being introduced on Sundays to replace the 197B, whose routeing it adopted throughout), the 280 at Sutton and the 277 at Poplar and Clapton, but the last-mentioned was obliged to fall back from Poplar to Cubitt Town due to the prohibition of buses heavier than RTs from the narrow swing bridge connecting these two points on the Isle of Dogs; new local route 277A continued RT operation. On Sundays the 130A at Croydon lost its RTs for DMSs spare from the 197, and at night the N84 was converted from RM to DMS at Poplar, using stock from the daytime 277. Finally for 5 January, the 132 at Bexleyheath had an upper deck restored with DMSs replacing its SMs.

On 2 February the third of the trio chosen for crew-DMS operation, the 149 shared between Edmonton and Stamford Hill, received its Fleetlines. On the 23rd Barking's 179 was upgunned from SMS to DMS and on 1 March Cricklewood's N94 was obliged to assume crew-DMS operation due to all its RMs from the 16 having departed. The following day saw Alperton DMSs tasked with fighting their way through Sunday-shopping crowds to Wembley Stadium Market beyond the usual terminus of the 92.

Between 4 and 19 January DMS 1500 embarked on the first publicity tour of the UK by a DMS; under the banner of London Entertains '74, its seats were replaced by bookshelves and London landmarks were painted on its upper-deck windows. At each stop on the tour it displayed slides of London on a screen mounted between the doors. After completing this task it entered service at Cricklewood.

Top left: **The 144 was a long and busy route shared between Wood Green and Walthamstow, but was duly passed for OMO and on 5 January 1974 DMSs took over; here at Gants Hill is Wood Green's DMS 574 (MLK 574L), already based here since the 221's conversion.** *David Wilkinson collection*

Above left: **The most vulnerable portion of the roof dome of Sutton's DMS 732 (TGX 732M) has taken a bit of a hiding two years after its allocation for the 280 on 5 January 1974, but the bus would see its short life (six years) out at just this garage.** *Haydn Davies*

Left: **There is next to nothing in this post-industrial Isle of Dogs backdrop of DMS 100 (EGP 100J) during 1977; regeneration is a decade away. Allocated to Poplar for the 5 in April 1971, it was still there in time to assume the 277 on 5 January 1974, or at least the part of it cleared for DMS OMO.** *Haydn Davies*

Left: Allocated to Stamford Hill, DMS 1607 (THM 607M) on Lambeth Bridge on 2 October 1974 has almost finished its long journey to Victoria. After nearly a year's filling in on this busy crew route, it would be reallocated in December to Croydon when displaced by a purpose-built DM.
David Wilkinson collection

The conversions of January, effected by new DMSs releasing RTs, were followed by a spate of slow deliveries and a stoppage of Aldenham repaints that month due to industrial action; if it wasn't the manufacturer, it was the operator – the 1970s in a nutshell! By the end of 1973 LT found itself 6,822 staff short, leading to a 5% cut in bus mileage operated as compared to 1972, and further industrial action as 1974 progressed would hit deliveries and the supply of spare parts, producing a vehicle shortage which would bite hard in the second half of the year. With no labour pool to draw on (despite the appearance of the first female bus drivers at the end of 1973) and not the money to pay them despite a pay deal thrashed out in August that turned a modest surplus into a large deficit, there was no easy solution. Still, on 19 May LT sent DMS 1659 into action during the Syon Park Gala Day as a recruitment vehicle; DMS 835 had already participated in the Easter Parade in Battersea Park and finally, DMS 833, while hardly a veteran and not to become one, participated in the HCVC London to Brighton run on 5 May.

Despite the DMSs' chief use at present being to replace Merlins, the core of the MBAs performing to their best intended role on the Red Arrows received an unexpected reprieve when the LTPC objected to their proposed replacement on these services by DMSs and suggested that new DMSs go to replace Swifts instead, an option which was later taken up under different circumstances. To this end DMS 1601 was returned to fleet livery and no further notion of double-decking the Red Arrows was ever entertained.

Delayed by three months due to knock-on effects from the aforementioned host of industrial difficulties, a small scheme anchored on points north-east of Ponders End took place on 23 March, converting Enfield's 191 (plus the Sunday service on the 135) to OMO DMS (ex-RT) and upgrading the W8 from MBS to farebox-fitted DMS to accompany its transfer

Above: DMS 1630 (THM 630M) was new to Enfield for the conversion of the 191 to OMO on 23 March 1974. Three months later it is seen at that route's Chingford terminus of the time.
Tony Wilson

ENTER THE LONDONER

Right: The time had now come for repaints, ideally spaced at the halfway mark of the initial Certificate of Fitness, and on 21 May 1974 Shepherd's Bush's DMS 5 (EGP 5J) is going through the process at Aldenham. *Bob Greenaway / Online Transport Archive*

from Enfield to Edmonton. At Thornton Heath, the anomalous Sunday-morning journeys that were all that remained of the 109 on that day of the week were converted from SMS to DMS operation.

In March 1974, with an eye to eliminating the remaining RTs as well as the troublesome Merlins, London Transport firmed up its 1975-76 order; at a cost of £10 million, 679 Fleetlines were to be delivered, which it was envisaged would be split between DMS and DM configuration but with all to be bodied by Park Royal. LT had already inspected Metropolitan prototype NVP 533M, taking it for test runs in the London Bridge area while housing it at Chiswick. Hedging its bets against DMS unreliability, and disregarding the likely outcry by British manufacturers against what was an essentially a foreign competitor (the Volvo Ailsa also being looked over at this time but rejected due to engine access considerations), LT took the opportunity of the Commercial Motor Show in September 1974 to finally confirm an order for 164 Metropolitans, all of which were to be bodied by MCW as the MD class. For the first time, real competition was in the offing for the DMS.

With crew-operated DMSs, and now purpose-built DMs, completely negating the Fleetline's intended purpose as laid down in the Reshaping Plan, still London Transport attempted to sell the unwilling public on OMO; during the spring and early summer of 1974 the Bromley SMSs on the 227 (from 3 June) and Bow's captive allocation of DMSs for the 10 (from 20 May) were modified for a three-month period to publicise the split-entrance aspect of fare-paying by painting the rear half of the entrance doors yellow (since January) and 'directing' boarders thus via specially-shaped yellow side adverts with a dropped panel and a roundel-cufflinked hand showing the way. It didn't work, passengers knowing that they risked embarrassing themselves in public against a (probably) recalcitrant machine, only to be prevented by a barrier from turning back from it to try again with the driver, who thus took on most of the work that the machinery was supposed to free him of. AFC takeup thus did not increase sufficient to prolong the experiment beyond its three-month period. It has been said that the presence of inspectors to assist with the machinery somewhat compromised the experiment.

In January 1974 an important change was made to the way running numbers were displayed on bus sides; rather than each route taking a series from 1 upwards, garages introduced a distinct block for each route. Cricklewood began to use black plastic plates with self-adhesive white numbers rather than the traditional stamped metal plates, and during the spring red plates with white numbers were introduced and became fleet standard. On the sides metric measurements began to replace Imperial weights, though fitfully and inconsistently; Park Royal DMSs from about DMS 836 onwards were billed at 9700kg or 9850kg and MCWs at 9950kg, though the latter were also labelled in tons, hundredweight and quarters as '9 14 0' or '9 7 0'. Repainted buses received metric figures.

Seasonal route 137A was reintroduced on 12 April to furnish the Flower Show and subsequent weekend events in Battersea Park till 23 September; Victoria's DMSs did the

44   THE LONDON DMS

Left: **A stylised beckoning hand shows passengers exactly where to get on Bow's DMS 1333 (MLH 333L) if they still fancy their chances against the automatic fare machinery located over the nearside front wheelarch. This shot was taken at London Bridge Station on 25 May 1974.** *C. Carter / Online Transport Archive*

honours and between 1 July and 31 August a weekday evening service was added. The Round London Sightseeing Tour took on a new batch of DMSs, releasing its incumbents indirectly to Barking for the OMO conversion on 20 April of Barking's 145 ex-RT; as part of this scheme the 23 on Sundays was treated to DMSs at Upton Park and Poplar. Now that the changes postponed from 1973 had been implemented, Merlin replacement could get under way in earnest. 18 May saw three upgrades from Merlin; Sutton's 293 and Merton's 152 and M1. The latter route's initial batch was rotated within a few days for buses more suitable for farebox operation. On Saturdays DMS-operated route 61 was pushed through from Chislehurst to Eltham to replace SMS-operated 227 on that day of the week. On 1 June the 79, 79A and 182 at Alperton were converted from MB to DMS (other than leaving SMSs on Harrow Weald's

Below: **Barking's DMS fleet swelled during 1974 as first the 179 was converted and then the 145. DMS 1626 (THM 626M) was one of the new deliveries for the former, but when seen at Ilford during 1977, had not managed to pick up a repaint, as was normally customary after three or four years.** *David Wilkinson collection*

Above: **Merton's flat-fare M1 was upgraded from MBS on 18 May 1974, introducing the likes of DMS 872 (TGX 872M). In this 1978 shot, the birds have been at it!** *Haydn Davies*

Wembley High Road is absolutely empty, if you can imagine such a thing, in this autumn 1974 Sunday shot of Alperton's DMS 700 (TGX 700M). This bus had been new to Stockwell as a Round London Sightseeing Tour bus but rotated out after the customary six months to upgrade the 79 from MBs. *Haydn Davies*

Sunday allocation on the 182). Southall's 282 was converted from MB to DMS on 27 July and North Street's 247A was removed from its forays round the Hainault Industrial Estate, a change not to be formalised until November.

Several significant mechanical developments characterised 1974, despite Aldenham having to wait for its guinea pigs due to a strike by the Central Distribution Service at Chiswick which halted the supply of spare parts to garages. In June DMS 864 was taken from the delivery line to Chiswick, where it received a Rolls-Royce Eagle 220 engine before taking up service at Turnham Green garage in November. Progressing from the trials with DMS 88, DMS 1665 was fitted at Chiswick during August with a mock-up engine compartment constructed of wood and fibreglass, featuring a pair of air-intake and exhaust chimneys angled at 45 degrees (although this bus would resume standard configuration in October, this would become familiar to us as the B20's engine compartment). DMS 884 was displayed at Olympia under the banner of the Castrol Motor Extravaganza from 23 July to 13 August (although, to actually get into the building, it had to have its wheels replaced with smaller wheels from an RT!) But the most important advancement was taken with a view to future policy in the teeth of noise problems (among other things) with the existing DMS, something which was likely to fail impending legislation (as had already been the case with the early Leyland engines), and which constituted a major complaint of the public, irrespective of whether they travelled in

Gardner- or Leyland-powered DMSs. DMS 854, officially taken into stock on 23 April, was kept back by Leyland for conversion into what was boldly to be called 'quiet bus' specification. This involved constructing a true end of the type mocked up on DMS 1665, whereby air would be taken in through the offside chimney and exhaust released through that on the nearside, which was slightly narrower. The redesigned engine compartment would be soundproofed with fibreglass-type material, hopefully baffling any racket put out by the turbocharged Leyland O.690 engine to be fitted. Even so, it was more than a little untidy with its asymmetrical vents and six-inch protrusion beyond the existing rear of the body necessitated by the turbocharger, with the attendant overheating problems.

Pending the completion of the move of Fleetline chassis construction from Coventry to Leyland in 1974, buses were constructed on both production lines, allowing deliveries to pick up; 53 came into stock in July and seventy were being stockpiled at Aldenham by August. Those DMSs stored at Chiswick were fitted there with fareboxes. The August registration change from M to N introduced two new blocks of SMU-N, booked from SMU 721-799N and SMU 901-999N, though unusually they would be curtailed after 19 and 47 members respectively; for the Park Royal intakes DM 948 commenced a new series at GHV 948N, with the awkward 'thousand', DM 1000, to be GHV 500N and then picking up from GHV 1N onwards; MCWs would take a GHM-N series starting with GHM 740N.

Above: **27 July 1974 saw Southall's 282 converted from MB to DMS operation, and on September 1974 we see DMS 1667 (THM 667M) in Yeading.** *John Laker*

The angled chimneys of the prototype 'quiet bus' are clear in this February 1978 shot of DMS 854 (TGX 854M), which had entered service at Cricklewood only three months previously after extensive trials that prompted a follow-on order for 400 B20s. *Tony Wilson*

Right: **Here came the DMs, and the only indicator that OMO had stalled was the lack of 'PLEASE PAY AS YOU ENTER' instruction on the front. Cricklewood's batch for the 16 were the first into action, and the garage continued to receive top-ups for some time after the initial need had been fulfilled; hence in the lead in this two-bus shot coming up to Victoria on 1 May 1975 is DM 1090 (GHV 90N), new in April 1975, leading DM 941 (SMU 941N), one of the original intake.**
David Wilkinson collection

Below: **Seen at the foot of the hill atop which is Alexandra Palace, DMS 874 (TGX 874M) was new into Wood Green in October 1974 and would spend all seven years of its Certificate of Fitness there.**
Haydn Davies

From 14 September the first DMs started entering service, intended fleetnumbers spanning DM 918-1247 (Park Royal) and DM 1703-1832 (MCW). They could be easily identified by their plain fronts with no 'PLEASE PAY AS YOU ENTER' admonition, while inside a three-bench seat replaced the AFC cabinet and a glass panel separated the forwardmost passenger from the doorway, rendering capacity H44/27D + 5. Concurrent with the display of DM 940 at the Commercial Motor Show from 20-28 September with blinds for the 16, Cricklewood was their first deployment, the conversion of the 16 and N94 (until 3 October) allowing the stopgap DMSs to be fitted with AFC machinery and redeployed to Wood Green for the W3 (converted from MBS on 22 September). Routes W1, W2 and W4 followed on 6 October, with lazy blind displays carried for these short routes, and the following day Cricklewood's own flat-fare requirements were rationalised with the transfer of the off-peak service on the 616 to the largely-parallel (and DMS-operated) 32. This was also the day the 134 at Muswell Hill was converted from crew-DMS to DM, and finally the 149 was treated, its DMs (shared between Edmonton and Stamford Hill) phasing in between 31 October and 5 December. All of these routes shared Park Royal and MCW-bodied DMs, although some swaps

Left: **DMS 915 (SMU 915N) was also new to Wood Green for the takeover of the W1, W2 and W4 from MBSs. During 1976 it is seen heading west through Hornsey with stablemate DMS 888 (TGX 888M) behind as a W3.**
Haydn Davies

were subsequently undertaken to rationalise the batches. The first few DMs of the MCW batch were built as DMSs and then converted. On 5 October the introduction of a Sunday service on the 39 from Battersea allowed the Sunday-only 19A to be withdrawn. DMS 1681 was LT's participation in this year's Lord Mayor's Show.

An aesthetic change which probably brought the DMS family into maturity was the relocation from DM 918 (Park Royal) and DMS 1698 (MCW), those considered to start the 1974 batches, of the front numberplate from the centre of the towing hatch to above it, right at the bottom; this was to forestall buses having the wrong vehicle's panel refitted after attention. Very few DMSs from the 1-167 batch were treated thus, it looking most uncomfortable, but upon overhaul the new position was rendered standard and probably the easiest way to identify an overhauled bus from distance. Uniquely among the early batch, DMS 83 was fitted with a later front with wider-separated headlights.

Even after trying and failing with white bands, which were beginning to disappear upon routine inter-overhaul repaint after two or three years, and phasing in the white fleetnumber/white solid roundel livery, LT still saw a need for improvement in the presentation of the DMS. And how it came, when in September

Left: **The second conversion from crew DMS to dedicated DM was the 134, shared between Muswell Hill and Potters Bar, although this time Potters Bar specialised on Metro-Cammells, turning in their three early Park Royal deliveries in exchange for three MCWs that Muswell Hill had taken. Turning out of Potters Bar garage's forecourt for what was still a long journey south despite the removal of the Victoria extremity is DM 1720 (THM 720M).**
David Wilkinson collection

ENTER THE LONDONER

Above: **On 3 March 1975 Brixton's DMS 46 (EGP 46J) shows off its new white-topped livery. The effect was so positive that it was adopted as standard.**
Tony Wilson

1974 Brixton's DMS 46 was repainted with white upper-deck window surrounds. This simple treatment changed the look of the DMS at once, bringing it just that little bit of variance that distinguished it from the dull and lazy all-red that had done nothing for the type's appearance and reputation. After a few days on loan to Abbey Wood to show the new livery off to south-east London passengers on the 177, it returned to Brixton.

During the summer of 1974 experiments were undertaken at Abbey Wood with a handful of DMSs fitted with a foot switch that opened the doors instead of a button; after operating favourably alongside unmodified DMSs, this was adopted as standard, Battersea's DMS fleet being done first. Meanwhile, white plastic ribbing began to be fitted to the horizontal grab rails on all DMs and DMSs to comply with new DofE regulation affecting all vehicles licensed to carry more than eight standees.

Two Plumstead routes were double-decked on 10 November, the 99 and 122A losing their MBs for DMSs, while on the 30th a small scheme at Southall took off the 232 and converted its partner 232A from RT to DMS operation. Continuing the advance of buses into the fast-developing Thamesmead area came new route 272 on 30 November, its Abbey Wood DMSs supporting the 177 east of Woolwich along its roads and then turning left at Abbey Wood Station. This was the last route change of 1974, though the RLST fleet was rotated again that month, Stockwell's expelled examples going to garages with particular shortages of DMSs. The entry into service of Rolls-Royce-engined DMS 864 at Turnham Green did not, unusually, merit a new code. Performance of this 12.17-litre powerplant, displacing 220bhp at 2100rpm, was satisfactory, though with the extra power by comparison with Gardner and Leyland units, fuel consumption was a little higher.

Despite continuing to struggle with the DMS family when deliveries of the type (and spare parts for them) weren't held up by strikes, the infamous three-day week occasioned by the miners' overtime ban, and then, once they were actually in service, having to contend with fear of suspicious packages and/or outright terrorist acts, not to mention hooliganism against staff and vandalism (or even arson) against vehicles and property, London Transport could count itself satisfied that at least the new DMSs had allowed most of the Merlins to be withdrawn by the end of 1974. With one eye on the future, LT was keeping a hand in the development of British Leyland's B15 project, a double-decker which, while not as rigid in specification as the corresponding single-deck National, was intended to incorporate as much development to LT's preferences (specifically a lower floor, a transverse engine and improved suspension and noise reduction) as had been denied the organisation since the squashing of the FRM.

Left: **DMS 724 (TGX 724M)** had been at Southall since October 1973 when the 282 had been one-manned, but on 30 November 1974 it added the 232A to its collection. *Haydn Davies*

Below: **Once DMS 761 (TGX 761M)** had finished its stand-in work on the 16 (see page 41), it was fitted as intended with the innards to its AFC cabinet and reallocated to Plumstead to take over the 99 and 122A from MBs. Still looking smart during the following summer, it is seen at Woolwich, General Gordon Place. *David Wilkinson collection*

Accordingly, LT announced by the autumn its intention to take one or two B15s on evaluation once construction of four under way at Park Royal was complete. Deliveries for 1974 had totalled over 400 Fleetlines, half of which were DMs. As befitting any class fortunate enough to reach one thousand in strength, DM 1000 was the subject of a handover ceremony at Park Royal in December, LT's Chairman, Sir Richard Way, taking delivery of the new bus.

CHAPTER THREE

CONCERNS AND CREWS

1975

The conversion of Hendon's 183 to OMO from RT on 4 January 1975, made possible by the completion of rebuilding work on the garage, was to be the last one-manning at all for the moment. DMs were now arriving in force, and on the weekend of 25/26 January they poured into Holloway and Muswell Hill. The former replaced RMs from the 17, 214, N92 and N93 and RTs from the 168A and allowed the shortfall to assume control of its allocations on the 4, 104, 172 and 253 at weekends. The allocation into Muswell Hill took over the 43 and at weekends the 102 (this latter change lasting, however, only till 23 February due to union personnel rejecting it). Stamford Hill's Sunday share of the 253 also became DM-operated.

This weekend's changes affected Wandsworth routes 295 (extended from Wandsworth Garage to Clapham Junction) and 295A (this Saturday-only service withdrawn) and 296 (a new route introduced to link Roehampton, Bessborough Road with Wandsworth via Dover House Road and Putney so that the 85's shortworkings to the estate could be withdrawn) and finally at Muswell Hill, where the W7 became the last of

Right: **DMS 1566 (THM 566M)** began life as a stand-in crew bus on Potters Bar's 134, but once a DM had arrived to replace it was fitted out for OMO as intended and put into Hendon for the one-manning of the 183 on 4 January 1975. In April 1976 it is seen heading away from Golders Green.
Tony Wilson

52 THE LONDON DMS

Left: **During 1975 Holloway became a major user of the dedicated crew-operated DM class, taking examples of both Park Royal and Metro-Cammell bodywork. The 17 was converted on 26 January but DM 1086 (GHV 86N) was allocated in June, spending six further years there before its particularly premature withdrawal and sale. On 1 April 1977 it is captured at the Elephant & Castle, unfortunately carrying a via blind for the 19.** *David Wilkinson collection*

Below: **On 23 February 1975 DM 1775 (GHM 775N) arrives at the 168A's Clapham Junction terminus, emerging through the mid-afternoon shadows on an otherwise perfectly sunny winter day. This Holloway bus would also serve its career at no other garage, but lasted two more years than DM 1086, additionally becoming a D for its final eighteen months.** *David Wilkinson collection*

the Reshaping-vintage 'Wood Green' routes to dump its MBSs for Fleetlines, in this case using former crew examples displaced from the 16, 134 and 149 and converted at Aldenham to flat-fare format.

The murder of Merton conductor Ronald Jones while at work on 20 January led to a series of actions taken to combat the increasing prevalence of vandalism and violence on London's buses; after an all-out strike on 29 January in sympathy with the conductor on the day of his funeral, a contract was placed with Redifon later in the year to fit two-way radios to 200 buses in the hope that all crews would be capable of contacting help quickly. Part of this was the installation of a mode in which buses' headlights were flashed and the horn blared. Authority to arrest suspected offenders

CONCERNS AND CREWS

Left: DMS 903 (SMU 903N) is in this mid-1975 view halfway along the very short but always busy W7 route operated by Muswell Hill. It had been new to Wood Green but would spend the rest of its life at its new garage. *Haydn Davies*

Below: **DMS 1610 (THM 610M)** was taken from Peckham with DMS 1614 and put into Camberwell on 23 February 1975 for the double-decking of the 42. It is seen at Aldgate on 24 April. *R. C. Riley*

for not giving their name and address on public transport was granted from 1 August, and from 1 December police personnel were granted free travel on buses and the Underground from 1 December.

Cricklewood's Sunday-only 245A was upgraded from SMS to DMS on 16 February, two years later than originally intended, and a similar double-decking on the 23rd replaced the 42's MBs with eight DMSs gathered from all over and put into Camberwell; the 45, however, was converted from RM to DM, the buses into Walworth soon falling out with severe gearbox problems to the extent that within five months, only seven of the 27 DMs allocated could be put into the field! If they could handle it, they crept out on the 12 on Sundays as well. Similarly, the DMs recently deployed to the 134, 149 and Holloway's doored crew routes had to be subbed by RMs from time to time, sometimes in strength. Blame can be apportioned here to Leyland, for amending the design of the gearbox brake band (already a major source of increased wear and subsequent vehicle failure) coincident with the move of production from Coventry to Leyland, which had already thrown delivery timetables out of likelihood of fulfilment, but LT were not consulted (or proper testing had not been carried out) and were thus caught out when the conversion of routes like the 45 should have been just a routine change from one type of vehicle to another. Coming hard on the heels of the spare-parts shortages and continuing engine breakdowns, this was unacceptable and led to LT's decision to seek out new manufacturers, British or even foreign concerns, such was the depth of reliability that had now been reached.

Left: **Whatever the type of bus to be found in London, its lifelong foe is parked cars; DM 1790 (GHM 790N), allocated new to Walworth for the conversion of the 45, is just about managing to do its job one day three years later, though some wing mirrors might have sacrificed themselves in the process. This bus was never repainted or converted to D and spent its whole six-year career at Walworth.**
John Parkin

Below: **Following the conversion of the busy inner-city 45 to DM on 16 February 1975, the Walworth allocation on it was apt to let its new buses wander to the 12 on Sundays, and such a working is demonstrated in Oxford Street that summer by DM 1786 (GHM 786N).**
Haydn Davies

Right: **DMSs 463-467, the five with glider doors, had been kept together as they moved from their first garage, West Ham, to Brixton, but when the S1 was converted to DMS operation on 23 March 1975, DMS 467 (MLK 467L) alone came back. It is seen shortly before repaint in November 1975, which would turn the red entrance doors yellow.**
David Wilkinson collection

During February 1975 West Ham's DMS fleet had their nearside windscreen wiper replaced by a pantograph unit as on Nationals, with the view to seeing whether these should become fleet standard. March saw the end of MCW's DM deliveries and DMSs resume from DMS 1833; a short industrial dispute had held things up a little. Some repainted DMSs came back from Aldenham during February with gold fleetnumber transfers and further examples had to make do with the large transfers from numberplates, which looked most uncomfortable in this role, until more white Johnson numbers could be printed. Four Holloway DMSs (55, 59, 61 and 62) were noted carrying their front numberplates between the narrowly-spaced headlights of this batch, again looking unhappy but at least permitting the right number to be recognised when towing! Conversely DMS 904 was one of a later fair few to wear its numberplate in the lower position; it would not be the first time DMSs' numberplates migrated up, or down!

On 1 March the Saturday run beyond Bexleyheath garage to Slade Green was switched from the 122 to the 132, while at Hornchurch the 252 was converted from SMS to DMS and the 165 pointed off its normal route at certain times to provide a service to the Mardyke Estate on the Dagenham-Rainham borders.

Right: **Replaced at Muswell Hill by brand new DMSs from the same month of deliveries as those into Wood Green, DMS 809 (TGX 809M) passed to Bromley on 27 April 1975 to help upgrade the 126 and 138 from MBs. On 2 July 1976 it is still hard at work on this task.**
R. C. Riley

Left: **The Round London Sightseeing Tour's regular rotation of Fleetlines now put examples of the DM class into service; here laying over at Waterloo on a sunny June day in 1975 is Stockwell's DM 1072 (GHV 72N). Once again, the blind boxes not needed for this route have been blacked out. Once its RLST spell was up, this bus remained at Stockwell for the 168.**
D. T. Elliott

Croydon was next to receive an allocation of DMs, these crew-operated Fleetlines displacing the last RMLs to have entered service from the 130, 130B and the Saturday portion of the weekend 130A. The 79 at Alperton was introduced on Sundays. On 22 March it was again time for the Round London Sightseeing Tour's fleet at Stockwell to rotate out, but this time all that was available new was DMs, so it was these that replaced the six-month-old incumbents over a two-week period. On 23 March Brixton's 133 and Sunday 57A were converted from RT to DM operation, night route N87 also taking on DMs, but at Stamford Hill the N83's official conversion to DM did not settle, RMs continuing to turn out in practice. At West Ham the S1 was converted to farebox DMS operation, its intake for this route coming from all over the fleet, but the garage had to borrow two buses from Wood Green on Saturdays until 1 June. Yellow ultimate blinds were displayed on anti-clockwise journeys over this frying pan-shaped route. In the absence of seasonal route 137A this year due to the closure of the Festival Pleasure Gardens at Battersea Park, 28 March saw the introduction of seasonal route 74X from Victoria with three DMSs, which took passengers from Baker Street to the London Zoo at the north end of Regent's Park. This was rendered daily from 24 May and three new

Left: **Brixton's 133 was converted from RT to DM on 23 March 1975; the garage used a mix of Park Royals and MCWs for this task, with the former bodywork represented at the Elephant & Castle on 22 April by DM 1064 (GHV 64N).** *R. C. Riley*

CONCERNS AND CREWS

57

Above: **Metro-Cammell DMS deliveries resumed in the spring of 1975, and their first order of business was to double-deck the W21 at Walthamstow. That October at Walthamstow Central we see DMS 1838 (GHM 838N) in front of West Ham's Routemaster RM 2132 (CUV 132C) on the 69.** *Geoff Rixon*

DMSs put into Victoria for it. On 20 April the 281's Sunday OMO roster was upgraded from SM to DMS with vehicles spare from the 90B and 267.

Merlin relegation continued with the conversion from MB to DMS of Bromley's 126 and 138 and Holloway's 143 on 27 April, though MBs continued to assist DMSs at Plumstead on the 99 during the first half of the year. The arrival of farebox DMSs for Walthamstow's W21 on 1 June allowed this garage to take over from Wood Green the task of loaning suitably-equipped Fleetlines to West Ham's S1 on Saturdays. The W21 was originally to have been treated to DMs from the current intake but fitted with fareboxes; indeed DMs 1076-1079 were put into Walthamstow to train for this route until the union put its foot down and new DMSs were allocated after a two-week postponement, again with black-on-yellow blinds to denote anti-clockwise journeys. One of the more severe cuts to have accompanied the opening of the Victoria Line was ameliorated somewhat on 14 June when the 134 was projected south again from Warren Street to Tottenham Court Road.

Right: **During the 1970s London Transport was experimenting with ways of identifying distinctive workings to the passenger awaiting buses at a distance. Black-on-yellow blinds were the chosen method, expanded from isolated ultimate panels to the entire set. In the case of the Croydon-operated flat-fare C-routes, they replaced white-on-blue panels, and during 1975 DMS 1389 (MLH 389L) with the new setup poses beside original-blinded DMS 1388 (MLH 388L) at West Croydon.** *Haydn Davies*

58   THE LONDON DMS

Left: **Brixton's DMs from the 133 were used on the 109 at weekends, as seen north of Croydon by DM 1061 (GHV 61N) during March. The main conversion that month was of Croydon's 130, exemplified by DM 1799 (GHM 799N) new the same month, and behind both of them is CJN 435C, a Southend PD3 loaned to London Transport at the most critical point of its vehicle shortage.** *R. C. Riley*

May deliveries were slow due to industrial action at both Park Royal and MCW, which didn't help the need to return two MCW-bodied DMSs a day for front end modifications. In June two DMs (1825 and 1831) then in course of delivery became the test rigs for a test at Aldenham of new number blinds with suffix letters of an increased size (to about two-thirds of the number they followed), answering criticism by the LTPC of the legibilty at a distance of such suffixed routes' number blinds. While blinds with larger suffixed numbers were printed thereafter, it was by no means universal practice. The C-routes at Croydon, meanwhile, took new yellow blinds from 12 May to reduce confusion with the 130 group since the conversion of those three routes to DM. The lack of DMSs at the moment necessitated the putting into service at Merton of seven new DMs for Derby Day work on 4 June; once their work was done they moved on to Holloway.

On 23 June the weekday service of Holloway's 4 was converted from RT to DM operation,

Below: **After the weekend allocation on the 4 gained DMs on 26 January, the rest of the route was converted on 23 June. Two days after displacing an RT, Holloway's DM 1054 (GHV 54N) is seen at Waterloo blinded for a garage run.** *R. C. Riley*

while on 19 July the opportunity was taken to use some of Brixton's crew Fleetlines on its Saturday allocation on the 109. The 285 was double-decked at weekends, ex-SMS (Fulwell on Saturdays and Norbiton on Sundays) and on the 20th the 276 at Walthamstow was upgraded from MB to DMS. The 275 would have been done on this day but was postponed for a fortnight to allow for the completion of tree pruning.

The 172's conversion to DM was completed on 3 August with the input of yet further Fleetlines into Holloway and now Camberwell, the latter putting them to use at weekends on Saturday- and Sunday-only route 40. Double-deckings that summer took in North Street's 66B and 103 and Walthamstow's 275 (ex-SMS, all on 3 August) and on 30 August Potters Bar's 84 (ex-MB), the latter prompting the use of DMSs on the 284 rather than MBs when FRM 1 was not available. The 31st then saw Wandsworth and Stockwell receive their first DMs to replace the 168's RTs, in a reversion of the intended order of conversion of this and the 4 and 172. Something of a failure in the face of the vehicle shortage, the 296 was withdrawn on 13 September after just eight months.

Not what you would call an auspicious year by anyone's reckoning, despite the GLC's approval in July of LT's ten-year capital investment programme, 1975 was bracketed by two considerable fares increases, while the spare-parts shortage and general unreliability of modern vehicles combined to create a desperate situation which, it was felt could be eased only by the extraordinary expedient of hiring coaches from private operators to fill in on up to 32 routes during peak hours. Routes 125 and 270 were subjected to this from 1 September, neither of which were DMS-operated, but it was significant that 19 of the 32 routes to be chosen were. As it happened, Union opposition caused this plan to be abandoned, several journeys on over a hundred routes seeing cancellation instead, while towards the end of the year shuffles were undertaken between garages with excess capacity (Holloway, Stockwell, Camberwell and Willesden) to those with insufficient (New Cross, Leyton, Croydon, Poplar and Walthamstow), and recruitment was suspended altogether at some garages. LT was already looking ahead to the delivery of the 679-strong next order for DMSs, which were all to be in the white-top livery of DMS 46 and all with two-leaf glider doors, though 200 of the body order, all of which was to have been by Park Royal, were now transferred to MCW. Even then, LT had not given up on the idea of building its own buses, a concept which had served it so well in the past for good or ill; the passage through Parliament of the London Transport (Additional Powers) Act on 2 May 1975 had restored to LT some of the powers taken away by the Transport (London) Act in

Below: **DMS 1910 (KUC 910P)** was one of the 84's new fleet of double-deckers from 30 August 1975, and on 21 June 1976 is seen at St Albans alongside London Country's MCW-bodied Atlantean AN 103. Perhaps London Transport would have had success with the Atlantean, or struggled to adapt it as much as they did with the Fleetline, but those particular ANs were from a batch diverted from another operator entirely and London Country adapted to them rather than the other way round. *R. C. Riley*

60 THE LONDON DMS

Left: DM 1126 (KUC 126P) was one of the Wandsworth allocation from new on the 168, converted to DM operation on 31 August 1975 in concert with Stockwell. By September 1977 this bus was still resident at Wandsworth, and is seen that month outside its home garage. *Photobus*

1969, which specifically spurred along what became known as the the XRM project. Among other things, this was a plan to design a shorter, lighter-weight bus with up to four axles (a three-axle Bedford VAL coach being purchased for experimentation) and the engine in a position of the operator's choice, with production models envisaged by the early 1980s. Until such time, if LT could no longer physically build its own buses on its own premises, it could at least attempt to subvert ongoing problems with DMS deliveries; particular displeasure at this time was evinced with the Leyland-badged chassis now coming into service as opposed to those manufactured under Daimler at Coventry. And LT was hedging its bets with the order for MD-class Scania Metropolitans imminent and work continuing on Leyland's own B15 project, which would become the Titan; a demonstrator was now complete and would be with LT by the end of 1975. Accordingly, the Rolls-Royce engine fitted to DMS 864 and the Sevcon automatic transmission control unit fitted to DMS 136 in 1975 remained under observation.

Right: The 40 was a Saturday- and Sunday-only route, the main effort being entrusted to weekday route 40A. Still, there were enough DMs spare from the conversion of the 172 to take over the 40's Camberwell allocation, as depicted during March 1978 by DM 1113 (GHV 113N) at Aldgate. The Poplar allocation remained with RMs. *John Parkin*

CONCERNS AND CREWS

The original Speedbus idea of a Marble Arch-Hackney route was replaced on the drawing boards by a north-south route from Parliament Hill Fields to Peckham, although the Metropolitan Police, working closely with LT and the GLC, were insistent that the restrictions proposed over so extensive a route could not be enforced. The flat-fare concept, meanwhile, seemed to have more legs in it than did AFC, passengers having no choice but to tender the correct change under the eyes of the driver, though at the attendant risk for LT's revenue of them underpaying and not being caught. Even so, the concept of multi-use tickets began to come into play during 1975, the DMSs on Muswell Hill's and Wood Green's flat-fare W-routes having a ticket canceller fitted at Aldenham in August advance of what would be known as 'Multi-Ride'. This made its debut on 14 September 1975, by which a card with capacity for thirteen journeys could be inserted into the canceller and the appropriate segment cut out, with no limit as to time or route used.

Night route N97 from Turnham Green was one-manned on the night of 19/20 September, after which (on the 28th) Potters Bar received more DMSs for the 242, seeing off further Merlins; this conversion should have been concurrent with that of the 84 but for the continuing delay in vehicle deliveries; industrial action at both Park Royal and MCW meant that neither dual-sourced option was entirely safe! Both 84 and 242 ran beyond the GLC boundary where local fares applied, so the AFC cabinets were roped off on their DMSs and drivers issued all tickets. Upton Park's 238 was converted to DMSs on Sunday on that date. The next big allocation of doored crew buses, however, was to Chalk Farm's 24, which on 19 October was converted from RML to DM; the garage's Sunday share

Top left: Potters Bar gained a reputation for well turned-out buses, and could really open them up on rural routes like the 242 across the roof of the border into Hertfordshire. DMS 1896 (GHM 896N) was allocated new in September 1975 and is captured at work a month later. *Haydn Davies*

Above left: Another Potters Bar bus at its best, DMS 1899 (KUC 899P) is captured in strong winter sunshine at Clare Hall, South Mimms one weekend in December 1976. *Tony Wilson*

Left: DMs were now sweeping through central London, and the 24, converted on 19 October 1975, was a particularly ambitious choice for these already slower and more complicated doored buses. **Chalk Farm's DM 1170 (KUC 170P)** reposes at Pimlico in June 1978. *Tony Wilson*

Left: Chalk Farm took the opportunity to put the 24's Sunday shortfall of DMs on the 3, personified at Crystal Palace on 24 October 1976 by DM 1117 (GHV 117N). *R. C. Riley*

of the 3 followed suit. A week later three night routes received DMs, Wandsworth's N68 and N88 pair and Stockwell's N81. Some weekend double-deckings were implemented, that of the 125 (Finchley) and 231 (Enfield) on Sundays, Holloway's 239 on Saturdays and Potters Bar's 299 on Saturdays and Sundays, all from SMS. Due to the vehicle situation, Stockwell's DMs were withdrawn from the RLST on 1 November, the OMs of Obsolete Fleet continuing in their stead. Stockwell's piece of the N87 was converted from RML to DM operation to complete this route. Further SMS displacements came to pass on 16 November, routes 147 (Upton Park) and 181/181A (Stockwell) receiving new DMSs. On the 30th the Croydon allocation on Sunday-only 59 became a DM operation, Streatham retaining its RMs. This was to have coincided with the conversion of the 130 group in March but was objected to by the union.

Below: A little before the tide of single-deck withdrawals turned against the SMS fleet, there were isolated individual upgrades of their routes to DMS operation. One such was the 181 and its Sunday counterpart 181A from Stockwell, which received new DMSs on 16 November 1975. Here at Victoria on the following 31 March is a smart-looking DMS 1932 (KUC 932P). *R. C. Riley*

Below: **On 20 August 1976 Hanwell's DMS 1955 (KUC 955P) passes Boston Manor station, eight months after the conversion of the E1 and E2 from SMS operation. These Reshaping-era flat-fare routes had struggled under the Merlins that had commenced them and fared no better under the shorter Swifts, but the input of DMSs settled them; often in these cases, all it took was the extra seating capacity provided by the good old double-deck bus.**
John Laker

As at Wood Green, the Ealing-area E-routes spawned by Reshaping had become unreliable and unpopular under their Merlins, and on 7 December the E1 and E2 were upgraded to DMS; the E3 had to remain single-deck (SMSs replacing MBSs) due to Fleetlines being just too high to get under the railway bridge at Acton Lane.

The conversion to DM operation of the 24 had been carried out with a view to properly examining the effects on boarding times of doored buses in central London rather than the allocation hitherto of Fleetlines apparently willy-nilly; from 14 December a second route was converted to DM on this basis, the 29 shared between Wood Green and Holloway and paralleling the 24 for some of its length in town so that measurements could be taken at specific points along each route. At weekends, Wood Green's excess DMs were employed on the 123 on Saturdays and 141 on Sundays. In spite of the rapid and widespread penetration of the DM class during 1975, their unreliability necessitated continued appearances by Routemasters, particularly on the 149 and 168.

As the staff shortage eased, vehicle problems now came to the fore; where DMSs were concerned, things had got to the point where new Fleetline chassis, stored at Chiswick due to the late delivery of new bodies for them, had to be stripped of parts to keep other examples running. By September 1975 the supply of bodies was four hundred behind that of chassis! Some DMSs, sidelined early in their careers by any combination of failures that characterised the type's first few years, ended up cannibalised at their home garages. A significant number thus lay idle for several months to several years and some never ran again at all, a notorious example being DM 931, which was robbed for parts at Cricklewood. None of this was helped by the first of two consecutive hot summers which caused overheating. Merlin withdrawal fell behind, with recertifications having to be undertaken and even MBSs being recertified as MBAs for Red Arrows. It was even felt necessary to look abroad for new parts suppliers, an order for piston rings being placed with Federal Mogul of Southfield, Michigan, USA. A smaller-scale expedient was to purchase five more

Left: **On 20 August 1976 Hanwell's DMS 1960 (KUC 960P) is seen in West Ealing on the E2. Both buses pictured would last here until replaced by Metrobuses in 1981, but only this one would be overhauled for further service in the capital.** *John Laker*

Rolls-Royce engines, which would be delivered in 1976 for fitting to incoming vehicles.

The end of the '1972-74' order for 1,600 DMSs (a quarter of which had turned out to be DMs) was in sight, but the pace of deliveries lagged sufficient for London Transport to switch between its sources on the fly according to their capacity; accordingly, the last thirty DMs that would bring to a close the '1972-74' order, DM 1218-1247, were diverted from Park Royal to MCW. Attention could then be turned to the '1975-76' order, which would be arriving straight after. Due to MCW's commitment on the MD class, deliveries of which had started in December 1975, all of the 1975-76 Fleetline order were to be bodied by Park Royal, but the continuing production delays there prompted the transfer of 200 bodies to MCW, a total quickly increased to 300, minus thirty subtracted from MCW in exchange for their taking on the bodying of DMs 1218-1247. Thus 170 DMSs (1968-2057 and 2167-2246) were to have standard MCW bodies, DMS 2058-2166 being bodied by Park Royal. There were Leyland and Gardner engines in both batches, while of the 400 B20s, DMSs 2247-2346 would be the MCW contingent and DMSs 2347-2526 and DMs 2527-2646 Park Royal.

It was decided to adopt the 'white top' livery for the 1975-76 order (including MDs), but not for repaints, as it was difficult to apply white over red unless existing paintwork had been fully stripped. Nor would overhauled examples wear the new colours, but this wasn't to be for a couple of years yet anyway. As well as white-top livery, DMSs 1968-2526 and DMs 2527-2646 would specify two-piece glider doors as standard, the entrance door's panes folding over one another to the front and those in the entrance door opening to either side. Fluorescent lighting would now be in the blind boxes, and a pantograph windscreen wiper would replace the single wiper in the nearside half of the windscreen, ensuring rather more sweep and less likelihood of the unit just hanging lifeless as often seen, its point downwards. The basic LT code for this specification was DM7, with the usual prefixes and suffixes as modifications ensued. Externally, they were badged at the rear as LEYLAND / FLEETLINE and bore chassis codes in Leyland's fashion as FE30AGR (Gardners) or FE30ALR (Leylands), FE30ALR Special denoting the B20.

Below: **On 14 December 1975 the bold step of converting the 29 to DM was undertaken. This lengthy and extremely busy trunk route was shared between two garages, Holloway and Wood Green, and DM 1182 (KUC 182P) was one of the latter's intake. It is seen on the following 5 March in Wilton Road.** *R. C. Riley*

CONCERNS AND CREWS

1976

1976 began with the introduction of DMSs to the 616 on 12 January in place of MBSs, an act which would have taken place eleven months earlier if plans had kept to the letter. Cricklewood was also in the news when on the 31st the 16 was split in half, new DM-operated route 16A taking half the service to the new shopping centre at Brent Cross. This important new landmark had several local services extended to serve it, including DMS-operated route 182, but this latter change, which incorporated an extension to Brent station (renamed Brent Cross later in the year to match the new shopping centre) was reversed on 19 May due to the objections of locals in Western Road to buses. Another objection, this time by Hertfordshire County Council and Hertsmere District Council, forced the cancellation of a planned conversion of the 292 from DMS to SMS so that the 231 and 299 could be double-decked in the interest of equalising vehicle types at the affected three garages; as it turned out, the 231 had to wait till October for new DMSs and the 299 never got them at all, only the weekend share deriving from spares from the 84.

Part of the 31 January programme in the Walthamstow area involved the projection of the 278 from Leyton to Walthamstow and, at night, the extension to Victoria of the single route N84 journey to Charing Cross. On 7 March the meal reliefs of four DMS-operated night routes were livened up through the diversion of route N68, N84, N88 and N93 to or via Liverpool Street.

Right: **The new Brent Cross shopping centre was an immediate hit and became a local landmark and focal point. Sensibly, from the outset it was lavishly provided with buses, links being provided from all directions. That from central London took half the 16's service from the Neasden direction, buses diverting the other way once north of Cricklewood. Heading back into town and having reached Hyde Park Corner is Cricklewood's DM 924 (SMU 924N).** *David Wilkinson collection*

Right: **Not all the routes added to Brent Cross were a success; the projection of the 142 and 182 to the simultaneously-renamed Brent Cross Underground station had to be pulled back within months due to residents' objections. Setting off from the already busy bus station during October 1976 is Alperton's DMS 288 (JGF 288K), based there since new and the beneficiary of a repaint the previous November.** *Tony Wilson*

66

Routine repaints reached the first of the MCWs in February; a slight hitch where the BESI-fitted examples at Clapton were concerned meant the bottom quarter of the nearside roundel had to be sliced off so as to accommodate the BESI grilles.

One last push remained for the DM class as this batch of 460 vehicles began to approach its end – the mighty 207, shared between Hanwell and Uxbridge. The former's RMLs departed on 28 February and the latter's on 28 March. Slow deliveries were the cause of Uxbridge's deferment, though it needed only twelve DMs to Hanwell's forty-nine, and even then loans came from existing DM sheds until all the MCW-bodied batch of thirty were in service.

Above: **Since introduction in 1960 to replace the trolleybuses, the 207 had spent eight years each with RMs and RMLs, and from 28 February 1976 DMs began to phase in, first from Hanwell. Completing the last leg of its long slog from Shepherd's Bush is DM 1813 (GHM 813N), coming into Uxbridge town centre on Leap Year Day, 29 February 1976. Although most of Hanwell's DMs were new Park Royals, this one was an earlier MCW new to Walworth and is still carrying its code.** *John Laker*

Left: **DM 1230 (KUC 230P) was one of the thirty-three new Park Royal DMs that, together with nine MCW-bodied transfers from around the fleet, restocked the 207 at Hanwell. On 29 February 1976 it is sharing Uxbridge forecourt with that garage's RML 2512 (JJD 512D), itself shortly to be replaced by a new DM (from a choice of five Park Royals and seven MCWs) and transferred to Upton Park.** *John Laker*

67

Left: **Four of the last standard DMs joined Stockwell for the Round London Sightseeing Tour in April 1976; DM 1215 (KUC 215P) was the only Park Royal of the quartet, and is seen passing Mansion House in July.** *R. C. Riley*

Below left: **Thirteen new DMSs were allocated to Holloway to convert the 239 from SMS on 21 March 1976; these were the first Park Royals of the '1975-76' batch and the highest-numbered-but-one of Holloway's intake was DMS 2071 (KJD 71P), seen at Euston in May. It can be seen how odd is the tapering-off of the white relief into the upper-deck windows on the Park Royal body.** *Tony Wilson*

Two south-west London changes that midwinter added DMSs to the 57's Saturday runout on 28 February and extended the 233 from Roundshaw to Wallington Station on 1 March. On the 21st Holloway's 239 was converted from SMS to DMS, somewhat alleviating a shortage of the type of their scheduled Saturday workings at Holloway. 10 April saw the 189's shortlived extension to Esher pulled back to Hook, while two Uxbridge SMS routes to gain DMSs at weekends were the 223 on Sundays and the 224B on Saturdays, and at Enfield, new route 217B was introduced between Enfield Town and Ninefields North. Battersea's seasonal 137A operated again in 1976, but only on 18/19 April.

Loughton received its first DMSs for the conversion from MB operation of route 20 on 25 April, which also encompassed the 167 on Sundays. This date also saw the Wembley Market runs of the 92 and 182 withdrawn. On 9 May North Street's 66 shed its SMSs for DMSs, Stonebridge's 112 following likewise on the 23rd and the weekday service on the 285 at Fulwell gained Fleetlines on 12 June. A new section was added to the 241 on 13 June when it was taken out of its V & A Docks terminus and rerouted westwards to the Kier Hardie Estate. On 4 July two New Cross SMS routes, the 70 and 188, were double-decked. The 91 was extended in service from its Wandsworth Bridge stand to the safer forecourt of Wandsworth garage on 13 June.

Left: **A Saturday double-decking brought Uxbridge DMSs to the 224B on that day of the week with effect from 10 April 1976. Its original livery was looking tired by the time of this shot at its home garage, and a repaint was duly implemented in October.** *Haydn Davies*

Right: **12 June 1976 saw the 285 at Fulwell upgraded to double-deck operation. Although the intake of DMSs comprised new examples, all of them had been licensed at other garages and transferred in. The Hatton Cross area is certainly looking parched from the legendary long hot summer as DMS 1976 (KUC 976P) swings through on 21 August on its way to Kingston.** *John Laker*

Below right: **DMS 1980 (KUC 980P) was another transfer into Fulwell for the 285, though it was recorded at Elmers End and Merton before coming here. The neatness of the new standard lower rear design and the MCW bodywork's interpretation of the white-top livery combine on this wander to the 267 at Hampton Court, also on 21 August.** *Geoff Rixon*

The publication in April of LT's Annual Report for 1975 bemoaned the fact that OMO was only up to 40% due to MB replacement by new DMSs despite the staff and vehicle situation both having improved sufficient to see off the hired coaches on the 125 and 270 after 2 April 1976. This wasn't sufficient to ward off a 50% reduction in LT's operating grant requiring a fares increase (implemented 20 June) or the suspension of recruitment, but the falling pound at least boosted tourism. The introduction of Multi-Ride ticketing was to be split between four manufacturers of cancellers for installation during early 1977; Wood Green's existing flat-fare set-up was by passimeters whereas buses at Muswell Hill could accommodate both flat fares and graduated fares but with the machinery set to the former mode.

From DMS 1968 and 2058 respectively, the first of each bodybuilder's batch of the '1975-76' order, there was a revised rear light arrangement with four lights (including a pair of white lights for reversing) set into a taller unit, metal-edged and tapering at the top and bottom. Inevitably, the clusters appeared on accident-damaged bodies and recertifications. Park Royal bodies also demonstrated a subtle variance in the application of the white-top livery by comparison with MCW bodywork; while the beading above the upper-deck front windscreen on MCW bodywork allowed the white to continue all the way round the buses, on Park Royals the lack of beading prompted them to curtail the white by tapering it off into the front upper-deck windows; this had not been the case with DMS 46, but it allowed another means of visual identification between Park Royal and MCW bodies.

Right: **All Loughton's intake for the 20 on 9 April 1976 were transfers rather than new buses; DMS 1555 (THM 555M) came from New Cross and had begun its career as a crew bus out of Potters Bar. It's letting the side down somewhat with a floppy windscreen wiper as it passes through Loughton with DMS 1695 (THM 695M), similarly drafted in for the 20, heading the other way.** *David Wilkinson collection*

New Fleetlines were now badged as Leylands, despite the embossed 'D' for Daimler still existing on wheel hubs. One hundred DMS bodies from the upcoming order were transferred in January 1976 from Park Royal to MCW, whose output otherwise segued from DM 1247 to DMS 1968 in April. Improvements to the basic specification included strip lighting throughout, the carrying in the saloon of a fire extinguisher and the creation of a lockable flap over the rear blind handle on the rear wall downstairs. After a long spell with just Leyland engines, a batch of Gardner engines was included in this order, to be fitted to DMSs 2038-2057 and 2167-2246 (MCW) alongside DMS 2128-2166 (Park Royal). Alarms, plus a two-way radio link to the bus control centre at Mansion House, were specified from DMS 1943 onwards. Of the five Rolls-Royce engines purchased at the end of 1975, one was fitted to DM 1199 in March 1976 for onward transfer to Hanwell in April, with DMSs 1968, 2059 and 2120 from the current order following in June for allocation to New Cross, Turnham Green and Fulwell respectively. All were in service by August, with a spare engine to be used on rotation as needed, and were of marginally differing specifications for close observation by Chiswick, that on DMS 864 additionally being derated to address the kind of engine noise output problems that the Leyland engine was becoming notorious for. DMS 854, meanwhile, continued to be the subject of noise-reduction experimentation of its own. Duly fitted by December 1975 with a rear end assembly like that mocked up on DMS 1665, it carried a turbocharged Leyland O.690 engine rather than the O.680 fitted to its fellows. Moving in September 1976 to British Leyland's experimental department in Leyland in Lancashire, it had become the prototype for the B20. Despite doubts by LT over the cost of the project, 400 B20s were ordered, to be included at the tail end of the current deliveries. Where shrouds were concerned, DMSs 786 and 1694 from Wandsworth had theirs removed altogether at the beginning of 1976, affording a provincial appearance but enabling easier access to the rear window for cleaning purposes. A few DMSs went on to have this done over their lifetime, but not as many as the usefulness of the modification would suggest.

Its concession to the market and to the whims of politicians by ordering off-the-peg vehicles having burned it so badly, London Transport began to think again about specifying its own designs, or at least wresting back as much of the ability to do so as it could. In connection with the XRM project that had been in gestation in one form or another since the removal of LT's freedom to design its own specifications, LT took unserviceable DM 1787 out of Hanwell on 22 April 1976 and sent it to the National Engineering Laboratory at East Kilbride, which fitted it with hydrostatic transmission. This theoretically enabled the engine to be mounted anywhere due to the supply of oil to traction motors affixed to the rear wheel hubs (or even inside the wheels), propelled by an engine-driven pump through flexible tubes. If successful, this could cure the weight-distribution and engine overheating problems suffered by rear-engined buses, and if the engine was side-mounted (under the staircase being felt to be the ideal position), allow a flat,

Below: **Repaints carried out to DMSs in the middle of their seven-year Certificate of Fitness brightened them up no end, and, where previous liveries and fleetnames had existed, standardised them all on the current model with white filled roundels and white fleetnames. Battersea's DMS 405 (JGF 405K) was repainted in October 1975 and is seen the following 14 May with the Houses of Parliament as a backdrop. Despite the route 39A blind being carried, this day was a Friday and thus '39' should be being shown; in any case, both the 39 and its Saturday counterpart had been extended through to Putney Bridge Station in the DMS era.** *R. C. Riley*

Left: **New in June 1976, DMS 2004 (KJD 4P) was allocated to Catford in July, ready for the conversion to DMS of the 108B on 15 August, and on 10 October is seen outside its home garage; this was a Sunday, so the 124A came out to play. This bus would spend seven years at Catford before finishing its career at New Cross, but subsequent use as a trainer prolonged its life until 1991.** *R. C. Riley*

level floor for maximum passenger-carrying potential at an optimum weight. Leyland's own B15, which was the real-world answer so far to LT's mechanical intentions, was now in service alongside DMs on the 24 and provided helpful comparison figures with them during a legendarily hot summer which did its best to incapacitate newer buses where the RTs and Routemasters kept right on working.

By June 1976 DMSs could now boast two thousand members, despite stock numbers having romped towards the 2100s with the concurrent delivery of Park Royal bodies in that range; the registration split from DMS 1999-2001 was KUC 999P, KJD 500P and KJD 1P. AS the plate change came around, blocks in the OUC-R and OJD-R series were reserved; DMSs 2025-2057 would carry OUC 25-57R and OJD 123-503R were made available for as many DMSs were delivered before time ran out. In August the final configurations for the final DMS deliveries were firmed up; after concurrently-delivered Gardner-engined DMSs 2128-2166 (Park Royal) and DMSs 2167-2246 (MCW), the last four hundred would be B20s, Leyland's classification for the 'quiet bus' concept experimented upon with DMS 854. Of these, DMSs 2247-2346 would be MCW-bodied and DMSs 2347-2526 Park Royal. The final Fleetlines of all would be Park Royal-bodied DMs 2527-2646. It would have been good for LT and for the B20 alike if one had been ready in time to be shown off by Leyland at the Commercial Motor Show at the end of September 1976, but DMS 2147 had to do the honours instead; perhaps fittingly, photography of it was impeded by a wall.

Shortlived route 277A came off on 7 August when the 277 was extended once again beyond Cubitt Town to Poplar over the once-contentious bridge. To allow driver changes at Edmonton, the W8 was projected in service beyond Lower Edmonton to Tramway Avenue, while not far away, a number of Wood Green flat-fare DMSs were fitted with transponders to allow them to beat cars into the stand at Northumberland Park station. More SMS-to-DMS conversions during the summer of 1976 were Catford's 108B (15 August, postponed from 25 July), Streatham's 249 (29 August) and Loughton's 167 (12 September), but one DMS (more often as not DMS 2036) replaced a more noble vehicle on 30 September when FRM 1 was withdrawn at Potters Bar after a collision while working the 284. This arrangement was formalised from 19 November.

On 9 October the two halves of the 10 were linked up again, with the 10A coming off and the 10 operating throughout from Victoria to Woodford Wells, the latter terminus (after a six-day pause for lack of toilet facilities there) representing a diversion from Woodford Bridge. The Victoria workings from the 10A passed to the 10. At the Essex end of this route, two Loughton routes had their northern ends transposed so that the 20 now operated to Debden and the 20A (converted from RT to DMS OMO) terminated at Epping. The 10's extension to Woodford Wells covered the 20A over these roads and facilitated a one-manning that had been planned since 1973. Another OMO conversion for 9 October was of Seven Kings's 129, now that this garage had been rebuilt to handle buses of larger dimensions

CONCERNS AND CREWS

Right: **DMS 2190 (OJD 190R)** looks pristine in this summer 1977 view recording the 129's OMO conversion on 9 October 1976, but the bus itself was already on its third garage, having started at Wandsworth and then spent three months at Wood Green before coming to Seven Kings. Like most of the pre-B20s of the '1975-76' order, it was to enjoy only a very short life in the capital, in this case completing just six years in London Transport ownership. *Haydn Davies*

Below: Route 10A was withdrawn on 9 October 1976 and the 10 restored to Victoria. Earlier, Victoria's DMS 1299 (MLH 299L) rests at Aldgate on 18 February. *R. C. Riley*

than its previous 100% allocation of RTs; the introduction of the 129 on Sundays allowed the 169C to be withdrawn. Refreshingly, DMS deliveries had picked up by this time sufficient to cover all the requirements for these conversions. With an eye to maintaining those already in service, Chiswick stepped up its gearbox overhauling regime from 55 a week to 75 a week, subcontracting where feasible to fully get to grips with the design change suffered during the factory move. LT stated that 1,200 gearbox failures had been incurred as a result, exacerbated by the failure of overheating alarms. Aldenham works, meanwhile, was planning expansion so as to overhaul the SM family, then the DMSs and amid all that, extra-heavy overhauls for 1,000 RMs. All this hard work had finally knocked down the NBA issue after such a long time of desperate shortages.

For the same subsidy-reduction reasons as the 9 October changes in Essex, a similar round of rationalisations hit the Surrey borderlands on the 23rd. In Sutton a shuffle was implemented along the 80/280 corridor running north to south beyond the GLC border; in the DMS class's favour was new route 280A, which picked up the 280's service to Walton-on-the-Hill so that the 280 could divert over the 80 to Lower Kingswood; it took a while of wrong or no suffixes being displayed till sufficient blinds were in place. Enfield garage, meanwhile, gained more DMSs on 24 October when the 121 lost its RFs and the 231 its SMSs. On the 31st additional DMSs (2035, 2037, 2038 and 2154-2156) were added to the RLST in place of Obsolete Fleet's OM-class ex-Midland Red BMMO D9s. Manufacturing progression in November saw MCW finish DMS 2057 and move on in fleetnumbers to DMS 2168.

As 1976 came to a close further SMS-to-DMS upgrades encompassed the 294 (North Street, 7 November), 21A (Sidcup, 5 December, including the 228 on Sundays) 223 and 224B (both Uxbridge from 12 December, matching the weekend arrangements on these routes).

Although 1976 had seen the easing of the NBA figures from 900 to 200 buses with a view to elimination entirely in 1977, the year had had its own problems, not helped by a second fierce summer and the overheating problems resulting. Battered on one side by the total failure of its DMSs, whether or not that was a catastrophe of its own making, and on the other side by the ever-unsympathetic press that cited a likely cost of £30,000 per bus, London Transport released a statement in November 1976 that confirmed the withdrawal of the SM family and that after that, the DMSs would also go. In a Hirohito-like understatement, the wording was that the DMS 'had not proven a complete success in London service' and that no more would be ordered. What that implied was unclear, as premature withdrawals would arouse even more ire, given that the cost of like-for-like replacements by 1980, the time this process was likely to have started, would be £30,000 per bus. While the MD class was entering service to not particularly much more acclaim other than slightly increased reliability, it was the doored crew aspect of congested central-London routes that was sabotaging any real hope of success of both the DMS and MD families. Without solid orders on the horizon (the Titan and Metrobus still being on the drawing board or present only in penny numbers, and the XRM project in its infancy), the best LT could do was to start to think about overhauls, and in April 1976 DMS 1 entered Aldenham works. Even so, this bus was in such an advanced state of deterioration that it was still there by year's end. Considerable difficulties were reported to the extent that doubts were entertained about the feasibility of doing every member of this batch, the problem lying in LT's dogged insistence on being able to separate the bodywork for attention on a float separate from the chassis, just like previous types. Unfortunately, Park Royal's bodywork was not designed to do this, the word not having gone out to that concern to make its bodies detachable until it was too late, so while the body on DMS 1 was dismounted relatively cleanly, putting it back onto the chassis was a different matter; the bodyside members buckled so badly that the vehicle was almost wrecked. Clearly, dismounting was not going to be an option, on Park Royals at least, and to overhaul them at all was going to have to be done on a whole-bus basis, for which there wasn't the room at Aldenham at present. The 2/1DM batch spanning DMSs 118-367 was represented in pilot overhaul by DMS 118, which entered works on 13 December 1976.

At least in some terms was London Transport looking to the future; in August 1976 DMS 2121, destined to go into service at Streatham on the 249, was delivered with a new design of seat moquette in orange, brown and yellow, originally intended to adorn Speedbus vehicles. Whatever the choice of double-decks that would take London Transport into the 1980s (a plan being announced on 29 November 1976 to purchase 450 alongside 210 single-deckers and ratified by the GLC in December), that would be what they would wear. LT was still racing against the intended discontinuation of New Bus Grant, the GLC pressing the need to replace unsuitable off-the-peg buses despite the risk to the B15 project caused by Leyland's concomitant difficulties which had forced central Government to pump money into that manufacturer and LT to seek GLC permission to take an 18% stake which would allow it to specify buses to its needs. XRM development was still proceeding in the person of DM 1787, albeit with not as encouraging results as would have been wished. The hydrostatic transmission concept was designed so that the pistons in each wheel would activate to provide the energy needed to set the bus in motion, but acceleration was achieved by cutting out two of the pistons to increase oil flow to the others. Efficiency, unfortunately, was a little lower. A second stage could recoup fuel lost by acceleration (which in towns was up to 70%) rather than disengaging a flywheel – but it was discovered that a huge example would be needed to bring this off. Each time braking was required, the wheel motors would effectively be converted to pumps, delivering oil to hydraulic accumulators via the main swash-plate fuel pump for simplicity of control, slowing down vehicle and storing energy for acceleration. Fuel costs were not felt to be a problem, but reliability was paramount. All things considered, a smoother ride would be offered and more room released for seating if the XRM had four smaller wheels with independent suspension.

Below: **Uxbridge's route 223 assumed daily double-deck operation from 12 December 1976, providing more work for buses like DMS 1348 (MLH 348L). A one-garage bus that spent all seven years of its Certificate of Fitness at Uxbridge, it was the beneficiary of a repaint in February 1977 and is seen at Uxbridge station that September.** *Photobus*

CONCERNS AND CREWS

CHAPTER FOUR

THE B20

1977

First up for 1977 was the extension to Ilford of the 247A and the appearance of crew DMSs on the night 177, which retained crew operation as distinct from the daytime OMO service, both from 8 January, but the first major OMO conversion came on 26 February in the form of the 75 out of Catford, which was supplied with second-hand DMSs. The 124's peak-hour journeys beyond Eltham to Woolwich were withdrawn at the same time. In March six new DMSs were allocated to Merton temporarily for the M1 so that Multi-Ride cancellers could be fitted to its existing fleet, passing on to West Ham after this was done.

Not long after its reunification the 10 was cut back at its Essex end, losing the Wanstead-Woodford Wells section and the Victoria allocation. Also on 19 March a significant change of mind finally recognised the failure of doored buses to cope adequately in central London and accordingly returned the 29 to RM operation; its DMs were transferred to the 141 instead, Wood Green's staying put but Holloway's transferring to New Cross to fulfil that garage's allocation plus five DMs made spare from Stockwell by the arrival of five new DMSs for the RLST. A scheduled cross-working theoretically supplied one DM to the 53, by now restocked fully with MDs. So much for the OMO theme of the W-routes; the extension of the 29 from Wood Green to Enfield Town daily rather than Southgate allowed the W1 to be withdrawn, the W2 to be withdrawn at weekends (more than replaced by the 144's extension from Turnpike Lane to Muswell Hill Broadway) and the W4 to come off on Sundays.

Below: **It's not a particularly nice March day in Penge as Catford's DMS 1427 (MLH 427L) typifies the runout on the 75 following its conversion to OMO on 26 February 1977. This bus had been based at Catford ever since transferring from Thornton Heath six months into its London career, and would remain at Catford until turned into a trainer in 1980.** *David Wilkinson collection*

Left: Wood Green's DMs from the 29 seamlessly transferred to the 141, which covered most of the same roads north of Manor House. DM 1159 (KUC 159P), however, was a transfer from Holloway to New Cross, the 141's other garage, and is seen in May 1978 on the route's central London section by St Paul's. *R. C. Riley*

The 123, ceding to the 29 its roads beyond Winchmore Hill to Enfield) was one-manned with Walthamstow DMSs, some new and others nearly-new, and its one-time trolleybus-replacement partner 275 picked its way further eastwards with an extension from Claybury Hospital to Barkingside, while the 278 pushed north from Walthamstow Central to Chingford Mount. In this sector, night-time saw the N96 one-manned with Leyton DMSs replacing RMLs, and finally for 19 March, Potters Bar's 284 was withdrawn.

January 1977 saw the delivery of the first B20s with Park Royal bodies, starting from DMS 2347 onwards; they were stockpiled at Aldenham until enough were available to institute a new policy of converting garages to this sub-type rather than individual routes for ease of standardisation. Bexleyheath was the first recipient, from 11 March. Production versions of what had been decided following experimentation with DMS 854, the 'quiet bus' configuration of the B20 DMS attempted to reduce the volume of noise output by baffling

Below: DMS 2366 (OJD 366R) from the first intake of Park Royal-bodied B20 DMSs looks pristine on 28 February 1977 as it poses at Chiswick before allocation. Although over fifty of its fellows in this general number block would be sent to Bexleyheath, this bus would enter service at Enfield in July. *John Laker*

Left: West Ham added nearly-new DMSs to its fleet on 20 June 1977 to convert the 162 from SMS, and, as is only right, buses like former Enfield DMS 2133 (OJD 133R) visited all of the garage's DMS routes, one of which was the 241. This shot shows it leaving Stratford. *Haydn Davies*

Below left: Heavy construction is ongoing behind DMS 2136 (OJD 136R) at Aldgate during 1977, which would change the familiar backdrop to bus photographs at this location. New to Enfield, it was dislodged from there to West Ham for the 162 on 20 June 1977, but in this shot has turned out on the 5. *R. C. Riley*

it and effectively redirecting it upwards; thus, instead of the twin engine shrouds (which were occasionally removed to facilitate cleaning of the rear window), two angled chimneys were fitted, the nearside one slightly narrower than the offside. The bonnet was redesigned, the whole protruding outwards six inches from the lower deck, and since the design inhibited the driver's view out of what was already a difficult spot, a wide-angle lens was incorporated in the glass of the rear window. For passengers looking out of the back to see if their next bus was coming up behind, most of what they saw was a reflected fisheye version of themselves, but it did seem to help the driver, and to make sure, the lit-up 'REVERSING' light also made its way to the edge of the engine compartment, overlooking the bonnet lid above LEYLAND / FLEETLINE plates.

Quiet it was not, unfortunately – if anything, the B20 DMS was even louder than the standard, emitting a frantic whine akin to a hairdryer, with the concurrent drop even further in reliability. A particular issue was the siting of the power-steering fluid filler tank above the engine cowl, which was difficult to see to refill, and if thus overfilled the overflow would drip onto the engine! Fires of this nature thus became the leading cause of B20 casualties in years to come, and in the short term Bexleyheath's examples were soon falling out in large numbers, what would now be retrospectively termed 'standard' DMSs being drafted in to cover for them – a situation which would endure for all six years of B20 DMS operation at Bexleyheath!

DMS 1 was outshopped from Aldenham on 15 March, after an overhaul which had lasted eleven months and with no success in rendering the body and chassis distinct entities

Left: DMS 862 (TGX 862M) spent all eight years of its life (1974-1982) at Merton, plying the uneventful flat-fare M1 route as shown at Morden during 1977. *Photobus*

Above: **Enter the B20, troubled from the outset. DMS 2361 (OJD 361R) was new to Bexleyheath and is seen on 19 June 1977.**
C. Carter / Online Transport Archive

Below: **DMS 2220 (OJD 220R) represents the DMS in London Transport's Easter parade of 10 April 1977. Its long-term home (and indeed its only garage after that) would be Sidcup.**
Bob Greenaway / Online Transport Archive

for treatment separately. Unfortunately, it came out of works in all-red, though still with yellow doors, heralding future policy, and unresolved water-ingress problems discovered once it had returned to Shepherd's Bush caused it to be delicensed again for a few days. A small but significant external change was the replacement of the push-out front upper-deck opening windows with pull-in Beclawat units like the rest, while the little-used external PA system was also taken out. The numberplate was also restickered to put the numbers closer to the suffix letter in line with legal requirements, as was often done at repaint or when road wear had rendered them illegible. Despite clamouring by passengers for improved side blinds and a half-hearted promise by LT thus to retrofit early DMSs, this was never done. Blinds were at the forefront also when Uxbridge's SMS fleet and the BLs at Edgware were fitted with blinds including all the DMS services at those two garages so that the single-deckers could stand in where fit, but the drivers refused to operate them.

Three oddments for the spring saw the RLST's Fleetlines (comprising from March, DMSs 2203-2207 still with 'PLEASE PAY AS YOU ENTER' transfers to replace DMs taken from the 168) once more backed up by OMs from 2 April (until 5 November), the 137A pop up again on 10 April (with six Battersea DMSs and two borrowed from Wandsworth) and DMS 2220 in fleet livery form a reticent contribution to the Queen's Silver Jubilee parade through Hyde Park on the same day, otherwise the province of 25 silver-painted RMs. On 23 April the 154 was rerouted via Carshalton Beeches station. 21 May, however, saw a major route one-manned in the form of Sidcup's 51, its nearly-new DMSs now running an increased service to incorporate the Green Street Green journeys of the former 51A; further to the east, the 229, which took the RMs displaced from the 51, was split, new route 269 (with Bexleyheath DMSs) commencing between Woolwich and Sidcup Garage; unfortunately, due to the inability of the DMS class to negotiate Murchison Avenue in Bexley, this road was abandoned. On 20 June Upton Park's 162 was converted from SMS to

THE B20

77

Right: **Upton Park's DMS 1921 (KUC 921P) heads down East Ham High Street after the garage had added the 162 to its existing DMS-operated portfolio on 20 June 1977. This bus had been allocated new for the 147 the previous autumn.**
David Wilkinson collection

Below: **Having seen off all but the Red Arrow variety of Merlins, the ongoing DMS deliveries turned their attention to restoring the upper deck to SMS routes. The 70 and 188 were New Cross's responsibility, and DMS 1979 (KUC 979P) was well bedded in by the summer of 1977.**
David Wilkinson collection

DMS, although 36 hours elapsed before the first Fleetlines dared venture out once trees were lopped in their path. So followed the 238, a West Ham operation. Vehicles for both Upton Park and West Ham were sourced from Enfield following its progressive conversion to B20s.

London Transport's Annual Report for 1976 was published in April; while recording a small surplus above breaking even, it castigated the reliability of off-the-shelf buses, though the NBA figure was now down to 300 and crew shortages were at 12%. Gearbox life was improving, units on a DMS now likely to last fifteen months rather than six weeks, with the hope of getting this to three years. Brake linings, however, lasted 8,000 miles compared to a figure of five times that for an RT, wearing out in six to eight weeks rather than in six months. Even so, route C5 had not actually run at all since 28 February 1976 due to a shortage of serviceable vehicles.

One idea put forward by the LTPC in the interests of cutting down boarding times was the introduction of pavement conductors from 2 October 1977 at bus stop F in Powis Street in Woolwich, where DMS-operated routes 51 and 96 boarded. It only lasted two days due to representation about the risk of attack and theft but resumed on 7 November until Christmas, unfortunately making insufficient impact to continue. Where staff security was concerned, bus radio fitment had reached two-thirds by this year, with whistles issued to conductors at Middle Row and Brixton in August and 250 (out of a total so far of 400) pocket radios issued to inspectors. An aesthetic change from March turned the colour of running number plates to yellow with black text, while the white-band livery was very thin on the ground now following repaints. Obliquely related to the DMS story were seven open-top Daimler Fleetlines new to Bournemouth and hired from Obsolete Fleet for the RLST; they were known as the DMO class.

Enfield was the second garage to receive B20 DMSs, the vehicles released from 9 May onwards passing, like those of Bexleyheath, around the fleet to top up allocations. Two new B20s (DMSs 2431 and 2433), however, were seconded to Merton to assist in Derby Day duties on 1 June. The last standard DMS, Metro-Cammell-bodied DMS 2246, was delivered in

THE LONDON DMS

June and MCW now commenced its own 100-bus batch of B20s. DMSs 2161, 2162 and 2170 were fitted with Clayton Dewandre power hydraulic brakes in January 1977 and DMS 2224 followed in May, this bus being additionally loaned to South Yorkshire PTE for trial between 8 June and 15 July alongside Fleetlines with similar-looking MCW bodies diverted there after delays with the original Alexander order for 60; it is worth noting that SYPTE became a solid user of Rolls-Royce engines, specifying them for their later batches of Metrobuses and Dennis Dominators due to their hill-climbing properties. All four hydraulic-brake DMSs were allocated to Fulwell that July – and that would not be the last we would hear of the SYPTE DMS lookalikes.

The GLC elections of 5 May 1977 returned the Conservative Party, with the corresponding swing to the right that saw first the Speedbus plans cancelled; this possible showcase for the DMS family had foundered in the face of shopowner resistance to bus lanes impeding the parking of potential customers; fourteen bus lanes themselves were removed within twelve months. The new GLC administration did, however, concur with some of LT's longer-term plans like Busplan, which was intended to rationalise and standardise route variations in the interest of the passenger rather than for

Above: **Gleaming new DMS 2465 (OJD 465R) plies the 107 through cheerful suburbia on behalf of Enfield garage.** *Haydn Davies*

Below: **The rear of the B20 is slightly asymmetrical, as demonstrated by Enfield's DMS 2412 (OJD 412R), laying over at Carterhatch shortly after entry into service.** *Haydn Davies*

the perceived convenience of the operator, and universal ticketing when it could be made practicable. Routes that competed with the Underground could be shortened despite differing needs of each kind of passenger, the proportion of OMO would creep up again and subsidy would be reduced. Still, relations remained sour, LT accusing the GLC of interference and the GLC accusing the latter of profligacy, and so it went on.

By mid-1977 London Transport was looking nervously at the imminent expiry of the CoFs of the earliest DMSs, necessitating their putting through overhaul once Aldenham works could be made ready for them and replacements were available from new deliveries; with the recent abandonment of any idea of overhauling the Swifts, the time had to be now, and indeed two new lifting hoists were installed at Aldenham at a cost of £10,000 apiece so that chassis could be steam cleaned and inspected. DMS 3 was delicensed for overhaul on 25 July; however, fellow early DMSs from Shepherd's Bush's inaugural intake had to be relegated to training duties or storage, while the problems encountered with DMS 1's overhaul forced some early DMSs to make do with recertification only to clear the backlog; this bought them an extra year before needing to go into works themselves. Finally, from August early members began to enter works, overhaul anticipated to take eight to ten weeks but to a lesser extent than on comparable RM-family vehicles, affording them only three years' worth of renewed CoF and thus not really solving the availability problem which was still prevalent. Only fourteen more were to enter works by the end of 1977. They were replaced at Shepherd's Bush by new B20s from MCW's batch then in delivery. These spanned the last year-letter registration changeover to affect DMSs, DMS 2268 taking THX 268S and DMS 2473 THX 473S, from a large batch of numbers booked in this series and also applied to incoming LSs, not to mention the impending successors to the DMS fleet in the form of the first Titans and Metrobuses. The B15 had finally been christened with this re-used name upon its formal launch on 30 June 1977, while the Metrobus, five of which were now ordered, was a home-grown development of the Metropolitan. Repaints, meanwhile, had now come up to the numbers spanned by the DM class, DM 956 being the first to go into Aldenham for a repaint, on 9 August 1977. Even so, penny numbers of white-banded examples from the 118-367 batch remained to be repainted, most of these seeing belated relicensing during the year after long periods out of use.

DMSs 2227 and 2433 were fitted in June with advertisements of a new type whereby much more of the bus side was covered; on the offside, the panels were extended down the staircase panel to form a T shape. This necessitated

Right: **Battersea's DMS 2227 (OJD 227R) inaugurated the T-side advert; in this case, a second version after an earlier attempt on behalf of Motofill oil had to be snipped at either end to fit along the bus's side. The rear aspect is seen on this lifelong Battersea bus (although six years wasn't to be that much of a life!) on 23 October 1977.**
C. Carter / Online Transport Archive

Left: The Air India advert on DMS 2478 (THX 478S) proved so likeable when combined with the existing white upper-deck relief of the later DMS that it was a shame no more were done. On 27 November 1977, a month after having been added to Stockwell's Round London Sightseeing Tour complement, it touts for business at Piccadilly Circus with Leicester Square in sight. *C. Carter / Online Transport Archive*

the relocation of the offside roundel to a most awkward position squeezed into the thin panel behind the driver's cab; in self-adhesive sticker form, the standard filled roundel just fit. DMS 2227's nearside ad for Bird's Eye and offside panel for Moltofil 90 filler were painted on, but self-adhesive pre-printed vinyl sheets were subsequently developed. The success of the T-side ads meant this look spread rapidly, the first bulk contract (after the initial deals with Bird's Eye and Moltofil, who had paid for the prototypes, fell through) going to Rothmans cigarettes for 100 buses, the ads to be on each side of the buses. Meanwhile, the entertaining early-1970s trend of painted all-over adverts, so widespread on Routemasters until discontinued from September 1975, had singularly failed to include so much as a single DMS – they just didn't seem to have the cachet, or the evocative shape, of their rear-entrance forebears, to be trusted to convey an advertiser's message to where it counted. Yet in October 1977 DMS 2478 was delivered with a wraparound for Air India, where the white surmounting the upper-deck windows was extended between-decks to carry a line of temple-like images in ochre/saffron. Its livery applied at the British Airways depot at Chiswick (including a silver stripe), DMS 2478 was allocated to Stockwell for the RLST, keeping the scheme until September 1980. No further takers came forward for this style of advert.

Multi-Ride was introduced on Croydon's C-routes and on Merton's M1 on 17 July. DMSs continued their march through the East London-Essex borders with their introduction to the 139 (North Street) and 148 (Barking and Seven Kings) on the 23rd, both with nearly-new examples and the last of the standards.

They were on the move in north London too, a programme on 20 August converting Enfield's 217 and 217B from RT to B20 DMS and introducing similarly-operated 107A over the eastern end of the old 107, which now fell back to Enfield Highway (Red Lion). To make way for these changes, Enfield ceded the 191 to Edmonton on weekdays and partially on Saturday.

On 10 September the 34, shared between Palmers Green and Walthamstow, lost its RTs for OMO DMSs and the 212 at Palmers Green also received DMSs to replace its Swifts. Rebuilding at Palmers Green now permitted larger vehicles, and Palmers Green's new DMSs were not only its first of the class, but B20s to join that select club of garages operating them, though

Below: The North Circular Road was a traffic nightmare almost as soon as it opened, and LT's planners have had to be careful assuming that a single route can handle more of it than traffic will actually allow. Such was the case with the 112, which has been split twice in its lifetime. The first eastern answer, Palmers Green's 212, was treated on 10 September 1977 to DMSs, B20s like DMS 2461 (OJD 461R) starting off the type at that garage. It is seen threading its way through Brent Cross's concrete. *Haydn Davies*

THE B20

Above: **DMS 1299 (MLH 299L) was transferred to Walthamstow on 10 September 1977 to help one-man the 34 in concert with Palmers Green. Not long thereafter it is seen heading north through Whetstone, but would not end up lasting the decade out.**
Haydn Davies

two (DMSs 27 and 38) came from Shepherd's Bush, which was beginning to disperse the early batch far and wide. Stockwell's regular recycling of RLST DMSs replaced DMSs 2203-2207 with B20s 2475, 2476 and 2478-2482, DMS 2478 carrying the Air India livery. DMS 2464, meanwhile, was the first normal-service B20 at Stockwell, it and fellow new B20s displacing standards on the 181 and 181A in November. At Southall, the 274 was converted from RT to DMS and the Sunday shortfall put onto the 120, both changes taking effect from 1 October. Completing the rout of crew buses from Seven Kings was the OMO conversion on 15 October of the 150, which not only lost its Ilford-Becontree Heath section to an extension of the 129, but abandoned Lambourne End to bus operation altogether due to the need for a reversing manoeuvre at the pub here, which a conductor-less bus could not manage.

Not quite a B20 garage by October 1977, Chalk Farm put two into service on the 24 at this point; one was DMS 2488 from the current sequence of deliveries and the other, significantly, was the prototype, DMS 854, which now marked its service debut on 18 November but appeared

Right: **10 September also saw the 274 at Southall one-manned. Most of its new complement consisted of new or nearly-new DMSs, including DMS 2160 (OJD 160R) which had bounced around a bit since new the previous October before settling at Southall.**
Haydn Davies

82   THE LONDON DMS

Left: Based at Seven Kings since the OMO conversion of the 129 on 9 October 1976, DMS 2031 (OUC 31R) now turned its attention to the 148 on 23 July 1977. It is seen laying over at Dagenham with another DMS beside it. *David Wilkinson collection*

thereafter comparatively infrequently. Both buses, neither of which had yet had AFC equipment fitted, were modified by the fitting of a luggage rack over the nearside wheelarch in the interests of determining whether this would create a greater area of circulation at the front and thus make one last desperate stab at reducing boarding time with doored crew operation, which had long been proven patently not to work. The two converted B20s invariably did not solve the problem, and were transferred to Cricklewood in January 1978. Another doubtful method of fare collection, that using ticket cancellers, was stepped up during 1977, though problems were encountered with the German-manufactured Landis & Gyr (Elgeba) equipment intended for buses on routes S1, S2 and S3; using an early form of scanning and optical character recognition rather than the brute chopping motion of the Almex-specified alternatives, it was deemed unsatisfactory and canceller implementation was put back to 2 October on the S-routes. The other sources for the equipment were Control Systems (routes M1, P1, P2 and P3) and TEL (C1, C2, C3 and C4), and their operation was put into use on 17

Left: Upon the OMO conversion of the 217B, the last route to have been created using RTs, the two-bus Sunday service was extended from Enfield Town to Oakwood, where DMS 2442 (OJD 442R) is seen when new. *Tony Wilson*

83

Above: **On 13 November 1977 Finchley's 125 was converted from SMS to DMS operation. DMS 568 (MLK 568L), passing through Whetstone, had been at Finchley since new and never worked anywhere else.** *Haydn Davies*

July, coinciding with an across-the-board 15% fare rise; the retention of the former fares if one bought the multiple tickets was the hook here. During October a similar system was prepared with the throughput of North Street DMSs to and from Aldenham for fitment of Multi-Ride cancellers in preparation for a programme to be implemented on 26 February 1978. Two B20s (DMSs 2282 and 2283) were allocated temporarily to Hornchurch while their normal DMSs were going back and forth to Aldenham, and went on to perform the same role at North Street before moving on to Wandsworth in March 1978.

Right: **After an overhaul that took a year and eventually necessitated the purchase of specialist equipment that really should have been foreseen (and budgeted for) when the vehicles were designed, DMS 1 emerged from Aldenham in March 1977, returning to Shepherd's Bush. However, the conversion of that garage to B20s that autumn obliged it to move on, and Merton became its steward. On 23 September 1978 it is seen setting off from the 152's Hampton Court terminus of the time.** *Geoff Rixon*

Left: Metro-Cammell's 100-strong contribution to the B20 order comprised DMSs 2247-2346, and the first examples were allocated to Shepherd's Bush just in time for its early DMSs' CoFs to expire en masse, necessitating overhaul. DMS 2267 (OJD 267R) was new in August 1977 and is seen at the northern extremity of the 220 shortly after. Shepherd's Bush had evidently completely given up on the problem of side blinds through the expedient of painting over the panel meant to be used for destinations.
Haydn Davies

Weathering a bottleneck in production from both bodybuilders as 1977 waned, Park Royal completed its B20 DMSs in November 1977. The final examples (including a handful fitted with fareboxes for the 616) were allocated to Cricklewood during December, again with the intention of displacing early editions to overhaul, though for the moment early DMSs suffering CoF expiry were stored at British Airways' facility at Chiswick and at Clapham. The last location named was a former garage used as a museum since closure and now as a storage facility, but shortly to be elevated once again (albeit on a temporary basis) to a full garage. Production then switched to DMs; the appearance of the first of these at Cricklewood for the 16 and 16A in December marked that lucky shed's third complete turnover of new Fleetlines in three years, and on a local basis enabled a little relief from fellow members of the class taking their place in the queue for repaint at Aldenham, which had obliged the odd RM coming back to cover duties on routes like the 149. At the moment, B20 deliveries to garages were segregated by bodywork, thus Stockwell took Park Royals, but MCW-bodied examples, trickling in extremely slowly, finished Shepherd's Bush in November and started at Brixton that same month. By that time the early members leaving this garage were at last beginning to pass through works for an overhaul which would take three or four months each, the hoists at Aldenham now installed and fully operational. The overhaul of DMS 118 of the '1970' batch was finally completed in October, this bus (also in all red like DMS 1) leaving for Merton (albeit to be partially deroofed there almost immediately), where the rout of the SMS continued with the conversion to DMS of the 57 and 200 on 13 November. One of Merton's intake, which spanned the entire stock number series of the standard DMS variety, was DMS 1. Finchley's 125 was converted from SMS to DMS on the same day, including in its new intake B20-displaced cast-offs from Enfield, Stockwell and Shepherd's Bush. As 1977 came to a close, the end of Fleetline deliveries was in sight, and, as if to underscore the end of the beginning for the class, only one DMS remained in service with a white band. This was New Cross's DMS 188, which had skipped its routine repaint due to being laid up at Bexleyheath until being repaired and returned to service in June 1977, and it managed to hold out in this livery till 12 October 1978.

By December 1977 DM 1787 was ready to undergo road tests, which would continue into the first half of 1978. Christmas oddments saw Wandsworth put out not only its DMs on the 28 but two crew DMSs too. DMS reliability was still poor enough that the extreme measure was taken to add SMS 809 to Stonebridge's complement, but drivers vetoed it and it was taken away again.

It was now coming up to 1978, the year by when all crew-operated vehicles were supposed to have been replaced according to the Reshaping Plan. Far from having accomplished that, the Merlins were all gone, the Swifts were departing against a completely intact Routemaster family and over two hundred RTs were still in service, which themselves bought at least another year's reprieve through the recertification for a year of sixty-five of them, due to the need for new DMSs to replace older examples going into overhaul rather than RTs!

THE B20 85

1978

1978 was the year of 'Busplan '78', a coordinated route-change programme that in three stages attempted to standardise workings daily and increase mileage into the bargain, but the year started with a few OMO conversions as of routine; Southall's 120 and Sidcup's 228 received DMSs on 28 January, the former replacing RTs and the latter RMs, while the 160/A at Sidcup were upgraded from SMD, the purge of the Swift now extending to these ill-fated semi-single-door conversions. At Turnham Green the N97 was projected to Heathrow Airport, providing a new and immediately popular link.

MCW's DMS output was almost at an end; from January B20s with this bodywork were put into Wandsworth, releasing several to Holloway to let that garage's early numbers stack up inside Clapham awaiting their turn for overhaul, further displacing stored examples to Aldenham. CoF expiries were now occurring faster than new or cascaded buses could be allocated to replace them; a tentative order placed in February for 50 Ts and 50 Ms was soon increased to 250 Ts and 200 Ms, and as a matter of urgency fifty SMSs were selected for recertification to forestall any need for their own replacement in the short term. Still, the bottleneck was about to ease when in January DMSs 3 and 5 were outshopped, going to Leyton and Bexleyheath respectively; the latter was an interesting placement reflecting the struggle that garage was enduring with the reliability of its B20s; many more would follow during the class's spell there, beginning with DMSs 16 and 21 from March's output of just five buses. DMS 23, 30 and 49, meanwhile, were recertified at Clapham with two-year tickets. Repaints had now reached MCW's DM block, with RMs found substituting for Walworth's contingent on the 45.

MCW's participation in the DMS story having finished with the completion of DMS 2346 and its delivery on 23 March as the last of the DMS class, B20 DMs now took up the thread. They were certainly flavour of the month in February; only two years after its conversion from RT to RM, the 109 started receiving new crew-operated Fleetlines on the

Above: **At the start of 1978 Brixton exchanged its entire fleet. Its early DMSs went in for overhaul, to be replaced on the 50 and 95 by new Metro-Cammell-bodied B20s. DMS 2279 (THX 279S) was one of them, and is seen on 3 May 1978 heading south through Brixton.** *Geoff Rixon*

Right: **At the same time, Park Royal was turning out the last of its B20 DMSs, which began entering service at Cricklewood, also with the intent of displacing its early models to overhaul. New in January 1978, DMS 2513 (THX 513S) makes ready to depart Golders Green on 13 August. The Sunday-only 245A was withdrawn with the second phase of Busplan '78 on 28 October.** *John Laker*

THE LONDON DMS

Left: **Wandsworth rotated its early DMSs out for overhaul at the start of 1978, receiving brand new MCW-bodied examples like DMS 2338 (THX 338S), caught in May 1979 during a spot of construction at Euston.** *Photobus*

1st, the Brixton allocation taking DMs first between this date and 3 March, while additional numbers displaced standards from the 133 in the interests of standardisation. DM 2546 was briefly allocated to Chalk Farm before taking up service at Brixton, while Stockwell was added to the list of B20 DM recipients, taking several between March and August. Having put into service the first of the B20 DMs and then being compelled to stand aside as other garages got in the way, Cricklewood resumed its intake as DMs climbed into the 2600s.

On 26 February 1978 LT launched its Multi-Ride network in the London Borough of Havering, all the DMSs for locally affected routes having been equipped with Almex-manufactured cancellers at Aldenham over the winter, minus ten DMSs (293, 442, 477, 479, 481, 483-485, 488 and 2239) based at North Street for the 139, which was not part of the network. This time a 'MULTI-RIDE' sticker was carried under the blind box on affected buses to drive the point home to passengers, and if it speeded up boarding, steps could then be made

Below: **Having restocked its OMO routes with Metro-Cammell-bodied B20 DMSs, Brixton proceeded to standardise on the type, both replacing the existing DMs on the 133 and adding to them via the conversion of the 109. DM 2543 (THX 543S) is seen on its way north on 8 March.** *R. C. Riley*

Left: Fulwell's unremarkable route 270 exchanged its buses three times in the space of a year, first converting from SMD to BL, then to DMS and finally to M. DMS 196 (JGF 196K) had been based at Fulwell since April 1977 and would end its career there. *Haydn Davies*

to extend the concept to trunk routes. While singularly failing to reduce boarding times, the money-saving tickets, priced in multiples of 10p, had an unintentionally adverse effect in that they were so popular with the public that they actually reduced revenue and had to be increased in price from the fares increase of 18 June! Anticipating this, the cancelling mode of operation was discontinued from the P- and S-routes on 22 April and the equipment removed from buses within two weeks.

On 9 April the 270 at Fulwell, having lost its SMDs for BLs only on 28 January, was converted to DMS operation.

Busplan '78's first stage opened on 22 April and hit the dwindling RT family hard; the fairly large concentration to be found in south-east London was broken up with the DMS OMO conversions of Catford's 54, Bexleyheath's 89 and New Cross's 151 and 192. The 132 was rendered a circular by taking over the 89's Eltham leg and the 122A was extended west of Woolwich to Queen Elizabeth Hospital. Tidying-up of weekend-only routes incorporated the 40A into a now-daily 40 and the 160A into a daily 160, while the 126's Sunday extension from Eltham to Bexleyheath was withdrawn. An extension of Stonebridge's 112 to Palmers Green replaced the 212 and that of Barking's 199 northward to Ilford removed the need for the 291. The 147's journeys beyond Redbridge to Leytonstone were replaced by the extension there of the 148, but the 129's Sunday service was withdrawn, and at the southern end of the 147, its peak-hour projections beyond East Ham to Royal Albert Dock were taken off. In town the 5 was extended from Clerkenwell to Bloomsbury and the 55 was projected from Aldwych over the river to Waterloo during peak

Above left: The 120 had undergone a straight RT to DMS conversion on 28 January 1978. DMS 1682 (THM 682M) had already been at Southall since April 1974. *Haydn Davies*

Left: The 192, one of five RT-operated routes remaining in the Lewisham area as late as 1978, was converted to DMS OMO on 22 April. DMS 1989 (KUC 989P) had operated out of New Cross since July 1976, but when this picture was taken passing Lewisham Odeon, could not muster a side destination blind. *David Wilkinson collection*

Right: **Having just become able to work the 173, Poplar's DMS 179 (JGF 179K) reposes at Becontree Heath alongside Barking's RT 778 (JXC 141), still going strong on the 87. In September the DMS would be taken into overhaul and outshopped to Abbey Wood three months later.**
Haydn Davies

hours; in the early mornings the 177 was taken off the Embankment to work via Fleet Street instead. Upton Park's 173 was reallocated to Poplar so that it could take on West Ham's 238, in the interests of reducing garage journeys. The extension north of North Street's 103 brought DMSs to Stapleford Abbotts to help out hard-pressed BLs on the 247. In south-west London the 213 and 213A were revised so that the latter gained a Norbiton share and overall precedence; the 213, despite passenger protest, was reduced to middays only and no further east than New Malden. Uxbridge's 224B was introduced on Sundays amid a general increase to incorporate withdrawn route 224 and Palmers Green's 261 was one-manned with DMSs. At West Ham, DMs replaced RMs on the 262, stock coming from Brixton for the most part, while such a conversion also applied to Upton Park's 101 on the 30th; DMs for this purpose were taken from Cricklewood. Stonebridge's 112 was projected past Brent Cross to Finchley, Manor Cottage Tavern during the day on Mondays to Fridays, necessitating the addition of one DMS. The rationalisation of routes under Busplan '78 accompanied some service reductions, thus accommodating the difficulties being suffered with the DMS family, and only four more were needed on aggregate after 22 April – not that the plans were accepted in general by London Transport's busmen, who indicated their protest with a series of lightning strikes over the ensuing week, staggered to cause maximum disruption.

Below: **The 213 and 213A pair were rationalised on 22 April 1978 with the former being reduced heavily owing to little custom along its Traps Lane dedicated section. On 20 May consecutive Norbiton DMSs 639 (MLK 639L) and 638 (MLK 638L) show off each route's via points, but the 213 by then usually displayed a blank panel.** *Geoff Rixon*

THE B20

89

Right: **Almost forgotten despite only needing two buses, the 151 succumbed to OMO DMS on 22 April 1978. DMS 712 (TGX 712M), seen at Kidbrooke after the conversion, had been new to New Cross and never worked anywhere else.**
Haydn Davies

Below: **DMSs were now coming out of Aldenham overhaul, breaking up the established numeric blocks and spreading them far and wide. DMS 6 (EGP 6J) was outshopped in April 1978 and went to Fulwell, on whose 267 it is seen at Hampton Court on the 23rd of that month.** *Geoff Rixon*

Abuse from the travelling public quickly put a stop to that, however, reflecting the thin line between the workforce's willingness to fight for improved conditions and its obligation to the public. All this caused the third stage of Busplan '78 to drift into 1979, by request of the union.

Now 100% DMS since the 22 April 1978 changes, Bexleyheath was slowly recovering from the reliability problems of its B20 DMS fleet, although not enough to avoid having to take on standards as reinforcements, and by the spring it was Enfield's turn to suffer, Wandsworth not having such a great time either. The rate of DMS overhauls was 18 in and 14 out in May and 29 in and 17 out in June; finally picking up speed, but for enthusiast purposes increasing variety through the spreading of these early examples to every corner of the fleet. *LT News* reported the plan to achieve the overhauls of seven DMSs a week for four-year tickets now that Aldenham staff were familiar with the different methods needed for this type and had all the equipment they needed after an 18-month delay in its delivery. By June only eight of the first 117 DMSs had not entered Aldenham, these being long-term sick; from that month members of the DMS 118-367 batch started going in, and also, most significantly, DMS 1449 as pilot example of the MCW batch. Also into works in June was DMS 46, taking its experimental livery with it, while the last white-banded example in service, New Cross's DMS 188, was sent for overhaul in October. DMS 88 went into works in June, coming out in October with its Ricardo sound-baffling modifications intact. Otherwise, the DMS 1-117 batch had their illuminated 'NO ENTRY' signs

THE LONDON DMS

Left: **The 132 route has wandered seemingly all over the landscape since its introduction. The only stable section has been its Blackfen-Blendon core, which remained thus even when the route was transformed into a circular with the Busplan '78 first stage. Displaying the yellow ultimates needed to impress the new format upon the passengers is Bexleyheath's DMS 2390 (OJD 390R) during the summer of 1978.**
Haydn Davies

removed upon overhaul, the type's dual-door operation being considered familiar enough to passengers by now. Despite the overhaul process prolonging the life of those DMSs treated, the spares situation was as bad as ever due to industrial action carried out by twenty suppliers, with brake drums, road springs and heater components in particularly short supply. All this combined with recruitment problems to cause a doubling of lost mileage since the previous summer; if it wasn't one thing with the poor DMS, it was another! Accordingly, Routemasters were frequently seen on DM-operated routes 43, 133, 141, 168 and 172 during the year.

On 6 May the Saturday-only 233A was withdrawn, route 233 taking on its remit to Wallington as an extension. The night of the 26th/27th saw the last RTs removed from night duties, Barking's conductors requesting crew DMSs on the N95 and N98 for safety reasons. On 18 June Muswell Hill's 244 was converted from SMS to DMS operation, taking newly-overhauled DMSs 10, 32, 55, 56 and 107 and the N99 at West Ham went from RML to DM on 10 July, albeit in this case unofficially.

As DM deliveries wound down, output from Park Royal assuming a truly glacial pace once the spring had started, the RLST fleet was rotated for the final time, Stockwell's B20 DMSs

Left: **The 262 was one of the shortest-lived DM operations in the class's history, but the route would still fall prey to OMO before the Fleetline was done in this part of east London. DM 920 (SMU 920N) was replaced at Cricklewood by a B20 in December 1977 and came to West Ham, where it spent until 22 April 1978 as a trainer. Seen that summer in central Stratford, it would leave for New Cross when the 262 regained RMs.**
David Wilkinson collection

THE B20

Right: **Merton's DMS 1922 (KUC 922P) reposes at Mitcham on 18 August 1978, in the same week as DMS production finally came to an end upon the delivery of DM 2646. The deceptively sleepy-appearing 200 had been converted from SMS the previous 13 November and would manage to hold on to Fleetlines for the next decade; and with two further 'post-LT' operators at that!** *Haydn Davies*

moving out for six new DMs (2631, 2633-2636 and 2642) that were intended to be broken in on the Wimbledon tennis services on loan to Merton (already experienced with B20s through the licensing there of new examples to work on the Derby Day service), but in the event not used, help from six other garages coming instead. One of the displaced, DMS 2478, had already lost the silver band it had carried in sympathy with the Jubilee celebrations a year earlier, but kept its Air India advert upon transfer to Palmers Green. Advertising may never have reached its highest potential on DMSs as opposed to RMs, but the offside configuration lent itself to imaginative T-side adverts, which commenced with a pitch by Rothmans' cigarettes (including Government-mandated health warning!) and which by mid-year had mushroomed to hundreds of vehicles for a variety of contractors. An aesthetic change as well as easier on the eye for control was the introduction of yellow running-number plates during the year.

On 23 August 1978 DM 2646, the very last 'Londoner' of all, was delivered. The passing of the torch fleetwide from Fleetlines to a mix of Metrobuses and Titans had now begun, but no quicker at this stage than the last of the DMSs.

Right: **DMS 1441 (MLH 441L) had been at Upton Park since new in 1973, but from 22 April 1978 added the 238 to its quiver on transfer from West Ham. It was repainted in October and looks smart in this Plashet Grove shot taken not long after that.** *Haydn Davies*

Right: **The charred remnants of DMS 1248 (JGU 248K) have been brought into Aldenham following its fire at Burgh Heath.** *David Wilkinson collection*

Below right: **The weekday parents of Sunday-only routes 57A and 59 had evolved away from them; in the case of the former almost unrecognisably. Brixton's DM 2551 (THX 551S) sees out this route in Streatham garage's forecourt.** *David Wilkinson collection*

While the DMS family had racked up scores of casualties, buses lying semi-derelict out of sight at garages with parts removed for years in some cases, outright withdrawals had never yet been the case until 17 August 1978, six days before the delivery of DM 2646 would have seen all 2,646 members in stock. Allocated to Sutton and operating that day on the 280, DMS 1248 sprung an electrical fault at Burgh Heath and was burnt to a crisp.

Following a spot of rebuilding at Thornton Heath sufficient to allow DMs, that garage's share of the 109 went over on 27 August to match the Brixton allocation treated earlier in the year, albeit with standard versions predominantly displaced from Stockwell's 168 by the last of the B20 DMs; the rest were formerly engineering spares from other garages. Similarly from RM to DM went Thornton Heath's allocation on the 130 on Sundays as all Routemasters departed that garage.

Stage 2 of Busplan 78 was implemented on 28 October, taking off the 17 in favour of an extension northwards of the 45 (and the introduction of a Holloway DM allocation). Battersea's Saturday-only 39A was withdrawn and the 39 introduced on Saturdays.

Changes to the Brixton Road corridor saw Sunday-only routes 57A and 59 both withdrawn and the 109 reinstated on that day with Thornton Heath DMs; the night-time DMS on this route was replaced by a DM. Reductions to Brixton's DM complement on the 109 by sixteen vehicles released enough DMs to enable Wandsworth to standardise its crew-operated Fleetline roster on the B20; its earlier ones topped up numbers at Thornton Heath, whose workings on the 109 increased by six. The removal of the 13 and its RMLs from Muswell Hill meant that DMs (now including B20s) had to return to its Sunday share of the 102. Still, there were now no spare DMs available to prevent RMs from having to

Right: **London Transport retained its obsession with standardisation, even if in some cases it took a while for shared routes to fall into line. The 109's Brixton allocation had been DM-operated since the beginning of 1978, and on 28 October Thornton Heath took its turn, though of course with non-B20s. DM 943 (SMU 943N) came from New Cross and is seen at Croydon, North End on a sunny day to best show off its repaint.** *David Wilkinson collection*

THE B20

Right: **Heavy reductions to the 109 when the 159 came back into the ascendancy over their shared corridor on 28 October 1978 obliged Brixton to reduce its DM fleet. Four of them were transferred to Muswell Hill, commencing the B20 era at that garage. DM 2533 (THX 533S) was one of them, and is seen at the Golders Green stand of the 102, once again DM-operated on Sundays.**
Haydn Davies

be requisitioned to form a semi-official spares contingent at Potters Bar (route 134), Muswell Hill (the 43 and 134) and Upton Park (the 101); the Routemasters were strangers now at the former two sheds. Yet the other side of the coin was return appearances by Wood Green DMs on the 29, straying from the 141! Any bus was better than no bus, as the passengers boarding rogue RMs on the 24, 45 and 141 at this time would have said.

Croydon's weekend-only 130A was replaced by the introduction of the 130B, with DMs on Saturdays and DMSs on Sundays; Croydon also picked up the 130 on Sundays on transfer from Thornton Heath. This accompanied a rationalisation of the Addington-area express routes, which became just C3/C4 on weekdays and C1 on Sundays, the C2 coming off altogether. The 154 had its allocations altered, Sutton replacing Thornton Heath on Saturdays and Croydon coming off on Mondays to Fridays. The Saturday Wallington extension of the 233 had proved successful enough to warrant its introduction on weekdays during the peaks, but fellow Croydon route 197A was withdrawn. Elmers End passed the 194B to Thornton Heath in exchange for the 289. New Cross's 70 was introduced at weekends and diverted at Deptford to reach Lewisham instead of Greenwich, really coming into its own with

Right: **Differing from the 197 through its haring off to the north once having reached West Croydon from Norwood Junction, the 197A remained a Monday to Friday route for all eight years of its existence. Seen in the person of Thornton Heath's DMS 235 (JGF 235K) outside its home garage on 9 March 1978, the route was withdrawn without replacement on 28 October. Straight after that, DMS 235 went into overhaul, which bought it three and half more years in London.**
R. C. Riley

94

Left: **At the very top of the world, or rather where London Transport's red buses shade off into open countryside at Hammond Street, is where we see Edmonton's DM 1026 (GHV 26N) during August 1979. The 283 was a new route intended to partially one-man the 279, but the timetable couldn't be made efficient as an OMO route so it bowed with DMs, and after two years it ended up incorporated back into the 279.** *Tony Wilson*

a simultaneous extension from Waterloo to Victoria. A diversion through the Pepys Estate near Surrey Docks was planned (and included on blinds) but did not come to fruition.

On the Hertford Road the 149 was extended from Edmonton to Enfield Garage, while the 279 underwent an interesting convolution in that the Sunday-only 279A, hitherto a way of giving OMO drivers on the 259 work on Sundays, was converted from DMS to RM and its Tottenham share replaced by one from Enfield. At the northern end of the 279, new route 283 (DM from Edmonton and operating from Lower Edmonton to Hammond Street) was created to allow the 279 to fall back to Edmonton and disappear entirely on Sundays (hence the 279A); the simultaneous extension of the 149 from Edmonton to Ponders End Garage saw 13 more DMs put into Edmonton garage, most of which came from Muswell Hill's last standards. DM participation left the 253 when Stamford Hill converted its Sunday mix to RMLs only, though RMs were the staple.

At Cricklewood the 245A was withdrawn and replaced by the introduction of the 245 on Sundays; also in that sector the 83 and 183 swapped routeings in Hendon so as to bring the former past its operating garage at Hendon, while the 125 lost its remaining projections past North Finchley to Golders Green and the 143

Left: **On 13 August 1978 DMS 807 (TGX 807M) out of Hendon lays over at Golders Green on the 183, which on 28 October 1978 underwent a minor but not insignificant intermediate rerouteing in the Hendon area.** *John Laker*

THE B20

Right: **The 101 in its heyday used to field over sixty buses, but with the docks mothballed and only tentative plans to revitalise the area with housing, the route needed just 16 DMs when it came time to convert from RML. Upton Park's DM 939 (SMU 939N) has just dropped its passengers off at North Woolwich's ferry terminus on 1 October 1979, but, like the 262 in the same general sector, DMs were not to last long and the 101 would regain its Routemasters four weeks after this photograph was taken.** *I. Thomas / Colour-Rail.com (BUI30531)*

was reallocated from Holloway to Hendon, which took seven DMSs (three each from Putney and Fulwell and one from Cricklewood). South of the river, a spot of cutting back took off the 249's weekend extension beyond Clapham Junction to Battersea; instead the 295 was projected to this point. At Norbiton, the remnant 213 was withdrawn and further to the west Fulwell's 281, OMO on Sundays, was extended from Twickenham to Hounslow daily. Foreshadowing a trend, routes 168 and 172 were taken out of the Embankment and rerouted down the Strand.

By taking the PVR down by 5%, a spares margin was created with the 28 October programme which allowed the DM and DMS classes to breathe more freely in the face of multiple failings that had almost crippled operations hitherto. The Primary and Supplementary schedules devised at this time were discontinued, totals generally being rounded down to reflect vehicle availability. Still, a spares margin of 14.2% for the DM class and 19.1% for the DMS hardly made for good economics, when half that is considered tight today.

Right: **Only the Saturday and Sunday rosters of the 299 were DMS-operated when this picture of Potters Bar's DMS 541 (MLK 541L) was taken at Southgate, contingent on the availability of buses spare from the 84 and 242. When those routes had to resume single-deckers in 1979 to free urgently needed DMSs, the 299 followed suit.** *John May / Online Transport Archive*

THE LONDON DMS

Left: Willesden's 226 would be its only DMS outpost, taking eight on 12 November 1978 to upgrade the route from SMS. DMS 154 (JGF 154K) had spent its first seven years as a Fulwell bus, but was overhauled between August and October 1978 so as to take its place on the 226. During April 1980 it is seen in Harlesden. *David Wilkinson collection*

11 November or thereabouts saw the first Metrobuses join forces with Cricklewood's DM fleet on the 16 and 16A and the following day saw the 226 at Willesden upgraded from SMS to DMS, using eight overhauled DMSs which included in their ranks DMS 1449. This bus had actually successfully had its body separated at Aldenham, the MCW body having been designed to permit doing so, but to overhaul the MCWs would have necessitated the addition of another production line at Aldenham with yet a new set of specialist equipment. By now overhauls were proceeding at a rate of 20 a month, examples leaving garages for overhaul being replaced there simultaneously by outshopped examples with slightly lower stock numbers. DMS 2396, meanwhile, visited Leyland in October for modifications to its air-cleaner intake resulting in the addition of another grille on the nearside bonnet stack.

On 4 December the first official conversion from DMS began when Hornchurch's routes 165, 246 and 252 began taking Titans. Nothing, unfortunately, could outpace CoF expiries, and shortages were biting at the end of the year, particularly at south-east London garages Abbey Wood, New Cross, Peckham and Catford. The death knell for the DMS came at the end of the year when LT officially announced that withdrawals would be commencing in 1979; as hard as they'd tried to adapt the vehicles to their standards, whether it be overhauling or what have you, the reliability issues were too much to keep wrestling with for that much longer when attention was being focused on the new Ms and Ts, which had teething problems (though nowhere near as severe) of their own.

Even with an overhaul, the early DMSs would be coming up to midlife by the end of the CoF it conferred, which is when they would have been withdrawn anyway under normal circumstances; plenty of RT-family buses had racked up little more than a decade, after all. As it happened, while the early DMSs and the B20s survived to achieve something approaching a normal lifespan in service, it was the middle order that would be devastated.

Above: Titans made their debut in regular service on 4 December 1978, beginning at Hornchurch and commencing the process of chasing the DMS westward, back towards town. One displaced was DMS 646 (MLK 646L), which transferred to North Street when the prolonged conversion of Hornchurch was completed in October 1979, but is still carrying Hornchurch's 'RD' codes when espied in South Street in December. DMS 2157 (OJD 157R), coming past, left this month when the introduction of Ts to North Street obliged it to move on and DMS 646 followed it out in March 1980. *I. Thomas / Colour-Rail.com (BUI30654)*

THE B20 97

CHAPTER FIVE

WITHDRAWALS AND OVERHAULS

1979

On 26 February 1979 DMS 251, derelict at Catford for over five of its seven years of age, was hooked up to a wrecker and towed to Wombwell Diesels' scrapyard at Barnsley. Thus began the withdrawal and disposal of the DMS family, undoubtedly controversial to observers of the bus scene, whether they numbered enthusiasts or politicians. Included in the first round of disposals, which were divided between Wombwell Diesels of Barnsley for scrap cases and Ensign of Grays for onward sale, were former Leyland-engined pioneer DMS 132, the five early examples carrying two-leaf doors (DMSs 240 and 463-467) and the last in stock with a white band, DMS 284. The opportunity was thus taken to dispose of a handful of other hopeless cases, led off by DMS 1906 (damaged in March at Potters Bar) and the first B20 withdrawal, DMS 2433, which had managed no more than a year in service before being damaged by fire. But this wasn't the record – Bexleyheath's DMS 2387 ceased to function after just four months, the same length of time it spent in store before being allocated, and never worked again!

Below: **DMS overhauls are in full swing on 16 September 1979, as evidenced by this visit to Aldenham. This one has needed so much done to it that it's impossible to even guess at its identity other than being a Park Royal.** *Bob Greenaway / Online Transport Archive*

As DMS stocks began to deplete, future policy was drawn up as to which sub-types would be favoured over another when it came to overhauling. Where possible, MCW-bodied DMSs suffering CoF expiry were to be sold as runners rather than overhauled, as it had been determined that setting up another line at Aldenham just to separate the MCW bodies from their chassis in the manner of DMS 1449 was not cost-effective. Thus did large numbers of the early MCW DMSs begin popping up in strength around the country, West Midlands PTE in particular taking eighty via Ensign and keeping them for four more years – about the length of time they would have survived in London with an overhaul of the kind affecting Park Royals. Only the best Park Royal-bodied examples would thus be retained beyond their initial CoF expiry, whether by overhaul or recertification work on a more limited basis to produce a two-year ticket. Some thus were resuscitated after many years out of use, most notoriously DMS 141, which had sat idle since 1973, and three more had spent five years out of service. Even so, DMS overhauls were to be reduced so that extra RMs could go in.

By the spring of 1979 repaints were coming up to the originally white-topped examples, slowly but steadily reducing this attractive livery. Having already failed to specify the white-top livery for DMSs going into repaint, London Transport effectively cancelled it altogether from early 1979 when the first new Ms and Ts appeared in dreary all-red after only a few of each class had worn it. The incongruous and superfluous yellow on the entrance doors, however, would endure for another twelve years! Painting of a different style was evident when DMSs 400 and 405 were made use of in the Great Children's Party in Hyde Park on 3 June; due for repaint anyway, the two buses were arranged side-by side and separated by scaffolding for kids to climb up on and do their worst with water-based paints.

They called the winter of 1978/79 the Winter of Discontent; on top of strikes by ASLEF and other unions, which were demanding a 20% pay rise by April (they settled for 14%), the climate itself was particularly tough, with long spells of snowy weather which saw buses freeze where they were left due to the refusal of local authorities to grit roads; the drop in temperature caused bus components to crack, with the DMSs being particularly badly affected. The NBA figure for January/February was up to 600, and one truly terrible day, 16 February, saw more than a dozen garages unable to put any buses out at all.

Above: **As the future of the DMS family was determined, hard choices had to be made as to which sub-types would be retained and which disposed of, and these categories fluctuated over the years. One sub-classification that would be particularly unlucky was the DM, none of which would be overhauled (other than one fluke). Some of them, like Holloway's already tired-looking DM 1098 (GHV 98N) captured along the 104 on 8 July 1979, would not even manage to be repainted before withdrawal.** *Geoff Rixon*

WITHDRAWALS AND OVERHAULS

When the weather eased off, 1979 marked the 150th anniversary of the placement into service of London's first stage-carriage horse buses by George Shillibeer, and to mark this twelve RMs and DM 2646 (because British Leyland insisted a Fleetline was chosen) were painted into an approximation of the green and yellow livery used, with a red cantrail band. Wearing 'OMNIBUS' fleetnames like the rest, DM 2646 was particularly distinguished, even without the ability to include the red window pans of the RMs, and took the opportunity to advertise Leyland's upcoming products – the National and the Titan – on its front and sides. After the formal launch at 2 March at the Guildhall, its deployment, like the RMs, was in three stages to particular routes from particular sets of garages, viz Cricklewood for the 16 between 3 March and 1 June, thereafter the 43 and 134 out of Muswell Hill (2 June-31 August) and finally the 109 and 133 from Brixton between 1 September and 30 November, in a late change from plans to use it from Thornton Heath on the 109 alone. All its allocations were to specific running numbers, though while at Cricklewood it was sometimes seen on the 16A and N94. Between those duties DM 2646 made sure to participate in the Easter Parade through Battersea Park on 15 April and the commemorative road run to Hyde Park on 8 July, plus clocking up appearances at five garage open days and finally at Aldenham on 16 September before repaint into red on 9 January 1980. The garage open days were a 'hearts and minds' component of the decentralisation imperative that LT hoped would restore its reputation among the public, and were continued for some years thereafter.

The year had begun with the 99's extension finally from Erith to Slade Green via hitherto unserved roads on 13 January, but the first big event of 1979 was the conversion of Fulwell from DMS to M beginning on 19 March and encompassing routes 270 and 285 by 12 April, followed on 13 April by the 281 on Sundays.

Top left: The treatment of DM 2646 (THX 646S) to Shillibeer livery almost stole the show from the twelve RMs that were otherwise detailed to carry it. The first of three allocations during 1979 was to Cricklewood's 16, on which it is seen at Hyde Park Corner on 18 March. *Geoff Rixon*

Above left: British Leyland may have been 'leaders in passenger transport', as the advertising proclaimed, but LT had struggled with its products for the last decade, particularly this one. DM 2646 (THX 646S) being the last DMS, the bills either side of the blind box advertised the company's latest products, the Titan and National, both of which would have happier innings. It is seen in Old Street in July, when allocated to Muswell Hill. *Geoff Rixon*

Left: The third deployment was to Brixton's 109 and 133, but the weather has turned by the time DM 2646 (THX 646S) is seen swinging into Moorgate. *Geoff Rixon*

Of the DMSs displaced, the Clayton hydraulic brake-fitted quartet moved en bloc to Norbiton.

Busplan's third and final stage was implemented on 31 March, saving 74 buses to make 442 in total over the three stages, and its big surprise was the reversion of route 106 from DMS to crew operation with RMs; this extreme decision had been made as a drastic attempt to solve both the chronic unreliability of the DMSs, and to stave off impending CoF expiry on them. The OMO drivers transferred to crew work retained their OMO rates of pay. Ealing Hospital, just to the east of Southall, was treated to bus services from 31 March, the 92 coming in from Southall Garage and the 83 from Hanwell Broadway (its DMS-operated Sunday service, however, reaching the hospital only between 1100-1900 hours). The Sunday Brentford-Syon Park service on Hanwell's E-routes was switched from the E1 to the E2. The service into the isolated Wapping region was transferred from the 67 to the 22A, but at its northern end the 67 was extended from Stamford Hill over new ground via St Ann's Hospital to Wood Green. Part of it was put into Tottenham on Sundays to give work to that garage's drivers displaced from the 106. The 283 at Edmonton had been slated for one-manning at this date but this was cancelled; like fellow DM-operated routes 18, 149 and 168A at the moment, it had been seeing rogue RM appearances in strength.

Planned for Stage 2 but postponed following objections by local residents was a round of reductions in the Surrey borderlands based on Sutton. Here the 164 was one-manned with DMSs and the 164A withdrawn, routes 280A and 80A being re-rerouted over its former roads in the Tattenham Corner region. Brixton's 95 was extended to Tooting Broadway on Sundays and the 181 (moving today from Stockwell to Merton) dwindled further, losing its roads from Clapham Common to Victoria. It almost came off altogether but for a campaign to save it. Stockwell received a proportion of the 44 in compensation. The 295 was extended on Mondays to Fridays over its Saturday roads beyond Clapham Junction to Battersea Park Station. The Sunday-only 181A was withdrawn entirely. Not far from this sector, the

Above: **The reversion of the 106 to crew operation on 31 March 1979 was the most visible indicator of the DMSs' failure, and it was wondered how much further this could be taken. As it turned out, OMO would return, three years but a lifetime in political terms later, with the rather more reliable Titans. DMS 710 (TGX 710M) had come to Hackney only as recently as June 1978.** *David Wilkinson collection*

The takeover of Fulwell by Metrobuses in the spring of 1979 made all these DMSs redundant. DMS 1940 (KUC 940P) is only passing through in this 9 June portrait taken round the back of the garage, while of the rest pictured, DMSs 196, 370 and 369 were sold and DMSs 372 and 373 were reprieved for overhaul. *David Wilkinson collection*

Right: **Sutton's 164 was one-manned on 31 March 1979, absorbing the 164A. Sutton's DMS 763 (TGX 763M), transferred in for the purpose, is coming up to Sutton Station.** *David Wilkinson collection*

Below: **In this March 1979 shot DMS 295 (JGF 295K) has had it; it didn't manage to clock up four years in service before being sidelined at its second garage, Fulwell, at the end of 1975 and never revived. This is where it's snapped for posterity shortly before sale directly to Wombwell Diesels for scrap.** *Geoff Rixon*

168A gained a new northern terminus, being diverted at Holloway to Hornsey Rise, rather than Finsbury Park, so as to assist the 14 on this sector.

DMS movements with the 31 March programme finally expelled non-B20s from Bexleyheath and Wandsworth, some going to Sutton to join overhauled examples for its route 164 requirements, but overhauls had dwindled now that withdrawals were in progress; sixteen DMSs were sold in March. At this point North Street's replacement of the DMS type with Ts and Fulwell's similar endeavour with Ms were in full swing. Reductions to Shepherd's Bush's 220 allowed the transfer of six of its DMSs to Bexleyheath, introducing MCW-bodied B20s there and breaking the monopoly hitherto of one body or the other at the B20 sheds; Wandsworth followed in the opposite direction by taking Park Royal-bodied DMS 2496 made spare from Stockwell by the route 181 reductions. Other than those specific conversions, the spare vehicle situation was so acute that those DMSs released from the 106 and from the M or T conversions were deployed to cover CoF expiries where needed, all over the fleet. North Street's departing DMSs had their Multi-Ride cancellers removed first at Aldenham, three (DMSs 649, 652 and 780) subsequently showing up at Edmonton on the 149 in crew mode without the stickers removed! DMS 780, of course, had started out there as a crew bus. Holloway and West Ham also pressed DMSs into service on their crew routes, at least giving the passengers a chance by taking off the 'PLEASE PAY AS YOU ENTER' transfers. During April, the situation at Potters Bar and

Upton Park had improved to the extent that the RMs drafted in to support those two garages' beleaguered DMs at the start of the year were sent away again.

Finchley undertook some exercises for 31 March, withdrawing the Sunday-only 240A (covered by an extension of the 221 from North Finchley to Edgware on Sundays to match its weekday service) and extending two peak journeys on the 125 from Finchley Central to Hendon Bell following representations about the withdrawal of the leg to Golders Green the previous October. Its most unusual endeavour was new limited-stop route 296, its single DMS linking Finchley Central with Copthall Sports Centre at the behest of Barnet Council. It was to prove singularly unsuccessful, not helped by it only beginning during the mid-afternoon outside school terms, and lasted less than seven months. White-on-blue blinds were carried.

Above: **Finchley's DMS 2012 (KJD 12P) may have been showing the best of leafy suburbia in this summer 1979 shot, but there are only three passengers on board, and custom that poor doomed the second 296 from the outset.**
Haydn Davies

Left: **Fulwell's DMSs had already been replaced by Ms and it wouldn't be long before Southall's DMSs, like DMS 435 (MLK 435L) at Northolt, gave way too.**
Haydn Davies

WITHDRAWALS AND OVERHAULS

Above: **The 18 and 24 exchanged their vehicles in a neat swap; DM 1055 (GHV 55N) came from Chalk Farm to Stonebridge and is seen approaching Wembley in April 1980.** *Haydn Davies*

Below: **DM 1143 (KUC 143P) is operating Stonebridge's Sunday share of the 266 through North Acton but a side blind has somehow found its way into the front box.** *Haydn Davies*

Busplan's raison d'être was to eliminate non-standard workings deemed in the interest of the operator rather than the passenger, at the same time removing suffixed routes where possible; thus did the orphaned 224B and 232A become 224 and 232 now that their parents had faded from memory.

On 22 April the 24 at Chalk Farm regained its RMLs, the discarded DMs moving to Stonebridge for the 18. Despite their unpopularity in central London due to unreliability, one advantage of DMs was that their doored configuration perhaps sealed in conductors from the likelihood of assault, which is why they were specifically requested on the 18, which ran through parts of town filling up rapidly with violent undesirables. Knock-on effects at Stonebridge put DMs onto the 266 on Sundays and at Chalk Farm allowed the Sunday 3 to revert from DM to RM, while Holloway's DMs on the 253 on Saturdays also gave way to RMs. To match Westbourne Park's Sunday status on the 18, Alperton's share on the day also took on crew-operated Fleetlines from 13 May, though in their case it was DMSs.

DMSs from the main Park Royal batch (368-917) began to move into Aldenham for overhaul as 1979 progressed, though blocks from those numbers were being gutted as withdrawals took away those in the worst shape. Sutton's early MCW contingent delivered for the 213 group seven years earlier now fell out en bloc, but as runners were sold to Ensign, the Essex dealership which immediately saw resale prospects in these unloved buses. Cannily, and foreshadowing the trend of a decade later, one of them would remain in London, this being DMS 1256, which under the ownership of Ted

Left: Most DMS casualties came from neglect and parts shortages, but a greater proportion than earlier classes fell out from fire damage, and almost all of it was isolated to the same place, the overworked and overheated engine. DMS 2433 (OJD 433R) ended up looking like this after catching fire on 10 May 1979, and never worked again. The open day at Aldenham permitted passengers to witness its shame, but it was to be another four years before DMS 2433 was actually sold. *Bob Greenaway / Online Transport Archive*

Brakell's dealership in Cheam and with a white band applied, operated on the Round London Sightseeing Tour from June alongside the last of the B20 DMs from Stockwell (of which four were added on 7 April) and an eclectic collection of oddments from Obsolete Fleet. With the London features that had troubled them so much in the capital removed (the exit door, the semi-automatic gearbox and door interlocks), the first of eighty MCW-bodied DMSs (most of the JGU-Ks and a number of the MLH-Ls) subsequently entered service in Birmingham with WMPTE. One of them was not DMS 1612, a March fire casualty from Hendon, and on 10 May the first B20 to find itself damaged beyond reclamation by fire was Enfield's DMS 2433, operating as E10 on the 107. Rear-end fires would form an alarmingly high proportion of the casualties accruing to B20s, due to the tendency of hot oil to drip onto the engine.

It was relatively easy to predict the order of withdrawals by recalling the date of entry into service and adding seven years for CoF expiry; LT thus anticipated large numbers of DMSs unavailable at once and had to hold their breath for their replacement either by overhauled

Left: DMS 383 (JGF 383K) was under overhaul when Londoners were allowed to glimpse Aldenham's inner workings on 16 September, but DMS overhauls were actually tailing off at this point as LT wondered whether it wouldn't be more cost-effective just to withdraw all of them. They wouldn't have that luxury, and indeed the year's hiatus cost them even dearer. DMS 383 was outshopped to Catford but only managed two more years in service, half that afforded by the CoF awarded upon leaving works. *Bob Greenaway / Online Transport Archive*

WITHDRAWALS AND OVERHAULS

examples or by others released from garages converted progressively to M or T operation; either option was progressing with agonising slowness and CoF expiry wasn't slowing down. Bromley and Battersea had their original fleets replaced in May as the former's MCWs were withdrawn and sold and the latter's readied for overhaul. Outshopped DMSs were split between these (DMS 141 at Bromley going back into service for the first time in six years!) and four other garages with early members to rotate, Catford, Merton, Finchley and Putney.

One of the most important changes ever to occur to London buses, and one which certainly negated all the advantages that the DMS family was supposed to convey, was implemented on 27 May during the Spring Bank Holiday; the discontinuation finally of automatic fare collection, as part of a productivity deal agreed with the Union to accompany a pay increase that was settled in June at roughly 14%, paid for by a 7.5% fares hike implemented on the 17th. Revenue from the machinery by then had dwindled to a pitiful 4%, and for all the (very slight) improvement in boarding times offered by the self-service concept, the machinery could never be made reliable enough to justify its continued use or trust in it by passengers who would rather deal with a human being, and resort to vandalising it if they couldn't. All AFC cabinets were barred off, the buttons were panelled over and the turnstile removed and passengers were directed to pay the driver, conventional OMO becoming the standard. Those employees tasked with handling the machinery and its contents were redeployed, where practicable as conductors. The DM class would then be converted, it was intended, to enable them to work OMO as well. The Multi-Ride concept was continued for a little while longer, but that too fell by the wayside in early 1980.

With DMS withdrawals gathering strength, it was proposed to suspend overhauls of the type while Ms and Ts could be deployed to replace them; however, this policy came back to bite them when Ms and particularly Ts did not arrive in sufficient time to outpace withdrawals of CoF-expired DMSs, and some desperate measures had to be taken while the likes of West Ham repaired long term-delicensed DMSs as fast as they could. Bexleyheath found itself so short of serviceable DMSs during the spring that from 23 May it was supplied with some redundant SMs, which were put onto the 132 ostensibly as a short-term measure meant to last only a week (thus no blinds were printed for them) but which remained there for the rest of the year while modifications were carried out on Bexleyheath's DMSs. Palmers Green, meanwhile, was struggling badly in May, with half its B20 fleet delicensed sufficient to have to

Below: **Flexibility has been a watchword for London bus operations distinctly discounted by London Transport; despite the efficiency of standardised operations and allocations of specific types, sometimes any bus beats no bus at all. The passengers of Edmonton's DMS 1339 (MLH 339L), not to mention its conductor on this crew-operated route, will have had to fight their way past the now disused automatic fare collection machinery in this May 1979 photograph, but at least they all got to where they were going.**
Haydn Davies

Above: **Fulwell's DMS 1363 (MLH 363L) looks healthy enough in this 5 May 1979 shot near its home garage, but more money could be got for it through sale, and it subsequently worked as West Midlands PTE 5574 before returning to town as a Cityrama tour bus.**
Geoff Rixon

accept two J-registered examples during June. Barking undertook a swap in June to move out some of its early Park Royals, while the non-standard nature of B20s at certain sheds was overlooked when one-day events needed loans, such as to Hendon on the occasion of the Pinner Fair on 30 May and a lone B20 (DMS 2250) into Merton to help out on the Derby Day service on 6 June. Nobody even minded too much when DMS 1338 was pressed into service as a crew bus on Holloway's 4 during June; better any bus than no bus!

30 June saw the 107 swallow up the 107A once again and the Telegraph Inn journeys transferred from the 85A to the 85. On 25 June the 173 (Poplar) and 244 (Muswell Hill) took on new LSs, the latter displacing its small band of early overhauled DMSs; the 173 would have to assume single-deck operation before long anyway as it was scheduled to be extended to Stratford via a low bridge at West Ham station. Still, DMSs left the 267 at Fulwell between 25 May and 16 June, completing the conversion of that garage to M and making that garage the first to lose the DMS type altogether. Fellow Cardinal District garage Norbiton was next in line for Metrobuses, treating the 211 (ex-SMS) on 15 July, the 213A on the 16th, the Sunday share of the 285 on the 29th and the 131 between the latter date and 27 September when the last three DMSs at Norbiton, used as engineering spares, were stood down. The Clayton examples thus needed a new home, and this was Thornton Heath.

After an eleven-week break DMS overhauls resumed at Aldenham in July, DMSs 378, 385, 392 and 402 entering; Hanwell was now recertifying others without a repaint, while the expiry of CoFs into the 400s and resulting sales now hit Bow's route 10 contingent. Standards were tightening somewhat in that Aldenham rejected some of those sent its way and returned them to garages with instructions to get them

Above: **DMS 618 (MLK 618L), seen swinging into the 131's latter-day West Molesey terminus on 4 August 1979, was displaced from this and other Norbiton routes by a Metrobus in September and moved on to Leyton, but lasted only until the following April.**
Geoff Rixon

WITHDRAWALS AND OVERHAULS

Below: *Otherwise a solid SMS user, Southall garage prepared for the conversion of routes 195 and 273 to permanent double-deck by treating their Sunday services first. On 27 August 1979 DMS 24 (EGP 24J) heads for Ruislip Lido; it had actually come back to the same garage following overhaul in the furst half of 1978.* John Laker

Bottom: *Southall's DMS 767 (TGX 767M) had started as a crew bus but had come to Southall in November 1974; it is seen in Ruislip Road, Greenford.* Haydn Davies

actually fit for overhaul. Some of these thus never did make it to works. The sluggish pace of overhauling due to this and the fact that CoFs were still expiring, however, produced a critical shortage of DMSs by the autumn, and the class's situation was further imperilled when British Leyland announced the closure of Park Royal works and the effective end to Titan production after the first batch. Plans for as far off as 1984 had already been drawn up (and were confirmed at the end of the year at an LT conference held in Eastbourne about future direction) envisaging a need for 2000 more buses to replace the DMS family between 1981 and 1984, by which time it was hoped that the XRM, of whichever configuration being experimented with (though to be fixed at a length of 28ft) proved preferable, would be in production and a decision could be made as to whether it would replace the Metrobuses and Titans, or the RM family. In the short term, though 100% OMO was still the ultimate aim and it was not intended to convert back to crew any more OMO routes than was strictly necessary, bearing in mind the vehicle availability situation, Routemasters were being acquired back from London Country, where they were intended to replace DMs and MDs in central London and thus put an end to the failed concept of doored crew operation. Not that the MDs were any luckier than the DMS family in the grand scheme of things; although somewhat more reliable than DMSs, they were suffering problems of their own, most notably with corrosion, and a number of accident casualties had already been taken out of service and stored. It was announced that they too would be sold after their seven-year CoFs had expired, but not before being reallocated to quieter work away from central London. One DM to meet an early fate before it had been decided what to do with the DM subclassification was Holloway's DM 1757, which was deroofed under the low bridge at Finsbury Park when returning light to Holloway after a journey on the 4 on 14 August. It experienced the ignominy of being displayed at the Aldenham Works open day on 16 September, alongside fire victim DMS 2433, before joining the ranks of buses sold to Wombwell Diesels at the end of the year.

It seemed that every problem that LT managed to stem was exacerbated by another one popping up; even a second fares rise of 12.5% on 9 July, accompanied a little earlier by an enormous (54%) increase to Havering fares, failed to make the case to resume OMO conversions until a solution to boarding times that was better than Multi-Ride could be found. At least MCW was on the ball, talks opening to fill the gap left by Leyland by increasing the order for Ms by 100.

Now that new deliveries of Ms and Ts omitted the white roof relief and repaints had caught up with the DMS 1968+ numbers which had carried it from new, slowly it started to disappear. At Southall, DMSs had come to the Sunday rosters of the 273 on 20 May and the 195 on 29 July, but Ms then turned up here too, taking over both those two routes' Sunday services plus the 92, 120, 232, 274 and 282 in their entirety between 17 September and 19 December.

On 1 October 1979 London Transport put into effect plans it had been hatching for two years to decentralise its perceived monolithic and remote form of operations into eight geographical districts, each with its own

District General Manager, Operations Manager and Engineering Manager. The rationale was to bring operations closer to the passenger and thus increase his morale, and while the new structure would have little effect on DMS deployments at the moment, it would go on to dictate which of Metrobuses or Titans replaced them. Already Forest District was specifying Titans and Cardinal District Metrobuses, so it was not difficult to predict which garages would be next in line. On the buses themselves, paper posters (not stickers) were devised and posted from 10 December; DMSs had theirs in the wide panel nearside between the entrance door and the first downstairs window. Underscoring the power of the unions at the time to prohibit the carrying out of even the most seemingly trivial tasks, the job of garage billposters was to deal with paper posters only, so stickers were not used and the paper posters faded. This neat on-paper (so to speak) exercise was less so in real life, as the fourteen existing traffic areas, on which the new Districts' borders were based, remained in use. The concurrent placing of the existing engineering districts into the new system left Forest without a parent engineering garage, so Upton Park, otherwise geographically within Tower, assumed this role. This sort of divide-and-rule mentality would be continued with progressively more severe results in the next decade, but the effort put in at this stage steadily beat back the NBA figures once again.

Autumn changes involved the withdrawal of the 296 (29 September) and on the 30th, the necessity of converting Bromley's 61 from DMS to LS due simply to the availability at the time of Leyland Nationals from the current order for 140; double-deckers would not return for five years. The delay in Titan production and resulting delivery to Hornchurch, exacerbated by modifications being carried out to existing Ts in stock from an extensive list, forced LT to make plans to release DMSs by converting Leyton's 55 (and N96) to SMS operation from 7 October, though this plan was cancelled two days beforehand as enough Fleetlines were scraped up just in time to replace Leyton's CoF expiries; mostly from Southall (replaced by Ms) and from Bromley (replaced by LSs). Thus did the SMS last a little longer, recertifications to this type allowing more than most to achieve a reasonably normal ten-year lifespan for a modern full-size single-decker. West Ham converted the 262 from DM to RM operation on 14 October after less than two years; the displaced DMs going to relieve shortages of the type elsewhere. The RMs here came from trainers made spare by buses dislodged from the failed Shop-Linker route. Two weeks later Upton Park's 101 regained Routemasters on the 28th, many of its DMs passing to Edmonton

Left: **DMS 211 (JGF 211K) had an eventful 1979. Beginning the year in works, it came out of overhaul in February and was allocated to Putney, but in June was transferred to Barking, where it is seen on that garage's short 156, still carrying Putney's 'AF' codes. In September it made a further move, to Poplar, and in December found itself back at Aldenham, delicensed pending another transfer. That turned out to be to Croydon, where it spent the rest of its career in the capital.** *David Wilkinson collection*

WITHDRAWALS AND OVERHAULS

Above: **One of the Fleetlines displaced from Bromley when the garage's double-deck OMO complement was unceremoniously replaced by LSs was DMS 88 (EGP 88J), which had retained its Ricardo sound-baffling equipment through overhaul and outshopping to Bromley. On 12 October it is seen at Bromley South; after the conversion it would transfer to New Cross.** *R. C. Riley*

where appearances of RMs on the 149 throughout the year had threatened to make a mockery of the route's officially-allocated DM type. Plenty went to New Cross to alleviate shortages that had grown so extreme there that crews were running their buses into the garage early in protest. When Stockwell's RLST component was stood down for the winter, its DMs went to top up numbers at Muswell Hill.

The rest of Bromley's DMS fleet was removed with the loss of the upper deck on two more of its routes (126 and 138) on 21 October; again LSs took over. Sutton's 80 and 80A received a boost on Sundays when spare DMSs replaced BLs. On 5 November, North Street became only the second London Transport garage to start taking on Titans; it had taken until 25 October for the last DMS to leave Hornchurch. North Street's roster comprised routes 66 (Mon-Sat) / 66B (Sun), 103, 139, 175 (Sundays only), 247A and 294. Three routes lost their DMSs for SMSs in November; Uxbridge's 224 on the 10th, Potters Bar's 84 on the 17th and Camberwell's 42 on the 24th. The 299's weekend DMS operation was converted on Saturdays to SMS, the 242 at Potters Bar able to spare enough DMSs only to keep them both double-deck on Sundays. Uxbridge's and Potters Bar's were spread all over, the remnant of Uxbridge DMSs in the high 1300s expiring and being sold, while Camberwell's exiled DMSs joined forces with early Park Royal overhauls into Croydon to replace the garage's expired original members in the 500s and 1300s; the cancellers from the expired C-route MCWs were removed and refitted to the incomers comprising DMSs 177, 183-185, 187, 189, 193, 200, 211, 217, 220-224, 233 and 235-238. To mark them out at the garage for the convenience of the engineers, the letter 'C' was painted on the offside corner pillar by the cab. Despite withdrawal at this point DMS 1332 was kept hold of, due to its hydraulic braking, and escaped sale through its move to the Experimental Department at Chiswick the following April. Croydon was intended to have its 197 converted to SMSs displaced by new LSs, but this did not come to pass.

On 3 December Holloway's 239 also took on SMSs to replace DMSs, the maligned Swifts having one last chance as their traditional routes otherwise began to be colonised in earnest by Leyland Nationals. Finally for 1979, the march through Cardinal District of the Metrobus completed Southall and next encompassed Turnham Green, which on 19 December converted the 91 (and night N97) from DMS to M in one fell swoop. additionally completing the 267, whose Fulwell majority had already been done. Holloway and Turnham Green split their DMSs predominantly between Elmers End and Croydon, plus a couple to Clapton, whose original allocation in the mid-500s was now falling out. Two of Turnham Green's expellees were Rolls-Royce-engined, and these joined

Left: **Desperate times called for desperate measures, and this far north of the border it wasn't considered too detrimental to have to convert routes to single-deck so that their DMSs could be redeployed where needed more. The 84 was one such sacrifice, converting to SMS on 17 November 1979 and obliging DMS 1902 (KUC 902P), seen at New Barnet Station, to transfer to Wood Green. In this case, the reign of SMSs on the 84 was to prove temporary and DMSs returned on 27 September 1980.**
Haydn Davies

two more gathered at Putney since March. The hill-climbing properties of the engine were put to good use on the garage's route 85.

As DMS replacement began to accelerate (a total of 357 being sold by the end of 1979) London Transport held a management conference in Eastbourne in November to determine future direction. While the eventual aim was to achieve 100% OMO (perhaps with flat fares) despite the fact that the cost of implementing it would eat up the projected £48m in savings, a short-term plan was announced to buy back the Routemasters sold to London Country and use them to replace the DM class (and the MDs) on crew routes in central London. LT's political masters at the GLC, however, turned down LT's 1980 budget outright due to its failure to meet the mileage target set, and questioned maintenance procedures, not to mention the economics of overhauling altogether, given that the press would not get off LT's back about the policy of selling off DMSs.

Below: **357 DMSs were sold in 1979, beginning the wholesale withdrawal of the type. One of the year's casualties was DMS 1266 (JGU 266K), seen looking in at least passable condition along Bromley's 126 on 26 March 1978; however, it was sold for scrap even before Bromley's three DMS routes had to assume single-deck LS operation.**
Haydn Davies

Right: **At the turn of the decade came Alperton's slot for DMS-to-M replacement. This February 1980 view of DMS 1479 (MLH 479L) alongside brand new M 189 (BYX 189V) shows the lineage clearly; MCW had simply ported its existing body onto its own, rather better chassis.** *Haydn Davies*

1980

Three weeks into the new decade came another retrenchment for the fast-dwindling DMS class; Alperton's conversion of routes 79, 79A, 92, 182 and 297 (and on Sundays the 18 (crew-operated) and 83 (OMO) to M commenced on 24 January, although industrial action by the Craft Alliance union concerning the level of overtime payable for new-vehicle transfers from Aldenham, not to mention a strike by steelworkers, dragged out this conversion until 13 July; the same issue prolonged Hendon's conversion of routes 143 and 183 from DMS to M (10 February-15 June) and the input of Titans into North Street (finally completed on 20 July). At this point it was the turn of Wood Green's DMSs in the 1400s to fall due for replacement, and this was accomplished with DMSs leaving Peckham and Hendon. In March members at Catford and Walworth in the 1400s were delicensed and replaced with earlier vehicles, including DMS 1 on transfer from Merton to Catford. Overhauls had by now dwindled to single figures per month, but recertifications were still going, now encompassing the best of the MCWs in the 1400s batch from April, while repaints were ploughing through the 1975/76 order and approaching the 2000s. The early overhauled examples now merited second repaints, which started taking place in March even though not all DMS-family buses had received a first repaint and those that hadn't were showing it.

Right: **Recertification certainly took less time than the comparable overhaul, even with the CoF extent penalty in the longer term; DMS 1440 (MLH 440L), come into works from Upton Park, would leave for Edgware once done.** *John Laker*

THE LONDON DMS

Left: Displaced from Plumstead by an MD, DMS 1567 (THM 567M) came to Merton in April 1980 and is seen in Kingston on 17 August to replace one of the 131's original batch now fallen out with CoF expiry. However, this bus's ticket didn't have much longer itself and it was withdrawn in October. *Geoff Rixon*

A different choice characterised Peckham's DMS removal when it was decided to convert for OMO several MDs made spare from the reversion to RM of the 36 group over that winter and into the spring; thus did the 78 and night routes N85 and N86 assume MD operation on 24 February. Further OMO MDs ousted Plumstead's DMSs on 27 April, taking over the 99 and 122A. They were despatched mostly to Merton, whose batch of Park Royals in the 600s delivered for the 131 in 1973 were now at an end.

B20 DMS 2373 out of Bexleyheath was written off in a head-on-collision on 28 January when an HGV skidded into it at Lower Belvedere; the DMS's cab was pushed into the body right back to the staircase and the driver had to be cut out.

To accompany a particularly hefty fares increase put into effect on 24 February 1980, the Havering Multi-Ride system was discontinued; as had so many fares experiments of the past, it had done nothing to speed up boarding times to match those of rear-entrance crew operation. It was still thought that flat fares of some sort would be the ultimate answer, so a 20p flat fare was instituted in Havering and Harrow instead; by inflation or design, fares were all now in multiples of 10p. Statistics published during January gave the DMS a 6.5mpg figure and a 'seat mpg' of 450 (DM) or 430 (DMS); the RML's comparable figure was 550 and the RM gave a thrifty 7.2mpg; clearly no competition.

During February 1980 those early DMSs overhauled in 1978 started going through

Left: Already fielding the majority of the MD class of Scania/MCW Metropolitans, Peckham decided to make them their standard double-deck OMO bus, converting for dual-purpose operation MDs released from the 36 group and allowing DMSs like early DMS 76 (EGP 76J) to leave. Now allocated to Wood Green, this bus is seen underneath the A406/M11 junction at South Woodford in April, but is letting the side down through its display of a via blind for the W2. *Haydn Davies*

113

Left: **DMS 565 (MLK 565L) was sent by Tottenham for recertification in February 1980 and in this 24 April view at Aldenham, the work is nearly complete. It would be allocated to Catford in May and spend the next two years and three months there.** *John Laker*

Aldenham for intermediate repaints, but at the same time the members that had been recertified rather than overhauled began to be withdrawn, cutting gaps in the very earliest hundred stock numbers. A programme of three-year recertifications commenced in anticipation of future service requirements, this lesser work covering DMSs rather than RMs. 26 Park Royals in the high 500s and 600s and 18 MCWs in the 1400s and 1500s were recertified during the year, while eight DMSs were treated to proper overhauls in the interests of resuming them for the class if deliveries kept falling behind.

Turnham Green garage may have been closed to service buses after 9 May 1980, but it was kept in use to serve as a conversion centre; after RMLs going into service were fitted with radios there before heading to Cricklewood to displace DMs, the garage became the base for DMs to be fitted for OMO capability. Under this programme, DMs would be fitted with powered Almex baseplates on the driver's cab edge to enable them to accept Almex E ticket machines.

The drift back into town of Routemasters, having proven so successful with the 36 group, now began to expand as RMLs were made available following the bulk purchase of London Country's examples and their sending through overhaul at Aldenham. On 24 May the 16 and 16A at Cricklewood were converted from DM to RML and the N94 to crew M (or crew DMS officially). Cricklewood's DMs were sent via Turnham Green to Muswell Hill, standardising that garage's DM complement on the B20 and enabling those displaced to top up spares at nine DM-operating garages. However, among these were the first DMs converted at Turnham Green

Above left: **Two routes to lose Fleetlines in 1980 were the 143, whose Hendon garage, epitomised by DMS 805 (TGX 805M) took Metrobuses, and the 16A, converted to RML in lieu of DMs like Cricklewood's DM 2627 (THX 627S). Both are at Brent Cross during February 1980.** *Haydn Davies*

Left: **After conversion to D format, Croydon's D 950 (GHV 950N) remained able to work the 130 whether in crew mode on weekdays or OMO on Sundays, as in this September 1980 shot on the Addington periphery. However, its DMS-like 'PLEASE PAY AS YOU ENTER' lettering wasn't in the spirit of flexibility.** *Haydn Davies*

for dual OMO/crew mode, and four went to Catford and three to Poplar. At this point, the vehicles were still coded DM and only a few had 'PLEASE PAY AS YOU ENTER' transfers applied at front, but something more obvious had to be devised over and above the fitment with Almex baseplates and cab-edge cash trays. To emphasise the current DM class's continuing availability for crew operation, two brackets were fitted beginning in June to DMs passing through Turnham Green, to make it clear to the boarding passengers exactly whom they were to pay. On the outside came a two-piece metal plate with a hinged strip that turned over, the undisplayed portion to lie against a pair of magnets. The top panel displayed 'PAY DRIVER' in black capitals on yellow background, and the reverse read 'PAY CONDUCTOR' in white on blue. A similar instructional plate was fitted to the driver's cab, the turned-over section being secured with a hinge. Although this in effect rendered them DMSs, the order went out to recode suitably-fitted DMs to D, which stuck once examples started appearing with it in June 1980 – producing endless confusion among observers of the type and officials alike, which, it will be hoped, will not be the case in these lines, which will refer to routes not officially allocated the specific DM class as operated by 'DMSs' or 'crew DMSs' as fit! The first five were done at the end of June – DMs 1008, 1019, 1144, 2626 and 2628 – and even then Holloway mistakenly recoded DM 1008 to DS 1008 and never got around to physically changing it. Once Ds were taken out of service, they reverted to DM class on paper before sale, their D kits transferred to either newer ex-DMs or new Metrobuses and Titans. The OMO-fitted MDs for the 78 also had the external brackets, as did all subsequent M and T deliveries. 145 DMs had become Ds by the end of 1980, though not all had external D kits and some even had PLEASE PAY AS YOU ENTER transfers. DM 2582, transferred from Cricklewood to Muswell Hill on 24 May and reclassified D in August,

Above: **Transferred to New Cross in August 1980, D 1006 (GHV 6N) has no markings at all when seen at the Bricklayers Arms on the 177.** *Haydn Davies*

Below: **Elmers End's D 1167 (KUC 167P) on 17 September 1980 shows an intermediate approach of applying the 'PAY DRIVER' sticker to the bodywork, as the bus was unlikely to turn out on the 12, the garage's only crew route.** *R. C. Riley*

WITHDRAWALS AND OVERHAULS

Right: **Prototype B20 DMS 854 (TGX 854M), seen at Marble Arch in April 1980, was about to suffer the fate of all crew-operated Fleetlines at Cricklewood when on 24 May RMLs would sweep in to oust them from the 16 and 16A. This bus would pass to Catford and spend three more years in service there.**
Haydn Davies

Below: **The DMS stock in the eastern half of the capital began to deplete during 1980, departing Hornchurch, North Street and then Barking and Seven Kings to tie up the first Titan order. DMS 707 (TGX 707M), having worked for all but its first six months at Barking, was displaced when that garage's OMO routes received Ts during the summer and is seen at Dagenham prior to that. It looks no more careworn than seven years of service would suggest, especially after having been repainted as recently as August 1977, and indeed it would go on for 16 years' further service with three more operators.** *I. Thomas / Colour-Rail.com (BUI30165)*

was fitted during that month with a farebox for exclusive use on the W7 and had the 'PAY DRIVER/PAY CONDUCTOR' vinyl removed from its frontal D kit and 'PLEASE PAY AS YOU ENTER'/'exact fare please' transfers applied underneath instead, producing rather a clumsy result. Brixton took three, DMs 2611, 2626 and 2627, as Ds to join their unaltered DMs. Otherwise the converted Ds started popping up all over the fleet, to be treated no differently from their DMS counterparts.

DM-operated route 18 was not one to gain back open-platform buses, this route still being still considered too dangerous a pitch, so its Stonebridge allocation was converted between 2 and 19 June from DM to crew M, the Sunday operation on the 266 following likewise. The displaced DMs, shortages of which had already been catered to by putting into service early several of Cricklewood's incoming RMLs on loan, plus some of its own DMSs straying from the 112, went to top up DM allocations at nine

Left: **Both these DMSs are beyond help when espied at Wombwell Diesels on 8 June 1980, the first still recognisably a Metro-Cammell and the one behind it nothing but a Christmas tree. What useful pieces still remained after the blowtorches had been at them were returned to London Transport.** *R. C. Riley*

other DM-operating garages, as had those from Muswell Hill. Even as DMs were being taken off front-line service and reconfigured to D spec, an investigation into boarding times carried out in April 1980 justified their replacement; the time taken to board a doored crew bus clocked in at two seconds flat, which although better than the 5.5 seconds needed for graduated-fare OMO buses, four without change and under three for Havering-style flat-fare, was still double the 1.1 seconds it took to board an RM.

The first of an intended 69 DMSs were converted into permanent trainers beginning in June 1980 so as to release the RMs currently used back to service. The modifications, carried out at Aldenham, included the fitting of two nearside mirrors, two offside mirrors, a brake handle and a bell push behind the driver's cab, repeat indicators on the front window ledge and the single seat from behind the staircase upstairs brought down and mounted dead centre in the gangway for the instructor to sit on. Many would go on to serve seven years in this capacity before, even more incredibly, returning to service. Their seating had otherwise been retained pending this eventuality.

Once the dispute affecting the entry into service of new Ms and Ts had been resolved in June, the huge backlog of buses waiting in store could be released, and a rash of planned conversions were able to be completed. On 1 June Willesden's 226 went over from DMS to M operation, the DMSs leaving for a variety of deployments to cover CoF expiry. On 17 May the 139 was transferred from North Street to Seven Kings in the interest of improving its reliability, converting it from T back to DMS, while the 148 pased from Seven Kings to Barking, just in time for the conversion of that garage's OMO routes from DMS to T operation beginning on 1 June. Crew DMS operation left the N98 with its transfer to North Street under crew Titans. Barking's routes comprised the 145, 148, 156, 169, 179 and 199, plus the 23's Sunday OMO operation and crew-operated night route N95, and was finished by 31 July; the next day Seven Kings began taking Titans, this garage operating OMO routes 129, 139, 148 and 150. and its last DMS left on 15 August.

Below: **April 1980 sees North Street's DMS 1886 (GHM 886N) at Stapleford Abbotts, the very periphery of north-east London where a terminus of the 103 had been established since 22 April 1978. Fifteen months after this picture was taken, that leg would pass to the 175.** *Haydn Davies*

WITHDRAWALS AND OVERHAULS

A deliberately-set fire at Catford garage on 14 September damaged DMSs 216 and 388 (which was sold for scrap) and affected DMS 2172, the foreshortened chassis of which survived to become a mechanical demonstrator to various authorities. Never regaining a body, it survives today under the ownership of The London Bus Museum in Brooklands.

A Pay and Productivity Agreement was signed with the Union in June which at a stroke changed again the role of the DMS family. Under its terms, paid for with a 20% pay rise, flexibility was increased so that similar types of vehicle were now permitted to turn out on the same route if suitable blinds were carried, as long as crew buses did not turn out on OMO routes. That was set to put a stop to the rigidity of type allocation that had forced gaps in service due to there being no appropriate bus available and the unwillingness (which varied from garage to garage) of staff to take out unscheduled buses without the proper remuneration, and would see the explosion over the next few years of strange visitors of unauthorised types to a host of routes. Potters Bar led the way by adding their newly converted Ds to the 84 and 299's complement otherwise scheduled for SMSs since November 1979. RMs thus substituted where needed for DMs on the 141 and 149, with DMs returning the favour on the 12, 29, 190, 253 and 279. As 1980 continued DMs could be seen on RM routes 35, 40, 68 and 159 and RMLs on the 168A.

Top: **On 17 November 1980 New Cross's DM 1174 (KUC 174P) is in Downham Way. The 141 would remain DM-operated for another two years, its Fleetlines occasionally being backed up where needed by RMs.**
R. C. Riley

Above: **DMs had wandered to the 253 ever since they were new at Holloway, and Stamford Hill's examples, like DM 989 (GHV 989N) near its base in August 1980, eventually did the same. No longer needed on the 149, it would transfer to Poplar in September.**
Geoff Rixon

Right: **It's the end of the line for DMS 657 (MLK 657L), late of Elmers End, as it arrives at Wombwell Diesels in June 1980. Ironically, both vehicles pictured next to it, SM 1 and RT 1798, survive today.**
R. C. Riley

THE LONDON DMS

Left: The Isle of Dogs area was still post-industrial wasteland by the time the 56 was introduced on 21 June 1980, so the route can't be blamed for being a little ahead of its time; still, it was felt worth celebrating its first day with balloons and streamers on Poplar's DMS 1905 (KUC 905P). *Haydn Davies*

On 21 June new route 56 commenced with Poplar DMSs, linking Aldgate and Poplar (with extensions to Limehouse) via the Isle of Dogs. Having got rid of its crew Fleetlines, Cricklewood now replaced its OMO DMSs with Ms between 6 and 10 July (routes 32 and 245), then took the fareboxes out of the 616's DMSs to fit to further new Ms for this flat-fare route between 21 and 31 July. The B20s from here once again ejected all non-B20s from Bexleyheath, Palmers Green and Enfield but once again had to cede to them when DMS 845 appeared at Enfield. Other ex-Cricklewood B20 DMSs, including prototype DMS 854, crossed the river to strike up a new allocation at Catford. DMS 1 was one to move out, passing to Walworth (though it did return in December). The availability situation had eased enough by 14 July to give the 42 back its

Below: Standard DMSs lingered at Cricklewood for as long as the B20s did, but all departed when Ms took over. DMS 1883 (GHM 883N) is at Marble Arch on 27 April 1979. *R. C. Riley*

Above: **DMS 134 (EGP 134J) was an early DMS drafted into Camberwell to give the 42 back its upper deck. It is seen at the Bricklayers Arms in March 1981.**
D.T. Elliott

Right: **On 10 August 1980 the 149 began converting from DM operation to the marvellous RCL class, but on this first day we see a choice of MCW-bodied DM 1736 (SMU 736N) or Park Royal-bodied DM 972 (GHV 972N) heading south into Shoreditch. DM 1736 would transfer from Stamford Hill to Edmonton and DM 972 would pass from Edmonton to Wood Green, but neither of them would become Ds.**
Geoff Rixon

DMSs, early overhauled examples being sent from their spell of helping-out at Bexleyheath. A handful of DMSs were put into Thornton Heath on 20 July, a week earlier than planned, to double-deck the 115, and a spirited week at the end of July saw all DMSs leave North Street by the 21st, Alperton by the 24th and Barking by the 31st. Edgware, suffering CoF expiries this month, took on a number of the ex-Alperton DMSs. Due to the destruction by fire of Alexandra Palace on 10 July and the rerouting until 2 September of the W3 via Hornsey, a single DM (or DMS) from Wood Green operated a free service between Wood Green Underground and BR stations (the latter now known since 1982 as Alexandra Palace) from 21 July, paid for by Haringey Council.

The 149 at Edmonton and Stamford Hill now took its turn to lose its DMs, but this time it was the plush RCL class that took the honours, treating the Stamford Hill allocation on 10 August and the Edmonton share following between 27 September and 12 November. Crew DMSs or RMLs assumed the N83 at night. On the 17th the mighty 207 began converting from DM back to Routemaster after four years, but Hanwell, which started first, received a mix of RMLs and RMs up to 31 October and Uxbridge didn't take its RMs until 20 October; all DMs had gone by 15 November and, where not added to existing DM operators, were put through the D conversion process at Turnham Green ex-garage and allocated where fit. One such was Rolls-Royce-engined D 1199, which after leaving Hanwell in August (as a DM) was allocated to Putney as the last to join its fellows concentrated there since the reduction in numbers by one (DMS 864, which was withdrawn and sold after its engine seized; the unit was retained 'just in case' but was not subsequently repaired or refitted). Croydon and Merton took more than a few ex-207 D conversions as well, to cover for CoF expiries to their MCWs in the 1500s range of stock numbers, as did by Sutton in September (replacing its Park Royals numbered in the 700s). No DMSs were overhauled in September so that RMLs could pass through works; six DMSs were recertified in October and eight in November.

27 September heralded a large programme of changes, mostly in Leaside District in north London. At Potters Bar the 84 reverted from SMS to DMS operation, but the 298A and 299

Left: **DMS 220 (JGF 220K) was written off in an accident during June 1980 while working out of Croydon; the extent of the damage is clear when the remains were espied at Aldenham in July.** *Tony Wilson*

were withdrawn altogether and the 298 one-manned with DMSs (Palmers Green giving way to Potters Bar and Wood Green) and extended northwards to South Mimms over the old 299. The other end of the 298A was attached to the 121, turning this four-bus local route into an important suburban service linking Chingford and Turnpike Lane the long way round; Palmers Green replaced Enfield, adding three B20 DMSs. This also obviated the need for the W4. Palmers Green's 261, meanwhile, was withdrawn to allow the 84 to extend over it to Arnos Grove. At Edmonton the DM-operated 283 was withdrawn, RMs on the 279 and 279A resuming the more flexible and easier-to-control through service beyond the border to Hammond Street, and the 149 started gaining further RCLs to complete this route's conversion from DM by 12 November. Enfield's 135 was one-manned with DMSs, gaining an extension from Brimsdown Station to Enfield Lock in lieu of the previous journeys to industrial lands north of Brimsdown; the 231 was extended up from Carterhatch to Brimsdown in support. On Sundays the 217B was diverted to terminate at Chase Farm Hospital instead of Oakwood.

Below: **The 261 found itself withdrawn with the 27 September 1980 programme; prior to that upheaval, Palmers Green's DMS 2463 (OJD 463R) heads south through New Barnet.** *Haydn Davies*

Left: On 12 April 1980 Holloway's DMS 68 (EGP 68J) sets off from King's Cross and would remain able to work the 263 for another two years, as it was just the Finchley allocation converting to M this autumn. *Geoff Rixon*

Below: Schoolchildren pile onto Merton's D 957 (GHV 957N) on the 152A, the service hived off specifically for them when the main 152 otherwise fell back to Surbiton. It lasted only a year and was not replaced when withdrawn; blame its cross-border nature. *Haydn Davies*

Finchley was included in the 27 September changes, its 125 and 263 having begun to convert from DMS to M between 2 September and 20 October and the 221's DMSs being last to go; all the garage's Fleetlines were out by 20 November, DMS 2479 being the last. Changes were also made south of the river; Merton's allocation on the 131 was withdrawn on Mondays to Saturdays, relegating DMS operations to just Sundays. Merton's 152 was rerouted past Tolworth to run to Surbiton, a new 152A taking over at peaks to the former Hampton Schools terminus but reflecting the reduction of operations beyond the GLC border that was underscored by the withdrawal of some of the BL-operated services in this area. Croydon underwent revisions to its Addington-area express routes, taking off the C1 and C5 and introducing the C3 on Sundays, on which day of the which the 234B was also withdrawn, leaving it Saturday-only. At New Cross, the 53 officially gained a DM complement on top of its scheduled crew MDs, but lost its DMS-operated 192 to Plumstead's MDs. In the area served by this route the 177 was clipped east of Woolwich and its roads to Thamesmead transferred to new local route 178 with Abbey Wood DMSs; this allowed enough slack to extend the 177 towards town as far as Waterloo. At Uxbridge the 224 began taking back DMSs. More trainers were done by September, while DMS 1444 was an unusual MCW-bodied flat-fare conversion to join the overhauled Park Royals on Croydon's C-routes due to the writing-off of DMS 220 after an accident in June. The C5 had actually not operated since being 'temporarily' withdrawn on 28 February 1976 owing to the vehicle shortage; this just formalised the status quo.

122　THE LONDON DMS

Left: Edgware's single-deck roster was completely revamped at the end of 1980, converting first to DMS and then to Ms. D 1141 (KUC 141P) came from Edmonton in August and was converted to D for this purpose; it reposes in its home garage's approach road in November, and once its work here was done it was transferred to Walthamstow. *Geoff Rixon*

Edmonton's DMs were all out by 12 November; the 'proper' DMs gathered at Wood Green to release its own DMs for D conversion and reallocation elsewhere. As 1980 waned Edgware began converting to M, though most of its services used SMSs; the conversion of the 292 between 22 October and 7 November (brought forward to forestall a rash of prohibitions dished out by DoE inspectors during October) allowed that route's DMSs to edge Swifts off the 186 and 286 and appear a little later on the 142 before further Ms arrived to bring double-deck operation back to all these services, plus three others worked by SMSs. DMSs 154 and 2145 and D 1040 left Edgware at the end of November, the conversion being completed officially on 8 December. Hanwell simultaneously took enough Ms for the E1 and E2, commencing on 23 October and taking a month. The fact that all the DMSs from the current batch converted to trainers were in use by 15 November permitted the release of enough RMs to replace the DMs from the 168, shared between Wandsworth and Stockwell; DMS OMO remained on Saturdays. Thus did night services N68, N81, N87 and N88 follow on an official basis at least, though the reality was more like Round London Sightseeing Tour DMs on the Stockwell-based services (N68 on Saturday nights, N81 and N87).

1362 DMSs, 436 DMs and 143 Ds were in stock by the end of 1981; 348 Fleetlines had been sold and 148 DMSs converted to D format. As 1980 closed it had become clear that the DMSs would not be replaced in due course by XRMs; the abandonment of the project was recommended by LT's Chairman in September and endorsed by the GLC. Ms and Ts were felt reliable and cost-effective enough to continue at the spearhead of new double-deck deliveries by themselves, and all the work that had gone into the XRM was redirected to their own improvement. To this end, DMS overhauls were formally restarted in December, stock numbers selected leaping into the 800s (Park Royal) and 1600s (MCW).

Right: Another first-time DMS service was the 286, with DMS 2119 (KJD 119P) demonstrating in November 1980. It had come from Catford to Edgware in July, and subsequently followed D 1141 to Walthamstow. *Haydn Davies*

WITHDRAWALS AND OVERHAULS

1981

On 2 January the DMS family passed its tenth birthday in service; already 705 of the original 2,646 had been sold with not much more hope held out for the rest to still be around by 1985.

The conversion of the E-routes at Hanwell from flat-fare DMS continued in the third week of January with the receipt of the last Ms of the 1980 order; the displaced flat-fare DMSs were despatched to perform like-for-like replacements of their expired counterparts at Merton on the M1 and at Edmonton on the W8.

Doored operation was progressively removed from the 53 as 1981 opened, its MDs and DMs leaving New Cross in favour of RMs between 17 January and 26 February and obliging the N82 and Inter-Station Night Bus to take crew DMSs. Holloway's 4 followed to kick off the extensive 31 January programme, which threw up another surprise conversion of a DMS route back to crew operation in the form of Leyton's 55, which shed its DMSs for RMs and ceded its Bloomsbury-Waterloo section to an extension of the 5 so that it could follow the 38 to Victoria. This was the centrepiece of a series of changes based on the Walthamstow region; RM-operated 69 was curtailed at Chingford Mount and new Walthamstow DMS-operated 97 introduced to replace this section to Chingford; new partner 97A also commenced from this point but took the eastern track vacated by withdrawn flat-fare route W21. The other end of this circular became new route 212, again with Walthamstow DMSs, and finally new route 158 was introduced to partially one-man the 58. Losing all its RMs and crew operation, Walthamstow now became 100% DMS and boasted, if that was a word that could be used to describe the DMS, the biggest allocation in the fleet.

In the Stratford region West Ham's 241 broke free of the Keir Hardie Estate with an extension to Canning Town and the 278 was rerouted to Stratford rather than Chingford Mount. The conversion of the 55 to RM unfortunately forced the busy N96 to assume LS operation, as these were now Leyton's only OMO vehicles.

Below: **Walthamstow gathered DMSs from far and wide for the introduction of four new routes on 31 January 1981. DMS 377 (JGF 377K) came from Camberwell and shows off the new 97 at Walthamstow Central during August.** *Haydn Davies*

Right: **New route 158 combined the northern extremities of the 58, still RM-operated at the time, with the southern end of the 230 (which was one-manned). DMS 1844 (GHM 844N) was an indigenous Walthamstow bus and is seen in Leyton during August, the same month it was taken in for overhaul.** *Haydn Davies*

124

South of the river, the 72 was converted to OMO; as Riverside could not accommodate DMSs, Shepherd's Bush took over, putting back into service ex-Wandsworth and Stockwell B20 Ds displaced at the end of 1980 from the 168. Abbey Wood's 177, 178, 198 and 272 discarded their DMSs for MDs, helping to furnish Walthamstow with its increased requirement. A spot of reallocation gave the 220 a Sunday Wandsworth allocation and took the 191's Enfield allocation off on Saturdays. However, some routes were losing so much money that LT was considering applying to the Boroughs through which they passed for support; those operating DMSs were the 112, 160, 189, 234, 234B and 244. No help was forthcoming, not surprisingly, and these routes had improved sufficiently by May to drop the idea.

Above: **Abbey Wood became the second garage after Plumstead to take on the MD class in its new guise as a suburban OMO vehicle. During January 1981 DMS 171 (JGF 171K) plies through bleak Thamesmead; on the 31st of that month it found itself transferred across the river to Walthamstow.** *D.T. Elliott*

Left: **A number of former Wandsworth and Stockwell B20 DMs were converted to D and sent to Shepherd's Bush for the one-manning of the 72 on 31 January 1981. Nitpickers will note that the 'PAY DRIVER' sticker on D 2541 (THX 541S), seen at Hammersmith shortly after, is on the other half of the flip-over plate than is customary.** *Haydn Davies*

WITHDRAWALS AND OVERHAULS

Right: **At one point it looked like the GLC was intent on reversing the DMSs' contribution entirely by not only bringing back ex-London Country Routemasters to see off DMs, but converting routes back to crew altogether. Only three ended up thus converted, and the 5 was the third of them. West Ham's DMS 1537 (THM 537M) rests at Waterloo in March 1981, a month before the 5 took RMs, but this bus would remain based at West Ham until ousted by Titans in mid-1982. It became better known as a trainer and its final days as such are depicted on page 227.**
D.T. Elliott

January 1981 saw DMS overhauls resume in earnest. After treating the best seventeen Park Royals in the 800s and twenty MCWs in the 1600s, which were due for imminent CoF expiry, intake otherwise leapt over the remaining unoverhauled members of the 1972-74 batch, dooming them to impending withdrawal, and Leyland-engined MCWs in the middle 1800s started going into works, chosen for the Leyland engine's better heating properties in both cab and interior. The 'DM' batches were not to be treated at all, nor their D-class derivatives, the first unaltered DMs starting to be withdrawn during the early part of the year. Within eighteen more months a concerted effort had seen most of the MCWs between DMS 1833 and 1967 overhauled, followed by the best Leyland-engined examples from the stock numbers spanning DMS 1968-2037, though their service career in London would ultimately be cut short for reasons unanticipated at the time. Almost forgotten, meanwhile, since its departure for the experimental shop at Chiswick in April 1976 was DM 1787. Unfortunately, the advancements applied to it in Scotland had proven distinctly ahead of their time, any hope of relocating the drive shaft and thereby the engine through its regenerative-braking concept having been hampered by a severe lack of speed and the accompanying reduction in fuel capacity from an already low 6.5mpg to a clearly inadequate 4.5mpg. After the project was officially abandoned, DM 1787 was restored gradually to standard format, converted to D and licensed for service on 1 January 1981, being allocated to Uxbridge.

February thus saw the official cancellation of the XRM project, LT declaring itself unable to fund through current budgets the extent of design, development and tooling needed for a bus of design likely to be limited to the capital, but at the same time declared itself broadly satisfied with the progress of the Metrobus and Titan and was bolstered by the enduring reliability of the increased Routemaster fleet. Titan production had been successfully, if belatedly, transferred within Leyland to Workington and orders could now be fulfilled again. It still looked as if all DMSs would be withdrawn by 1985, XRM or no XRM. Meanwhile, the programme to convert 69 DMSs to permanent trainers ceased in February after 55 had been done, seven of the other fourteen being considered suitable to send to overhaul and the rest sold. A change to advertising panelling specified vinyl panels rather than paper bills for T-side adverts, as the contracts were invariably for longer periods.

On 22 February the 194 at Croydon was converted from DMS to LS on Sundays and was increasingly operating Nationals on weekdays as well. On 21 March another DM route began its reversion to RMs, the Walworth share of the 45 incorporating Sunday schedules on the 12 and the Holloway share going over on 25 April, but it was the 5 that cast off OMO entirely on this latter date, ten years and eight days since its conversion to DMSs; it was revamped to take the 23's roads east to Becontree Heath so that the 23 (the Sunday service of which was also converted from DMS to Routemaster) could copy the 15 all the way to Ladbroke

THE LONDON DMS

Grove. Several of Walworth's DMs were put into Stockwell to see off the Obsolete Fleet OM class of BMMO D9s.

If it wasn't national politicians meddling with the operation and maintenance of London's bus services, it was regulation, ever more of it. From 1 April 1981 substantial changes were made to vehicle licensing by which the seven-year Certificate of Fitness would be replaced on 1 January 1983 by a yearly certification known as Freedom from Defect (FFD). Although all buses with current certificates gained an automatic extension to them till 31 December 1982, by which time they had to have the new FFD certificate, each bus would have to be allotted a 'birthday' which would serve as the date of its subsequent examination every year thereafter. Overhauling was therefore to be reconfigured to afford a four-year span between overhauls, which would now be known under the natty acronym of WASP (Works Annual Service Programme). Light-overhaul work done to achieve the yearly FFD between WASPs would be done at garages (hence GASPs), with each District having their own test centre. One could see this being used as a long-term plan to phase out overhauls (and Aldenham) altogether while piling still more bureaucratic pressure on an organisation already completely swamped by spurious paperwork. Repaints would accompany WASPs rather than in-between. To an extent LT was heading this off by dispatching DMSs from the 1800s and 1900s to overhaul while their existing CoFs had a year left on. Certainly the turnaround time had improved, the examples from the 800s and 1600s coming back to Merton just in time for unselected fellows in those blocks to suffer mass CoF expiry in March and withdrawal. Buses were now selected for disposal according to condition, not calendar age or CoF expiry, and DMs (and their derivative Ds) were excluded from consideration for overhaul. Thus some DMSs of a newer age and examples of those overhauled in 1978 were disposed of during 1981. All future vehicle policy seemed contingent on DMS CoF expiry, the 1982 order for 275 Ts being placed early and the last 75 of the 1981 order for Ms being held over into 1982.

Below: **DMS 2204 (OJD 204R) had entered service on the Round London Sightseeing Tour in March 1977 before being displaced by a B20 after six months and transferred to Merton, where it spent the next five years. One of its tasks was to inaugurate new Sunday-only route 77B commencing on 25 April 1981, and the following March it is captured at Raynes Park.** *Tony Wilson*

WITHDRAWALS AND OVERHAULS

Right: **Wearing two roundels, the original one exposed by the removal of a T-side advert, Sutton's D 1135 (KUC 135P) sets off from West Croydon on 22 April 1981. Three days later the 154 would be rerouted to take on the Roundshaw leg of the 233.** *R. C. Riley*

The ever-sensitive issue of fares could, where implemented to the dissatisfaction of the ever-pressed bus passenger, bring down governments, and so it proved when the implementation of a suburban short-hop flat fare of 25p on 4 April cost the Tories the GLC election the next month, in favour of a particularly left-wing brand of Labour that had plans of its own for the fare structure within London Transport.

A programme set in train on 25 April 1981 saw, amongst other things, the 77 group tinkered with, the 77 ceding its self-contained section south of Tooting to new Merton DMS-operated 127 and the 77A spawning a Sunday offshoot over its southernmost section known as 77B, again with Merton DMSs. Further to the south an attempt was made to bring buses to Beddington Lane with new Sutton-operated 254 during weekday peak hours, while the

Below: **DMS 2111 (KJD 111P) sees out the 233 on 22 February 1981.** *Malc McDonald*

Below right: **The 85A's Putney-Roehampton path was switched on 25 April 1981 to go via Dover House Road as new route 264. DMS 16 (EGP 16J) was the second lowest-numbered DMS to work out of Putney (the lowest being DMS 5) and on 22 March turns at Danebury Avenue.** *Malc McDonald*

circuitous 115 was withdrawn and its various parts appended to routes 127, 200 and 234A, the last mentioned now reaching Streatham from the south. Sutton's tally of DMSs also increased with the conversion from BL of the 80, while Thornton Heath's loss of the 115 was made good by adding a share of the 157, which was strengthened to allow the 154's section paralleling it to Crystal Palace to fall back to West Croydon. The 154 was rerouted via Roundshaw to swallow up the 233. Merton's Sunday allocation on the 293 passed to Sutton on that day of the week and the 200 received an extension on Sundays from Wimbledon to Wallington.

The 77 group's alterations allowed the 168 and 181 to be withdrawn entirely; the southern end of the 168 was attached to the 170, which was transferred from Wandsworth to Stockwell, introduced on Saturdays and extended over the 85A (withdrawn) to Roehampton; the 85A's aim was continued with new Putney-operated 264, which went via Dover House Road instead and simultaneously allowed cuts to be made to the 30 and 74. Stockwell's appearance on the 170 on Saturdays allowed the similar allocation on the 44 on that day to come off, plus the extension of the 295 east of Clapham Junction. All remaining DMs at Stockwell, both B20s and a handful of standards transferred from Walworth after the conversion to RM of the 45, were based on the Round London Sightseeing Tour alongside FRM 1, that great 'what might have been'.

At Holloway DMs ceased to operate, the N92 and N93 gaining RMs (or RMLs in practice), the 104's weekend DMs giving way to RMLs on Saturdays and RMs on Sundays. The allocation on the 172 was converted from DM to RM and the 168A (with heavy reductions) and 214 went over to OMO (DM to DMS). That was the end of the once-mighty DM class at Holloway, though many stayed put under the D code.

After several months' impasse while Titan production was transferred from Park Royal to Workington within Leyland's empire, the first examples of the Workington factory's products began converting Upton Park, beginning on 25 April with the 147, 162 and 238. Upton Park's DMSs were kept around to one-man the 262 on that date. The 58 at West Ham was converted to OMO on Sundays and the 40's weekend DMs were replaced by RMs. The federation of the 23 with the 15 was completed with its withdrawal beyond East Ham and corresponding conversion of the Sunday OMO service from DMS to RML; to restore the reliability of the roads eastward to Becontree Heath, the 5 was converted to crew operation on Mondays to Saturdays; only on Sunday did DMSs remain while they were still extant at Upton Park.

Above: **Rolls-Royce-engined DMS 2059 (KJD 59P) inaugurates the 264 at Roehampton, Danebury Avenue on 25 April 1981, but the route never really lived up to the logical progression of partially one-manning the 74 and lasted less than six years.** *Malc McDonald*

Below: **At the same spot on the same day came a new link into town in the form of the 170, now the province of Stockwell with DMSs like DMS 2464 (OJD 464R).** *Malc McDonald*

WITHDRAWALS AND OVERHAULS 129

Above: **DM operation dwindled substantially during 1981, but where shared routes were concerned, there were two instances where one garage's allocation came off considerably sooner than did its partner's. The 172's Holloway share lost its DMs on 25 April 1981 but Camberwell's stayed put another year, and it is the latter's DM 977 (GHV 977N) that we see making the protected right turn from Westminster Bridge into Whitehall on 20 July 1981.** *R. C. Riley*

Right: **Holloway's DM-operated crew routes were picked off gradually; the 168A was one of two of this garage's routes selected for OMO and dropped its conductors on 25 April 1981, together with its roads beyond Vauxhall to Clapham Junction. Seen at King's Cross that August, D 1179 (KUC 179P) had been converted to dual-format mode in time for this scheme, despite having been at Holloway since March 1980, before which it was DM 1179 out of Edmonton. Ironically, it had begun its career at Holloway before being transferred away.** *Haydn Davies*

130   THE LONDON DMS

Left: **The 214 was also one-manned on 25 April 1981; during the preceding winter, with frost on the ground, we can see the conductor inside DM 1737 (SMU 737N) as layover is taken at Moorgate. This particular bus would not survive the 25 April scheme and was sold in June.** *Haydn Davies*

Below: **The 262 was converted to OMO on 25 April 1981, having flirted with DMs before but officialdom now deeming the route appropriate for one-man operation. The service career of DMS 2230 (OJD 230R) spanned a very miserly five years and three months, all of it from West Ham, and it is seen looking rather threadbare in August 1981.** *Haydn Davies*

On 28 May the first B20 DMS entered works, even before the first of the 1975-76 batch was accepted; Bexleyheath's DMS 2351 was the pilot example of the B20 variety, although it came too early for three fellow B20s, which included MCW-bodied DMS 2247, to be accepted; they were returned to their garages in June. CoF expiry had by May reached both Park Royal and MCW batches of DMs, numbers of which were eaten into by subsequent selection of many for sale rather than conversion to D. During that month London Transport set up its own sales department known as London Bus Sales, seeing how well the likes of Ensign were doing for themselves with their former vehicles; Turnham Green would be used to

WITHDRAWALS AND OVERHAULS 131

Right: **1981's Wimbledon Tennis service operated from Merton used three of the small number of Park Royal DMSs in the low 800s to receive overhauls before policy changed to favour MCWs. Outshopped to Merton in March, DMS 806 (TGX 806M) still looks pristine as it tackles the hard climb up Wimbledon Hill on 23 June.** *Tony Wilson*

Below: **DMS 83 (EGP 83J) was the only early DMS ever to receive a front with the wider-spaced headlights. In this August 1981 shot it is allocated to Merton, where it finished its career.** *Haydn Davies*

bring the sales stock up to FFD standard and paint them in undercoat. Finally in July went DMS 1968 into works as herald of the 1975-76 batch; it came straight back out again, its Rolls-Royce engine marking it out as non-standard! Already the first DMS trainers were starting to fall out with CoF expiry while it was still valid, these buses having been recertified for a year upon conversion to this mode and this year now being up. DMS 2351 was the first B20 to be outshopped from overhaul, returning to Bexleyheath in August and to no-one's surprise, in all-over red.

The first examples of the 1981 batch of 300 Metrobuses were put into Finchley in May so that earlier Ms could ease a few more DMSs off Hanwell's E-routes. Then followed specifically flat-fare Ms into Wood Green from 4 June, removing the similarly-equipped DMSs from the W2 and W3, and after that, Muswell Hill's W7 was converted between 11 June and 15 August. At the other end of town, Uxbridge's 222, 223 and 224 were converted from DMS to M between 15 July and 10 September; D 1787 found itself withdrawn on 20 August and placed into store. Isolated early-summer

Left: **According to the district structure then in operation, Stonebridge would become a Metrobus-operating garage, though only its crew route 18 had been thus treated and the 112 remained with DMSs, like DMS 2094 (KJD 94P). This bus served a similarly short period of time as a London Transport bus, being withdrawn after the reallocation of the 112 to Cricklewood on 15 August and sold. It only ever worked from Stonebridge.** *Haydn Davies*

Below: **The new Westbourne Park garage opened on 15 August 1981 continued the doored-bus aspect of the 18, though with B20 DMs rather than Ms, as it was an Abbey District garage and thus not yet scheduled for conversion to newer types than Fleetlines. The 7 on Sundays was also rostered for DMs, at least for a while, and in September we see DM 2580 (THX 580S) at Paddington.** *Haydn Davies*

changes saw the 194 regain its Sunday DMSs on 18 June and, at Sutton and Merton, a DMS-operated service mounted from the 22nd to serve the Wimbledon tennis championships, won this year by John McEnroe. These garages controlled the Wimbledon Station leg of the service and used their own and loaned DMSs, specifically selected from recent overhauls and spruced up with dedicated Fred Perry posters all over, to join Norbiton Ms and LSs emanating from Southfields station.

A long-term programme to replace several garages with brand-new, purpose-built premises was now beginning to bear fruit. On 15 August Middle Row and Stonebridge closed, new Westbourne Park (coded X) under the Westway taking their routes. However, a problem arose here due to the standardisation policies maintained by the eight districts formed in 1980; Abbey District, in which Westbourne Park found itself, was not ready for Ms, which had been the major component of the 18 under Stonebridge, so a complicated three-way shuffle was set in motion. The 18 converted from crew M to DM, its B20 Fleetlines coming to Westbourne Park from Brixton, whose 109 and 133 were converted to RM operation using Routemasters displaced from Fulwell by crew Ms dispatched from Stonebridge. The highest-numbered of Brixton's DMs were transferred to Stockwell to take all non-B20s off the RLST. Westbourne Park also received the 18A from Middle Row, but although this route was officially converted to DM, Routemasters continued to prevail, as they did on new route 52A, which had been pencilled in for DMs on Sundays. Stonebridge's only OMO route, the 112, lost its DMSs upon transfer to Cricklewood with Ms, while just enough DMs remained at Brixton to go through conversion to D and continue to turn out on the N87 alongside DMSs in crew format. A week later Westbourne Park decided to put DMs onto the 7 on Sundays, but changed its mind on 4 October. Similarly cancelled was the conversion of Camberwell's allocation on the 172 from DM

Right: **The appearance of dual-purpose Ds at Shepherd's Bush with the one-manning of the 72 prompted the garage to put them out on the 12 if a Routemaster couldn't be made available. On 17 August 1981 in Oxford Street we see D 2634 (THX 634S). Ignore the 'PAY DRIVER' board; it's seven years too early for that sort of thing! In any case, the Almex E mount is empty.** *Geoff Rixon*

to RM, which was intended for 15 August but was held over into 1982.

Post-Productivity Agreement, crews were really getting into the swing of using suitable buses wherever they could be found, DMs now paying visits by autumn 1981 to Routemaster-operated routes 2B, 7, 12, 18A, 21, 29, 35, 53, 88, 93, 101, 109, 149, 155, 190, 207 and 253, as well as LS-restricted 289 and the 194 on Sundays. Three Brixton DMSs, 2279, 2286 and 2287, were fitted with D kits on the front so as to be able to properly demonstrate to passengers of the N87 that it was crew-operated; for this purpose they were coded DS, reviving the abortive code.

Over time all of Brixton's DMSs received the D kits, though remaining coded as DMSs.

Titans were now pouring off the production lines at Workington, and at the same time as they almost finished off Upton Park's DMSs in September, started work out of Walthamstow from the 15th of that month. Over eighty DMSs needed to be replaced here, from routes 34, 97, 97A, 123, 144, 158, 212, 275 and 276, and the conversion lasted into 1982. Withdrawals at this point were almost all DMs, the majority of the MCW-bodied DMSs in the 1900s released from these garages going for overhaul. Some of them lost their side shrouds on outshopping

Right: **And then there was the abortive DS class, instigated by Brixton when its staff felt the need to show passengers on the N87 that the doored buses they were boarding were still crew-operated. Here at Croydon, North End on 27 January 1982 is DS 2279 (THX 279S), complete with D kit.** *R. C. Riley*

134 THE LONDON DMS

Left: Hanwell's DMS 1942 (KUC 942P) heads south down Greenford Avenue during the summer of 1981, the last year of DMSs on the E1 and E2. Having been based here since new, it was starting to look tired and indeed was sent in for overhaul in August.
Haydn Davies

and even had their rear bumpers painted black to hide the oil and grease that dripped there. This time DMS 1968 did manage to make it through works with its Rolls-Royce engine intact, no chances being taken through the expedient of taking out the engine first and watching over it at Chiswick until the overhaul at Aldenham was complete. As 1981 wound down, the three-year tickets on the very first overhauled DMSs began to expire and they too joined their newer fellows in the queue for withdrawal. Some of them would just make it to eleven years in service – about normal for the provinces, frankly generous on a DMS, but not good enough for what London had become used to. Even Ds were not exempt, many now reverting to DM classification (though almost never having transfers amended to match) and departing for sale.

Between 19 September and 17 November Palmers Green received Ms for the 121 and its half of the 34, displacing its fleet of DMSs into overhaul to form the first major intake of the B20 and sending to Enfield examples to replace that garage's own B20 units going in, while mixed M/T operation on the 144 replaced the Fleetlines' hegemony when the Wood Green conventional-OMO routes (144, 221 and 298) were completed between 19 September and 20 November. After a conversion lasting ten months, Hanwell's E1 and E2 were finally completed on 23 November by the convoluted process of allocating new Ms to Finchley from 23 October, which displaced to Hanwell earlier ones of the approved mechanical configuration to see off the last DMSs there; DMS 1834 was the last to leave. Ms continued to sweep through Leaside District with their appearance at Potters Bar (routes 84, 242 and 298 between 19 November and 19 January 1982) and Enfield (routes 107, 135, 191, 217, 217B and 231) between 30 December and 22 March 1982. Two of its discarded overhauled standards restored the type to Bexleyheath (DMSs 1908 and 1909)

Below: DMS 1876 (GHM 876N) spent only three months at Potters Bar, coming out of overhaul in September 1981 in time for this picture to be taken on the 298, but departed in December when replaced by a Metrobus and subsequently took up at Elmers End.
Haydn Davies

WITHDRAWALS AND OVERHAULS

Above: **Metrobuses swept through Leaside District's DMS sheds over 1981 and into 1982; Edmonton's D 1076 (GHV 76N), seen in March 1982, lasted until that June.** *Haydn Davies*

and Shepherd's Bush (DMS 1953). DMS 2479 was the last at Palmers Green on 17 November and the only Fleetlines now remaining at Wood Green were seven Ds and seven DMs for the 141. Never a B20 garage but close to Wandsworth if it needed to pull reinforcements, Putney borrowed D 2638 in December 1981.

MDs had become the dominant players in a sizeable swathe of south-east London, and the programme of 31 October reinforced this; New Cross's DMS-operated 151 was withdrawn and fused with Plumstead's 192 to produce MD-operated 291, operated by the new Plumstead garage (PD). At Merton the 152A was withdrawn without replacement, that part of Surrey now becoming lost to buses, but one small victory for the still-diminishing Fleetline numbers was the conversion of Holloway's 239 from LS back to DMS operation, buses being transferred directly from Holloway. Part of the 184 on weekdays was transferred from Walworth to New Cross.

Overhaul could often replace a route's stock for no other reason than to refresh it and allow earlier (or later) buses to go into works; in November Streatham's complement for the 249 (DMSs 2005-2009) was rotated out and in came DMSs 1844, 1846, 1893, 1896, 1915, 1928 and 1930. Its low mileage since its experimental days counting in its favour, meanwhile, D 1787 became the only 'DM' taken into overhaul, in December 1981. Shepherd's Bush gained a little variety with the allocation of its first Park Royal-bodied B20, DMS 2377, following its overhaul between October and December. Other than overhauls, the healthy flow of new Ms and Ts meant that fewer like-for-like replacements were occurring as 1981 came to a close; large numbers of DMSs, from expired early overhauls to R-registered white-tops that weren't deemed fit to overhaul, started to pile up at AEC's former site and thence to at Ensign's yard in Purfleet prior to their sale to that concern, the latter complement supplying a seemingly endless number of cheap buses to fix up and turn around, to any specification wanted, for onward sale at a healthy markup compared to the low price they had paid LT for them. Thus, relatively few DMS-family buses were now going directly for scrap. At the end of 1981 there were 1,633 Fleetlines in London Transport stock (1,173 DMSs, 266 DMs and 194 Ds), a reduction of 306 on 1980. 99 DMs were converted to Ds and 38 Ds became DMs again, not forgetting the three DMSs (2279, 2286 and 2287 out of Brixton) that became DSs!

After several years of fare increases on London Transport buses, some coming twice a year, the Labour GLC administration had made reducing fares part of their pitch, and once elected on 5 May 1981, quickly set about it despite Government warnings on spending. As well as making sure to throw out Tory policies overnight, which had included a programme of OMO conversions intended for 31 October, plus lifting the overtime ban and increasing expenditure for recruitment, Ken Livingstone's administration carried over a particularly significant idea that it had nurtured for a long time (but which was Conservative-planned, incidentally) to rationalise fares into some sort of zonal, if not entirely flat-fare model, to accompany the fares reduction. On 4 October 1981 a structure was introduced, advertised under the 'Fares Fair' banner, by which fares were brought down roughly 32% as promised in their election manifesto, funded by the imposition of a supplementary rate within the GLC area amounting to 2%. Believe it or not, this was the first fares cut in London Transport history! Increased ridership resulted for the first time in many years, with the pressure taken off the tube, which for a long time had had to compete with buses by trading increased prices for quicker and unencumbered operation, and the majority of pass sales had been successfully divested away from the LT infrastructure to newsagents and the like. However, the London Borough of Bromley took the GLC to Divisional Court almost immediately, this tubeless borough reasoning that it was unfairly subsidising the rest. The case was dismissed on 3 November, but Bromley subsequently appealed to the House of Lords, which ruled in Bromley's favour on 17 December, effectively branding Fares Fair illegal as LT had a statutory duty to break even. It was feared that to restore the status quo, fares would have to be doubled, at a stroke driving away all the extra custom generated by the fares reduction and imperilling services to the extent that massive cuts, feared to be on the order of 25% of services, would have to be made in 1982.

Historians, and certainly this one, will debate till the end of time as to what extent each political extreme attempted to fight irresponsible profligacy with selfish intransigence, but between their two fists the poor passenger, as ever, got crushed. For London's buses the striking down of Fares Fair was a devastating blow from which they would never recover, setting off decisions in the highest places which would, in time, engulf London Transport itself – and for the DMS, it was very nearly the death knell altogether.

Above: **New Cross's DMS 1668 (THM 668M) plies through Kidbrooke in September 1981, with a home-made blind to join the lazy panel that's otherwise good enough for this short shuttle route that really needed to break its bounds, which it did when transformed into the 291 on 31 October.** *Haydn Davies*

Left: **On 31 October 1981 the 239 was converted back to DMS operation after two years under LSs, though the route was considered unviable and would disappear on 4 September 1982. DMS 2217 (OJD 217R), passing St Pancras, had been based at Holloway since February 1980, but would be withdrawn when the 239 came off, only just managing to make its fifth birthday in service.** *Haydn Davies*

137

CHAPTER SIX

B20 REPRIEVE

1982

Politics dominated the tail end of 1981 and into 1982 as the Fares Fair experiment was struck down by the High Courts, forcing fares to be doubled from 21 March. The GLC, which could otherwise have been expected to fight the ruling with the militancy for which its current administration was known, had no choice due to the legality of the ruling, but two strikes ensued nonetheless, on 17 February and 10 March, and it was made clear that crews would look the other way if disgruntled passengers tendered lower fares or none at all. As predicted, patronage crashed to the extent that economies would have to be made urgently, and plans were drawn up to cut up to 700 buses off the runout from 31 July – a bruising 15% – which would include some outright route withdrawals as well as renewed OMO conversions. Hard times were coming, and none more so than for the DMS family.

B20s left Enfield during January and February as Ms took over, all of its examples heading off to Aldenham for overhaul until the last one operated there on 22 March, though DMS 2516 remained licensed as a spare until 22 April. The supply of preferred MCW-bodied Leyland-engined standards for overhaul had just about run out in the face of increased numbers of B20s going in, so the newest of the Park Royals and MCWs expired by default and were sold after a poor six years. The highest-numbered standard DMS to be overhauled was DMS 2021, while the last standard taken into works was DMS 1987 on 22 December 1981. D 1787 remained the only standard DM to be overhauled, and it was outshopped to New Cross in February 1982. When the last one out of all was outshopped, DMS 1857 on 24 May, only B20s were treated from now on – and their own programme was shortly to be curtailed as the works geared up for the task of overhauling the Metrobuses and Titans, the first of which were approaching their fourth birthdays.

Right: **Loughton's DMS 2019 (KJD 19P) rests at Whipps Cross Hospital during August 1981; when Titans replaced it and its fellows from the 20, 20A and 167 in February 1982 it would transfer to Croydon.**
Haydn Davies

Left: West Ham's D 1730 (SMU 730N) had been available for OMO use since April 1981, eight months after arriving from Stamford Hill, and in this shot is operating flat-fare route S1. It would be one of the over 200 DMSs withdrawn with the 4 September 1982 purge, by which time a Titan had replaced it. *Haydn Davies*

Below: London Transport Museum visitors of a certain age will have fond memories of DM 963 (GHV 963N), which had been divided upon withdrawal and its front sixth installed there between April 1982 and 1993 with working controls, lights and Walthamstow blinds. On 7 November 1981 it is seen at Ensign's Purfleet premises undergoing conversion. *R. C. Riley*

Walthamstow's epic conversion from DMS to T was completed on 21 January (barring the relicensing in February of DMSs 2151 and 2176 as T cover until 30 March) and, between 26 January and 19 March Loughton received Titans for the 20, 20A and 167. Loughton's DMS 2117 infiltrated Wandsworth for B20 overhaul cover, but most of their small fleet passed to Thornton Heath, only DMS 2177 lingering as a licensed spare until 30 March, the same date Walthamstow's holdouts, DMS 2151 and 2176, were delicensed at last. B20s were beginning to leave works in strength now, DMS 2388 becoming the second (or third, if you count DMS 854) at Catford and heralding a flood during the spring. Standards were also outshopped to Bexleyheath in February, while the first B20 Ds began to enter Aldenham, D 2538 coming from Shepherd's Bush and D 2577 from Muswell Hill. As the overhauled early DMSs continued to fall out, the three-year tickets given them now expiring, one such to receive a very late alteration was DMS 88, whose Ricardo shrouds were removed in January 1982. During the year buses from various Districts were selected for fitment with tachographs so as to be used on private hire where full records of such journeys had to be kept by law. In Wandle these were DMSs, numbering at this point DMSs 1845 and 2010 from Merton, DMSs 2279 and 2305 from Brixton and DMSs 1892, 1899, 1916 and 1970 from Croydon.

One noteworthy DMS sale in February 1982 remained in London – sort of. The LT Museum, resited in 1981 from Syon Park to an ideally central location in Covent Garden and immediately popular despite the high entrance fees charged, installed the front sixth of DM 963 as a sort of driving simulator with working lights and blinds (Walthamstow issue) for kids (and adults!) to wind themselves.

Left: **Poplar and Clapton, joint operators of the 277, both lost their DMSs during 1982, and DMS 1883 (GHM 883N) served at both that year. Outshopped from overhaul to Poplar in July 1981, it left for Clapton in June 1982 and is seen later in the summer crossing the imposing swing bridge on the eastern side of the Isle of Dogs peninsula, before being replaced by a Titan in September.**
Haydn Davies

Below left: **The footbridge linking Edmonton Green with Lower Edmonton station became an unlikely local icon, featuring unforgettably in** *Some Mothers Do 'Ave 'Em* **and otherwise serving as a platform to photograph buses at this unusual angle. The W8 at Edmonton exchanged its DMSs for Ms in the spring of 1982 and DMS 910 (SMU 910N), seen in September 1981, was one to go.**
Haydn Davies

West Ham's 262 lost its DMSs for Ts from 21 February, though an industrial dispute over the amount of overtime payable for carrying out vehicle transfers dragged out this conversion (and those of the 241 (commencing on 25 March) and the 238 and 278 (from 3 April)) until 4 September; similar issues held up Poplar's switch to Titans on the 56, 277 and N84 (18 April-3 August, D 1027 and DMSs 2099 and 2233 proving to be their last) and the fitment of fareboxes to Ms for Edmonton's W8 (9 April-24 June) following the otherwise successful deployment of Ms to that garage's 191 and 259 between 24 March and 29 April. Edmonton's last Fleetline was DMS 1613, which last operated on 24 June. West Ham's conversion also comprised the 58 on Sundays, while the S1's farebox DMSs there were kept around until the route was converted to conventional OMO on 4 September. Meanwhile, the arrival of crew Ts at New Cross for the 174 and 175 allowed enough RMs to leave to begin ejecting DMs from Wood Green's allocation on the 141 beginning on 4 April and lasting until 17 June, when DM 1735 was withdrawn. Wood Green was impatient to get rid of its DMs, it seemed, this having been one of the garages taking full advantage of the flexibility agreement to stick out RMLs and even a crew M from time to time. A delay in new vehicle deliveries, however, caused the completion of New Cross's partner allocation to slip and not be completed until 4 December. Even so, between 4-7 June Camberwell's residual allocation on the 172, having had to wait a year since the Holloway share had taken RMs, was treated first and the DMs were withdrawn; they were stored in the former Abbey Wood garage before sale.

Left: By 1982 appearances of the 'wrong' strain of Fleetline away from their scheduled routes were commonplace. Serving as an example for a dozen routes that could fit this description is D 1230 (KUC 230P) of Merton garage. The 155 would become more familiar to the DMS family when it was converted officially to crew Fleetline operation in 1986 and one-manned that 25 October, but in this 21 June 1982 shot it's just another bus, and better any bus than no bus. *R. C. Riley*

Although the generation of the Ms and Ts had replaced DMSs on their OMO routes, the likelihood of Fleetlines making return appearances came to pass during 1982 with wanderings of Ds from the 141 to the 221 (Wood Green), the 134 to the 298 (Potters Bar) and the 134 to the 244 (Muswell Hill, until this latter route's withdrawal on 24 April). While crew-operated Fleetlines were still extant, they continued to visit the 2B, 3, 4, 12, 21, 28, 29, 35, 52A, 53, 88, 93, 149, 155 and 172 with Routemasters returning the favour on the 134 and 141.

DMS overhauls in March and April involved examples from Shepherd's Bush, Wandsworth and Bexleyheath going in and output coming out to those garages plus Brixton and Stockwell, while the dwindling number of standards continued the winnowing down of the early numbers. DMSs 1857 and 1859 were the last outshopped, going to Sidcup and Thornton Heath respectively in May. But from June, two new deployments for B20 overhauls showed the way to the future when Sutton and Merton started receiving examples, initially for their now familiar employment on the Wimbledon

Below: Another crew Fleetline sneaking onto a Routemaster route is DM 1100 (GHV 100N), seen on 19 April 1982 on the 35 at London Bridge. It was withdrawn when Camberwell's allocation on the 172, its normal haunt, was converted to RM during the first week of that June. *R. C. Riley*

Left: **As with their immediate predecessors, the final batch of flat-fare DMSs at Croydon had the letter 'C' painted into the corner pillar to distinguish them, as on DMS 1848 (GHM 848N) near Shirley on 12 August 1982.** *R. C. Riley*

Below left: **The 80A was a casualty of LT's spring 1982 to consolidate its outer operations behind the GLC border. Captured from an unusual viewpoint in Sutton and wearing the complicated ultimate blinds for this route is Sutton's D 1205 (KUC 205P) in March 1982.** *Haydn Davies*

tennis service, but thereafter released to normal service, with Sutton taking priority for more as the summer progressed. Meanwhile, a spot of rationalisation of the training fleet in June made several DMSs redundant, and they joined the large numbers staging through AEC's former site for storage before onward sale to Ensign. The expiry and resulting withdrawal of Croydon's second generation of flat-fare DMSs during the spring and summer obliged their replacement with newer examples in the 1800s, which inherited both their fareboxes and the practice of painting 'C' in white on the offside corner pillar.

The first inklings of the massive retrenchments to come involved the transfer of several sections of routes crossing the GLC border to London Country, which could operate them cheaper. Thus from 24 April Sutton's DMS fleet lost the 280A and its Sunday counterpart 80A, and suffered the pulling back of the comparable 80 and 280 routes from their roads south of Belmont; the 164 was similarly curtailed at Banstead so that its Epsom leg could pass to London Country as new route 418. To compensate Sutton, the Merton share of the 293 was transferred in, but that was all.

Only one Fleetline had held out at Upton Park throughout 1982, this being DMS 2134; it was finally withdrawn on 4 June. The previous day the conversion of Stamford Hill's 67 from DMS to Metrobus had commenced; its completion on the 22nd (with DMS 131 their last) saw the N83 generally assume RM operation though officially allotted a crew M. The reciprocal Tottenham share on the 67, plus that garage's share of the 259, took Ms between 17-28 June, D 1192 seeing that garage out. That was the whole 1981 batch of Ms accounted for, save for the last six which were put into Sidcup to begin comparative trials on the 51 alongside six new Ts and the garage's shortly-to-be-replaced fleet of DMSs; seven from the mid-2100s were

Left: **Tottenham's DMS 18 (EGP 18J) looks in decent enough condition in this 27 April 1981 shot taken at King's Cross, but by the following June its time was called as Metrobuses finished off Leaside District.** *R. C. Riley*

Left: **The winter of 1981-82 was fiercer than most, but enabled evocative shots of London buses in the snow that will be almost impossible for younger generations to imagine. DMS 107 (EGP 107J) demonstrates the occasional placing of early DMSs' numberplates smack between the headlights, which didn't look particularly attractive but ensured that the correct panel wouldn't be lost if it had to be removed. This had been a Sidcup bus since June 1979 and would be withdrawn in April 1982.**
D. T. Elliott

immediately got rid of, moving up the road to store in Abbey Wood and after that, Ensign. Despite the last-minute touches being put to the impending programme of reductions, LT still planned for the orderly withdrawal of its remaining DMSs, an order being placed in June for 210 Ts and 150 Ms to accomplish this.

On 22 July the 10 at Bow began taking Titans to replace the small band of Fleetlines operating there; all DMSs were gone by 4 September. As the summer continued, the Fleetlines at Camberwell (routes 42 and 188) were targeted from 26 July, Clapton's route 22A and 277 being treated simultaneously from 12 August, with just Walworth left to do in Tower District after that.

The delicensing of DMS 1 at Catford in September, where it was replaced by one of a steadily increasing number of B20s to come out of overhaul, underscored the limited future for the standard DMS. With an eye to reductions to their likely PVR after the autumn programme (the implementation of which, due to its sheer enormity, had to be put back during June from 31 July to 4 September) and thus the likelihood that only four more years or so remained for them, DMS overhauls were cancelled. DMS 2374 was the last B20 to enter Aldenham, going in on 26 July, although DMS 2343 was recorded in a little later. During this year FFD 'birthdays' were being established for existing buses in advance of the new legislation, which

Left: **Caught in mid-handover on 10 August 1982 at Victoria as the 10 at Bow went from DMS to Titan operation are DMS 402 (JGF 402K) and T 522 (KYV 522X). The DMS would be sold in December and spent the next two and a half decades as a catering vehicle for film sets, finally being scrapped by 2008.**
R. C. Riley

Right: **In the last full year of the standard DMS, some examples stood out, like New Cross's D 1063 (GHV 63N), which had a statement applied by the Bus & Coach Council warning against the current rash of cuts. In July 1983 it is seen at Greenwich on the 188, which would take its turn for conversion to T at the end of the year. The Plumstead Titan that was also part of this campaign asked Londoners 'Would you rather overtake me or 22 cars?'.** *Haydn Davies*

was already rendering traditional overhauls effectively superfluous.

Spanning July and August, New Cross's D 1062 and 1063, very late standard converts from DM, were given gold fleetnumbers, outlined bullseyes and a white band between the decks in the otherwise long-forgotten manner of the DMS 118-367 batch. While incongruous, these were the first showbuses of what would become a torrent in Jubilee Year, with the DMS not excluded. D 1063 went on to be treated with a bit more TLC than your usual member of the DMS family, being used as a political statement by the Bus & Coach Council with the forthcoming massive cuts and privatisation imperative in mind. It lost its white band to be branded with an advert which in large yellow letters on the offside reminded Londoners that 'We carry more passengers per gallon', warning underneath in white that 'we'd all miss the bus'; on the nearside was a more conciliatory 'Ease the rush, use the bus.' Stylised seats with passengers' heads formed four diagonal stripes; Plumstead's new T 569 had something similar.

Right: **The first of the B20 DMS intake at Merton was put to use on the Wimbledon tennis service, where the freshly-overhauled buses with their gleaming paintwork and dedicated adverts for Fred Perry sportswear would make the best impression. DMS 2435 (OJD 435R), new to Enfield, was outshopped from Aldenham in June 1982 and is seen in 2 July setting off from its new home garage. Jimmy Connors was this year's champion.** *R. C. Riley*

144   THE LONDON DMS

Right: **The 18A was just one of several routes withdrawn upon the 4 September 1982 programme, and its particular track was not replaced. This is Westbourne Park's DM 2581 (THX 581S), seen on the route's last day.** *Haydn Davies*

The 4 September programme marked the largest set of reductions to totals since the debacle of post-strike 1958; even despite negotiations that had seen 100 of the planned reductions reinstated, 13% of the runout vanished overnight, including several routes in their entirety; more than a few sections of road were abandoned and further routes succumbed to OMO. Although it was most notorious for the commencement of RM withdrawals, 4 September was the standard DMSs' Cannae, over 200 being withdrawn on this day and including a number of examples overhauled only a year earlier. Due to the clearance of stored DMSs from AEC and Abbey Wood to Ensign's premises at Purfleet, where they were stockpiled in advance of their formal sale to that concern, visitors could see the astonishing sight of over six hundred DMs and DMSs lined up on the muddy hardstanding there, listing against one another in various states of repair as those in the worst condition, including the various fire and accident casualties accruing to the fleet, were dismantled to refit those suitable for resale. And still there were more waiting to go, once more filling up AEC and now waiting their turn in two other dead garages, Dalston and the old Plumstead.

Changes to DMS-operated services on 4 September are as follows; Westbourne Park's B20 DM fleet lost the 18A and its Sunday allocation on the 18, while Chalk Farm's 46 found itself extended from Hampstead Heath to Swiss Cottage. Holloway's 104 was converted to DMS OMO but the 168A and 239 were withdrawn. At the southern end of the 168A the 170 was transferred from Wandsworth to Stockwell, although at the expense of its Aldwych-Euston section; Stockwell ceded its weekday allocation on the 44 to Wandsworth. Unusually, three

Above right: **The 46 gained an extension that obviated the need to project the 45 too far from its own central London remit. DMS 1887 (GHM 887N) passes through Kentish Town on 18 September.** *Geoff Rixon*

Right: **Holloway's 104 was another route to go over to OMO. On 11 November D 1831 (GHM 831N) rests at Moorgate.** *R. C. Riley*

were converted unofficially from RM to crew-DMS operation, Shepherds Bush's 72 lost its Tolworth Broadway-Chessington Zoo portion and the 220 fell back to Willesden Junction from the north.

Muswell Hill cast off its DMs, restoring the 43 and 134 to RM and withdrawing from the 102 on Sundays; Potters Bar's last Fleetlines similarly departed with the addition of RMs for its own piece of the 134. At West Ham, the last DMSs left with the conversion of the S1 from farebox to conventional fare with Titans.

South of the river, Croydon's Addington-area routes were revised so that the 130 received express journeys to replace the C3 and the 130B likewise to replace the C4; the 130 itself lost its Thornton Heath Garage-Streatham Garage leg to new RM-operated route 60 and both 130 and 130B were converted from DM to DMS OMO. The 234A was introduced on Saturdays to replace Saturday-only 234B but the parent 234 dwindled, losing its off-peak Purley-Hackbridge leg. Merton's DMSs didn't fare well at all, losing control of the 127, 152 and 189 to LSs, having to share the 57 on Saturday with the interloping Nationals and losing the 249 on Sundays. Sutton received DMs for the 93, using Muswell Hill's discarded B20s from the 43 and 134, and gave the 80 back a little dignity with an extension from Sutton to Belmont.

Above: **Wandsworth would regularly put its B20 DMSs out on the 28 over the festive season while it had them; one such working during 1982 is that of D 2632 (THX 632S), seen at Golders Green.** *Haydn Davies*

crew DMSs were now part of the 28 roster at the latter due to an increase in its allocation on Mondays to Fridays, though Fleetlines rarely appeared in practice (despite regular Christmas and Boxing Day workings over the last few years) and this was cancelled on 6 November. The N68 and N88 at Stockwell and Wandsworth

Above: **Holloway's route 168A ended with the 4 September purge, the planners reckoning that its path through the less-trafficked portions of inner north London was adequately served. D 1774 (GHM 774N), laying over at Waterloo on 16 March 1982, exemplifies the route in its final year, curtailed and one-manned and with little resemblance to the old 168 family's tram-replacement heyday. The bus itself would last until September 1983.** *R. C. Riley*

Right: **Like Bromley three years before, Merton's DMS fleet took its turn to suffer at the hands of the Leyland National, with three routes dropping a deck on 4 September 1982. On 2 July DMS 817 (TGX 817M), from the small Park Royal batch in this number series overhauled in 1980, calls at its home garage on the way to Mitcham. Behind it, on a Merton route that would manage to retain DMSs, is DMS 1621 (THM 621M), an MCW overhauled at the same time.** *R. C. Riley*

A Sutton allocation was introduced to the 157 on weekdays, but the 254 was withdrawn. All these changes made Sutton an 100%-Fleetline garage, though not quite all-OMO due to the 93.

Putney's small DMS fleet ceded the majority of the 85 to a new Norbiton M allocation and added a Sunday service to the 264; Brixton's 95 was pushed at its southern end to St George's Hospital in Tooting, but on weekends got no closer to town than the Elephant, while the 50 came off on Sundays altogether. The Thornton Heath allocation on the 109 was converted from DM to RM, completing the route.

In south-east London a switch between Plumstead and Bexleyheath gave the latter garage's DMSs the 122A on Mondays to Saturdays, and since this route was now withdrawn on Sundays, the 99 came in on that day. New Cross' 70 was hacked quite severely with the loss of its Surrey Docks-Lewisham section and the 177 abandoned its ambitions east of Woolwich, but in town the 188 was extended over withdrawn route 239 to King's Cross. At Catford the 124 and 160 were both withdrawn on Sundays, but the latter route begat new Sunday-only 160A to encompass them both; the 185 suffered too, losing its long-standing service to the southern bore of the Blackwall Tunnel. Sidcup saw its 21A shortened to run to Sidcup Station rather than Eltham and the 229 one-manned with DMSs to accompany a similar shortening that cost it its Farnborough leg in favour of taking over the 51's stand at Green Street Green.

Above right: **The 254 was distinctly ahead of its time and came off after just a year; although there are now shops and a tram depot in the Beddington area, in July 1982 the man getting off Sutton's DMS 2246 (OJD 246R) was disembarking into wilderness.** *Malc McDonald*

Right: **Busplan '78 may have standardised workings in the interest of passengers, but the reality of passenger and traffic patterns on different days of the week made this inefficient. The 124 and 160 at Catford, personified on 31 March 1982 by DMS 2139 (OJD 139R), thus had their Sunday services combined into a second incarnation of route 160A.** *R. C. Riley*

Right: **DM 1796 (GHM 796N) spent its entire London career at Croydon, having been delivered for the 130 family and exiting from those same routes after 4 September when they were one-manned. It is seen crossing the underpass on 17 August.** *John Laker*

If there was any merit at all to the massive reductions of 4 September 1982, it was that the reduced rosters could now be matched to available vehicles – but substantially fewer of them were from the DMS family. The DM class as such was now down to 36 buses on just two routes, the 18 at Westbourne Park and the 93 at Sutton, though the latter's B20s were quickly converted to D spec before year's end. There were no more transfers or reprieves for the remainder through D conversion after 4 September 1982; the standard DM fleets of Thornton Heath, Potters Bar and Croydon simply vanished.

Some sundry DMS activities during that tough summer were the appearance of Westbourne Park DMs on the 52 and 52A for both days of the Notting Hill Carnival; the transfer of B20s into Catford, displacing overhauled DMSs numbered in the 1800s to Merton, Putney, Battersea, Croydon and New Cross; the exit once again of non-B20s from Wandsworth and the withdrawal of FRM 1 as unobtrusively as had marked its career throughout. In June DMS 2205, after a year spent at the experimental shop at Chiwick where it was fitted with a gearbox manufactured by Maxwell, was put into service at Croydon.

Right: **The 134 was converted back to RM operation on 4 September 1982 and its B20 DMs redeployed from Muswell Hill. Seen on 29 July 1982 heading north from Warren Street, DM 2619 (THX 619S) would find itself converted to D and redeployed to Merton, there to spend the rest of its life.** *John Laker*

THE LONDON DMS

Left: **Coincident with the ongoing replacement of Sidcup's DMSs with new Titans was the withdrawal of the 51 from Green Street Green as part of the massive cutbacks. The last day the route would terminate outside the Rose and Crown pub was 3 September 1982, on which afternoon is espied a smartly-presented DMS 2021 (KJD 21P). Its overhaul, completed in February 1982 as one of the last standards done, enabled it to escape withdrawal for the time being, transferring after Sidcup to Bexleyheath. Titans would chase it out of there (February 1983) and out of Catford in turn (July) until final withdrawal from New Cross in December. However, it survived to be rebuilt as a Bexleybus, spending the period from January 1988-November 1989 there. After a spell as a sightseeing bus, it retired to New York in 1995 and was cut up there.** *R. C. Riley*

Below: **The Round London Sightseeing Tour was reallocated from Stockwell to Victoria with ten of its DMs (including DM 2586 (THX 586S), seen at Victoria on 26 July), plus FRM 1. The move would prompt occasional wanderings to the 2B.** *R. C. Riley*

The autumn saw the clearing-out of DMSs from the rest of Tower District; Clapton's last, DMS 1542, ran on 21 September, Camberwell lost its last (DMS 179) on 30 September, and finally Walworth was tackled, its routes 184 and 185 taking Ts between 16 September and 18 October; DMS 2127 was the last there. The comparison trials on the 51 having concluded after 31 October without a clear winner between the Metrobus and Titan, other than a mutual fuel and maintenance saving of 25% over the comparable DMS, Sidcup's whole roster now began converting from DMS to T, comprising the 21A, 51, 228 and 229 and taking until 23 December to complete; this marked the first incursion of second-generation OMO buses into Selkent District, whose specified type was to be the Titan. Unofficial stragglers, however, just about squeaked into 1983. On the 6th the Round London Sightseeing Tour was transferred from Stockwell to Victoria, taking ten DMs with it and, once they were fitted with blinds for all Victoria's routes, allowing them to wander to the 2 and 2B. Four were not needed for the winter requirement; they remained at Stockwell and began to turn out on the 88, including DM 2646. Non-B20 DM 1791 was one of these, and it became effectively the last

Right: **The great migration of the B20 south gathered pace during 1982, facilitated by overhaul. Sutton thus replaced its entire fleet, its intake including DMS 2502 (THX 502S), new to Cricklewood but having been put into overhaul from Bexleyheath when Ms replaced Cricklewood's DMSs. Gleaming from its overhaul, which was completed in July 1982, it is setting off from Kingston in the same month.** *Geoff Rixon*

'pure' standard DM used in exclusively crew mode; it was withdrawn in January 1983. By the end of 1982 crew-operated DMSs were firmly entrenched on night routes N92 and N93, and on the Saturday-night N81 roster. One eye-opening visit was of Holloway's D 1110 to the C11's King's Cross-Holloway garage shorts on 27 November, underlying a continuing need for capacity over these deceptively quiet-looking industrial roads. Finally, the last loose end of the year was tied up when New Cross saw off its last DMs from the 141 on 4 December.

During October, as B20 DMSs continued to be outshopped to Sutton, its remaining Ds in the 1200s were withdrawn and their D kits transferred to the B20s inherited from Muswell Hill for the 93; all were done by the end of the month. D kits were removed and refitted at Clapham, which also served as an inspection centre which determined whether Ds and DMSs made redundant would be kept or sold. The balance of the DMs made spare on 4 September were converted to D and sent south to introduce the B20 type to two new garages,

Right: **Migrating B20s also swept standards out of Croydon, though the state of some of them left something to be desired and would indeed not improve, as this was the point at which B20 DMS overhauls came to an end. D 2568 (THX 568S) had been made spare from Westbourne Park and put into Croydon in December 1982 (being converted to D at the same time) and is seen at the 166's Beckenham Junction stand on 19 October 1983.** *R. C. Riley*

Left: **The southward sluice of the B20 wasn't just into Wandle, Catford in Selkent District continuing to take large numbers on their way out of overhaul. On 24 September DMS 2505 (THX 505S) has just arrived, joining DMS 2514 (THX 514S) there since July.** *R. C. Riley*

Below: **The likelihood of certain sectors of society to exact violence upon bus crews forced London Transport to compromise by allocating doored buses in place of Routemasters on several night routes that were still crew-operated. Holloway's N92 and N93 had thus converted to crew DMS by the start of 1983; here at Trafalgar Square on 19 August 1983 is D 1830 (GHM 830N).** *Malc McDonald*

Merton and Croydon. With the decision from late 1982 to retain the B20s, it was becoming clear that a great migration southwards was in progress, with Wandle District to be their new, and perhaps ultimate, stronghold. DMS 2246, the last standard, was fittingly Sutton's last as well, departing on 3 December to leave the garage 100% B20 for good or ill. MDs were also departing in earnest by autumn 1982, their replacement by Titans at Plumstead following much the same pattern as any DMS-to-M or T conversion elsewhere.

DMS overhauls were now at an end; the last, DMS 2317, was outshopped on 3 December and sent to Brixton; a total of 194 of the B20 fleet had been overhauled. In the absence of further overhauls of the DMS family while Ms and Ts passed through, repaints commenced again, treating some Ds that gravitated to Croydon and Merton, followed by the RLST DMs. DMS 2381 became the first B20 actually sold despite a couple of dozen members having fallen out for various reasons; this was a fire victim and it departed for scrapping. DMS 2415 more or less invalidated its recent overhaul with a front-end collision into a shop; it never returned to service, and was replaced at Brixton in the short term by non-B20 DMS 2092.

Despite the overhaul during 1982 of 227 DMSs, stock numbers were now below 50% of their 1978 peak, comprising 834 DMSs, 282 DMs and 114 Ds for a total of 1,230. The sale to Ensign of 265 members of the DMS family in December and another 287 in January 1983, surely the largest volume of sales ever recorded by London Transport, dropped this below a thousand.

B20 REPRIEVE

1983

1983 was London Transport's Jubilee Year, and even with ominous forebodings for the future of the organisation as an intact, quality provider of public transport, all the stops were pulled out to give the public a superb show that both hearkened back to past glories and offered a glimpse into future developments.

Another blow against out-county operations sharply reduced services south and west of Kingston from 29 January 1983; the knock-on effect was that Norbiton LSs now joined Shepherd's Bush DMSs on the 72, although the latter no longer operated on Sundays and indeed fell back from Tolworth to Roehampton so that Norbiton could provision the southern end, now including live garage runs all the way to Kingston. To fill the space, Shepherd's Bush commenced new route 283, whose DMSs squeezed their way round the White City backstreets between Fulham Broadway and East Acton and back.

During February and March all of Victoria's RLST DMs were repainted, kicking off a small-scale but steady programme of repaints to the unoverhauled D and DMS members still in white-top livery. By March Ensign's DMS complement had grown to a staggering 675 due to the need to clear examples out of Aldenham so that Vic Berry could break RMs there.

Abbey District's conversion to M could now commence, Putney leading the way with the treatment of its 85 and 264 to Metrobuses commencing on 25 February. This saw off the last Rolls-Royce-engined DMSs in service, D 1199 having been taken off the previous December and DMS 1968 now being stood down in April. Four of Putney's escapees (DMSs 860, 2188, 2202 and 2232) became non-B20 infiltrators at Wandsworth before 2188 was returned to Putney in April, while chaotic scenes in the final months of DMS operation of these Wandle garages saw at least DMS 2329 of B20 stock loaned from Wandsworth to Battersea during April as its own standards prepared to depart. From 7 March continuing deliveries of Titans from the 1983 batch of 240 Titans, having come close to ousting the MD class from Plumstead, now turned their attention to Bexleyheath, where its stalwart B20s were still supported by a not inconsiderable number of standards on routes 89, 96, 99, 122A, 132 and 269. The B20s released were inspected for cleanliness at Clapham before onward transfer to Merton and Croydon, but on 31 March Thornton Heath became another operator of the type in the form of DMS 2391, to be followed in subsequent months by many more. Merton's overhauled MCW-bodied DMSs in the 1800s now started to come out of service, and in that condition made ideal low-age trainers to add to or displace existing examples.

Right: **In response to local demand in the Bloemfontein Road area tucked round the back of QPR football club, London Transport commenced new route 283 on 29 January 1983. Four Shepherd's Bush DMSs were scheduled, the new route proving popular enough to occasion the cross-link of a fifth from the 220 within four weeks. Here is D 2540 (THX 540S) on the first day.**
Malc McDonald

152

DMSs operated the Easter Sunday-only 137A for the last time on 3 April 1983, as Battersea's small fleet (of which six were used today) was due for replacement by Ms. DMS 2227 of inaugural T-side advert frame had spent all its life there, albeit just six years' worth.

A programme on 23 April could be said to have resumed the progress of OMO conversions that had tailed off in the previous few years, finally tipping it from 47% of routes so operated into a slim (52%) majority. Sutton lost its conductors with the one-manning of the 93, but it was felt

Above: From 26 February Putney started losing its DMSs for new Metrobuses, inaugurating Abbey District's conversion. Rolls-Royce-engined DMS 1968 (KUC 968P) is already menaced by a new M, while next to it at Putney Bridge Station in April is Sutton's D 2536 (THX 536S), itself soon to fall out with fire damage. *Haydn Davies*

Left: The six-year career of the B20 subtype at Bexleybus was about to come to an end upon the appearance at the garage of the first Titans. In that time they'd had overhauled examples come in, and filling that category is DMS 2477 (THX 477S), outshopped in July and seen on the 269 in October. It was transferred to Croydon. Some of Bexleyheath's original B20 DMSs had endured without either an overhaul or a repaint, while the B20 in general let itself down so badly that niceties like standardisation were overlooked and several B20-intended garages, like this one, operated mixed allocations. *Haydn Davies*

B20 REPRIEVE

153

Right: **Its path northward from Sutton having been switched from the Mitcham-Tooting direction to instead reach Morden via Sutton Common Road, the 80 was only recent to DMSs, but from 23 April 1983 the route really came into its own with a projection over the 93 to Putney Bridge Station. It was now the dominant route over this corridor, with 13 DMSs allocated to the 93's ten, and together representing a six-bus increase over the 93's PVR as a crew route. The 80 now provided a link to Sutton from Putney and Wimbledon, as exemplified by DMS 2518 (THX 518S) having arrived at Putney Bridge Station in the first week. With this programme, Sutton garage now found itself 100% DMS and 100% OMO.** *Haydn Davies*

that the route would not be able to handle its new role alone, so the 80 was extended from Morden to Putney Bridge Station in support. The OMO conversion of the 60 after just seven months in existence was accompanied by a reallocation from Croydon to Thornton Heath, which handed its weekday duties on the 157 to Croydon. Presaging future policy, the 190 was converted to OMO on Sundays, using Croydon DMSs.

Right: **OMO now came to the seven-month-old 60 route, together with an allocation switch from Croydon to Thornton Heath garage. On 23 April 1983, the first day of such a combination, DMS 1871 (GHM 871N) has just passed Streatham garage. Prior to giving it up, Croydon had stuck out on it an increasing number of Ds and DMSs with conductors.** *Malc McDonald*

154

Left: The multi-suffixed 77 family shed one of its variants on 23 April 1983, the Sunday-only 77B coming off altogether while the 77A was withdrawn south of Wandsworth. Prior to this, Merton's just-repainted D 2532 (THX 532S) is seen at the familiar Raynes Park stand on 28 December 1982. *R. C. Riley*

Sunday-only DMS route 77B was withdrawn and the 77A on which it was based pulled back to Wimbledon so that new Merton-operated route 156 could take over both this end and the roads of flat-fare route M1; the 164 was extended up from the Morden direction as far as Lower Morden and the 293 contorted eastwards from Morden to Hackbridge rather than assisting the 93 as far as Wimbledon. In Abbey District, Westbourne Park took back part of the 18 on

Above: Taking the 77A's place along the Wandsworth-Wimbledon corridor was new route 156 with Merton DMSs. As well as representing a partial OMO conversion of the 77A, its continuation to Morden allowed the M1 to be withdrawn. At the Clapham Junction end is DMS 2482 (THX 482S). *David Wilkinson collection*

Above: By the end of 1982 the N68 and N88 night routes shared between Stockwell and Wandsworth had assumed crew-DMS operation. On 21 August 1983 at Wandsworth is D 2577 (THX 577S) belonging to Stockwell. *Malc McDonald*

B20 REPRIEVE

Above: **DMS operation disappeared from the 263 with the withdrawal of the Holloway allocation; this route was repositioned northwards to partially one-man the 134 north of Barnet. While B20s were appearing at Holloway, the garage's regular fare still consisted of standards, exemplified by DMS 2036 (OUC 36R) on 25 June 1982; it would be withdrawn in September 1983.** *Geoff Rixon*

Right: **The treatment of Sutton's D 2593 (THX 593S) to a Jubilee livery involved the painting of a cream band amidships, which when dry was gone over in gold; simple but effective. Seen on the 213A that summer, it was also loaned to Merton at one point.** *Haydn Davies*

Sundays, while Holloway's DMSs left the 263 with the transfer of that service entirely into Potters Bar to help cut down part of the 134.

Streatham, with just the one route (249) became a B20 operator in May with the arrival of two ex-Bexleyheath, while Merton and Sutton continued to take standards on loan or as spares for their B20s. Battersea garage, meanwhile, had only fourteen DMSs to replace, and it took just three weeks for Ms to take over the 39 (6-27 May), DMS 1628 being their last on the 26th. Putney's conversion was interrupted by the need to cover for M 819, damaged in an accident soon after entering service and sent to MCW for repair, and DMS 1857 was reactivated after the last three, DMSs 2188, 2202 and 2243, were otherwise delicensed on 19 May.

In May appeared a most splendid vehicle which presented such a different appearance to the usual unrelieved box-like shape of the DMS that one wonders whether the simple application of its 1933-style Golden Jubilee livery to the buses when new would have afforded the miserable 'Londoner' a better chance at immortality. DMS 1933, its fleetname overriding the withering away of its fellows in that number block of the standard DMS fleet, was taken in March from its normal work at Catford and repainted in April to become DS 1933, reviving the code which had been supposed to but never did quite mark out DMSs that could work as both crew and OMO buses. Allocated to Thornton Heath from 9 May 1983 and generally turned out on the 60 (though with jaunts to OMO routes 64 and 194B as well as crew route 109, showing up the RMs now based thereon!), it wore a silver roof atop its red livery surmounted by lined-out white window surrounds on both decks and sported gold-leaf fleetnames (underlined LONDON TRANSPORT, no less, just fitting into the limited space available) and gold fleetnumbers. A chrome Daimler badge on the front and rear, plus a pair of red mudflaps, topped off the effect. And that wasn't the end of the humble DMS's participation in the Golden Jubilee celebrations. On 10 May D 2629 made its debut at Croydon in a completely different, but no less attractive livery. This was a modern interpretation of the the brown and cream of Croydon Corporation Tramways, which while

156 THE LONDON DMS

Left: DMS 1933 (KUC 933P), the absolutely marvellous Fleetline entrant in the Jubilee 50 celebrations. It's worth wondering whether the simple morale factor of a livery as splendid as this (even with the odd kink required to accommodate the differing heights in the beading) would have given the DMS, or any of its unfortunate contemporaries, a better chance. The code carried is 'DS', it will be noted, and bore some legitimacy, following on from the attempts by Brixton to give some of their DMSs a code more befitting that garage staff's flexibility in use, but like Brixton, crew operation was rarely carried out. *Geoff Rixon*

incorporated into London Transport in 1933 was celebrating its 100th anniversary, paid for in part by Croydon Borough Council, which was also commemorating the centenary of its charter. Immediately nicknamed the Chocolate Box, D 2629 in its two years in this livery racked up appearances on all Croydon's OMO routes, with the 130 group specifically excluded. It carried M/T type moquette on both decks. Yet a third, Sutton's D 2593, was treated to Jubilee finery on a smaller scale, first being seen in April with a cream band, which in June was painted over in gold. It carried adverts from the Bus & Coach Council and Jubilee logos. All three buses, and their numerous counterparts in the RM family plus Metrobuses M 57 and 359 and Titans T 1 and 66, were rallied at the numerous garage and works open days staged throughout 1983 by London Transport as we knew it in what would ultimately prove to be

Below: On 6 May 1983 DS 1933 (KUC 933P) is seen outside its home garage of Thornton Heath. *Geoff Rixon*

Right: The splendid 'Chocolate Box', D 2629 (THX 629S) celebrated 100 years of Croydon Corporation Tramways at the same time as LT's 50th Jubilee. The very sleepy 234 was its usual home, as seen on 18 August. *Geoff Rixon*

Below: The nearside of D 2629 (THX 629S) that summer. *Geoff Rixon*

Below right: D 2629 (THX 629S) would wander to the 197 as shown at Caterham on 22 July, but it was specifically prohibited from the 130 and 130B owing to the likelihood of vandalism. *Malc McDonald*

Right: DMS 48 (EGP 48J) had a far less auspicious 1983. Despite having been the longest-lived example of the early batches, lasting until December 1982, it was displayed at Chiswick open day on 2 July 1983 as an example of how to right a fallen bus using inflatables. *Malc McDonald*

158

its swansong year. Even Ensignbus got in on the act, painting one of their DMS acquisitions in 1933 livery and reclassifying it DF 1682 to emphasise its conversion to single-door. Less glamorous by far was the role played by another pair of DMS and DM in the Jubilee celebrations, DMS 48 and DM 1077, which were lowered to a prone position and raised again with the use of an inflatable airbag operated by a new Leyland Freighter breakdown tender in the service vehicle fleet.

The decisive Conservative election victory of 9 June 1983 prompted sterner measures against the political thorns in their sides, with a White Paper drawn up within six weeks to remove the GLC and similar local councils altogether. Despite the rejection of an early potential competitor in the form of the AMOS minibus application, LT was changing with the wind again, gearing up for further OMO conversions and on 28 June 1983 ordering the vehicles with which to do it – 240 Ts and 150

Above: **Ensign would process the vast majority of the DMS fleet upon its exit from London – in 1983, it seemed all at once! A visit to Purfleet on 7 June has turned up five identifiable examples from a stock of over six hundred awaiting conversion and resale. From left to right are DM 1150 (KUC 150P), DM 1064 (GHV 64N), DMS 2107 (KJD 107P), DM 1067 (GHV 67N) and DMS 1702 (THM 702M), all five of which went on to further service, DM 1064 even finding its way back to town under London Buslines' ownership.** *R. C. Riley*

Left: **You'd think DM 999 (GHV 999N) would not be long for this world from this view of it languishing unloved in Ensigns' yard on 6 July 1983 after acquisition in March, but after a spell as an in-house tour bus and a long period with one further subsequent operator, it would go on to become one of the privileged few DMSs in permanent preservation (see page 244).** *R. C. Riley*

B20 REPRIEVE 159

Right: **The great drive south of the B20 fleet to new homes in Wandle District continued during 1983, though with the ending of DMS overhauls, came about through straight transfers after replacement by new Ms or Ts. DMS 2515 (THX 515S) was transferred from Catford to Streatham in October, released by a new Titan, and the following 9 February is seen at Crystal Palace.** R. C. Riley

Below: **Just Elmers End remained to accept B20s by mid-1983, and this shot of DMS 1916 (KUC 916P) on 28 February allows us both to say goodbye to the standard DMS in this part of town, and to observe the occasional necessity of mixing types depending on availability, seen in the form of Leyland National LS 77 (OJD 877R).** R. C. Riley

Ms for 1984 and 335 Ms for 1985. The 'Just the Ticket' fares programme of 22 May had eased passenger fears by reducing fares by around 25%, while the Travelcard was quickly proving an enormous success that would perhaps facilitate further OMO by reducing the need for on-bus transactions, the Achilles heel that had plagued the DMS ever since its introduction.

The departure of DMS 1857 from Putney on 8 June was followed on the 17th by the input from Battersea of DMS 2049, which stayed until 8 July but lived on, now taking up B20 cover at Wandsworth. None of the garages selected for B20s had ever been able to avoid assistance by their forebears, even for a short time! The arduous task of replacing all of Bexleyheath's DMSs was almost at an end by June when two of its cast-offs took the B20 to Elmers End, the last Wandle garage still to accept the type, and was finally finished on 20 July when the last four were stood down, DMSs 2278 and 2372 last working on the 269, DMS 2395 on the 132 and

Left: Westbourne Park's DMs were instrumental in converting Holloway's DMS routes to B20 from the autumn of 1983. With Almex E baseplate fitted but not the accompanying 'PAY DRIVER'/'PAY CONDUCTOR' front plate in this November 1984 view in Upper Holloway is D 2564 (THX 564S). *Haydn Davies*

Below: Catford was a tough proposition for allocators; fielding over eighty buses on six busy OMO routes, the garage would need the summer, autumn and much of the winter of 1983 to clear out its DMSs, which were again a mix of B20s and lingering standards. Prototype B20 DMS 854 (TGX 854M) just survived into this era; it is captured reversing within the garage forecourt on 7 September, the month of its withdrawal. *R. C. Riley*

DMS 2443 on the 96 before being substituted by Titans during the day. Standard DMSs had persisted all the way to the end, DMSs 1908 and 2003 being the last representatives of the type to leave Bexleyheath.

Part of the Victoria allocation on the 2B was transferred to Stockwell on 25 June, allowing crew DMS appearances that had otherwise tailed off on the 88; the latter route's reciprocal Shepherd's Bush allocation had also cut down its use of DMSs since the 283 had been introduced. From 27 June a Sidcup-style twist took place when six Ts joined 14 Ms in ousting Westbourne Park's DMs from the 18; the displaced B20s were converted to D and sent to release older members from Chalk Farm between 15 August and 2 September (DMS 1614 being this garage's last), as well as the first example of the B20 into Holloway during the month. DMs 2548 and 2552 lingered into September at Westbourne Park and last worked on the 19th of that month, also making sure to see out latterly common RM substitution on the 28 before they left. The 18 was the last LT route officially to be DM-operated.

The mammoth job of clearing DMSs out of Catford fell due next, commencing on 25 July with over eighty buses, not all of them B20s, to replace with Titans. The standards were taken care of first, New Cross receiving several as well as the last two pre-B20s ex-Bexleyheath. Metrobuses, meanwhile, their own immediate future secure due to the doubling of 1985's order to cover the cancellation finally of Titan production, started appearing at Shepherd's Bush, taking over the 72, 220 and 283 from its B20 fleet. The displaced Ds and DMSs ramped up the conversion from standards at Holloway that had been begun by those DMs leaving Westbourne Park. Two B20 Ds fell out this summer; D 2536, another fire victim accruing to Sutton and DM 2559, which was transferred into the service vehicle fleet for use as a mobile survey control centre, fitted upstairs with office equipment powered by a generator downstairs.

B20 REPRIEVE 161

Left: **The dedicated flat-fare express routes linking West Croydon and New Addington were withdrawn with the 4 September programme and their remit incorporated into express journeys on the parallel 130 and 130B, which were converted simultaneously to conventional OMO. Its unlikely overhaul having allowed it to just edge its tenth birthday in service, Croydon's DMS 705 (TGX 705M) in New Addington in August 1983 shows the new format and accompanying black-on-yellow blinds.** *Haydn Davies*

Catford was almost done by October, its 74 workings being nearly covered by its long string of incoming Titans which had completed the first stage of the conversion by 26 October with the ejection of its final standard, DMS 1874; while continuing its long-drawn-out dispatch of B20s to Croydon, it managed to retain eight to the end of the year and beyond into 1984. Although it didn't particularly matter which kind of DMS could turn out on the Round London Sightseeing Tour, given the plethora of vehicles (including ex-DMSs) being used by the competitors to LT on this deregulated tour service, the input of DMS 2268 into Victoria in October was something different from the usual unaltered B20 DMs that had known no other work since delivery.

A small programme on 29 October saw the 95 taken out of its terminus at St George's Hospital, to some acrimony; the morning and evening services had already come off on 18 July. Stockwell lost its share of the N68, the N81 was withdrawn and a number of other night routes gained Saturday-night services to reflect increasing demand.

As 1983 wound down, the life of the overhauled MCWs from the 1800s and 1900s stock-number blocks was coming to a premature end, being progressively replaced from the Wandle garages Croydon, Elmers End and Thornton Heath and the two remaining Abbey District operators, Chalk Farm and Holloway. Of the Wandle sheds Streatham alone had held out with just one or two B20s, but in October their GHM-N, KUC-P and KJD-P DMSs were all replaced. By October Croydon could field

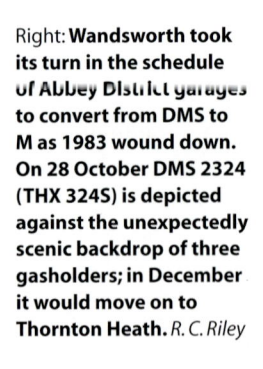

Right: Wandsworth took its turn in the schedule of Abbey District garages to convert from DMS to M as 1983 wound down. On 28 October DMS 2324 (THX 324S) is depicted against the unexpectedly scenic backdrop of three gasholders; in December it would move on to Thornton Heath. *R. C. Riley*

162 THE LONDON DMS

only eighteen standard DMSs to three each from Elmers End and Streatham, and the latter two's stock was soon whittled down, Streatham withdrawing DMS 1846 on 17 November and Elmers End keeping DMS 1950 till 14 December. Merton's last standard, DMS 1967, was delicensed on 1 December; it had spent its last months in service fitted with diagnostic equipment which allowed engineering staff to isolate problems more easily. It proceeded to a new role training staff in the use of BUSCO radio-control equipment. Thornton Heath withdrew overhauled Park Royal DMSs 806, 819 and 822 on 15 December and ended 1983 whittled down to, appropriately, DS 1933, while Croydon could put into action only DMSs 2017 and 2205. Over the river Holloway was reduced to DMS 2074 and D 1773. The opportunity was taken to rotate some of the withdrawn overhauled DMSs to replace earlier examples on training work and thereby fulfil an increased requirement for such vehicles.

Shepherd's Bush's conversion from DMS to M was officially completed on 23 November, DMS 2254, one to have worked there since delivery, being the last after one final turn on the 220 on 3 December, and on 23 November Wandsworth commenced its switch to Metrobuses on routes 44, 220, 295 and crew-operated night routes N68 and N88; it finished 1983 with 14 DMSs licensed. Simultaneously from 15 November, the final DMS-to-Titan conversion of 1983 began to encompass New Cross, affecting routes 70, 177, 184, 188, N82 and the Inter-Station Night Bus; the latter two services were still crew-operated at this time. Although its DMSs and Ds departed for sale, the garage retained eight standards into 1984, including the sole overhauled D 1787, which had led a charmed life since its return from a life of experimentation which failed to convince LT to go ahead with the XRM. D 1063 of this dwindling group, though having lost its admonitory advert, could now count itself the oldest DMS in service. There were now 660 DMSs left in stock as of the last day of 1983, comprising 507 DMS, 42 DMs and 111 Ds; the class as a whole had been reduced by 570 members during the year, with 32 DMs converted to D.

Above: **The R-registered standard DMSs were lucky if they achieved six years in service in London; accordingly Catford's DMS 2235 (OJD 235R) doesn't look like a withdrawal candidate when seen on 14 February 1983, but it only lasted until July.** *R. C. Riley*

Below: **Roadworks at the top of Dog Kennel Hill on 21 November 1983 are perhaps preventing D 1188 (KUC 188P) from running away on this scary gradient. Its conversion to D format had bought it time, but the arrival of Titans (heralded by the Walworth example closing up behind) at New Cross was now putting an end to this, and the Fleetline was delicensed at the turn of the year. It was scrapped before it reached its tenth birthday.** *R. C. Riley*

1984

As 1984 opened, with the standard DMS almost a memory, it was almost as if the pressure was finally off the type. Free from the impossible expectation of converting Londoners, passengers and busmen alike, to a mode of operation they did not want, the surviving B20s could settle down to a reduced role of dedicated conventional-OMO work in a relatively concentrated area that eased the maintenance and spares issues of the past, and in this task they performed as well as could be expected of any modern bus, achieving a lifespan just about on a par with provincial Fleetlines. Quite a lot of them clocked up ten unbroken years with their final garages, including an engine change in 1988 which bought them the vigour they'd never had. Perhaps LT had finally learned how to look after the things, or perhaps they had to, because nobody else was going to buy such a tarnished design as the B20 – at least not yet! And in their remaining eight years the B20 DMS fleet was even trusted enough to participate in the great upheavals mandated by government that eventually swept away London Transport altogether.

In advance of the kind of organisational restructuring that would split LT apart, conversely it was the removal of two of the Districts introduced on 1 October 1979 that kicked off 1984. Where DMSs were concerned Wandle remained intact, though Stockwell garage was removed from the likelihood of taking new Metrobuses through its transfer from Abbey into Wandle.

On 6 January Holloway's D 1773 was delicensed, followed on the 27th by DMS 2074, its last standard. The official transfer to training duties of Croydon's DMS 2017 on 6 January did not prevent it from continuing to turn out in service until it was last seen on 4 February, while Catford's five holdouts were reduced to three by the transfer to Croydon of DMSs 2457 and 2499. This trio, DMSs 2396, 2410 and 2505, finally came to the end of the road on 13 February, completing Catford at last. New Cross, its Titan stocks increased in January and February by the first examples of the final 1984 batch arriving early to get what discount remained on New Bus Grant before it was discontinued on 29 February, withdrew all but D 1063, which was finally taken out of service on 19 February 1984, but in the interim D 1143 had been reactivated and it was this one that sneaked out onto the 70 for one last finale on 14 March, allegedly unlicensed! The last Fleetlines at Wandsworth, DMSs 2322, 2326, 2328 and 2507, left on 20 March 1984, and that was Abbey District completed south of the river. Victoria's non-stage RLST DMs and DMSs, the latter category comprising two ex-Wandsworth buses (DMSs 2322 and 2328) drafted in without logos to cover increased summer schedules from 31 March, were scheduled for replacement by new PA-equipped Ms, and Chalk Farm and Holloway would follow later in the year. Jubilee-liveried DS 1933 could not last any longer as a non-B20 and was delicensed at Thornton Heath on 5 March. That left just one, Croydon's DMS 2205. It was the last Gardner-engined DMS in service as well as the only standard, but it survived due to its experimental Maxwell

Below: **By 26 October 1983 there were far fewer DMSs to be found if your fancy was to pan the camera across Catford garage's forecourt. Today there is only DMS 2499 (THX 499S), flanked on one side by T 842 and T 880, and on the other by T 860 and T 831. DMS 2499 would depart for Croydon in January 1984.**
R. C. Riley

gearbox, a modification which allowed it to continue in service for a full six years after its standard contemporaries had been consigned to history.

Changes in south-west London on 4 February took off Croydon's 234A and reduced the 234 to peaks only, the 127 (reallocated from Merton to Croydon) being the beneficiary through its extension south to Purley. The 213A, shared by Norbiton and Sutton with DMSs used by the latter, was renumbered 213 and reconfigured to serve four termini – Sutton Garage or Belmont in peaks as before, but now adding an extension to St Helier on weekdays and an ambitious Sunday run all the way over the 154 (withdrawn on this day of the week) to West Croydon! The Sunday service was routed via Wallington to cover new route 151, a weekday service introduced to serve the Wrythe Lane area; this allotted Sutton more work after the reduction of its share of the 213 and also helped the 127 eclipse the 234 family. On Sundays new route 127A took this service in a different direction once beyond Mitcham, terminating at Streatham Garage. The 200 was projected here from Mitcham, but fell back from Wallington to Wimbledon on Sundays in favour of the 127A.

Above: **Inevitably, when a route with a suffixed partner is withdrawn, the suffixed route adopts the original number after a suitable period has elapsed sufficient for the passengers not to be confused. Five years was thus about right for the 213A to last before transforming on 4 February 1984 into new route 213 – though, with four new termini, surely there could have been a 213A, B, C and D! Sutton became the junior partner in the 213, Norbiton increasing to compensate for its withdrawal from the 72 and Sutton making it all even with the new 151. DMS 2297 (THX 297S) is seen at the new St Helier Station terminus on the first day it was served.** *John Parkin*

Below: **The withdrawal of the 234A and downgrading of the 234 allowed the 127 to convert back to DMS and transfer from Croydon to Merton. On Sundays, however, it was withdrawn and replaced by a Sunday-only 127A which commenced from Streatham Garage rather than Tooting. Here at Purley Oaks in June is D 2601 (THX 601S).** *Haydn Davies*

B20 REPRIEVE

Left: **A second route of this number to appear in the Sutton area, new route 151 introduced on 4 February 1984 allowed the Wrythe Lane area direct connections with Sutton and Wallington; it was Sutton-operated with DMSs on Mondays to Saturdays and its western terminus was Worcester Park station. One day in June 1986 DMS 2311 (THX 311S) is shortworking to North Cheam.** *R. C. Riley*

Night routes were the focus of a large programme implemented on 13/14 April 1984. Victoria's DMs and DMSs from the RLST struck up new routes N2 and N11 over sections of their daytime counterparts, while the DMSs of Brixton and Thornton Heath shared new N78, which allowed the night 109 to come off. Stockwell's N87, which like the 170, had now commenced the AVE trials from 26 March, was one-manned and the Brixton allocation removed to accompany a reconfiguration which made it more like the daytime 77 to Streatham. Holloway's N92 was converted to OMO with extensions north and south, leaving the N93 as its sole remaining crew-operated night bus, but on 8 May the garage's first Metrobuses entered service. These were meant for the 104, 214, 271 during the day and N92 and N93 at night, and due to the getting in the way of three batches of unusually-specified Ms, the conversion was dragged out till February 1985; DMSs did not appear on the routes introduced to Holloway or one-manned there as the year progressed, and those withdrawn were either placed into store or filtered south to Croydon.

Having missed out on the 1983 celebrations, D 948, which had been converted to open-top at the end of the year to advertise possible sales in that format as a last-ditch attempt to convince prying accountants of the continuing viability of Aldenham and Chiswick, was deployed on a Catford-operated service introduced from 25 May to take visitors to see the Thames Barrier, which had recently been completed and was now in action. It also peformed on an ambitious service from Morden to the Thames Barrier. In July it was joined by D 1102, also open-top but in white with yellow entrance doors. Fitted upstairs with blue vinyl Ambla seating, both were to enjoy a long career with Selkent District and later the self-standing Selkent subsidiary of LBL, lasting until privatisation at the end of 1994 when Stagecoach elected to concentrate its London private-hire arm across the river.

Above left: **From 8 May 1984 Holloway's DMSs started to depart, though their replacement by Ms dragged out as various esoteric specifications of the M class intervened. D 2634 (THX 634S) is seen in Upper Holloway in November; it left for Thornton Heath in March.** *Haydn Davies*

Left: **On 26 August 1984 D 1102 (GHV 102N) is at Greenwich, carrying out its first season as an open-topper in plain white.** *Malc McDonald*

Above: **The author wasn't impressed to see his local Sutton B20 Ds repainted out of their white-top livery during the spring and summer of 1984, one after the other. D 2620 (THX 620S) succumbed in August and still looks fresh when seen on 14 October at the nicer end of Mitcham.** *Geoff Rixon*

On 29 June 1984 London Regional Transport (LRT) came into being under the tenets of the London Regional Transport Act 1984 given assent three days earlier. With the removal of 'London Transport' from the GLC, the body was now effectively nationalised, but under the terms of the Act it would be compelled first to separate its business sectors as 'arm's-length' holding companies and then to put routes out to competitive tender. LRT hadn't yet ruled out the idea to sell the B20 family until it sounded out the market for the buses soon after its establishment and discovered that demand was lower than ever; peak demand had passed with the saturation of the market by those standard DMSs already sold and new bus construction was at its lowest ebb yet. Despite the strong possibility of a steady drop in PVR as independents muscled their way onto the London bus scene, it was thus recognised that the DMS still had a role to play, and totals would hold steady for some years to come, introducing an ironic stability that the class had never really known.

With the conversion of Holloway under way and that of Chalk Farm imminent, Victoria took on new PA-fitted Metrobuses between 4 July and 4 August (this conversion also including the N2 and N11, which went over from the night of 12/13 July). Three of the DMSs displaced topped up Chalk Farm but, unusually, the DMs were transferred into the dedicated Tours & Charter fleet, dispersed between Victoria, Camberwell, Battersea and Holloway. The fitting to a large number of buses of all classes with wheel hub-mounted tachographs to record mileage during the year increased the commercial inspiration that was beginning to awaken in London as LRT's six Districts took notice of how potential competitors were marketing and selling first coach services, then open-top tour operations, two facets of public transport deregulated in that order as the 1980s progressed. As the deregulation of London tour work in 1984 immediately introduced furious competition, eight operators amassing over fifty DMSs between them, it was not difficult for those business-minded individuals to predict the possibility of hitherto staid stage operations being opened up in the same manner, so it made sense to get in at the front door, whichever side of the LRT/private-sector divide they were on.

As class after class of the AVE trials entered service on the 170, the displaced Stockwell DMSs were apt to turn out in crew mode on the 2B and 88. The reciprocal Victoria allocation on the 2B also saw crew DMSs while they were still available, but their spectacular swansong was the one-off appearance of DMS 2328 on Green Line 704 during the evening peak of 21 June – surreal as that was, it broke down and was almost replaced by a DM. Strange visitors for 1984 were otherwise all now in solid Wandle territory, DMSs with conductors subbing for RMs on the 109, 133, 155 and 190 (which would all go on to assume permanent OMO DMS operation), while LSs were helped out on the 152 and 289.

B20 REPRIEVE

Right: **The 170 gained more fame than its sleepy and under-resourced nature would have it deserve when during 1984, four trios of experimental buses gradually filtered into service in place of the incumbent Stockwell DMSs. This shot of DMS 2464 (OJD 464R), which stayed put at the garage, was taken in Whitehall, and it's immediately apparent that one of the Ls, Vs or Ms (as had entered service by the time of this shot in September, has lent one of its side blinds for use as an ultimate.** *Haydn Davies*

In June 1984 DMS 1 was donated to the London Transport Museum and DMS 1967 replaced RT 2958 as the traditional radio trainer, but a surreal combination of entertainment and the realisation of the most extreme parts of the DMSs' potential came on 4 August when Ensign supplied six of them as participants in a stock-car race held at Northampton and televised on *World of Sport*!

1984's incarnation of the Wimbledon tennis service employed DMSs from Merton, Sutton and this time Thornton Heath as well as Norbiton Ms, but this year DS 1933, still around at Thornton Heath for private-hire, featured just the once before being withdrawn again at the end of June. A shortage of DMSs at Sutton during July saw many loans from fellow Wandle garages, featuring among others DMS 2247 from Elmers End and DMS 2377 pressed into service from store prior to taking up an experimental role at Chiswick Works. But as the summer wore on, it was time for more DMSs to be replaced as the 1985 order for Ms commenced delivery; Chalk Farm's conversion from DMS to M (route 46 alone) was carried out between 30 August and 27 October.

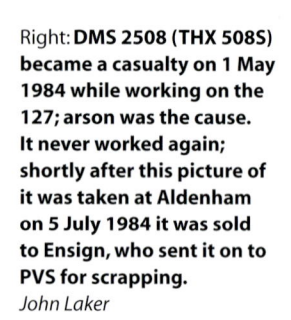

Right: **DMS 2508 (THX 508S) became a casualty on 1 May 1984 while working on the 127; arson was the cause. It never worked again; shortly after this picture of it was taken at Aldenham on 5 July 1984 it was sold to Ensign, who sent it on to PVS for scrapping.** *John Laker*

168 THE LONDON DMS

Left: As comprehensive plans were drawn up to increase vastly the extent of one-man operation, the remaining core of B20 DMSs in Wandle District would be earmarked to participate. The Sunday service on Croydon's 190 had been converted to OMO upon the 23 April 1983 programme, and one Sunday in June 1984 DMS 2412 (OJD 412R) works through Purley, with the implication (shortly to be fulfilled) that the rest of this outer south London route would be found suitable to lose its conductors. *Haydn Davies*

On 10 October the first thirteen routes were offered to tender under the provisions of the London Regional Transport Act. The decimation of London Transport was about to begin – but at the moment none of these routes included any operated by DMSs, nor was it yet evident that former DMSs were more than likely to return as cheap conveyances within the small budgets and low overheads of the independents, feared and derided as 'cowboys'. Bids were to be in by 11 February 1985 for commencement in July.

On 27 October the N78 lost its Thornton Heath allocation, while the DMSs still at Holloway saw their N93 extended to Hammersmith (in replacement of that section of the N92) and one-manned. The N87 lost its final half-mile between Streatham, St Leonard's Church and the Greyhound, within which stretch was Streatham garage, which closed for three years' worth of rebuilding; its only OMO DMS route, the 249, was reallocated to Clapham, which stocked it with Ms. The 200, Sunday 127A and night N87 were rerouted to terminate at Brixton garage. The Sunday forays towards town of the 131, which could boast Merton DMSs, were removed from the Embankment to terminate at Aldwych instead, commencing the progressive and inexplicable relegation of buses from this vital and indeed, purpose-built central London thoroughfare. Having cemented its path north of Morden since taking it over from the M1, the 164 was now projected during the peaks beyond Lower Morden to Wimbledon.

During the autumn of 1984 the fortunes of the DMS took another turn, this time for the better with the announcement by LRT that it intended to retain the B20 fleet in service for at least three more years (the low likelihood of being able to sell them for further service was not cited!). Two years having passed since the last DMS had been overhauled, a pair ex-Holloway were taken into Aldenham in September for trial WASPs, the works having been reprieved in July as long as it restructured itself to cut staff numbers by 40%. If the overhauls of DMS 2248 and D 2583, which hadn't been touched by year's end, proved successful, the rest would be done – 189 remained un-overhauled of the B20 fleet, though repaints, stepped up to reflect the DMSs' participation in the OMO programmes to be implemented, were progressing to the extent that fewer than 100 were still in white-top livery by the end of the year. In October thirty DMSs were plucked from the withdrawal ranks at AEC and converted to trainers at Clapham, these comprising most of the newest standards. Five more unaltered DMs were seconded to tours and commercial work in the last two months of 1984; DM 2586 going to Battersea, DM 2587 to Holloway and DMs 2585, 2589 and 2612 to Stockwell. Meanwhile, DMS 1887, unlicensed since May 1983, was loaned in October 1984 from sales stock to Ogle Designs of Letchworth for comprehensive studies to be undertaken concerning the boarding of buses, general safety and comfort standards and drivers' requirements, which would produce two surprises for the DMS family in the year to come.

By the close of 1984 plans were now in hand to extend OMO (or OPO, to give this form of operation a term coming increasingly into use) with a vengeance, and the exit of DMSs from Abbey District during the year had now

B20 REPRIEVE 169

Above: **The 190 was Croydon's penultimate crew route, but over the autumn half-term period went over to crew DMS operation. On 6 November at North End it sees a visit by the fine 'Chocolate Box', D 2629 (THX 629S).**
Malc McDonald

ensured enough spare to begin converting local routes to doored operation in advance of their eventual OPO conversion. First to succumb to crew DMSs in this way was Croydon's 190, going over between 19 and 27 October using examples made spare from Chalk Farm (plus indigenous 'Chocolate Box' D 2629, which liked to make its home on this route). Then fell Stockwell's 77A, needing 33 of them on weekdays and phasing in the discarded members of Holloway's, Chalk Farm's and Streatham's allocations between 16 November and the end of the year via a period in store at Clapham or at the newly-reopened Norwood garage. The weekend Stockwell share of the 77 assumed crew-DMS operation from around 1 December, though as more were taken in Stockwell ramped up its appearances of DMSs

Right: **Always rather unusual in its treatment of its long-established DMS fleet, Brixton broke the mould when, instead of sending away its Fleetlines displaced by the conversion of routes 50 and 95 to M, it kept them and used them to bounce RMs from the 133 instead, with attendant outings to the 109 and 159 also in crew mode. Calling at the Elephant on 12 September 1984 is DMS 2440 (OJD 440R).**
Malc McDonald

170 THE LONDON DMS

Left: The winter of 1984-85 proved eventful for Brixton's DMSs; having left the 50 and 95, they were now the mainstay of the 133, albeit with conductors now to evoke the route's six years under DMs. During weekends they spread their net to the similarly crew-operated 109 and 159, and on a hazy 27 December 1984 DMS 2467 (OJD 467R) heads south past Oval station, foglights ablaze. *Malc McDonald*

Below: The 159 on Saturdays and Sundays became a solid user of crew DMSs and even operated them officially until it was felt more appropriate to set aside enough RMs from the 109. There's barely enough room at the 159's long-established West Hampstead, West End Green stand for one bus, let alone one four feet longer than the usual RM, but on 9 December 1984 D 2611 (THX 611S) has wedged itself in. *Malc McDonald*

on the 88, and even on the 45 from time to time. Despite the conversion to Cummins-engined Ms of Brixton's routes 50, 95 and N78 between 19 November and 12 December, the DMSs there stayed put; the route to lose RMs was the 133, though the Brixton allocations of the 109 and 159 were just as likely to see Fleetlines with conductors and the Sunday roster of the 159 was even officially worked thus from 2 December. Finally the D kits on Brixton's DMSs could be used to their full potential!

549 DMSs remained in stock at the end of 1984, a total down by 111 on 1983; these consisted of 413 DMSs, 26 DMs and 110 Ds; 253 were scheduled for service, but this number was to creep upwards once again before long.

B20 REPRIEVE

1985

The first of four OPO programmes to be carried out in 1985 bowed on 2 February, and it took the proportion of OPO fleetwide from 52% to 56%. Along the Brighton Road new route 59 returned that number to familiar territory, operating between Brixton and Purley with ten Thornton Heath DMSs transferred from Holloway. The 109 thus fell back to South Croydon Garage and came off on Sundays altogether, the 59 adding not only this route's Sunday-morning journeys round the Embankment but an extension on that day of the week over the 166A to Chipstead Valley. Brixton now added a Saturday share to the 159, using its crew DMSs (until mid-March when both this and the Sunday share resumed RM operation). Further south, Croydon's 190 was converted to OPO using the same DMSs that had been phased in during the previous autumn, and to complete the changes relevant to Fleetlines, the 157 lost its Sunday Merton and Thornton Heath allocations to a standardised Croydon roster on that day of the week.

The career of the DMS at Holloway just made it across the fourteen-year anniversary of the one-manning of the 271 on 16 January 1971, but the garage's last examples, which still had that route to operate on, were delicensed on 21 March. Some of them, all from the D class, allowed fellow examples from Thornton Heath to join a growing number in storage at Clapham as potential candidates for overhaul. However, one, DM 2587, was despatched to Battersea in replacement of DM 2586, there to strike up a new London By Night sightseeing tour.

The decision to retain the B20 DMSs had prompted a resumption of the overhaul cycle discontinued in 1982, and to release enough examples both to Aldenham and to expected contractors Midland Red and British Leyland, new Ms were introduced to Croydon from 14 February. 189 DMSs were to be done, including all those not to have had a repaint since new, and the long-dead ones in store at Clapham were treated first. As it happened, DMS overhauls were cancelled again in April, due to the likelihood of excessive work having to be undertaken to turn around the wretched state of the ones that had been selected to go in first from the ranks of long-term stored buses, with twenty more such gathered during March. A Department of Transport snap inspection carried out on 6 February along the 77A road had already served prohibition notices on

Below: **Withdrawn upon Busplan '78 as a forgotten adjunct to the 159, the 59 was resurrected on 2 February 1985 as a partial OPO conversion of the 109; Thornton Heath DMSs were in charge, exemplified by DMS 2316 (THX 316S) at Streatham Hill on 22 April. During DMSs' tenure the 59 would expand to cover even more of the 109, only to be ruthlessly hacked down to a City of London shuttle without much of a future. By this time the white-top livery on DMSs was becoming very thin on the ground.** *R. C. Riley*

172 THE LONDON DMS

eleven of its DMSs, so time was of the essence – but Aldenham, already hit by planned cuts to its workforce in a last-ditch attempt to make it break even under new management (Bus Engineering Limited being convened from 1 April), refused, stating it had enough pressure to overhaul existing Routemasters, Ms and Ts. Instead it was decided to complete the sixteen contract overhauls under way at Midland Red's Carlyle works (eleven examples) and at British Leyland's Nottingham premises (the remaining five) and turn the FFD and accompanying heavy repair work over to Wandle's own garages instead (save Brixton and Thornton Heath, which pleaded pressure of existing work). Finally, repaints would be done at Clapham. Counting more as recertifications than overhauls in the classic Aldenham manner, it was intended that the work garner them three more successive FFD passes; D 2561 went through the procedure first, in May, 72 others passing through without fanfare for dispersal back to their own Wandle garage as needed between then and February 1986. Aldenham did feel prepared to take on a repaint contract, however, and subsequent repaints were done there rather than at Clapham, though not always at the same time as the bodywork repanelling. Wrong coding was prevalent on Ds hereafter, though it made no difference other than to enthusiasts (particularly this one, who it used to drive mad!).

Above: **The 77A at Stockwell needed three dozen DMSs to replace its RMs at the end of 1984. DMS 2435 (OJD 435R) was transferred from Streatham following its closure for rebuilding on 27 October, and the following July is seen sharing the Putney Heath, Green Man stand with DMS 2469 (OJD 469R), which had been at Stockwell since new. Neither bus shows any indication that they are crew-operated, obliging the driver of each to have to shoo boarding passengers away from him and into the body of the bus.** *Haydn Davies*

Left: **DMS 2339 (THX 339S) was one of the DMSs recertified in its home district of Wandle during 1985; in this 30 May shot the Sutton-allocated bus has required a new windscreen surround. The results can be seen on the following page.** *John Laker*

173

Above: **DMS 2277 (THX 277S)** was one of the overhauls contracted to Midland Red, who would appear to have done a perfectly fine job when the Merton-allocated result was seen attending the Derby at Epsom on 5 June, but Aldenham's workforce considered any outsourcing of their key work a threat. *Malc McDonald*

The Ms sent into Croydon as overhaul cover did not leave, however; moreover, further new ones arrived there in April, and mixed-type operation continued; this was something of a lapse in standards which heralded an inefficient era in which garages had to keep multiple stocks of spare parts. The impending onset of route tendering, the first awards being made on 11 April, meant that standards of presentation as a whole were about to decline sharply, cost being the main factor in just about everything, and Aldenham itself was already fighting for its life. In fact the structure of operations changed once again when on 1 April 1985 LRT's wholly-owned 'arm's-length' companies were unveiled and activated; legal lettering on buses now read London Buses Ltd, abbreviated hereafter to LBL. Engineering was now done by BEL (Bus Engineering Limited) on the same contract basis as other potential private-sector competitors, and LUL (London Underground Ltd) now ran the Underground. DMS 2177 was the sole Fleetline to migrate to BEL, continuing its role as a staff bus.

Between March and June 1985 Midland Red overhauled DMSs 2250, 2277, 2295, 2298 and 2401 and Ds 2535, 2537, 2612, 2632, 2636 and 2645, while British Leyland at Nottingham treated DMSs 2258 and 2335 and Ds 2562, 2584 and 2585. That made sixteen in all. ECW was set

Right: **And this is the result of the Wandle district refurbishments, in the form of DMS 2339 (THX 339S).** Having come in from Sutton, it returned there in July for this shot taken at Morden, but would be transferred to Stockwell straight after. *Haydn Davies*

174

Left: Open-top D 948 *SS Royal Eagle* (GHV 948N) is seen at the Thames Barrier on 2 June 1985, allocated to Catford. Both this bus and its partner D 1102 would later operate under the banner (and white-banded livery) of Selkent Travel. *Malc McDonald*

to overhaul two but passed them to Leyland. During the spring this contract-overhaul output found its way to Merton and Sutton for the usual Derby Day and Wimbledon specials, the orange Fred Perry adverts setting off the fresh coats of paint to their best advantage. Further Ms into Croydon in June released the balance needed for the duration until moving on to Norwood and allowing the DMSs to resume normal service. The overhauls, which at eight weeks had taken slightly less time than had been the case at Aldenham, were not generally considered on a par with Aldenham's standards, though the works was well and truly on borrowed time by now, with even Routemaster overhauls, less efficient than traditionally now that body changes were not able to be undertaken, beginning to wind down. One last accomplishment was the fitting to bus sides of advert frames to accept panels affixed to card inserts and thereby protect the paintwork as compared with the old pasted-on bills.

For the 1985 summer season, the two open-top DMs were reactivated in March and named, DM 1102 (to accompany a repaint from white to red) being christened *SS Royal Daffodil* and DM 948, itself with a new coat of paint, *SS Royal Eagle*, both to honour the old Medway steamers. They were used on the Thames Barrier Shuttle, once again operated out of Catford, while on the first of the same month an equally prestigious DMS returned to service – DS 1933, which could now count Thornton Heath's new 59 among its regular roster.

Right: DS 1933 (KUC 933P) was put back into service at Thornton Heath during March 1985 and on 3 June is seen at West Croydon on the 59. *Malc McDonald*

B20 REPRIEVE

This page: **DMS 2456 (OJD 456R)** was extensively revamped during 1985 in the interests of passenger accessibility. The alterations involved splitting and lowering the front entrance steps, adding a third step to the exit and straightening the staircase. All the modifications were set off by improved-visibility green handrails and the driver was not left out, being provided with a revised cab. The montage was photographed at Chiswick by the eventual owner of the bus today, who has preserved it in the same condition. *All: Stu Boxall*

Right: **With the 77A now OPO, the 77 couldn't be far behind, and indeed was converted on 1 February 1986. When that happened, Stockwell was obliged to switch DMS 2456 (OJD 456R) to the 88, but on 12 November it is seen at Clapham Junction, a full repaint having been provided since the above montage.** *Malc McDonald*

THE LONDON DMS

Stockwell's AVE trials could now boast their full complement of experimental vehicles following the introduction of the H class to the 170 on 4 March, but DMSs continued to appear as spares, providing a helpful comparison. Twin-staircase Volvo Ailsa V 3, meanwhile, joined the crew DMSs on the 77A on 18 March. Two DMSs intended for Stockwell, DMSs 2377 and 2456, had spent the latter part of 1984 at Chiswick's experimental shop undergoing the fitment of technological advancements that it was hoped would become standard on whatever buses were chosen as a result of the AVE trials. This was done in assocation with Ogle Designs of Letchworth, that innovative company that had brought us designs from Sir Alec Issigonis's Mini to Luke Skywalker's landspeeder from *Star Wars*. At an estimated cost of £250,000, DMS 2377 was fitted with an improved cab designed to follow the ergonomic recommendations from a committee of PTE chief engineers that carried forward earlier studies done by LRT's medical services board. The dashboard was modified with simplified controls, though one could not get much more stark than the deliberately sparse instrumentation traditionally specified by London Transport, and thus looked positively futuristic with its lit-up panels. To protect drivers against the increasing likelihood of assault by the passengers they served, provision was made for a perspex anti-vandal screen over the cab. The disused AFC cabinet was dismantled and the space over the nearside front wheelarch used for a luggage rack, while a spring-operated parking brake was fitted. It was put into action alongside the entertaining miscellany on the 170 on 18 March 1985 but results were not as promising as they could have been, drivers feeling that the alterations had left the cab rather cramped. DMS 2456, however, was substantially different. This was the real-world version of the 'London Bus of the Future' test rig constructed by Ogle and subjected to testing by sample passengers hired to represent a cross-section of passenger profiles. DMS 1887 had also spent time at Ogle's facilities to this end.

First and foremost, the staircase on DMS 2456 was increased in size to eight straight steps broken by a central landing; the extra room taken up obliged this to be resited over the offside wheelarch and the space normally underneath removed to the nearside luggage rack, which was increased in size to permit just two seats but allow passengers to stay closer to their small items of luggage. The steps in the entrance doorway, which was moved forward slightly, were redesigned on two levels, so that the forwardmost half had two steps and the rearmost three, permitting the easier boarding of a greater number of elderly or infirm, who had historically found boarding a little slower. In the exit doorway an extra step was added to make three, the handrails being lengthened and pointed further down to acknowledge how elderly passengers often turned around while disembarking so as to be able to hold on to the rails until completely off. The inward-facing three-bench seats over the rear wheelarch were replaced by two pairs of back-to-back seats, adding two to capacity where a similar figure had been removed at the front and rendering final capacity H41/23D. Inside, bells were rewired to ring just once when pressed, illuminating a 'Bus Stopping' sign on each deck. For visibility purposes, although anything but aesthetically, all handrails were now coated in non-slip bright green. The cab was similar to that of DMS 2377, though no further examples were fitted to Fleetlines. Not carried over from the mockup, nor specified on the 260 Leyland Olympians ordered on 5 June for 1986 delivery, were quarter windows extending further down than hitherto so that the driver could observe the kerb, though these features (and lower-set side blinds) eventually ended up creeping into bus designs by the end of the century.

Above: **The 189 had been the fourth route to gain DMSs and by 1985 was still around, but only just; its main effort mostly carried out by the 152, it was first converted to LS and then cut back heavily so that only its proprietary section along Burntwood Lane was retained, and served infrequently at that. However, from time to time Merton would put a DMS out, and one such on 28 July 1985 is D 2573 (THX 573S), repainted four months previously and still looking smart. The iconic 'We're backing Brixton' banner on the railway overbridge was a message of hope that didn't translate quite so well down on the ground; two months after this picture was taken a second major episode of civil unrest would unfold here.** *Malc McDonald*

Right: **The 133 had already spent six years with crew-operated Fleetlines and the second such combination would last a year until the inevitable OPO conversion on 2 November 1985. On 22 April Brixton's DMS 2463 (OJD 463R) pauses outside its home base for the once-over by the duty inspector before continuing to the 133's terminus of the time, the not particularly useful junction with Green Lane necessitated upon the closure of Streatham garage the previous autumn for rebuilding. The 133's terminus would change again upon one-manning, at the expense of the largely parallel 95.**
R. C. Riley

Below: **Stockwell had only come onto the 45 since 27 October 1984 and would withdraw again before nine months were out, but during its short allocation were apt to put out crew DMSs in lieu of the scheduled RMs. On 25 February 1985 D 2558 (THX 558S) is on the north side of Clapham Common.** *Malc McDonald*

A second major programme of route alterations for 1985 took place on 27 April. At Croydon the 234 was finally withdrawn, the 127 covering it with an extension from Purley to Selsdon during the peaks at which the 234 had operated. Sutton's 151 lost its off-peak service beyond North Cheam to Worcester Park, allowing resources to be added to an extension of the 280 north from Tooting to Wandsworth over the 220, which was reduced between these points. The 293 gained a Merton share again (to offset the 280's increase) and four DMSs each from Sutton and Croydon with which to work it, leaving Sutton operating at weekends only. The transfer of Stockwell's allocation on the 45 to Walworth precluded DMSs from turning out on it any more, as they had been in some strength during the early part of the year.

Right: **To consolidate crew changeovers at Elmers End on Sundays, their allocation on the 54 was switched to the 75 from 27 April 1985; here at Sydenham next day is DMS 2364 (OJD 364R).** *Malc McDonald*

Below right: **Now that the 119 was daily upon its OPO conversion, Shirley Way would have lost its Sunday service had not new route 194A been commissioned to fill the breach. Still, the route was two-headed, services to Forest Hill continuing without the need for yet another suffix. On 28 April Elmers End's DMS 2265 (OJD 265R) calls at Sydenham.** *Malc McDonald*

For some time, the 54 had had an anomaly of a Sunday-only Elmers End allocation instead of the usual Catford, meaning that DMS operation endured, but from 27 April this was transferred to a similar role on the 75 instead, bringing back Fleetlines to that route. Still at Elmers End, the 194 was withdrawn on Sundays so that new Sunday-only route 194A could assume the Shirley Way service vacated by the 119B upon its absorption into the regular 119.

Without doubt the most visible indicator of the enforced decline of London Transport was the debut of competitors as tendering was commenced. Saturday 13 July cost London Buses Ltd six routes, and one of them, the 81, was taken up using DMSs. Len Wright Travel of Isleworth, trading as London Buslines, was not afraid of the perceived reliability of the LT-specification Fleetline, and took nine of them supplied by Ensign and painted by them into a yellow and brown livery. As yet without fleetnumbers of their own, these comprised former DMs 928, 1007, 1019, 1033, 1040, 1064, 1078, 1083 and 1088.

Left: **Undoubtedly the beginning of the end for LBL and ultimately for unified bus operation in London, the first six routes were delivered to their new private-sector operators on 13 July 1985. Forgetting all the troubles the DMS family was saddled with, whether by reputation or experience, Len Wright's London Buslines took a punt on several nominal DMs purchased from Ensigns and painted into a yellow and brown livery for the 81. At least this first of the 'cowboys' brought back double-deckers to this route, which is busier than it looks; GHV 83N, formerly DM 1083, passes through Colnbrook on 20 July. London Buslines probably had the last laugh, as they went on to wring a full decade's work out of their DMSs!** *Malc McDonald*

Right: **The large number of DMSs into Stockwell for the 77A tempted the garage to stick them out on the other crew routes there, most notably the 88. Former Shillibeer D 2646 (THX 646S) crosses Marble Arch in March 1985, and in December would transfer to Sutton where it would spend the rest of its career.**
Haydn Davies

Below: **On 25 May 1985 DMS 1499 (MLH 499L) is eking out its days as a trainer, based at Brixton for the previous five years and seen in Downham under the stewardship of one of its prospective drivers. This was the lot for a sizeable number of the standard DMS variety by the mid-1980s, with even then nobody imagining that any of them could ever be put back into service.**
R. C. Riley

So much for memories of Jubilee Year 1983; two years on, with tendering under way and traditional facilities beginning to be cut away at every turn, its two Fleetline representatives were removed. Croydon Corporation Tramways-liveried D 2629, after cutting the tape at the opening of the extraordinarily hideous new West Croydon bus station on 17 May, was repainted red in July, the same month that Thornton Heath's DS 1933 was finally stood down, not to return this time. Still, one eye was on the future, however straitened it was set to be, with DMS 2456 licensed at Stockwell on 12 August, taking its new features to the public for the first time. However, due to the fact that its handrails funnelled boarders into the body of the bus rather than directly at the driver, it was put into service as a crew bus on the 77 (and 88, which enjoyed considerable crew-DMS appearances during 1985). DMS 1887, its work at Ogle thus done, was sold. Also in August Camberwell's DM 2643, treated to coach seating upon its overhaul in April, received the same white band between decks as

Selkent District's recently-acquired ex-WMPTE Titans, plus the blue 'SELKENT TRAVEL' lettering; partners DM 2641 and 2642 soon took this on as well. Otherwise the Tours & Charter fleet had been folded into LBL upon the latter's convening and its handful of B20 DMs were gradually taken off their private-hire duties at Victoria, Camberwell, Battersea and Holloway and readied for service. A renewed attempt to garner sales was made by treating DMS 2034 to yellow upper-deck window surrounds to serve as a sales publicity bus at AEC – it must have worked, because the bus was sold straight away!

Merton's 155 was converted to crew DMSs on Saturdays on 27 July, but on 3 August a programme was executed that would strike more conductors off LBL's payroll. The 77A was the major casualty, additionally losing its last projections from Wandsworth to Wimbledon, while the 77 now began to gain crew DMSs following the addition of a weekday Stockwell share, which at least meant that Merton could recoup enough DMSs to take back the 57 from its mix of LSs and add an extension to the 156 that took it as far towards town as Vauxhall. The 77 itself was rerouted to Euston alongside the 77A rather than eastwards towards Farringdon Street. The 164 lost its Wimbledon projections but its whole service west of Morden was now augmented to bring it to Raynes Park Station.

The final OPO onslaught of 1985, on 2 November, saw the 133 at Brixton lose its conductors to accompany rerouteing to Tooting over the 95, which was cut back severely to become a peak-hour-only route getting no further south than the garage. The 133 was supposed to have been one-manned entirely with Ms, but its existing DMSs had to form the bulk of the complement until the final Metrobuses were delivered at the turn of 1986. The 118, converted to OPO with new Ms on 27 April this year, saw isolated DMS appearances from 23 September onwards.

1986 was already looking ominous, despite 1985 having been a more settled year for the DMS than ever. On 15 November 1985 LBL announced that it would be taking in at garages most of Aldenham's current work other than heavy or accident repair and repaints, thus putting an end to the traditional London bus overhaul; with 300 fewer staff, Aldenham would now be expected to tout for its own contract work outside LBL if it were to survive. A second tranche of tenders placed out in July included DMS-operated route 127 and its Sunday counterpart 127A and 200, with a third batch of tenders due in from the start of December and also featuring two routes currently with DMSs, the 197 and 293. LBL would lose them all – and yet, thanks to three more private-sector operators, DMS numbers in the capital would actually increase. Battered and staggering as 1985 rolled into 1986, 'London Transport' could count itself damned lucky that the capital was not to be subjected to deregulation at this point, even though that the Transport Act 1985 endorsing this was given Royal Assent on 30 October. 490 DMSs remained in stock on the last day of 1985 (364 DMSs, 12 DMs and 114 Ds). 311 were scheduled for service, operating from Sutton (62), Merton (63), Brixton (8), Elmers End (14), Stockwell (55), Croydon (64) and Thornton Heath (45).

Above: In the absence of the traditional Aldenham overhaul, the DMS family had to make do with a smaller-scale refurbishment and repaint, which took less time and saved more money. The result on Merton's DMS 2329 (THX 329S), which underwent the treatment in October 1985, is satisfactory, even though the 'PLEASE PAY AS YOU ENTER' transfers and advertisements are still to be restored. On 15 November 1985 at Clapham Junction it is picking up the original part of the 156, which was otherwise extended from 3 August to commence from Vauxhall. *R. C. Riley*

B20 REPRIEVE 181

CHAPTER SEVEN

DECLINING YEARS

1986

The last day of 1985 saw the Alternative Vehicle Evaluation trials on the 170 officially brought to a close, and while an order for Ls had been placed in the interim without the trials having produced an official 'winner', the eventual moving on of the four experimental classes during the year would see the 170 effectively resume DMS operation and remain that way for another five years.

OPO marched on without pity; on 1 February 1986 the 77 was converted, using DMSs released from Brixton to Stockwell and Merton just in time by the delivery of the last new Ms of the 1985 order; this conversion would have been taken care of earlier had new Ms not had to be diverted to Southall after the fire there which destroyed or damaged over a dozen Ms. Stockwell's reduced band of conductors were given work on the 2B on Saturdays, using as many crew DMSs as RMs; the type had continued to turn out on this route and the 88 for most of the previous year, and DMS 2456 had to migrate to the 88 officially now that the 77 was OPO. The removal to store of DMSs 2420 and 2462 on 6 March meant that Brixton's conversion from DMS to M was complete; or so it looked…

Just making it into 1986 was the very last of the white-top DMSs that had so enlivened the class in its last two years of delivery. FFD work and the accompanying repaint having reduced numbers from thirty in September to just nine by year's end, this honour went to DMS 2486, which had been recertified at the end of 1985 but not repainted until the New Year; it last took the colours to London's streets on 14 January, although the 'white top' persisted on trainers until DMS 2181 was repainted in January 1988. The sizeable band of standard DMS trainers dotted about the fleet were coming due for repaint as well, DMS 1511 out of Sidcup being the first. The completion of the recertification programme was accomplished on 12 March with the output from Clapham of DMS 2305 and on 27 March DMS 2253 and DM 2640 formally brought to a close for the DMS the time-honoured Aldenham overhauling process. Other than contract repaints by BEL at Aldenham, garages would be on their own from here on in, and it was not long into the period of them doing their own heavy maintenance when it was announced in May that Aldenham would be closing altogether in November. Responsibility for the training fleet was already dispersed to the garages on 12 April.

As much of a threat to numbers as one-manning was tendering, which cost Croydon's DMSs the 127 and 127A on 22 March. The loss of this pair to London Country and the simultaneous cession of the 200 to Cityrama

Below: **After two years of eclectic experimentals, the 170 resumed its old identity as an unremarkable Stockwell DMS route during 1986 when the AVE buses gradually transferred away. DMS 2486 (THX 486S) was the last in service with the white-top livery, and in September 1984 is caught approaching Tibbets Corner.** *Geoff Rixon*

Left: **Until it gave in to the temptation to crack the London tendering market, Cityrama had been a stable tour operator. But they found out the hard way that operating DMSs on stop-start stage services in gritty south London was not the same as low-impact sightseeing work with genteel customers aboard. Cityrama had not introduced fleetnumbers by the time of this October 1986 shot, but GHM 836N would soon become known as 36. Ensigns had converted the blind boxes to full-width KM/NN specifications, producing a different 'face' than was familiar.** *Haydn Davies*

provided enough DMSs to commence the weekday conversion of Merton's 155 from RM, which was complete by 10 May (with the crew DMSs wandering to the Merton share of the 49 at weekends). Cityrama was a second new firm to use second-hand DMSs, though its versions were dark blue with a white band (to match those used on commercial sightseeing tours in central London) and had had their blind boxes altered to KM/NN configuration by Ensign, which also added a seat on each deck to render capacity H45/28D. They comprised former DMs 935, 937, 952, 958, 985, 1017, 1773 and 1813 and DMSs 1836 and 1892. No fleetnumbers were carried, and nor did ex-DM 1811 which topped up the allocation in May. On 12 April London Buslines added a second route, the 195, and used both the DMSs from the 81 and six new additions procured from Ensign, ex-DMs 962, 1026, 1036 and 1041 and DMSs 1869 and 1882. Yellow-on-black blinds were now fitted, and capacity was H44/27D. An irritant of the tendering scene applied to both routes in that Cityrama could not turn in Brixton garage and London Buslines could not turn in Hanwell, the 200 and 195 being rerouted to stand at Streatham Hill (Atkins Road) and Hanwell Viaduct respectively.

Below: **Six more DMSs were acquired by London Buslines for their take-up of the 195 on 12 April 1986; joining their usual Park Royal 'DMs' were two MCW-bodied DMSs. The blind boxes are unchanged, though the blinds themselves are yellow on brown. Seen at Charville Lane on the first day, GHV 962N, formerly DM 962, would achieve another seven years with this company, though the 195 would last only a single five-year term there.** *Malc McDonald*

Above: **Brixton's conversion from DMS to M had been completed despite the diversion of several new Ms to cover for the victims of Southall's Christmas Day fire, but only three months passed before DMSs made their comeback, personified by DMS 2253 (OJD 253R), fresh out of overhaul when seen outside its new home on 19 May 1986. Several of Brixton's Ms had gone to Clapham for the 37, and DMSs would eventually prevail altogether at Brixton.** *R. C. Riley*

Right: **The return of the DMS to Brixton from the end of April 1986 obliged the 118 to accept them now; the previous fleet had not had the route on their blinds. DMS 2469 (OJD 469R) was one of the first in, having transferred from Stockwell, and is seen on 27 April at Streatham Hill. The paint is still fresh from its recertification work carried out at Aldenham the previous Christmas in lieu of an overhaul, though the 'PLEASE PAY AS YOU ENTER' signwriting is not yet present. All the DMSs that had been sent away earlier in the year had taken Brixton's D kits with them!** *R. C. Riley*

Another unwelcome facet of the crumbling of unified red-bus operation in the second half of the 1980s was the complete throwing out of the window of any sense of standardisation, order or progressive modernisation. In order to supply Ms for the conversion to doored bus of the 37 at Clapham, DMSs had to be put back into Brixton only six weeks after that garage's conversion to M had seen them off! This commenced on 28 April and restored Fleetline operation to routes 50, 95 and 133 while allowing wanderings to the 118 on a more regular basis now that this one-manned route was included on blinds.

On 24 May Sampsons of Hoddesdon commenced what was to prove a miserable innings on LRT tenders when it took up route 217B, formerly of Enfield. The seven Fleetlines taken by this otherwise coach operator, former DMs 1030, 1119, 1120, 1122, 1762 and 1794 plus DMS 1881 came with KM/NN blind boxes converted by Ensign, and in two blue-based liveries with different proportions of red relief;

Left: **The graffiti writers who surreptitiously scrawled 'The cowboys are coming' on the interior fascia of a London bus travelled on by the author had good cause for concern when they faced Sampson's. This Hoddesdon-based coach operator contributed to the wholesale wiping out of Loughton garage's bus operations on 24 May 1986 when it took up the 217 and 250, and began to falter almost immediately. Perhaps it was just as well that the livery chosen for their six Ensign-acquired ex-DMs and an ex-DMS was strikingly attractive; GHV 122N (ex-DM 1122), seen at Upshire on the first day with its slipboard correctly turned to denote an LRT service (the obverse, for the 250, which had been taken out of the system, displayed the company logo) shows that even clashing colours like blue and red can mesh perfectly when separated by black lining-out. Curiously, Sampson's gave the punter in the Waltham Cross region a choice of two liveries; the second one was also blue, but with a single red band around the lower-deck windows. The black-on-yellow blinds would give the legislators of today a heart attack!**
Malc McDonald

DM 1119 alone had a broad red centre but the rest had two red bands outlined in black. Although the 250 and 250A had been taken out of the LRT theatre with their effective handover to Essex County Council on the same day (the 250A becoming 251), Sampsons won those too with Nationals, but when they used the DMSs, made sure to turn the 'London Regional Transport Service' placard in their front holder to the face reading 'Sampsons' in company colours.

A new night route accrued to DMSs on 21 June when Sutton was given the N54, carved on this night out of the daytime 154 and 157. This date heralded another tendering loss when Ensign stepped up for its first stage contract, the 145 (formerly with Barking Titans) and now provisioned with ex-DMSs in a particularly handsome blue and silver livery with black lining-out and silver Ensignbus fleetnames. This livery had been developed in 1985 and suited the nine chosen down to the ground.

Left: **Virtually all London night routes commenced at Trafalgar Square and probed outwards to the suburbs, but on 24 May 1986 a night option was given to the roads of the daytime 157, 154 and 164 under the number N54. Here at Sutton on 21 May 1987 is Sutton's D 2616 (THX 616S). The route was appended to the N88 a little while later.**
Malc McDonald

DECLINING YEARS 185

Right: **Having made its name first on tours services and then by converting the buses needed for them, it was well worth Ensign combining these two successful forays into a tilt at the London tendering market. The first of what would prove to be many such wins was the 145, taken over on 21 June 1986 with nine ex-DMSs refurbished from their own sales stock, numbers of which, after several years, were beginning to run dry. It goes without saying that the livery is amongst the best applied to any bus; it has certainly brought out the qualities hiding behind the likes of B 211 (GHV 69N), formerly known as DM 1069. Ensigns acknowledged the better parts of London Transport culture, like full blinds and running numbers, but used them more efficiently, and the variety offered by the company's ability to detach examples of the large London Pride sightseeing fleet for stage use provided the unpredictability that appeals to enthusiasts. With a wide blind-box conversion and white-on-blue blinds within, this bus is seen at Dagenham on 23 June. DMS operation by Ensignbus would last five years, and this one, by then known as plain 211 and under the later Capital Citybus fleetname, would be the last in service.**
Malc McDonald

Given an extra seat on each deck to render capacity H45/28D, they were numbered B 209-217 out of the former DMS 1424, DM 1020, 1069, 1074, 1101, 1114, 1118, 1793 and DMS 2000. 'B' denoted buses for stage service, where As were for tour work (including the London Pride fleet) and Cs belonged to Culture Bus, these being two sightseeing operations acquired in 1984 and 1985 respectively. The '2' in the fleetnumber stood for dual doors, with 100s reserved for single-doored versions and 300s for open-toppers. All are mentioned because as sure as dammit, every possible combination would turn up sooner or later on this initial Ensignbus route and all the others they were to win in the next few years! Taking their cue from their increasingly successful tour services, Ensignbus even featured tape-recorded music and local information aboard the 145's rolling stock.

The alteration of the 12A on Sundays into a 12B on 21 June handed it the Chipstead Valley extension of the 59, which fell back to Croydon. Any hope of crew DMSs on the 2 vanished with its one-manning and transfer from Stockwell to Norwood, while the 2B was cut between Baker Street and Golders Green. The OPO conversion of the 37 saw the return of a Stockwell share, on Sundays only and bringing the route its first DMSs.

Right: **The one-manning of the busy suburban 37 on 21 June 1986 brought back Stockwell, albeit as a Sunday allocation only; still, DMSs were new to the route. On 22 June, the first such Sunday, the photographer has managed to capture the author riding DMS 2252 (OJD 252R) eastward through Wandsworth. Within eight months DMSs would become the staple when Stockwell replaced Clapham as the majority eastern garage.**
Malc McDonald

Route 293 left the LBL fold on 19 July with its move to London Country, which also took up the 197 (featuring substantial alterations) on 9 August. Nine of the 293's castoffs gravitated to Croydon to reinforce the DMS fleet there so that the Metrobuses still based could begin converting the 68 to crew M operation in advance of its planned OPO conversion, and the 197's loss accelerated this process. The 16th saw vast changes based on Orpington, bringing us the Roundabout minibus network but also cutting further into LBL's operations. Metrobus of Orpington assumed the 61 as a debut contract, specifying one-time DMSs in a livery of dark blue and yellow and based at Green Street Green. Another company that didn't care for fleetnumbers as we knew them, its acquisitions, known by their registrations, used to be DMSs 1898, 1922, 1960, 1977, 2052, 2054, 2056, 2167, 2173, 2198, 2200, 2211 and 2243 and were also upseated to H45/28D. It didn't trouble Metrobus that there was a mix of engines, the highest-numbered nine being Gardner-engined. As well as this service and new route 361 added at a late stage to cover the southernmost section of the 261, the company's commercial 353, 354 and 357 were also taken into the LRT network on a convoluted 'under agreement' basis rather than full contracts, though due to a height restriction the 354 employed three new Bedfords purchased specially. Very quickly an oddment ensued, DMS 1469 (a.k.a. A 208) in an all-over advert livery for Hitachi coming on loan from Ensignbus's London Pride unit while accident-damaged DMS 1960 was repaired between 17 September and 11 October.

Above: **Crossing the border as it did, the 293 was a target for London Country and distant Dorking took it on 19 July 1986. On the previous 23 March, Sutton's DMS 2399 (OJD 399R) is pictured south of Morden.** *Malc McDonald*

The first tendering scheme to be built around a specific town network covered Orpington from 16 August 1986. Metrobus thus picked up its first contract. Not sporting fleetnumbers (Metrobus did not use them until 1998), OUC 56R, once DMS 2056, is at Bromley North during November. *D.T. Elliott*

Following a rash of increasingly nasty assaults on drivers, LBL instituted a fleetwide programme of assault screen fitment to every OPO bus between May and August 1986. The restriction of designs meant that the remaining AVE buses holding out at Stockwell were stood down on 31 August 1986, returning the 170 and N87 to DMS operation in practice. The balance of Sutton's former participation on the 293 was reallocated to Stockwell to this end. The advanced features on DMSs 2377 and 2456 did not exempt them, but due to their non-standard configuration, fitting a standard DMS screen to their rounded cab fascia was not cost-effective at the moment and they were restricted to crew operation, resuming service on the 88 in September.

As if Stockwell crew DMSs didn't appear unusual enough on the 2B, a Thornton Heath crew-DMS allocation was added on Saturdays from 25 October; this had migrated from the 68, which was one-manned on this extensive route-change day. Croydon's reduced share was predominantly DMSs, all but two of the Ms that had prepared the route decamping to Norwood for the other two-thirds of the total runout; no DMS had worked on the 68 prior to the OPO conversion. To make the numbers add up, the Croydon share of the 157 was transferred to Thornton Heath and the 194, when taken on from the closed Elmers End, demoted to LS operation (in theory at least, if imperfectly fulfilled in practice); the 194A was also assumed but stayed DMS until 7 December. No Croydon DMSs thus needed to move anywhere at all. Another route to lose conductors was the 155 finally, while the 131, which still covered the entirety of this route on Sundays with eight Merton DMSs to three Norbiton Ms, was pruned at both ends, losing its service beyond the Elephant to Aldwych and west of Hampton Court to West Molesey. The DMS-operated Sunday anomaly on the 75 remained thus with its transfer to Croydon, but the major effect of Elmers End's closure (cited bitterly as something that the direct impact of a V-1 bomb was unable to achieve in 1944) was the restocking of Brixton with Elmers End's fifteen DMSs so that Brixton's newest Ms could pass to Willesden for the 52. At night the N87 was bifurcated, a western leg being introduced in the direction of Raynes Park that was at first going to take the number N55.

No DMSs had been deemed fit for all-over ads in their London Transport days, but in October London Buslines' DM 1036 was treated to a yellow-based scheme for Telecom which didn't stand out too much from their usual buses. The takeover of several Essex County Council contracts in Hatfield, Welwyn and Harlow by Sampsons upon D-Day saw the spread of the vehicles acquired to work them, ECW-bodied Fleetlines, onto the 217B, with the DMSs often seen in the opposite direction. Metrobus suffered damage to another of its DMSs during the autumn; pending the repair of DMS 1960 in October, Metrobus took on loan Ensignbus C 224 (DM 1709) and acquired for spare parts DMS 1256, late of Brakell's, The Young Ones and Grange Hill TV fame, from its last berth as a hop-pickers' bus at Hewitt's Farm. Ensign helped out troubled London Buslines in November with the loan of B 217 (DMS 2000), while Sampsons, amid having to take hires from anywhere that could spare buses, treated former DM 930 to an all-over advertisement for the Cheshunt & Waltham Telegraph Gazette.

Studiously ignored by London, which had enough troubles of its own, was D-Day – the deregulation on 26 October of bus services in the rest of the country. This was set to throw bus services into absolute turmoil and change their pattern of ownership entirely. Passengers' resistance to the sundering of their established travel habits translated into mass abandonment of services, resulting into the release onto the open market of numerous second-hand buses, which the cash-poor upstart independents and forcibly-split NBC companies now in the process of being sold off bought in lieu of new buses, thus bringing the British bus manufacturing industry to its knees. Just about all the vast number of DMSs acquired by Ensign had now been sold on, and subsequent allocations of former DMSs to London-area independents would be in ones and twos, or re-acquired and resold by Ensign themselves.

Below: **Of the two garages remaining on the 68 after its one-manning, Norwood was stocked with brand new Olympians with more coming to ease out its indigenous Metrobuses, but Croydon remained wholly DMS with its own Ms leaving altogether, and it was not until the following January that new Ls were delivered to move on Fleetlines like DMS 2375 (OJD 375R), passing through West Croydon on 26 October.** *Malc McDonald*

THE LONDON DMS

Left: **To give work to the conductors made spare at Thornton Heath with the removal of that garage's share of the 68 upon its conversion to OPO on 25 October 1986, the 2B was put in on that day with crew DMSs. Taking its crews further into the West End than the 109 could go (although by now no further north than Baker Street, to which the 2B had been curtailed on 21 June) is DMS 2479 (THX 479S) at Marble Arch during January.** *Haydn Davies*

Below: Indistinguishable from its standard fellows, DMS 2205 (OJD 205R) with its Maxwell gearbox continued in service, leaving its withdrawn contemporaries behind by what turned out to be an incredible six years. Although no further such transmission was ever purchased and the company eventually went out of business, DMS 2205 (restored to original condition when relegated to training duties) was still to live a longer life than most of its type, passing to Big Bus and retiring to Philadelphia. It is seen in Croydon on 17 September 1986. *Malc McDonald*

More wistfully, after its valiant struggles with the DMS that had produced mixed successes by at least managing to overhaul several hundred of them, Aldenham Works closed its doors after operation on 14 November 1986; from now on, a temporarily reprieved Chiswick was to take on much of the more major tasks, though with the same proviso to break even as had doomed Aldenham. The last DMSs to be repainted at Aldenham were DMS 2270 and D 2611, both in October, while the licensing section and training school at Chiswick were closed, these functions passing to the Districts. FFD work was devolved to garages, with the full four-year recertification being carried out at District Test Centres, which for the DMS-operating garages meant Croydon at Wandle; pending the reopening in February 1987 of Streatham, which was slated to assume this role, excess space at Norwood was used. Abbey District, which counted Stockwell alone among its DMS garages, sent its vehicles to Ash Grove, but Abbey was soon to be removed from the roster of Districts anyway. In the absence of Aldenham, LBL had to cast about for repaint contracts, and in December DMS 2467 was sent to Gatwick Engineering as a pilot for such work. At Chiswick, BEL's sole DMS 2177 was used as the guinea pig to test the quality of the much-truncated works' new paint line, while a spot of outside work was garnered through the repair of London Buslines' accident-damaged DM 1078. Unfortunately, since the machinery at the relocated blind shop following the closure of Aldenham was not yet operational, printing had to be subcontracted to Norbury Brothers, which did not have the Johnson typeface and substituted one of no particular resemblance that proliferated on all London buses over the next year. However, reflecting a year of uncommon stability for the DMS in London as a whole, LBL's tally for 1986 was down by just one unit (parts donor DMS 2080), the total owned being 489. Of these, 78 were licensed trainers.

DECLINING YEARS 189

1987

The first change of 1987 fell in Ensignbus's favour; that company's win of the 62 introduced more DMSs from the depleting stocks still standing available in the yard at Purfleet. These were B 248-254 (ex-DM 1133, 1059, 1166, 1154, 1048, 1170 and 964), while four all-over advert DMSs were made available for stage service and took numbers in the B series, comprising B 203 (ex-DMS 1444 with ColorBus scheme for the London Dungeon), B 219 (ex-DMS 353 for the Trocadero), B 221 (ex-DMS 1469 for Hitachi) and B 224 (ex-DM 1709) and soon appeared on both this route and the 145.

From 29 January Croydon started taking Ls in strength as the last of the only order for Leyland Olympians poured in, ejecting the last two Ms but also 37 of the DMSs. The new Ls, 40 of them in number, could now be seen on the 68, 130, 130B, 190 and 194, though the latter was fitfully trying to remain LS-operated. On 7 February the closure of the temporary Clapham garage and the return of its staff to a reopened Streatham caused the 37 to be reallocated to Stockwell, rendering DMSs the predominant type alongside Hounslow's Ms; Stockwell abandoned the 77 to furnish this end but still took 13 DMSs spare from Croydon, while Merton took fourteen for its now sole runout on the 77. Streatham also gained the 50 and 118

Right: **Forever famous for fielding the last RTs to operate for London Transport, the 62 was not so sainted as to avoid the likelihood of tendering, and it was taken over by Ensignbus on 17 January 1987. Seven more DMSs were converted from sales stock and four all-over advertisement buses were made available; here at Upney on 28 February is the former DM 1059, B 249 (GHV 59N). It was renumbered B 229 that July but would not last the year out.** *Malc McDonald*

Right: **The 109 was one-manned on 7 February 1987, but the difficulty of perceiving this extremely busy trunk service as an OPO operation was ameliorated by taking the Blackfriars leg and transferring it to the 59 with the Brixton allocation; the 109 was additionally diverted away from the Embankment to stand at Trafalgar Square. During the summer of 1987 DMS 2512 (THX 512S) forms the meat in a B20 DMS sandwich outside Brixton garage, with fellow Thornton Heath bus D 2566 (THX 566S) on the 59 giving it a hand.** *David Wilkinson collection*

190   THE LONDON DMS

Left: 1987 was surely the year in which the drive to cut costs in 'London Transport' reached epic proportions, and the economy scythe now started ripping through the Sunday roster of crew routes. The closure of Clapham garage split the 137 between Brixton and the new Streatham; DMSs featured on the former's OPO allocation on Sundays alongside Ls from Streatham and its own dwindling number of Ms. Reposing at Crystal Palace in August is DMS 2260 (OJD 260R). *Haydn Davies*

from Brixton, removing the likelihood of DMS operation in favour of Ls throughout. The 109 was one-manned with Thornton Heath DMSs increased in number by 23 by further Croydon cast-offs, the Brixton allocation migrating to an extension of the 59 to Farringdon Street; with the laying off of Thornton Heath's last conductors, the short-lived DMS era on the 2B from that garage on Sundays came to an end. A new cost-saving gimmick was Sunday OPO conversion, which brought Stockwell DMSs onto the 88 and Brixton DMSs to the 137. Thornton Heath now had the largest number of DMSs in service.

The 166 at Croydon was downgraded to LS (again, like the 194 never quite discounting DMS appearances), while the 196 became another Cityrama route, using both the 200's DMSs and a handful of ex-South Yorkshire Fleetlines with ungainly ECW bodywork. At this point Cityrama introduced two-figure fleetnumbers, matching where possible the last two digits of their vehicles' registration numbers other than DM 1811, which had to become 81. Another DMS, numbered 8 (ex-DMS 863) was drafted into the stage fleet from the touring operation, its blind boxes restored, and painted in a new livery of two shades of blue; lighter around the upper deck and darker around the lower deck so that the midriff, when added in a base red colour, could accommodate advertising for holidays to Italy (offside) and the Caribbean (nearside), both on behalf of Pegasus Holidays.

Below: Stepping in after a late withdrawal by London Country South East, Cityrama assumed the 196 on 7 February 1987 as its second route. It added to the fleet nine ECW-bodied Fleetlines ex-South Yorkshire PTE and two DMS lookalikes new to the same concern, but the former DMSs belonging to the 200 soon pitched in. It was at this point that the fleet gained two-figure fleetnumbers, matching where possible the last two digits of their registration; accordingly former SYPTE 1522, seen heading north in August 1987, has become 22 (OKW 522R). *Haydn Davies*

Below: **Keeping busy during their delivery of a third of the B20 DMS order to London Transport, MCW had bodied 29 Daimler Fleetlines for South Yorkshire PTE using the DMS design! As with all PTEs, SYPTE had been battered by deregulation and by 1987 these were among very large numbers of fairly youthful second-hand buses for sale. Grey-Green were yet another company to fancy its chances in the swirling London market, and unlike most others, made a success of it. Ten DMS lookalikes qualify for this account by joining the fleet, albeit belying the company name with an orange, white and brown livery and a suitably corny fleetname, Eastenderbus, to salute the recently-introduced soap of increasing popularity. OKW 503R and OKW 525R find themselves together at East Beckton on 28 February, the first day, though both are going in different directions. Two more of them found their way to Cityrama at the same time.** *Malc McDonald*

On 27 March Ensignbus suggested making use of its DMSs running dead onto and off the 62 from Purfleet by operating them in service as a night route N99 following the 248 between Cranham and Romford on Friday and Saturday nights.

The final four Olympians, Ls 260-263, were coach-seated and displaced the ex-WMPTE Ts from the 177E at Plumstead, which in turn were dispatched to Camberwell to release the private-hire DMs for service (as Ds) during March; D 2643 lost its coach seats. Social problems in 1987, in addition to the need for anti-vandal plastic seats of the kind fitted to the rear upstairs in Stockwell's DMS 2313, had introduced graffiti of the New York MTA subway-car style; somehow, it was hardly as evocative on London's buses and attempts were made to control its furtive artists with video cameras fitted experimentally (and expensively) to a handful of London buses. Passengers were in some parts of town almost more likely to find DMSs covered in tags than displaying side blinds, which were variously plated over at Thornton Heath or painted over in red or black at Merton and Croydon. Routine repaints that could not be accommodated at garages were now subject to contracting-out, Gatwick Engineering painting three DMSs in February 1987 sufficient to win a major contract to do the rest. One such was DMS 2334, put back into service at Sutton after three years following an accident.

However, while the transfer of the 173 on 28 February to Eastenderbus, a novelty-named bus-operating offshoot of the Grey-Green coaching company, also brought DMSs back, these were not ex-London Transport but examples from the batch of lookalikes supplied to South Yorkshire PTE in 1977 and bought in its entirety by Ensign for dispersal. In an orange, white and brown livery belying Grey-Green's identity were as-yet-unnumbered OKW 501-503, 506, 519, 523, 525-528R. Two more of them, OKW 522R and SHE 507S, joined Cityrama with the 196's acquisition, numbered 22 and 7 respectively and in the new livery, which had been joined earlier by a white fleetname with red shadowing. Despite their usefulness in the short term, the DMSs and similar second-hand castoffs were jeopardising the very existence of Britain's bus-manufacturing industry; from 26 May six Leyland Lynxes joined the ex-DMSs on London Buslines' route 81, but otherwise very little new product was taking to the streets. London Buslines was learning the hard way that the reputation of the DMS wasn't just a popular myth; over the hard winter of 1986/87 the company was plagued so much by unreliability problems with its DMSs that it had to take on loan similar vehicles from Ensignbus between 2 March and May, including all-over advert DMSs, B20 (albeit latterly Gardner-powered) DMS 2407 and even Culture Bus examples before Ensign sold that latter operation on 1 April. As the roving DoT inspectors slapped PG9s on other wayward DMSs they found during the year, Sampsons were faring even worse, its Harlow tenders being taken away and, as part of myriad hires of coaches and buses, DMS 2216 from Davian (a card in the windscreen sufficing due to the lack of blind boxes on this bus) and even privately-owned DM 1023 in red livery and DM 1003 in white filled in on the 217B. Both Essex County Council and LRT took note of the problems and in June the 217B was one of the routes to be re-tendered early; incredibly, Sampsons won it back! London Buslines' risk taken in purchasing the new Lynxes was rewarded by LRT with a three-year extension added to the 81's contract term.

Serious industrial difficulty characterised the spring of 1987 as staff began to actively resist the new culture of reduced pay for increased work. As the centre continued to unravel and costs had to be pruned without regard to employees' considerations, so was ramped up the new wheeze of tendering by town-based networks. In April 1987 Norbiton won the majority share in such a scheme for implementation in the summer, but by the extraordinary method of taking 35 standard DMSs from the training fleet and refurbishing them for service in replacement of a like number of its nearly-new Metrobuses, thus copying the cheapest aspects of the 'cowboys' that were eating into LT's flanks with such apparent ease. As write-down costs had to be included in tenders, it gave bidders a competitive edge by gathering fully-depreciated buses in the specifically low-cost units to match the reduced wages paid to staff, again in the interests of outbidding the independents with their lower or non-existent overheads. All the reasons given for the DMSs' discarding in the first place were thus forgotten, and as soon as the contracts were confirmed, the vehicles selected for Norbiton started being delicensed from their training duties and sent to Stamford Brook for examination. Despite the first of several stoppages on 11 May, this was the likely course of policy and one which was sure to continue given the General Election result of 11 June, which returned the Conservative administration for a third term.

On 23 May the N54 was withdrawn, taking its Sutton DMSs to an extension of the N88. The N78, meanwhile, was projected from Croydon to New Addington, bringing the estate its first night buses. A supplementary leg under the same number was introduced to go via Streatham Vale. The introduction of the three Hs at Brixton at the end of May allowed three DMSs to leave for Stockwell. By the spring the 166 and 194 were mostly DMS, though from 6 June the former was formally split as five DMSs and four LSs. Crew DMSs from Brixton, meanwhile, were popping up on the 137 during weekdays.

June saw Ensignbus's fleet submit to renumbering, where the stage buses took blocks from B 209-219 (DMS 1424, DM 1020, 1069, 1074, 1101, 1114, 1118, 1793, DMS 2000, DM 1738, DMS 1469), B 222-230 (DM 1092, 1043, 1709, 964, 1166, 1154, 1048, 1059, 1170) and B 233 (DM 1133). A new all-purpose code of G was introduced to denote general purpose (Trocadero-branded DMS 353 becoming G 221), with an attempt to match the last digit of registration numbers where feasible. It wouldn't be the last time, either, as within a year the B codes had withered away.

Above: **Ensignbus B 217 (KJD 500P), formerly DMS 2000, works the new N99 onto or off a 62 when seen at Romford on 24 May 1987.** *Malc McDonald*

Below: **Large swathes of outer London remained to be served at night. On 24/25 October Raynes Park received its first night buses via a bifurcation of the N87; at Stockwell on 2 June 1987 is DMS 2419 (THX 419S). Further extensions were subsequently implemented.** *Malc McDonald*

DECLINING YEARS 193

With effect from 27 June, very slowly, Norbiton's intake of refurbished DMSs began taking over the 71, 85 and 213 in accordance with the new three-year contract terms (the 131 was lost to London Country South West on that day). The 65 was off-limits for the moment, due to the slightly higher height of the DMSs by comparison with the Ms they replaced meaning that they could not enter Kingston garage (reopened for Westlink minibus operations), although the fact that examples did manage to achieve this without damage meant increased appearances on the 65 on an official basis from 5 November, by which time all the DMSs used were in place. The Fleetlines, all Leyland-engined examples still owned by LBL and taken off training duties from April onwards, were treated to a rudimentary internal cleanup and service plus a repaint. The work was done by three separate concerns; Ensign's contribution comprised DMSs 711, 719, 1426, 1477, 1488, 1500, 1511, 1537, 1626, 1859, 1867 and 1900, of which all were painted by Kent Engineering save for DMS 1859, which was done at Chiswick, and were recognisable by the varied position of their roundels and unfamiliar characters on the numberplates on some of them. Bus Engineering Ltd (BEL) at Chiswick did DMSs 678, 717, 1447, 1473, 1837, 1873, 1889, 1901, 1904, 1950 and 2103 plus D 1804, with DMS 678 repainted at Kent Engineering, and Leyland at Nottingham treated DMSs 714, 819, 1852, 1862, 1884, 1890, 1936, 1990, 1993, 2006 and 2008. Those done at Chiswick were fitted with top-deck seats taken from withdrawn RMs, which took the DMSs' place as trainers. All AFC cabinets were removed and replaced by luggage pens and the buses re-entered service without adverts, DMS 2006 managing to dodge a repaint as well!

This page: Second-hand DMSs were perhaps all you could expect from these upstart new independents, but London Transport? The joke was over when during 1987 LBL took 35 ageing DMSs off the training work they had been employed upon for up to five or six years and readied them for service. Norbiton's treatment to the whole-town tendering network process was to prove fraught in the extreme, most of its existing staff not appreciating having to work for longer hours at less pay driving vehicles that had been condemned as unsuitable years ago! But, it seemed, it was that or disintegrate altogether at the hands of cheapjack outfits. Thus did the 71, 85 and 213 lose their nearly-new Ms for DMSs, commencing on 27 June 1987. Leyland at Nottingham prepared DMS 1990 (KUC 990P) (top, seen in July 1987, *Geoff Rixon*) **and DMS 1862 (GHM 862N) (middle, in Norbiton garage on 28 August,** *John Laker*), **but Ensign's contribution is given away by the non-standard numberplate typeface used to freshen up DMS 1477 (MLH 477L) (bottom, in Surbiton in July,** *Geoff Rixon*)

Left: **DMSs had appeared in crew mode on the Merton allocation of the 49 in recent years, but upon its OPO conversion on 11 July 1987 the route was reshuffled so that Streatham and Shepherd's Bush shared the Monday to Saturday roster and Merton had its entirety on Sundays. Thus did Fleetlines form that day of the week's staple, and on one such Sunday in April 1988 DMS 2440 (OJD 440R) passes a fairground set up on Tooting Bec Common.**
Malc McDonald

To standardise Norbiton under what was legally known as Kingston Buses Ltd with the 27 June programme, Sutton withdrew from the 213 and Putney from the 85; Norbiton's drivers themselves were scrambling to be transferred elsewhere after a very short time, given the lowered pay scales and increased hours now felt acceptable, and especially after the verdict of a case brought by the TGWU against LBL determined on 15 July that the new conditions, while stark, were not against the law. Repeated strikes thereafter placed in doubt the very future of Norbiton, LBL at one point deciding to surrender the garage's contracts altogether until a pay agreement was thrashed out by 21 September, but did force second thoughts on the area-based variety of tendering, at least with the straitened pay conditions. The concurrent award to LBL of the bulk of one more such scheme based on the Bexleyheath area, however, would affect London's DMS fleet in a most unexpected way when it was implemented, because not only would the very last of the LBL-owned stored DMSs be brought back into service *a la* Norbiton, but long-sold members of the class, incredibly, were going to be *bought back*!

The closure of Wandsworth garage on 11 July indirectly brought the DMS family more work; the 44 was transferred to Merton and the N68 and N88 at night passed to Sutton, which also took the 44 on Sundays (replacing Stockwell's share on that day), getting there via an extension from Mitcham over the 280. The 77 was withdrawn between Tooting and Streatham, while also at Merton the 156 was divided, passing on weekdays to Stockwell and losing its Raynes Park-Morden section so that new route 163 (LS-operated for now but with the odd DMS) could step in. The 49, otherwise the province of Shepherd's Bush Ms and Streatham Ms and Ls upon its one-manning, was transferred entirely to Merton on Sundays with DMSs. The 189, meanwhile, clinging on to life, was reallocated from Merton to Stockwell (being officially upgraded from LS to DMS after a spell of regular appearances by the double-deckers) and gained garage journeys in that direction from Brixton Station. In the absence of new buses and the sluggish pace that it was taking to get the revived DMSs into service at Norbiton, LSs from store had to be reactivated here to allow enough Ms to leave for Brixton, which could then supply Stockwell with nine DMSs and Merton four. In this part of town in particular, the presence of DMSs, Ms and Ls were never in sufficient quantities to permit one type to prevail over the other at the garages that now mixed them, and proportions of each would fluctuate as requirements were changed and changed again in the next half-decade. At this point in time, therefore, there were fewer DMSs at Brixton than there were Ms, and fewer DMSs at Croydon than Ls. Stockwell, fielding 89 DMSs, was now in the lead, with Thornton Heath and Merton 86 each.

Abbey District was removed on 14 August; no DMS-operating garages were affected this time, and in any case administrative functions were being further devolved to the garage level, with still further structural changes imminent. After a couple of years of unprecedented stability with comparatively few transfers and almost no sales, the remaining hard core of B20

DECLINING YEARS

DMSs could now belatedly count themselves accepted and useful members of the LBL fleet with still more that could be got out of them. In July DMS 2281 of Croydon was fitted with an Iveco 836.S11 engine rated at 175bhp at 2100rpm, the three-month trial proving so successful that 99 more were ordered. DMSs 2377 and 2456 continued in service with their experimental features as Stockwell crew buses on the 88, while Thornton Heath's DMS 2405 was treated after its repaint in July to a dot-matrix rear number blind, which operated perfectly until the bus needed to be used on the 194B, in which case '194' and 'B' would show for successive three-second periods.

For DMSs and LBL buses in general a new 'London Buses' roundel with a yellow bar was coming slowly into use from the summer of 1987 onwards, but where Leaside District was concerned, its most attractive livery of thick white band and black skirt appearing on Ms spread in July to its first DMS trainer, DMS 692, with several more coming in 1987. If a full repaint was not warranted, the band and skirt were applied locally. A large number of DMS repaints were undertaken by Gatwick Engineering on contract throughout the year, but garages were also repainting their own buses again by mid-year now that BEL had been offered for sale. As the year progressed, the long-lived Almex E driver ticket machines were replaced, garage by garage, with new Wayfarer units that printed a rectangular ticket with a sawtooth cut. These had been standard on tendered routes with independents since they first started, but were reliable enough to spread to standard LBL OPO buses. Stockwell and Merton were the last DMS-operating garages to use Almex Es.

A new tendered operator to the DMS emerged by a roundabout method when Ensignbus's A 104 (formerly DMS 1941) was loaned in the first days of July to Scancoaches, another small contractor, whose unusual Jonckheere-bodied Scania K92 single-deckers on the 283 were in need of assistance. It did not help that another of the DMSs hired, B 219 (ex-DMS 1469), was driven under the low bridge at Old Oak Common Lane in late July on the way back from the 283's East Acton terminus to the Harlesden base! Meanwhile London Buslines, which thought it could breathe a sigh of relief now that its similarly struggling DMSs were backed up by new Lynxes, lost three of them in a fire at its Southall premises on 28 July; DMs 928, 1019 and 1026 were destroyed while DMs 962 and 1078 were damaged and Telecom all-over ad-based DM 1036 was dismantled to repair them. Ensignbus loans to London Buslines during the spring included former DMSs 325, 589 and 1476 plus ex-DM 1043, and on its own turf sold B 209 (ex-DMS 1424) and G 220 (ex-DMS 1444) in July and replaced them with G 109 (ex-DMS 2219), from McMenemy, one of the A1 co-operative's participating companies, to whom they'd sold it in the first place). This bus would be subject to some most interesting experiments with its blinds in the years to come.

Below: **The N88 had already absorbed the N54 and with the closure of Wandsworth on 11 July 1987, passed entirely to Sutton with DMSs. On the night of 1/2 December 1987 at Whitehall, DMS 2518 (THX 518S) shows off the unusual ultimate blind that reflected the fact that 'KK' intermediate blind boxes weren't big enough to accommodate the number of via points needed on routes as long as this.** *Malc McDonald*

Right: Sampson's struggled desperately to maintain both their own 217B and a handful of Essex contracts won since. In fact the DMSs from the former had to be seconded repeatedly for use on these tenders and hires taken, whose three-track blind boxes could not display the suffix. In spite of this, the 217B was retained by the company under a new number, 317, shown in November 1987 on *Cheshunt & Waltham Telegraph*-promoting former DM 930 (SMU 930N), by an amendment to the blinds. *Haydn Davies*

And on 7 July outside the dead Bexleyheath garage, LBL officially launched what it called Bexleybus. In spite of the industrial-relations difficulties exacerbated by the provision of Norbiton's disgruntled staff with superannuated vehicles, LBL considered that the cost savings justified the means. This time it was seemingly determined to out-cowboy the cowboys by creating an entirely new identity which could not possibly be associated by the long-suffering public with staid old state-owned London Buses Ltd. Bexleybus was going to be different even down to the livery, a smart blue and cream recalling that of Eastbourne Borough Transport, probably because that was who applied it to DMS 2166, one of the last of the LBL-owned standard Fleetlines stored until earlier this year at AEC before being towed to Ensign for rebuilding to PSV condition. Two facets of Bexleybus struck observers as incredible – firstly, the planned reopening of a recently-closed garage (Bexleyheath) to replace a modern, expensively-rebuilt premises (Sidcup), and secondly, not only the recommissioning of these several derelict DMSs, but the repurchase of 14 DMSs from Clydeside Scottish, which had operated them in a modified single-door format that was decidedly non-standard; not that such considerations mattered in the savings-obsessed era of the day. Making up the double-deck complement at Bexleybus would be a batch of new Leyland Olympians unwanted by deregulation-hammered GM Buses but still finished to their specifications.

On 16 August Sampsons' 217B was renumbered 317, confusion having been caused to passengers by the inability of Sampsons' hired vehicles to display the former suffix correctly or at all. On the 22nd a scheme was implemented in the Croydon area which withdrew the 130B and transferred its resources (and Addington-area roads) to the 130 (minus the Sunday extension north, which became a Sunday service on the 60). The express legs of both were combined into new route X30 with a similar remit. The 64 was diverted at West Croydon to Thornton Heath Garage, new route 264 (Merton DMSs on weekdays and Croydon DMSs and Ls on Sundays) taking over the Tooting leg. Merton thus pulled out of the 157, giving its duties to Croydon.

Above: To counteract its extension deeper into the New Addington estate, the 64 was taken out of its run along the Mitcham Road into Tooting on 22 August 1987 and rerouted to Thornton Heath. DMS 2479 (THX 479S) is at Croydon on 29 May. *Malc McDonald*

Below: The express runs on the 130 and 130B were consolidated under the number X30. Though suited for the new Ls that had appeared in strength at Croydon at the turn of the year, the X30 also saw DMSs, as proven in August by D 2560 (THX 560S). *Haydn Davies*

Right: Surrey County Council played its part in the deregulation-inspired revamping of route networks across the country, and 31 October 1987 saw a handful of Sunday contracts knocking at Greater London's periphery awarded to LBL with Sutton DMSs. This was some small payback for what five years previously used to be proper London Transport routes sold away cheaply; on 8 May 1988 DMS 2394 (OJD 394R) with the new roundel is operating the 522, which on weekdays was known as 422 and which prior to 1982 used to be part of the 164. *Haydn Davies*

Below: On 14 November 1987 Ensignbus took resources from the 62 to give it a new partner known as 62A, which diverted from the south at Chadwell Heath to provide a service to King George's Hospital. Its DMSs like B 216 (GHM 793N), seen at Little Heath on the first day, were the staple, and like all their fleet, was beautifully turned out. *Malc McDonald*

The deregulation of buses outside London did not necessarily mean large operators being assaulted by cheap new upstarts; from time to time the 'arm's length' concerns themselves could gamble on commercial routes, and from 31 October Sutton did just this, its DMSs taking up morning and evening journeys on Surrey County Council routes 508, 520 and 522 (themselves descended from the London Country services that had expelled Sutton's own DMS services from the affected areas six years earlier!) plus a Sunday route 508 in the direction of Epsom. That night a single journey on the N68 was back-projected to start at Banstead, bringing night buses to that area.

14 November 1987 was Harrow Buses day, the second-hand buses for this unit being ex-WMPTE Volvo Ailsas and ex-GM Buses Fleetlines (the latest sales stock at Ensign's, given the plunge in ridership post-deregulation in Manchester), but on the other side of town Ensignbus introduced a 62A, which split off from its parent halfway through to run to Little Heath. A spot of autumn chopping and changing at this firm took out Bs 214, 228 and 229 and added B 232 (ex-DM 1142) plus a replacement B 214 (ex-DMS 2204) and B 229 (ex-DM 1079). On the 21st London Buslines took over the 79 (formerly 79A), though its DMSs now had to share their Southall premises with ex-GM Buses Fleetlines which phased in a simplified livery of yellow with just a brown skirt omitting the secondary brown relief; this spread in turn to the DMSs beginning with 1083 and 1882. Metrobus, on the other hand, upped the ante a little by specifying for the 261 eleven ex-West Yorkshire Olympians, only four years old but also made redundant by deregulation-related reverses; naturally, the DMSs already in place for the 61 could be counted on to make appearances, especially on Sundays where there weren't enough Olympians. At Grey-Green, the acquisition of the 125 and ex-GM Buses Fleetlines for it prompted the numbering of the existing 'DMSs' into a 500+ series to match their registrations. Two other routes were acquired, the 179 and 379, on which the former could admit DMSs. Norbiton was not without its own problems, it taking till October to get all of them into place. DMS 1904 was the last into service, while DMSs 1426 and 2103 had already required new engines.

THE LONDON DMS

Left: The 155 had finally succumbed to OPO on 25 October 1986, and a year later was involved in the partial one-manning of two more busy routes penetrating central London. To furnish the resulting 219 on 21 November 1987 (see below), Merton withdrew from the 155 in favour of Stockwell, who had lost several duties on the 88 upon its pulling back to Tooting. Before then, however, D 2583 (THX 583S), misidentified as a DM, wearing an ultimate blind with the increasingly prevalent non-Johnston characters and finally, missing its foglights altogether, calls at Balham on 2 November. *Malc McDonald*

The 137 was withdrawn between Oxford Circus and Archway on 14 November, Brixton's DMSs (and small remnant of Ms, plus three Hs) having held sole responsibility of the Sunday service since earlier in the year. Stockwell was given a Monday to Friday share of the 155, which additionally lost its daytime projections across the river to Aldwych; this was so that Merton drivers and their DMSs could be freed to implement a partial OPO conversion of Routemaster-operated 19 and 88 as new route 219 (Sloane Square-Mitcham). Among the intake into Stockwell, eventually, were DMSs 2396, 2410 and 2505, famous as the last DMSs at Catford but amazingly not to have worked since, having eked out the succeeding four and a half years as trainers. Spare parts were now available to refit long-disused standards for training work to replace them, which included erstwhile radio trainer DMS 1967.

Left: Having brought OPO to all but the most heavily-worked of crew routes in 1987, LBL changed its tack by cutting in half those that could not be one-manned, having to weigh this against passengers' need to travel into town from further afield. On 21 November the 19 and 88 lost their outer ends, which combined to form new Merton DMS-operated route 219. Here at Tooting Broadway on 15 October 1988 is Merton's DMS 2262 (OJD 262R). *Malc McDonald*

DECLINING YEARS

Big things were coming for DMSs in Wandle; as well as the Sutton area network being offered to tender at the end of the year, three more Croydon examples were fitted with Iveco engines. A deal had been struck with this truck manufacturer to supply and fit 100 units, an Iveco agent based off Lewisham Way in New Cross fitting the engines at a rate of one a day, first to Croydon's reduced allocation of 23 DMSs between November 1987 and January 1988 and then tackling Sutton's large fleet by mid-April. The resulting sound was quieter but stronger, a boom versus the Leyland O.680's whine, and the difference it made to performance was nothing short of spectacular; in fact, the engines were almost too powerful now for the buses! The conversions were referred to internally with 5DM6 engineering codes, probably the last amendment to the rapidly fading LT coding system where DMSs were concerned. A modification that marked out Iveco conversions to the observer was the cutting of an air-intake grille in the nearside lower side panel, replacing the function of the nearside chimney which was otherwise 'capped' with a solid panel only lightly perforated; not all received the latter accoutrement by any means. This theoretically bought five more years for the buses and released enough spare parts to keep the rest going now that Leyland was no longer producing spares for the B20. This was as long as the passengers didn't keep insisting on vandalising the buses provided for them – during 1987 twenty-one Thornton Heath DMSs were fitted with plastic seat backs upstairs, which perhaps forestalled graffiti but not treatment with knives! DMS 2205, though not the lone standard in service any more, went to Chiswick in September for fitting with an improved model of Maxwell gearbox and resumed service in December, though it would become the only non-Iveco at Croydon and thus even more non-standard than it was already!

At the tail end of 1987, for all the moves made towards sectionalisation of business units and then of operating areas under tender, LBL developed a corporate livery that, while weak in impact beside some of the outlandish affairs being dreamed up in the deregulation-mad provinces, made that little bit of difference from the dull all-red that represented the cheapest option every time. It was red with a grey painted skirt and 2in-thick white cantrail band applied with tape to save on white paint. To supersede both red and the Leaside livery, this 'tapegrey' scheme, in conjunction with the new roundel, spread rapidly, the first DMS to wear it being Stockwell's DMS 2380 in December. Having been painted already by Gatwick Engineering, it made the short trip to Clapham to have the finishing touches applied.

To allow Sutton to close for the day on Boxing Day 1987, the 93 and 164 were operated with Merton DMSs driven by Sutton drivers; the buses carried old RM side blinds in the via boxes.

Amazingly, DMS numbers increased in 1987; despite further sales, the acquisition of the ex-Clydeside DMSs for Bexleybus pushed numbers up by five to 494, of which 365 were DMSs, four were DMs and 125 Ds. Of these, 386 were scheduled for service.

Below: If there was to be any chance of the British bus industry surviving, operators had to start buying new again, even when it conflicted with the entire cost-cutting ethos of tendering. Grey-Green proved it had the wherewithal to succeed in the long term through its investment in six new Leyland Lynxes to operate the 179 and 379 from 14 November 1987, though they were backed up by ex-GM Buses Fleetlines and the existing ex-SYPTE DMS clones like 503 (OKW 503R) at South Woodford on 9 April 1988. *Malc McDonald*

1988

For all the troubles it would subsequently endure, Bexleybus at least had its entire fleet of 107 buses in place in good time for the start of operations on 16 January 1988. Even the fleetnumbering system was deliberately designed to move away from LT practice, all taking numeric fleetnumbers from 1 to 107. Of the DMSs, the ex-Clydeside examples (MCW-bodied DMSs 1492, 1580, 1610, 1649, 1656, 1657, 1669-1671, 1679, 1683, 1686, 1687 and 2021) occupied the numbers 77-90, followed by the existing Park Royal-bodied LBL DMSs 2063, 2064, 2068, 2074, 2108-2110, 2112, 2118 and 2121, DMs (or Ds) 1146, 1160 and 1195 and DMSs 2125, 2143, 2156 and 2166 as 91-107. The last numbered continued to wear plain '2166', as this was what it had been adorned with for the launch. While the single-door Clydeside examples (with a capacity of H44/32F other than DMS 2021 which was H44/29F) retained some LT features like their white-on-black

Above: The last act of the resuscitation of the DMS family for a London tendered operation proved even more extreme than refurbishing trainers – this time, not only were several virtually derelict examples still owned by LBL put back together by Ensigns, but a dozen were bought back! Perhaps the only bright spot in the notorious and ultimately cautionary saga of Bexleybus was the handsome livery, an attempt to make the poor punters forget that it was really LBL all along. Here is dual-doored DMS 2108 (KJD 108P), also known as 95 and seen on an ex-Kentish Bus route at Woolwich in April 1988. *Haydn Davies*

Left: The Clydeside buybacks had been nativised during their spell in Scotland, the centre doors having been taken out and the characteristic triangular blind box installed. This was modified to take KM/NN panels, but it was not worried about too much that there were now three distinct specifications of Bexleybus double-decker. Curiously, the ex-Clydeside DMSs, personified in April 1988 by DMS 1649 or plain 80 (THM 649M), retained their white-on-black numberplates. *Haydn Davies*

DECLINING YEARS
201

Right: **There were minor differences of fleetname placement between the ex-Clydeside and the LT-derived DMSs, as shown on 4 June at Woolwich by Bexleyheath's DMS 1580 or 78 (THM 580M), which unusually for an ex-Clydeside bus, is sporting a white numberplate. The 272 was one of the routes transferred from Plumstead, which filled its massive losses by taking the majority of the 53 as an OPO route.** *Malc McDonald*

Right: **DMS 2109 (KJD 109P) was also known as 96 and on 18 January 1988 is at Woolwich taking on passengers. After Bexleybus this DMS would have an unlikely second wind, as depicted on page 221.** *Malc McDonald*

Right: **No rear route number is evident on DMS 1492 or 77 (MLH 492L), even though providing one had been a mandatory component of any tender since its inauguration. The box has just been painted over in this case and could be easily restored, but for now the passenger aiming to board at this Bexleyheath stand would have to walk to the front of it to discover that it's actually on the 99.** *Andrew Jeffreys*

Left: The white-top livery that had cheered up the DMS so successfully made its final bow with the repaint in August 1988 of DMS 2181 (OJD 181R), the last straggler to carry it. Associated for all but the first year of its service career with Catford and for the majority of that garage thereafter as a trainer, the bus is caught on a bleak 15 January 1988. *Andrew Jeffreys*

numberplates, their Scottish Bus Group-style triangular-shaped blind boxes had to be replaced by a one-piece unit which, masked off, just about fit a pair of KM and NN blinds; the side and rear boxes had been painted over upon sale and did not return. On 81 and 86 (DMSs 1656 and 1679) the trafficator 'ears' had also gone, replaced in Scotland by BMAC 757 units mounted next to the sidelights, the shallow end pointing upwards, while 92 (DMS 1657) had BMAC 344 units more familiar to Ms and Ts. Clydeside's contribution, for which RMs were taken in part-exchange, reintroduced the Gardner engine to LBL service.

The LBL DMSs, all Leyland-engined Park Royal-bodied examples, also had KM/NN blind boxes but were fitted with reflective numberplates. Having languished outside at AEC's former site for so long, some of them were on the way to being reclaimed by nature, with grass growing out of them, and had to be strengthened where they stood before they could be safely towed out of the mud to be properly completed at Ensign! The positioning of their Bexleybus fleetnames was between decks where the ex-Clydesides, painted and vinylled by that concern before coming down to the capital for mechanical attention at Ensign, carried theirs below the blue midriff on each side. All Bexleybus vehicles, and indeed all buses operating in a wide swathe of south-east London, had Autocheck equipment fitted, yet another new innovation in fare-collection in operation in the affected area since 22 March 1987, by which magnetically-encoded passes could be validated in a choice of two readers at either side of the 'throat' between the front wheelarches. 'This is an AUTOCHECK bus' posters were applied either side of the blind box and on a single-line sticker above the entrance door, just to ram the point home; this reduced the capacity of the LBL reclamations from an already increased H45/28D to H45/27D. DMSs 2100 and 2158 were two that could not be reconstituted and their parts, including seats, went into refitting their siblings before the shells were scrapped.

Thus returning to DMS operation on 16 January 1988 as Bexleybus cranked into action were routes 96 and 99, joined by routes 178 and 272 all ex-Plumstead and new routes 401 and 469 created out of the knot of former Kentish Bus routes stranded in red bus territory. All but the last two had been the province of nearly-new Ls or only slightly older Titans, and all were immediately in trouble as the overoptimistic schedules combined with a shortage of drivers to create large gaps in service and overcrowding on the buses that did make it through. Local newspapers, never public transport's greatest cheerleaders, ripped into Bexleybus, castigating the elderly vehicles (one legendary report, entirely true, involved the need for the passengers of one DMS to dismount and push the wretched vehicle up a hill when it wouldn't do so on its own!). Management had made the fatal boast that it could operate DMSs as reliably as RTs, and even with assistance from the half of the fleet that was composed of brand-new leased Olympians, this couldn't be achieved. A strike on 4 and 5 February over wages took the entire operation off the road, a proposal by LBL for Plumstead to run the 272 with Bexleybus vehicles being turned down by the union, and it was not until mid-year, when a complete revamp of the schedule was implemented,

DECLINING YEARS

Right: **Some of the early tendered routes endured a wretched first few years as their owners learned the hard way that the LRT arena wasn't a licence to print money. London Country North East, one of the four inheritors of LCBS since 7 September 1986, should have known better when they bid for the 298 and 313 in north-west London, but it was strike action that killed them off in this sector, to the benefit of Grey-Green, which took over on an emergency basis and improved matters to be awarded longer-term deals. While buses were sourced, the company's own DMS-alikes appeared, like 506 (OKW 506R) at Enfield Town on 21 June 1988.**
Malc McDonald

Below: **Simple but effective, the Leaside livery of 1987 invariably found its way to the district's DMS trainers. On 27 May 1988 at Edgware bus station, Finchley's D 1062 (GHV 62N) even outshines the Metrobus next to it.** C. Carter / Online Transport Archive

that things settled down, by which time the damage was done. On 22 February new express route 472 was introduced to speed passengers between Woolwich and Thamesmead via the direct route, while for the ten months it was operated by Bexleybus before having to be given up, the 492, meant for LS operation, was known to see the odd DMS. So did the 269, very rarely.

After less than two years, the poorer of the earliest LRT contractors found themselves faltering; as early as 6 February London Country North East, plagued by strike action, had no choice but to hand back its 298, which was reassigned temporarily to Grey-Green; on the 22nd the 313 went in the same direction and both could now see visits by the South Yorkshire-derived DMS clones normally belonging to

Left: **Only the 65 had seen no DMSs, as they were felt too tall to fit through the side entrance to Kingston garage. However, when some managed it, DMSs appeared more regularly. During 1988 a 'KINGSTON BUS' logo was added, demonstrated by DMS 1511 (THM 511M) at KIngston in August.** *Haydn Davies*

Below: **Late in the day for an organisation which was definitely on its knees and soon to be broken into a dozen fragments, LBL introduced a corporate livery. The new 'tapegrey' scheme was red with 2in white band (in tape rather than paint) and grey skirt (jeered by cynics as hiding dirt sufficient to slack off on washing the buses). Concerted effort went into applying it so that a greater proportion of the fleet looked cared for than had certainly been the case since the running down of Aldenham. Croydon's D 2597 (THX 597S) demonstrates while it can still work the 157; that route was put solely into Sutton on 29 November 1988.** *Haydn Davies*

the 173. Change was coming to one of LBL's own tendered networks as well when during February a 'KINGSTON BUS' fleetname was phased in, this red-on-yellow text vinyl being of a size to fit perfectly over the roundel. DMS 1447, however, had one plastered over its front! Where LBL's tapegrey livery was concerned, there developed a measure of variety in that garages tended to apply it slightly to their own tastes, Croydon being one to just paint grey all the way round rather than allowing the lower mouldings to kink the skirt. Several DMSs gained the band and skirt over existing recent red paint jobs. DMS 2291, deroofed on 13 August 1987 under Finsbury Park station bridge, was converted to open-top by Kent Engineering (its new capacity being O44/28D) and painted into the Leaside livery to serve as a

DECLINING YEARS

205

Below: **Neither of the two overall advert liveries accruing to the DMS family were operated by London Transport or one of its unit-based successors. The further out of town they operated, the less LRT minded, and such was the case with the smart scheme for Mitsubishi carried by Metrobus's former DMS 2243 (OJD 243R) for two years. One would wonder at the morality of advertising buses' chief opposition in the form of a car manufacturer, but the influx of revenue was, then and now, much appreciated. It is seen at the Bromley North stand of the 61.** *Colin Byrne*

dedicated private-hire bus and regular trainer. Sutton, meanwhile, the rapid conversion to Iveco power of its DMS fleet completed in April, added some vim to its bid for the Sutton tendering network with the evaluation of three new looks; DMS 2409 went into a Leaside-like livery, DMS 2487 (still with the numberplate in the incorrect lower position) briefly gained a maroon skirt extending over the engine compartment and DMS 2408 from Merton was treated to 'Wandlebus' fleetnames. The bid proved successful, the network being awarded in its entirety in May, but as it turned out, none of these liveries, nor the fleetname would end up being used and they were all removed quickly. Metrobus, meanwhile, treated its ex-DMS 2243 to a ColorBus advert for Beckenham-based Mitsubishi dealer Saunders Abbott and Ensignbus achieved something which arguably should have been done in the first place when it fitted its A 103 (ex-DM 1720) with a KM/NN blind box at the rear so as to inaugurate its first Essex County Council contract, two Sunday-evening journeys on route 723, from 7 May.

The completion of the conversion of Croydon's DMS fleet to Iveco power necessitated the transfer of DMS 2205 to Brixton on 27 January, where it joined a motley collection of eclectic and experimental buses. DMS 1499 was scrapped at Norbiton but DMS 1985, intended for spares use, was deemed worthy of reconstruction. Not satisfied with the new 'cheesy' roundel, DMS 2296 of Thornton Heath gained a white filled roundel with 'BUSES' across the bar across its front; it helped that this was one of the very few B20 DMSs with its numberplate in the lower position. Otherwise, contractors were obliged to display the somewhat ridiculous outsize 'BUS' vinyl beside a huge roundel that was supposed to impress upon sceptical passengers that this non-red bus was actually legit and would take standard fares! Until standards were tightened up, Norbiton was apt to black out the side blinds of their DMSs, while Holloway trainer DMS 1909 had its front blinds panelled over altogether, ensuring that it could never return to service. One further attempt in the passengers' favour was the installation on Wandle District DMSs during March 1988 of holders for ring binders containing laminated farecharts, which could be flipped over by the boarding passenger until he found the fares for the routes he needed; this was accompanied by the final dismantling of the disused AFC equipment on DMSs after ten years of disuse and its replacement by a luggage rack. In April 1988 DMS 2308 from Thornton Heath was the first of only two to receive a pair of reflective numberplates, the black-on-yellow rear one being surmounted by a lightbulb bracket. DM 1159, converted to a mobile computer-training office during 1987 and painted white

206 THE LONDON DMS

Left: **A most unusual blind was specified for new route 389, which made its debut on 16 May as a replacement for much-missed links to Purley Way-area factories lost when the 130B had been withdrawn a year earlier. Thornton Heath's D 2643 (THX 643S) was one of the two dedicated buses, this and D 2642 being the only Fleetlines there to carry the panel, and is seen at West Croydon in August. Disregard the incorrect code carried – there were so many such misidentified that it barely registered any more!** *Haydn Davies*

and red at Chiswick that October, came into use during April 1988; with a diesel generator fitted beside the cab powering terminals fitted upstairs, it assisted the changeover at garages to computerised record-keeping systems.

Even after two of the hardest years in 'London Transport' history, LBL was wavering again about OPO, having come up against the sheer impossibility of tackling purely-central routes. For 1988 and into 1989, though 2% more of the network was pencilled in for one-manning, restructuring took preference, a plan being unveiled in January to split the Districts into several Units as free-standing subsidiaries in advance of privatisation. Warnings were made against deregulation by observers of its devastating effects outside London, and whether the B20 DMSs would still be around by the latest year set for deregulation was not certain as the buses passed their tenth birthdays. Already, however, surplus property was beginning to go under the hammer for that extra bit of revenue, BEL being sold to Frontsource in January 1988 and promptly flipped within months. Not that the science of garaging was any less fraught at the independents, March 1988 seeing London Buslines relocate from Spring Grove, Lampton to Fleming Way, Isleworth, and this wasn't to be the last base used by the DMSs operating with this company.

On 14 May revisions in south London removed the 190 on Mondays to Saturdays, its Old Coulsdon path being appended to the 50 instead; now starting from Streatham Garage in lieu of Stockwell Station, this route was given a Croydon share, thus reintroducing DMSs. The mile-long gap between Streatham and Brixton garages was filled with an extension south of the 59's northern section plus an extension north of the 60 to Brixton Station. The main point, however, was to make redundant some of the 159's conductors by taking most of the route off on weekdays between Streatham (Green Lane) and Thornton Heath so that new OPO route 250 could take those roads. To address complaints about the loss of a link to factories on Purley Way after the 130B's cutting-back the previous August, a peak-hour-only route numbered 389 was introduced between West Croydon and Thornton Heath and set going with a single Thornton Heath DMS equipped with a lazy blind.

Having belatedly developed some teeth by actually following through on threats to strip underperforming operators of their contracts, LBL declared itself sick of Sampsons finally, and on 2 July reassigned the 317 back to LBL at Enfield from whence it had come. Most of Sampsons' unfortunate Fleetlines hadn't even managed to make it to that date, although four of them were picked up by Ensignbus and added to their fleet, joining a third-hand acquisition which became 228 (DMS 415 ex-Hedingham); the class codes at this firm were now discontinued. 109 (DMS 2219) was a second to receive a full set of KM/NN blinds at the rear and with 103 (DM 1720) was put to work on new commercial route 349 from 24 June. Cityrama, still struggling with the 200, were taking Ensign DMSs on hire during the

DECLINING YEARS 207

Above: **The unfortunate Sampsons got bad enough press at the time that their unhappy innings needs little more slating in these pages; some operators just weren't up to the task set for them, but such is the dog-eat-dog world of competitive business that was changing the whole ethos of bus operations at the time. In any case, the buses were easily recycled; the former DM 1762 (GHM 762N), departing Enfield Town on 21 June 1988 in Sampsons' dying days, returned to Ensign and was swiftly returned to traffic as that company's 252.** *Malc McDonald*

Right: **The appearance of open-top buses on stage service was extremely rare until tendering, but Ensignbus from time to time took advantage of warm summer days to bring out special guests; one such in August 1989 was 315 (JGF 315K) on the 145.** *Haydn Davies*

summer, including DM 1166 and two (DMSs 1624 and 1684) belonging to Brakell's. DMS 1684 then went into Ensign's fleet as 234. Grey-Green started applying its new and more appropriate livery to its second-hand acquisitions during May. LBL's own 'cowboy' operation at Kingston Bus put DMS 1985 into service in May after it was determined to be good enough to rebuild rather than use for parts, though it didn't merit a repaint and was photographed once with the ultimate blind box held on by gaffer tape! DM 1196 and DMS 1450 were kind enough to supply the parts. Despite having made the repainting of DMSs their own, Gatwick Engineering switched its remit to RMLs during the year and subsequent DMSs were repainted at garages again. The point was made to use tapegrey-liveried buses on the Derby Day (from Merton) and Wimbledon services in 1988, Sutton and Merton featuring again on the latter with loans of two DMSs each from Croydon and Brixton. The two Plumstead Ds at Selkent took up the Thames Barrier run again, while Leaside's summer route 333 starred open-top DMS 2291. This bus provided a belated fillip to the DMSs' reputation with an overseas trip to The Hague and Rotterdam between 1-5 July.

Meanwhile DMS 2456 found itself fitted with an assault screen of its own and began working on the 77A from 15 April, but on 8 August was transferred from Stockwell to Brixton ostensibly for the 189, which had been withdrawn in its current form on 6 August but reborn exactly a month later as a Brixton-operated schoolday-only route, its path round outer portions of Balham and Tooting otherwise falling under the remit of new minibus route G1. DMS 2377 remained a crew-operated bus on the 88 until October, when it too was fitted with an assault screen and cleared for all Stockwell's OPO routes. On 13 August the 88 was split into two overlapping sections, the Stockwell DMSs on Sundays now being able to get no further west than Oxford Circus and thus not to the new terminus at Turnham Green.

Ensignbus was the major beneficiary of the closure of Hornchurch garage on 24 September following the loss by LBL of all the routes operating therefrom, taking up the 165 (and its new offshoot 365), 246 and new route 446; all could see DMS operation until the 165/365 received brand new Metrobuses, and frequently after that as well. Among the intake were DMSs formerly belonging to Southend and retaining

Left: **In the worst scenarios, tendering reverses could wipe out the entire roster of a garage and force it to close; such had been the case with Loughton in 1986, and so fell Hornchurch on 24 September 1988. Ensignbus upped the ante for contractors by specifying brand new buses, but until these were delivered, the company had to operate its existing DMSs on the 165 and its new counterpart 365. 233 (KUC 133P) had come with the 62 at the beginning of 1987 and is seen at Romford on 8 October.** *Malc McDonald*

their colours, 206 (DM 1106), 208 (DM 1008), 231 (DMS 620), 236 (DMS 1476), 237 (DM 926), 251 (DMS 820) and 255 (DM 1015) plus former Sampsons 235 (DM 1794), 238 (DM 1030), 239 (DM 1119) and 252 (DM 1762), which were all backed up by ex-London Country North East ANs. Frontrunner South-East, the East Midland-owned establishment that had won the 248 and 252 at the same time, had cut a deal with Grey-Green to use its drivers intended for the 24 prior to that service's takeup on 5 November, but very occasionally the DMS-lookalikes belonging to the 173 would be pressed into service on the 252.

However, after a comparatively quiet 1988 for the DMS family within LBL, a fourth major town-based operation was created, based on Sutton and known as Suttonbus. This time, lessons had been learned, just about; the routes were not tinkered with too heavily and the vehicles were Sutton's incumbent DMSs. Following the rejection of the proposed liveries carried by DMSs 2408 and 2487, D 2589 had been experimented upon during August, gaining a yellow SUTTONBUS logo across the front, of a size big enough to necessitate the removal of the numberplate to directly below the windscreen, thus displacing D kits on vehicles

Left: **Ensignbus was quickly acquiring a reputation for deploying all sorts of wild stuff on its increasing roster of routes, all pulled from its ever-extensive sales stock and treated to the marvellous blue and outlined silver. Even DMSs it had prepared for other companies found their way back, such as 237 (SMU 926N), which took its not dissimilar and no less attractive Southend livery into London service for a spell; it passes under Romford station bridge on 8 October 1988.** *Malc McDonald*

DECLINING YEARS

209

so fitted. Instead of a grey skirt, a mushroom colour was applied, complete with the garage's phone number, 01-644 8811, emblazoned across the towing panel in yellow. Whether and how wide to add a cantrail band was still unclear, so the bus received a 2in yellow band on the nearside and a 4in one on the offside. The narrower version was chosen, but application to all vehicles (again using rolls of tape to save money on paint) proved very sluggish.

Industrial action relating to reduced pay scales slowed the implementation of the new contracts, unfortunately, forcing a postponement from 29 October to 26 November. Norbiton, however, was ready for its own part, which involved taking off the 213's Sutton-St Helier section so that the 154 could be rerouted via Green Lane to serve the estate in its entirety. To fill that gap for the four weeks until Suttonbus could sort itself out, a Sutton-St Helier shuttle was mounted with Sutton DMSs, still under the number 213. The 213 also had its epic Sunday extension to West Croydon altered to follow the 154 via Roundshaw rather than the 151, which was introduced on this day of the week (though only as far west as Sutton Station).

Once the labour problems at Sutton had been addressed through a revised pay offer, Suttonbus bowed in earnest on 26 November and the changes could now take place. First, the 93 regained the ascendancy along its own corridor as the 80 was pulled back to Morden so that it could gain an extension from Belmont to Banstead instead, at the expense of the 164, which shifted northwards through a permanent extension to Wimbledon, incorporating the 157's roads between Morden and Raynes Park. In this region the 163 was now transferred in from Merton and converted from LS to DMS. Also to regain DMSs was the 152, like the 163 passing from Merton to Sutton. The rerouteing of the 154 via St Helier allowed the 213's Sutton assistance and St Helier section to be withdrawn; concentrating on its core section, the 213 allowed the 151 to be diverted at North Cheam to reach Lower Morden via the previously unserved Tudor Drive. The 44, though giving up its Sunday Sutton allocation, was projected through to Sutton to permit the withdrawal of the 280 on that day of the week; the 280, though passing through Sutton, was not to become part of Suttonbus and was reallocated to Merton. To make room there, the 264 was transferred entirely to Thornton Heath, the Sunday Croydon buses coming off likewise; Thornton Heath and Croydon thus ceded the 157 to Sutton. Stockwell came off the 155 and Streatham off the 50 other than on Saturdays. Sutton's complement of DMSs had now increased by fifteen, not all of which were Ivecos, and to help them out on the 163 live garage runs were added to that route from its Morden teminus via the 164.

While Sampsons had acknowledged their faults while attempting to keep their service running, Cityrama took the brave step of asking

Below: **Since its introduction, the 264 has bounced back and forth between the local garages at either end of its straightforward Tooting to Croydon routeing. On 15 October 1988 Merton's Monday to Saturday contribution was represented at Tooting Broadway by D 2530 (THX 530S), incorrectly coded but at least carrying the new LBL livery. Both Merton and Croydon would come off on 26 November in favour of Thornton Heath daily.** *Malc McDonald*

210 THE LONDON DMS

Left: After toying with the name Wandlebus, LBL settled on Suttonbus for its Sutton-area tendered network. Knowing that there would be a skirt, whatever its colour (black and maroon having already been tried and rejected), Sutton began moving its DMSs' numberplates up to below the windscreen – in two decades, they had migrated higher and higher! Upon the advent of Suttonbus, the 80 found itself withdrawn north of Morden, so thereafter DMS 2258 (OJD 258R), seen at Wimbledon Village on 15 October, would only be able to reach this point on the 93. *Malc McDonald*

LRT to be relieved of the 200 due to not having the resources to run it, and on 3 December Norbiton took it up instead; while LSs were the scheduled type, the Kingston Bus DMSs were known to participate occasionally. Boro'line, meanwhile, hired six Ensignbus DMSs to train drivers for their win of the 188 in 1989; Ensign also put them to use on a Christmas lights service in December, despite selling 251 (DMS 820) during the month.

The following Monday, 5 December, then saw the institution of LBL's new subsidiaries, which began applying their logos straight away pending the issuing of their O-licences on 1 April 1989 to become fully-fledged companies in their own right, just ripe for privatisation when the time came, be it during or after deregulation (the timetable for which, however, slipped to beyond 1990 following general industry unease about the 7% drop in passenger numbers since D-Day in the rest of the country). Of the DMS operators, Wandle District divided into two, London General (whose logo was a B-type bus in profile) taking Merton, Sutton and Stockwell garages and South London (personified by Tower Bridge) taking Croydon, Thornton Heath and Brixton. Selkent District begat Selkent the company, including Bexleybus, and London United incorporated Norbiton, but it was significant to note that all the hitherto autonomous units and their liveries would be coming under this eleven-Unit structure from now on, retaining or regaining the tapegrey livery; even at almost the close of its life, the ideal of unified London bus operation still had merit in it. Still, one of the DMSs' most recognisable features, the white-top livery, passed into history in 1988 with the repaint of Leaside trainer DMS 2168, one of 126 Fleetlines thus to be smartened up during the year. With new engines and new work, finally the reduced core of B20 DMSs (or ex-B20s, if they were Iveco-powered!) were pulling their weight, FFD passes rising from 92% to 96% in each half of the year. There was even enough confidence to mount completely crazy ideas like Thornton Heath's astonishing addition of DMSs to North Street's N98 roster on New Year's Eve, taking the buses thirty miles from home with no problems encountered.

Below: The 'divide and rule' imperative that was severing LBL's operations across geographical lines affected shared routes; strike action at Sutton prevented the intended rerouting of the 154 through St Helier, so from 29 October to 26 November a shuttle from Sutton to St Helier Station was performed with a Sutton DMS carrying a lazy blind; here at Sutton on 12 November is D 2589 (THX 589S), with the experimental 4in painted yellow band. *John Parkin*

DECLINING YEARS 211

Below: **Perhaps inspired by the autonomous nature of Bexleybus, the management of Norbiton introduced a new identity for its mixture of Ms and DMSs from February 1988. Kingston Bus was not terribly inspiring, but the black skirt that started appearing a year later as an accompaniment was, even if cynics scoffed that it was just there to hide oil spills from the back of DMSs. Here at Kingston is a weary-looking DMS 1904 (KUC 904P).** *Colin Lloyd*

1989

Very little affected the remaining DMSs' routes in 1989; on 25 February the 293 was split across Morden, the Hackbridge leg becoming new London & Country-operated 393 and the rest now terminating at Merton Abbey Savacentre instead. From February 1989, for no particular reason, Norbiton's DMSs and Ms started receiving black skirts, perhaps to match the Kingfisher livery on LSs that had inaugurated a commercial route numbered K10. DMSs 1477, 1626, 1837 and 1904 were the first, followed by DMS 1426 and 1884 by April. After well over a decade, there must have still been a pair of push-out opening front upper-deck window pans lying around, because DMS 1889 was fitted with them during March. DMS 1960 and 2173 of Metrobus made do with no opening front windows at all, these Fleetlines having received fixed glass panes upon accident repair late in 1986. DMS 2312 at Thornton Heath gained a pair of reflective numberplates by March; of the angular 1970s style as well, and paired this with push-out windows. On 4 March 1989 Croydon took its participation off the 75 on Sundays and Grey-Green lost the 379 to Eastern National Citybus.

April's Fool's Day 1989 saw the establishment of the LBL subsidiaries' own O-Licences and the amendment of their legal lettering to match. Where front fleetnames were concerned, London General for the most part adopted Sutton's practice of relocating the numberplate higher to admit the 4in-high one-line version of the logo, but South London determined that it just about fit on the front panel and generally left their plates alone. Occasionally the bigger version of Tower Bridge from the side logos would be cut up and added to the front. To take the DMS family through to the end of the decade in what was otherwise its quietest year ever, a second order for 101 Iveco 836.S11 engines was placed (including one for DMS 2456) and began being fitted from March 1989 at a rate of six or seven a week, taking care of the rest of Sutton's allocation that had been increased upon the implementation of Suttonbus, followed by Thornton Heath's DMSs, then the ten remaining at Brixton and finally three out of Merton. This time the work was undertaken at Walworth.

Right: **The breakup of LBL was now under way in earnest; from 5 December 1988 eleven units were set going in replacement of the five districts, and had a more prominent identity designed to take in the four or five years envisaged before deregulation and privatisation. South London Transport tended not to go in for relocating their DMSs' numberplates, as the logos just about fit on the buses' flat fronts – but try not to worry about why Tower Bridge was chosen as a logo when none of the unit's routes actually went near that structure! September 1989 sees Thornton Heath's DMS 2309 (THX 309S) passing Streatham Common.** *Haydn Davies*

Left: London General was the western half of Wandle, and operated the DMSs from Sutton, Merton and Stockwell garages. To accommodate the B-type bus logo, DMSs had to have their numberplates relocated in the manner of Suttonbus vehicles; Stockwell's DMS 2393 (OJD 393R) demonstrates at Euston during April 1989. *Haydn Davies*

Below: The impetus in the late 1980s had been to shorten route after route, disregarding passengers needing to come into town from further and further afield as accommodation close to their places of work grew ever more unaffordable. However, on 17 June 1989 this process was thrown into reverse, when the 249, introduced in 1972 as a one-manning of the 49's southern end, was withdrawn and the 49 re-extended to Crystal Palace! Surely it couldn't last, and it didn't – less than two years, in fact. This Chelsea capture of D 2578 (THX 578S) in tapegrey and DMS 2408 (THX 408S) in all-red hopefully persuaded Merton to address the spacing on its Sunday-only share, which continued during the period of the extension. *Haydn Davies*

On 15 April the Autocheck fare-collection system in south-east London was discontinued, having proven yet another failure in reducing boarding times. Bexleyheath's DMSs were given a barrier across the right-hand side of the entrance door in order to direct passengers to the driver, before the removal of the equipment within a month saw their lower-deck capacity increased by one seat, as before its fitment.

A three-year contract was granted to the London General subsidiary of LBL to operate the 200 from 3 June; it was taken up with Ms from a yard at Colliers Wood coded AA, but as this was an outstation of Suttonbus there was an outside chance of DMSs popping up on loan, and all of them could in any case turn in Brixton garage again. Somewhat less orthodox were occasional appearances of Sutton DMSs on minibus route 352 from July, with white-on-magenta blinds; Colliers Wood's Ms returned the favour with wandering to the 152 at schooltimes. Repaints to Sutton DMSs had spread the yellow band of the intended Suttonbus livery further by mid-year than had been the case at the outset of this network.

A surprise reversal of established route-shortening patterns on 17 June extended the 49 (still with a Sunday Merton DMS allocation) over the 249 to Crystal Palace; as part of this the 219 was rerouted at its northern end to

Left: **The desire to emblazon the post-'London Transport' identities on passengers' minds took precedence over any need to combine them with the new livery, still by no means universally applied. Thus, the appearance of customised DMS 2456 (OJD 456R), transferred from Stockwell to Brixton in August 1988 and caught at Oxford Circus, straddles two vastly different worlds.** *David Wilkinson collection*

terminate at South Kensington Station rather than Sloane Square; it had actually been turning around at the south side of Battersea Bridge since 19 January due to the damaging of that structure by a barge.

Although the ethos of tendering had been to split up the perceived monopolies and subject their hidebound practices to the efficiency of competition, the small operators favoured so highly in the early rounds of tendering were by 1989 giving up or seeking the financial backing of richer parents, which could divest unwanted portions at will – or acquire them, leading to the likelihood of monopolies coming straight back again! The fast-growing Stagecoach group had bought East Midland on 1 April, and on 1 July sold its Frontrunner South East operation to Ensign, which actually commenced operations the previous Friday night as Frontrunner packed up by 9 pm. The new acquisition comprised double-deck routes 248 and 252, and a point was made of spreading the company's blue and silver buses to these services as soon as possible, which included the DMSs once blinds were produced that included all routes now operated. Schoolday route 550 was restricted to single-deckers but open-top 358 (DMS 158) was put out on 28 June, a day of rail strike action when everything else was unavailable! Ensignbus added four DMSs to its fleet in July from Black Horse Buses, to whom it had sold some the year before; thus brought back was DMS 820 but this time under the number 240, while DMSs 1856 and 1949 returned as 256 and 249 and DMS 1371 became the second 251. Between them they helped replace 217 (DMS 2000), which was written off in a bad accident and scrapped. All-over ads continued to drift to normal service, including 102 (DMS 1682 for Pritt Stick), 104 (DMS 1941 for Fuji audio tapes) and 211 (DM 1069 for John Bull bitter), though 221 (ex-DMS 353) now went into fleet livery.

Above left: **The full Suttonbus treatment included a yellow band, as seen in September 1989 on D 2591 (THX 591S), one that returned to Sutton to restore the 152's upper deck.** *Haydn Davies*

Left: **This was more like what we got for the majority of Suttonbus DMSs, however, just the skirt and no band at all; and, from the start of 1989, London General logos eclipsing the marketing name. D 2615 (THX 615S) nonetheless looks smart as it plies the 164 south in February 1989.** *Haydn Davies*

A further possible pitch for independents' DMSs was the 90, created from the 90B as a new London Buslines contract on 19 August and otherwise using new Leyland Olympians. Former DM 1041 lost its Hitachi advert for fleet livery in August 1989, while stablemate ex-DM 1007 was a lone Fleetline to receive green handrails inside, an adornment unique only to DMS 2456 and omitted by the time DiPTAC came along in 1991. DMS 2456, meanwhile, was treated to an Iveco engine in August 1989, though Brixton would continue to operate both Leylands and Ivecos and even Merton would take three. Further east, DM 948 for 1989 received Selkent Travel livery complete with a grey skirt.

Bexleybus had settled down somewhat from its rough opening weeks after a timetable revision, but from August 1989 enough Titans were now available to begin easing out the worst of the unit's DMSs, six of the incoming Ts even adopting Bexleybus livery and the numbers of the buses they replaced before a foot was put down and the rest came in existing red livery.

August also saw the input into Merton of two Metrobuses, but the DMS's innings there, almost twenty years of it, was not yet threatened. Merton did, however, lose a dozen DMS workings on 2 September with the transfer of the 57 to Norbiton on tender. Fourteen Merton DMSs, despite being Leyland-engined, left for Brixton where, in what was becoming distinctly silly down at South London, they displaced Ms to Streatham which in turn sent Ls to Croydon to assume the 197 group and 403 from 28 October! The regaining of the 197 group thus obliged Croydon to hand much of the 50 over to Streatham. At night in this programme the N78 was split in two, new route N69 (with Brixton DMSs and Ms) being introduced to give Green Lane a night bus service terminating at Norwood Junction. Stockwell's N87 was extended from Raynes Park to Surbiton via Hook, bringing night buses to those locations for the first time. Finally, London & Country took the 196 from Cityrama, finishing off that company as an LRT contractor.

Above: **Now 'grey-green' to match its company name, 502 (OKW 502R) loads up at Stratford on 4 February 1989.** *Malc McDonald*

Below: **Bexleybus's DMSs lasted barely two years. The ex-Clydeside examples were sold first, DMS 1679 (THM 679M), a.k.a. 86 in this August 1989 shot, leaving in November. The rest were replaced by red Titans, and the last was withdrawn on 24 February 1990.** *Malc McDonald*

DECLINING YEARS

Above: **The division of LBL into eleven meant that subsidiaries could now compete with one another for tenders, and one such transfer was that of the 57 from London General to London United (with Norbiton Ms) on 2 September 1989. Prior to the change Merton's D 2532 (THX 532S) is seen on its way to Kingston.** *Haydn Davies*

Below: **Ensignbus 220 (JGF 325K) was once DMS 325; when caught at Marks Gate on 5 January 1991 it had had 'DM' garage codes added to denote the company's new Dagenham premises.** *Malc McDonald*

During November a further shuffle of the vehicles that had moved around to supply Croydon with Ls indirectly supplied Bexleyheath with enough Titans to allow the withdrawal of ten more DMSs. Service reductions to Stockwell's 77A and 156 on 25 November allowed ten DMSs to transfer to Brixton, increasing its complement to the detriment of its Metrobuses and thereby to Streatham's Ls. Brixton's DMS fleet was now predominantly Leyland-powered.

Two garage changes affected independent DMS operators at the end of 1989; first London Buslines moved once again on 9 October to Bridge Road, Southall, while Ensignbus had by now expanded enough to require additional premises, and on 18 November opened a new depot at Chequers Lane, Dagenham (DM). The 145 was first in from Purfleet, and on 2 December routes 62, 62A and N99 were similarly transferred. The newer buses in the Ensignbus fleet (Metrobuses and Olympians) tended to take predominance over the DMSs on the 62 on Sundays from this time, however. 221 (formerly known as DMS 353, and now with an ad for Evan Evans Tours) was a first re-registration for a DMS, gaining GVV 205 for more prestigious work on the Christmas lights service this December, though it padded that out with mundane runs on the 165. A six-month contract was awarded to Ensignbus for route 347 from 30 October 1989.

216   THE LONDON DMS

Left: There were by now relatively few new routes given to DMSs, but one such was the 250, transferred to Brixton on 6 January 1990 to take the place of the 133. This situation would last less than six months, but here setting off from Brixton, Stockwell Park Walk on 24 February is DMS 2278 (THX 278S), missing a white relief band.
Clive A. Brown

Below: The 166 found itself sawn in half on 6 January 1990 and its eastern roads turned over to new minibus routes 366 and 367, but as it turned out the former still needed big bus support at schooldays, hence the appearance of buses like Croydon's DMS 2374 (OJD 374R) at Beckenham Junction during the summer term. The Tower Bridge logo crammed onto the front is the larger-sized variant meant to accompany the side fleetname!
David Wilkinson collection

1990

1990 proved altogether more exciting than 1989 for the DMS family within LBL, only five days elapsing before a major programme. On 6 January Brixton's most important OPO route, the 133, was lost to London General with new Volvo Citybuses (VCs) from Stockwell; to take its place the 250 was moved in from Streatham, allowing DMSs to predominate and removing the possibility of Ls. Brixton was also added to the 159 on Sundays once again. Croydon's 60 swapped its northernmost roads with those of the 118, so that the former now terminated at Clapham Common and the latter at Brixton Station. The 166, its DMSs now just about in command after some years with LSs as the main complement, was hacked to terminate at Shirley so that a new minibus pair numbered 366/367 could take over to Beckenham Junction via unserved roads. One compensation was the addition of a schoolday double-deck working to the 366, performed by a yellow-blinded Croydon DMS or L (usually the latter) as fit, but as Shirley Way was effectively vacated by the 166, part of the 194B was rerouted along this thoroughfare. After nearly three years as the routes low enough on Croydon's food chain to have to make do with LSs, enough DMSs and Ls were put into Croydon to return the 166 and 194/194A to that particular double-deck mix.

The other major batch of new double-deck buses accruing to LBL on 6 January 1990 were the 23 Ls designated for RiversideBus at Stamford Brook; the shuffle of contract types it took to put them onto the 237 released Ms to Norbiton which in turn allowed about two-thirds of its DMSs to be withdrawn and three sold. Despite the re-tender of Kingston Bus's routes for implementation in the coming autumn and the DMSs' looming end, several had been repainted at the end of 1989 and black skirts continued to find their way on.

DECLINING YEARS 217

Right: **DMSs continued to depart Norbiton during 1990, in advance of the planned loss of much of Norbiton's runout after just three years of the Kingston Bus network. D 1804 (GHM 804N), seen on Westminster Bridge with London General fleetnames applied over its existing all-red (and with its foglights pulled out), had come to Merton in January 1990 after being displaced by a Metrobus sent from Stamford Brook after the re-ordering of that garage as an entirely contracted operation.** *Peter Horrex*

Below: **The ex-Bexleybus motors weren't the only standards to make a late flourish for the type at Merton; the garage made use of several displaced from Norbiton by the release there of Ms displaced by the RiversideBus scheme at Hounslow on 6 January. DMS 1447 (MLH 447L), in full tapegrey with London General logos, sees the non-B20 out for the final time at Euston.** *David Wilkinson collection*

However, four of the withdrawn examples (DMSs 1447, 1890 and 2008 plus D 1804, the last named actually referred to as such now) were transferred to Merton for continued service. Emblazoned with London General logos over the red livery, they turned out as fit though were meant for route 219, and as time went on some even received white tape bands and/or grey skirts (D 1804 and DMSs 714, 1447 and 1890). With the move of D 2547 to Sutton, DMS 2406 remained the only Iveco at Merton, and that bus would take its place in the garage's history books before long.

Ensignbus continued the move of its operations from Purfleet to Dagenham, sending the 252 there on 6 January and the 248 on the 20th. Open-top No 306 (DMS 886) was blown over onto its side during the storms of the 25th. Somewhat more usual risks were catered for in January with the sale of former Bexleybus DMS 1657 to the Metropolitan Police Training College at Hendon; this bus replaced DMS 1621, which had been there since 1984. The buses' purpose there was to train aspiring officers in the process of tackling recalcitrant passengers.

A massive scheme centred on the Hackney area on 24 February brought Kentish Bus a host of tendering victories that indirectly allowed the full replacement of Bexleybus's DMSs with cascaded Titans in red livery. The last one in service was 91 (DMS 2063) which operated on 23 February, the last ex-Clydeside model on 4 February having been 88 (DMS 1669) which had worked alone since the turn of the year after a late reprieve – but this wasn't quite the last we'd see of the blue and cream colours as such. The independents' DMSs were also beginning slowly to drift away, Metrobus standing down former DMS 1960 after 31 January despite having DMSs 2052 and 2167 repainted by Markelly Coachworks at Dartford. London Buslines' examples were considered spares only by this time, their appearances on the 81 and 90 being as backups to the newer types only. In February Ensignbus withdrew five of their stage-service DMSs (nos 212, 217, 228, 236 and 251) while placing an order for 24 new Dennis Dominators, mechanically descendants of the Fleetline, in the interest of seeing the rest off by the summer. And finally, included in Grey-Green's order for Volvo Citybuses arriving in February were six single-doored examples intended to replace the 173's DMS clones; four (504, 509, 510 and 527) were sold in March and the rest gradually gained fleet livery (in appropriate grey and green!).

Although the need to give Sunday work to the DMSs working on the 39 from 1972 had spawned a 19A over part of the 19, the parent route had never been threatened by DMSs until 24 February, when by a roundabout method put into place to equalise work between garages following the loss of so much LBL work, Merton gained a share of the Sunday OPO roster.

On 31 March the 389, all one bus of it, was lost to London & Country, and on 2 April the 77A's school projections beyond Wandsworth to Putney Heath were curtailed at Tibbet's Corner and bent back on themselves through hitherto-unserved but heavily-populated Southfields streets, though the route still got to Putney Heath on Sundays. Further pruning to the 88 cost this route its Clapham Common-Tooting section on 28 April, although the Sunday service continued through to Mitcham and Colliers Wood (and now extended at the other end to Marble Arch). The 155 was diverted to Vauxhall to partially one-man this section of the 88, losing its Elephant & Castle terminus to new route 355, operated jointly with the 155 by

Above: **When espied in Rosebery Avenue on 16 September 1990 Merton's D 2575 (THX 575S) had no foglights and a completely wrong code; by then the latter was more common than the former, even though the order actually to remove foglights would not go out until 1993, after the DMSs' time had ended. The 19 belatedly took its place as a DMS possibility with the introduction of a Merton allocation on Sundays on 24 February 1990.** *Malc McDonald*

Below: **Never quite getting as close to town as passengers still needed since the withdrawal of its service beyond Elephant to Aldwych, the 155 was now altered again to divert from Stockwell to terminate at Vauxhall. To take up the service to Elephant & Castle (but not, unfortunately, any closer to town than that) came new route 355, originally to have been numbered 155A were it not for the falling out of favour of suffixes. Merton's DMS 2350 (OJD 350R) heads a convoy southwestward during August.** *Haydn Davies*

DECLINING YEARS

Right: **What should replace the Merton DMSs sent out to Stockwell but some of the most extraordinary DMSs to see service in the two decades of the class's history. Collecting four ex-Bexleybus standard Fleetlines and knowing they would only be needed in the short term, LBL didn't consider it cost-effective to repaint them other than across the front, where their LBL tapegrey jarred horribly with untreated Bexleybus colours! The presence of Ms at Merton allowed KM blinds to be used, as on DMS 2143 (OJD 143R), turned short at Tooting Broadway on 9 May 1990.** *C. Carter / Online Transport Archive*

existing Merton DMSs (and the couple of Ms based there). In the person of London General, Stockwell took back the 196 on permanent transfer from London & Country's six-month stand-in period, using DMSs until a second batch of new VCs could be delivered. And what should replace the Merton DMSs sent temporarily to bolster the 196 at Stockwell? After Bexleybus had turfed out its Fleetlines, four still with valid FFDs were placed in store at Colliers Wood and incredibly, readied for service. Unable to justify running them in full Bexleybus colours but equally unwilling to go to the expense of repainting them for such a short-term gig, Merton adopted the bizarre half-measure of repainting the fronts only in LBL tapegrey, as if the passengers wouldn't notice! Blind stocks existed from those printed for Merton's two Ms to fully supply the KM/NN boxes on D 1160 and DMSs 2109, 2112 and 2143, and suitably fitted, they went into service from 28 April again on every OPO route operated by

Right: **Grey skirts were applied to two of the half-and-half Bexleybus/ London General DMSs, producing a hopelessly confused appearance. The nearside aspect of this oddity of oddities is shown at Mitcham in May 1990 by DMS 2112 (KJD 112P), with numberplate (albeit a white one, not known at this garage or at any other than Bexleyheath) relocated to the high position to make room for the London General fleetname.** *Tony Wilson*

220   THE LONDON DMS

Left: Even a frontal repaint only would have been a bit of a waste of money if the four ex-Bexleybus DMSs at Merton had only worked for the three weeks it took London General to await the delivery of the 196's new VCs, but they were brought out again in July for another week while other Merton buses were deputised for Flower Show duty. Operating the park and ride at Hampton Court on a superbly sunny day is DMS 2109 (KJD 109P). *Geoff Rixon*

Merton. Their white numberplates hoisted to the higher position to admit London General fleetnames, and with black fleetnumbers and garage codes inked onto the correct positions in marker pen, their appearance was undeniably and unforgettably surreal. DMSs 2112 and 2143 even received a grey skirt all round, and all four wore LBL roundels on the cream part of their livery. In concert with three more standard refugees from Norbiton (DMSs 714, 1500 and 1889), they allowed five of Merton's existing stock (DMSs 2472 and Ds 2564, 2618, 2635 and 2644) plus another five that came from Brixton (DMSs 2278, 2303, 2318, 2330 and 2339) to move to Stockwell for the 196.

As it turned out, the blue and cream DMSs would only last at Merton until not long past 12 May, when the conversion of the 39 to minibus and its split into two released enough Victoria Ms to commence a new allocation by that garage on the 77A, which made spare sufficient Stockwell DMSs to replenish Merton. The ex-Norbiton ones remained a little longer, while the VCs for the 196 were duly delivered and put into service during June. However the ex-Bexleybus DMSs had one last hurrah when they were pulled out of storage at Walworth at the end of June and returned to Merton to allow a number of the ex-Norbiton standard DMSs to carry passengers to and from the Hampton Court Flower Show (11-15 July) on attachment to Fulwell, complete with London United fleetnames for the duration. The red-fronted DMSs then joined in themselves on this work, after which all of them were withdrawn and the balance of the Stockwell loanees, some of which had also done duty on the three flower-show Park & Ride services, came back to Merton. DMS 1447 was the last interim standard at Merton, leaving in August. The balance of the ex-Bexleybus Fleetlines were stripped to keep both Merton and Norbiton compatriots going as long as they could, additional withdrawn standards being gradually taken apart on site at Sutton and Stockwell to to refit existing B20s.

Above: The London & Country contract on the 196 following the demise of Cityrama was only a short-term measure and London General secured its next term with the promise of new Volvo Citybuses, as had displaced Brixton DMSs from the 133 on 6 January. But until they were delivered, DMSs stood in, on loan from Merton. Here at Brixton on 24 May 1990 is D 2635 (THX 635S). *Malc McDonald*

DECLINING YEARS 221

The standard DMS would not survive beyond 1990 with LBL, its resuscitation at all having been something of a fluke, but the one that had survived all the way through, Brixton's DMS 2205, was finally taken out of service in April, losing both its Maxwell gearbox and Gardner engine to become a Leyland-engined trainer with Voith transmission. Merton's B20s (and Leyland-engined they still were) were already having to look over their shoulders even while the activity there was supplying the 196, as four more Ms were added to the two already based during April. Bexleyheath's were all gone and the announcement in May that Norbiton would be retaining only the 71 and X71 set the clock ticking on the remaining DMSs there. Metrobus's gradual intake of Olympians over three years was intended for steady upgrading of the age profile, though new blinds reached the Fleetlines in June; unfortunately, not to Johnson font. And a significant change to London's infrastructure from 22 April altered the time-honoured 01 dialling code to 071 and 081; rather than amend the phone numbers on the front of their DMSs to 081 codes, Sutton removed them altogether. At this late stage in the DMSs' career came a modification that was as practical as it was aesthetic; the appearance from about March 1990 of new rear light clusters of a square-edged, one-piece glass design incorporating the same combination of lights for ease of rewiring. Most Ms and Ts received them from the same time.

Ensign's DMS fleet commenced routes 348 and 449 on 21 April with open-toppers, while one of the afternoon journeys on the 550 could see them; Metrobus's contingent shared the 358 with Lynxes and helped out on new route 356 commencing on 26 March.

Even very late in the day for the DMS could come significant movements, dictated now by tendering and its obsession with newness, whatever the consequences. On 21 July 1990 the South London subsidiary of LBL retained a clutch of tenders based on Thornton Heath and Croydon, having banked on being able to furnish them with vehicles younger than seven years old. At this time, these were Ls, South London operating over half of the 260-strong batch that had formed LBL's last order. Thornton Heath operated nothing newer than DMSs, all the Ls being concentrated at Croydon and Norwood while Ms held court at Streatham, with just a few still remaining at Brixton. So, to supply the tendered routes 50 (introduced on Sundays to replace the last vestige of the 190), 60, 250 (transferred in from Brixton) and 264 (plus the 64 on Sundays) with Olympians, an extraordinary shuffle was implemented which continued the muddled mix of classes at South London, only in a different ratio. Having dropped all its Ls at the beginning of the year, Streatham was now obliged to get rid of several of its Ms so that a handful of DMSs could replace them! Into Streatham then, increasing the proportion of the type on the 59 and striking

Right: **Upheaval of the local buses wasn't all Kingston had to put up with in the late 1980s and early 1990s; the town centre's roads were revamped so as to create a pedestrian mall out of Clarence Street. The resulting one-way system became something of a racetrack thereafter, but the repositioned London Road allowed for good nearside photography, such as of Sutton's D 2621 (THX 621S) in October 1989. It has received London General fleetnames to supplant the outmoded Suttonbus frontal adornment and phone number, but the paint is fresh and unusually is topped off with the intended yellow band.**
Tony Wilson

222　　THE LONDON DMS

Left: Sometimes tendering could get plain silly. Burned by the cheap option being taken by operators who would then find their elderly vehicles breaking down, LRT started tightening up conditions by specifying an age limit. Where LBL subsidiaries were concerned, this often meant breaking up neatly organised standard fleets, and no such situation was more absurd than the 21 July 1990 programme, in which, in order to furnish Thornton Heath with Ls, Ms and DMSs had to be shuffled with the result that Streatham had to take on Fleetlines, thus stepping backward another generation in just three years since the garage had been open! Streatham's DMSs could be recognised by the narrow numbers on their blind sets, and D 2605 (THX 605S) looks suitably awkward when espied at Clapham Junction on 11 May 1991. *Malc McDonald*

up more regular appearances than hitherto on the 49 and 118, were DMSs 2249, 2285, 2294, 2309, 2316, 2337, 2359, 2405 (with dot-matrix rear blind jammed on '109'), 2502 and 2514 plus Ds 2597 and 2605. Thornton Heath lost the 109 to Brixton and Streatham (both of which could field DMSs on it) but retained a number of Fleetlines for non-tendered route 194B, and a knock-on effect removed the final Ms from Brixton, rendering it all-DMS (plus three Hs).

The 159, now permanently withdrawn south of Streatham High Road, was reallocated to Brixton on Sundays with DMS operation, while the 137 on that day of the week passed to Streatham, continuing the possibility of DMSs. In total, Streatham gained twelve DMSs, Brixton nine and Croydon nineteen, while Thornton Heath lost 38. Olympian numbers were strengthened at South London not just from reallocating existing examples but by also

Left: DMS 2277 (THX 277S) heads down Park Lane in March 1990, prior to the transfer of Brixton's Sunday DMSs on the 137 to Streatham. The legal lettering sticker has a grey background, anticipating the colour of the skirt meant to be underneath it. *Haydn Davies*

DECLINING YEARS

Right: **The southward path of the 12A was as busy as any built-up area in south London but was stymied by the need to operate single-deckers due to low bridges in Addiscombe and in Old Lodge Lane. But now that the offending obstruction in the former location had been removed LT could now reconfigure the service; out went the 12A and its Sunday counterpart 12B in favour of new Thornton Heath L-operated 312. But for the final Sunday of the 12B, and the next day, Bank Holiday Monday, L 1 and D 2588 (THX 588S) operated. Here is the latter at Forest Hill.** *Malc McDonald*

pulling examples from Plumstead, where Ts began making their way back to that garage. It wasn't just South London that was subject to these awkward schemes!

A second stage of the Croydon-area scheme was set in motion on 1 September, the most significant aspect of which was the ability now to add an upper deck to the 12A / 12B (combined as new route 312 with Thornton Heath Ls) now that the Addiscombe Road bridge that used to carry the Woodside-Selsdon line had been demolished following the line's closure in May 1983. For the last day of the 12B, 26 August 1990, which in fact stretched to two days since the following day was a Bank Holiday Monday, DMS 2282 (later replaced by D 2588) and L 1 turned out with full blinds. Thornton Heath transferred its share of the 59 to Croydon in compensation and converted the Sunday remnant from DMS to L operation. Other than fifteen DMSs into Croydon, the point was made to gather Ls for the 312 without having to shift too many vehicles around this time, Still, the odd Fleetline was known to pop up on it and on the tendered routes at Thornton Heath, which were normally strictly segregated. At Croydon,

Right: **Restoring buses to at least a small sector of the Beddington area abandoned in 1982 with the loss of the 254, a second route of that number and its partner 255 were successful enough to have their LS complement upgraded on 1 September 1990 to a DMS, though under the sole number 255. Powering through a set of roadworks at West Croydon bus station on the 12th is Croydon's DMS 2256 (OJD 256R).** *John Parkin*

224 THE LONDON DMS

Left: **Ensignbus 102 (THM 682M) had been more famous as DF 1682, the 'other' 1933-liveried DMS, but by the turn of the 1990s had taken on an equally attractive livery when drafted into the main fleet, despite having been converted to single-door (hence the fleetnumber in the one hundreds). It is seen in Romford on 16 June 1990, by which time the 252 was normally operated by Alexander-bodied Leyland Olympians.**
Malc McDonald

Below: **Pity the poor 88, withdrawing battered towards town; on 28 April 1990 a further section was hacked away from it with the loss of all roads south of Clapham Common (except on Sundays, where it continued to penetrate past Tooting to Mitcham and Merton Garage, necessitating some most unusual ultimate blinds). Stockwell's D 2611 (THX 611S), with a surviving 'PAY DRIVER' strip added in the air intake, calls at Clapham Common on 26 August.**
Malc McDonald

the hitherto LS-operated 254/255 pair was consolidated as 255 with a single DMS.

Ensignbus reallocated the 165 from Purfleet to Dagenham on 18 August; due to a shortage of Olympians from the 121-128 batch, DMSs filled in on the 252. The 449 was withdrawn on Sundays on 25 August and altogether on 26 October. 109 (DMS 2219) received an all-over advert for PFH phones and 104's Fuji scheme was replaced by one for IBM in connection with this year's Wimbledon tennis tournament; both were predominantly white. 223 (DM 1043), meanwhile, looked 'one-eyed' through the fitment of a plain glass panel on the front upper-deck offside.

On 22 September the 88, having run in sections for some years, was formally split, the Shepherd's Bush half taking the number 94 and the 88, still with Stockwell DMSs on Sundays, now going no further west than Marble Arch with further pruning to be done at the southern end only a week later.

Above: The cruel nature of tendering gave Norbiton's Kingston Bus operation little future by taking three of its routes away, and it was a miracle the garage stayed open at all, coveted as it was by supermarket chains (it eventually became a Wickes). Destined to be the last Kingston Bus DMS in service is DMS 711 (TGX 711M), seen in Galsworthy Road in August 1990; its route 213 was lost to Sutton on 29 September. This bus was one of the ones with a black skirt, but had since had it painted over (not quite thoroughly enough!). *Haydn Davies*

Right: Colliers Wood outstation received its first DMSs when the resources of routes 152 and 163 were transferred in from Sutton on 29 September 1990. Five months later they'd go with the buses to Merton, and even after that the 'AA' codes lingered enough to fulfil this page's photographic requirements; sporting them (not to mention a most unattractive repurposing of some numberplate transfers in lieu of the correct Johnston fleetnumber ones) is DMS 2260 (OJD 260R) at Raynes Park on 6 April 1991. *Malc McDonald*

Kingston Bus's three-year contract term was now up and with it passed Norbiton's remaining DMSs; the new order bowed on 29 September, costing the unit the 65, 85 and 213 and placing the garage's very viability in serious doubt. The 213, though returning to Sutton under a new London General contract, was converted to Ms, introducing Metrobuses to that garage for the first time, though both this and new route 413, created to sectionalise the Belmont bifurcation, were quite capable of fielding DMSs and often did. Norbiton's last Fleetline was DMS 711, which operated until 3 October and was also the last standard DMS in service with LBL. The proportion of Ms at Merton was increased substantially with castoffs from Norbiton, allowing the first bona fide B20 withdrawals other than by attrition; these were still useful as trainers and started being converted thus. Routes 154 and 155 were introduced on Sundays, respectively finishing off the 213's extension to Croydon and the 88's last projections south of Clapham Common. In order to free space at Sutton for the return of the 213, the 152 and 163 were farmed out to Colliers Wood, introducing that small outstation to its first DMSs in the form of fifteen transferred from Sutton and stripped

226 THE LONDON DMS

Left: **After so many years of confusion as to just which direction the 213 would hare off in once it reached Cheam from the west, at least one of its extremities was sectionalised on 29 September 1990 when new route 413 took over the peak-hour duties to Belmont and introduced them all day. It was meant to share the new allocation of Ms put into Sutton for the 213, but the garage's DMSs were blinded for both and turned out regularly, as has DMS 2462 (OJD 462R) on 29 August 1991 when espied in Carshalton. The panel is a lazy blind.** *John Parkin*

Below: **As the London Buses Ltd central identity continued to wither, its new subsidiaries flexed their wings as best they could, and the most freedom they were allowed in this respect was in terms of their trainers, which sat the turn of the 1990s still largely consisted of DMSs. Hounslow-based DMS 1537 (THM 537M) looks most smart in its London United scheme of red and two greys as it crosses Hampton Court Bridge in October 1990.** *Geoff Rixon*

of their Suttonbus logos. London General side logos invariably appeared on Sutton's DMSs when lower-deck repaints were carried out. The transfer of the 163 removed the need for the garage journeys beyond Morden to Sutton. A shortage of OPO double-deckers in the autumn compelled Streatham to operate its DMSs and an increasing number of Ms with conductors on the 159 during weekdays until four RMs could be reclaimed from sales stock at Fulwell in November.

Some of the withdrawn DMSs' fates in the second half of 1990 were varied; as well as six moving to Leaside and one to Hounslow for training, where their blind boxes were plated over (DMSs 1426 and 1537 additionally receiving a new livery with a broad grey band in the middle and RiversideBus fleetnames), over a dozen were despatched to the Department of Transport's Fire Research Centre in Borehamwood during the autumn for controlled destruction; Brixton's DMS 2320 was compelled to join them after it caught fire at Redhill on the way back from FFD work at Eastbourne on 28 September. Other than that, B20 repaints ceased that month.

Ensignbus had a busy year, first reconvening its operations under the Frontrunner O-licence for sale to Whitehall Investments, which deal fell through; this would have seen the dwindling cohort of DMSs among the fleet take on London Suburban Buses fleetnames. The opening of Lakeside on 23 October, which was to have seen an extension from the west of the 165 and 365, was instead carried out with new commercial route 565, plus three others and a night route introduced locally to feed it. Having put in sterling service in refutation of the accepted wisdom that they could not, the DMSs still available to Ensignbus began to make their exit as 1990 wound down, being replaced by 24 new Dennis Dominators, themselves mechanical kin to Fleetlines. On 1 December the 62 was cut back again to Marks Gate, but was rerouted at times to rove off in the other direction, to Collier Row. Against the withdrawal of seven DMSs during the year (nos 206, 218, 221, 226, 231, 252 and 256), 27 survived into the new era under Hong Kong Citybus, which bought Ensignbus on 29 December and rechristened it Ensign Citybus. Meanwhile, after five years of operation, London Buslines now felt it had a fleet big enough to require identification by fleetnumbers, to which end the surviving DMs gained 1007, 1033, 1040, 1041, 1078 and 1083 to match the stock numbers of their London Transport days, though DM 962 became 1062 and former DMSs 1869 and 1882 were slotted in as 1069 and 1082; one of them (1083) even received the new London Buslines livery designed by Best Impressions and inaugurated on the latest batch of new Northern Counties-bodied Olympians for route 92, acquired on 10 November 1991 and soon added to the DMSs' portfolio.

At the very end of the DMSs' career, which was looming fast, an edict went out in November 1990 to repaint all entrance doors red; the only DMSs known to receive this treatment were Stockwell's DMS 2266 and D 2563 and Thornton Heath's DMS 2500 and they looked surprisingly uncomfortable. As Merton lost 18 DMSs during the month, the first examples began to be readied for sale; Thornton Heath suffered a shortage which it addressed by borrowing DMSs from Croydon, and further accident victims, like Sutton's D 2552, were left unrepaired. Perhaps with an eye to the myriad of things that could be done with a DMS if someone were to buy the not particularly elderly B20 fleet, London Underground Ltd's marketing arm had DMS 1515 rebuilt into an extraordinary contraption known as Supercar for a TV commercial extolling public transport in association with the ad agency GGT; while the front remained familiar, the middle was now a 1973 stock Tube car (including Piccadilly Line map) and the rear a Class 321 EMU cab!

Below: **On 27 August 1990 London Buslines' GHV 83N is still going, sighted at Edgware, and at the end of the year would take on the number 1083 to match, albeit without the class code, the fleet number of its days as a London Transport DM.** *Malc McDonald*

1991

Despite it being now 20 years since the DMSs had bravely entered service on 2 January 1971, their anniversary year was to prove devastating as tendering losses progressively released enough Metrobuses and Titans to make feasible their final replacement, and indeed two were sold in January 1991. From the 27th of that month Ms began pouring into Stockwell, taking over the 37, 77A, 156 and 170, plus the 88 on Sundays and N87 at night. This was in advance of a massive scheme planned for 25 May and centred on Wandsworth, but even in advance of that date changes were implemented which still involved DMSs. On 2 February the 137 was subjected to cost-cutting by means of hiving off the southernmost section as OPO route 137A, which swelled to cover the entire evening and Sunday service on the 137; Brixton DMSs were allocated on weekdays, with Streatham in charge on Sundays with its mixed DMS/M contingent. What was left of the 95 was withdrawn and Brixton came off the 109 so that the whole route could become the responsibility of Streatham, which gained seven more DMSs and seven Ms to make up for the garage going 100% OPO with the concurrent loss of the RM allocation on the 159.

Left: **Even this late in their career the DMS would have a role to play in the eternal London Transport game of cutting corners, however roundabout the method. It must have been at least partially cost-effective to go to all the trouble of sending the 137's RMLs home after the evening peak and replacing them with DMSs under the number 137A; this new service was commissioned to take over the southernmost sector of the 137 and then grow to cover the whole route after 8 pm and on Sundays. Here on 11 May 1991 is Brixton's DMS 2412 (OJD 412R); Streatham Ms (and the odd DMS while they were based) operated alone on Sundays.** *Malc McDonald*

Left: **The 95 could have picked up the gold medal for longest continuously-operated DMS route, except that Brixton had spent two months without the class during 1986 and the 95 had been a feeble peak-hours-only route from about that time. Such services never last, and on 2 February 1991 the 95 was taken off, to be replaced by additional strength on the 109 and 133. On the route's last day, Brixton's DMS 2335 (THX 335S) heads south down the Brixton Road.** *Malc McDonald*

DECLINING YEARS

Above: Perhaps the saviour of the DMSs' reputation and proving it not just with words but with operation of a sizeable number, Ensignbus started winding down their fleet at the end of 1990 as 24 new Dennis Dominators arrived to replace them. 237 (SMU 926N) duly exchanged its Southend colours (see page 209) for company livery and lasted in service until January 1991. The previous May sees it hard at work on the 365. *Haydn Davies*

On 23 February 1991 Colliers Wood and its allocation on routes 152 and 163 were subsumed into Merton's runout, adding more DMSs to that garage for a little longer. The 156 was also taken back from Stockwell on Sundays from 2 March. Perhaps the final alteration to a DMS-operated night route took the N87 off the Kingston By-Pass on its way to Hook on 27 April and pushed it instead via the 131 through Kingston to Hampton Court. Meanwhile, in the debits column was London Buslines' 195, which was lost to CentreWest on 13 April.

Ensign Citybus withdrew seven DMSs (nos 210, 213, 220, 222, 230, 232 and 237) in January 1991 now that all its Dominators were in use on the 62 and 248, but was experimenting with new liveries, repainting 211 (DM 1069) in yellow and silver but with red outlining replacing the black. Also in March Metrobus withdrew former DMS 1922 and returned ex-DMS 2243 to fleet livery. London Buslines treated at least the lower halves of its DMSs to the new company livery (save 1033 and 1078, which were sold in June to a new tour firm which would soon become famous as the Big Bus Company), but LBL had stopped repainting DMSs some time since and DMSs 2311, 2413 and 2417 from Croydon had managed to make it into 1991 still in unrelieved red. Other than the lucky escape of a few DMSs to training work to displace the long-lived standards and a few more to private-hire and school contract work around the fleet at places like Stamford Hill, Holloway and North Street, most sales of the unfortunate DMSs, which comprised exclusively for the moment the Leyland-engined ones, were to PVS. At the same time Metrobus sold former DMSs 2054 and 2173 in part-exchange for Lynxes to improve the age profile on the 356, while Grey-Green scrapped 528 after an accident at Stratford on the 173. This company had added the 103 to its quiver on 6 January, taking it over with its Olympians from County Bus, and sure enough the DMS lookalikes were put out when nothing else was available.

Right: Stockwell had become a latter-day stronghold of the DMS as one after another well-resourced route was one-manned, but from the end of January 1991 Ms started taking over. The repaint red of the entrance doors of two of them to accompany a policy change was a surprise so late in the day. Looking more than a little awkward (and how would the poor passengers know where to get on?), D 2563 (THX 563S) turns into St John's Road, Clapham Junction on 11 May 1991. *Malc McDonald*

THE LONDON DMS

Stockwell's DMSs did not survive the implementation of the Wandsworth scheme on 25 May, but Merton kept hold of enough to feature on some of the new routes introduced on that day; the 270 and 344, combining the former extremities of the 220/280 and 44/170 respectively, fielded the occasional DMS while Merton still had them, their replacement by Ms dragging out beyond the end of 1991; the 344 was Merton's responsibility on Sundays and the 280 was pulled back to Tooting to offset an extension south to Belmont, while the 355 was repositioned at its southern end to terminate at Mitcham. Despite losing their Sunday-only allocation on the 19, DMSs also made their first appearance on the 22 when the Sunday Victoria allocation was transferred into Merton; that garage's 77 was rerouted south of the river to Waterloo and the 219 now terminated at Sloane Square rather than South Kensington. Helped by Titans into Norwood of all places, Streatham could now take back enough Ms to render the year-long assistance by DMSs a historical footnote; DMS 2305 was the last to leave.

Above: **Following its purchase by the CNT Group of Hong Kong, Ensignbus was renamed Ensign Citybus and new liveries were experimented with to bring the company closer to its new Citybus parent. This yellow and blue affair was applied to 109 (OJD 219R) in the summer of 1991, but didn't meet with approval from on high, and by the time the eventual Capital Citybus identity came in, with allover yellow buses, the DMSs had gone. The 347 was a commercial route on the edge of town, serving Dagenham Asda as this bus is seen doing in October.** *Tony Wilson*

Left: **Probably the last route to receive a debut allocation of DMSs was the rather unlikely 22, RML-operated on weekdays but without the resources at Putney to fully man it on Sundays; on 25 May 1991 the Victoria allocation was removed and Merton struck up a share. While Ms were the expected staple, the number of DMSs left joined them, and here at Piccadilly Circus is DMS 2410 (OJD 410R), taking the type into the West End for not much longer.** *David Wilkinson collection*

DECLINING YEARS 231

Below: Nobody could have imagined the strict segregation of Metrobuses and Titans by district upon their allocation being disrupted, and it wasn't really even the replacement of the district structure by pre-privatisation units that forced LBL to allocate its buses where they were needed, standardisation be damned. Damaged by ongoing strikes by London Forest staff against impending pay cuts and longer working hours conferred by this subsidiary's retention of their tenders based on Walthamstow garage, LT cancelled their contracts and wound up London Forest altogether, as a result freeing up nearly 200 Titans. As route after route departed for new operators (mostly Capital Citybus), Ts began to take over from DMSs at first Brixton, then Croydon garages. Not to last much longer on the Sunday OPO roster on the 159, therefore, is DMS 2311 (THX 311S), seen outside its home in November. Not only have its foglights completely gone, but unusually, the holes have been plated over! *Haydn Davies*

Ensign Citybus, for so long storming through the ranks of red-bus operations in east London, actually lost a route on 22 June; its first, the 145, followed by the N99 on 13 September. Almost at the end of DMS operation another livery experiment was undertaken in August with 109 (DMS 2219) as the guinea pig. Yellow down to below the lower deck windows and blue below that, the colours were separated by a red band. Neither this nor the livery on 211, nor a wild two-in one scheme of green-and-silver/red-and-silver applied to a Metrobus were adopted, a yellow livery with red bands appearing instead, and only a dozen DMSs remained by the time it was introduced. Their last hurrah was to concentrate mostly on the 252 in October and November to make available as much yellow stock as possible to fully man the routes newly acquired from the collapsing London Forest up to and including 23 November 1991. 109 in its experimental livery even popped up on the 97 on its first and fourth day with Capital Citybus, as the company was now called, running from Dagenham until the new depot at Northumberland Park depot (NP) was ready to be opened. Six DMSs left in September (nos 208, 209, 219, 225, 235 and 238), leaving eleven with the intent for them all to go by the end of 1991; the best place to find them was the 347 route on the eastern edges of town. While they could still run the 165/365, those routes were repositioned on 14 September to set the 365 north of Romford and the 165 to the south; the 252 was withdrawn between Romford and Gidea Park. On 23 November Ensign's second route, the 62, also returned to Barking with the Ts that had manned it before and the 62A was withdrawn at the same time. Maybe the last quirk here was an inward loan, for a change, of DMS 2200 from Metrobus, thus thanking the company for all the DMSs it had sent in the opposite direction during the early fraught years of operation! Following the conversion to Darts of the 358, Metrobus could now field just three DMSs as spares, and they were used on the 261 on Saturdays, which had a higher requirement than on weekdays.

The final blow was now descending. The last Leyland-engined DMSs in LBL service were withdrawn during June, these being part of Merton's fast-depleting allocation that was cut down to single figures (Iveco-powered) by August, when the total of B20s left in service fell below 200. The Leyland engine had survived at least long enough to be withdrawn at the same time as Ivecos started being taken off. On 31 August four of Sutton's routes were altered so that the 151 was restored to Worcester Park, allowing the 413 to convert to minibus operation and reach Lower Morden in its place, while the 80 was projected southwards from Belmont to serve two new prisons built on the sites of closed hospitals and the 213 gained the 151's schoolday projections to St Helier, Glenthorne School. The opportunity, often taken, for Sutton's DMSs to work on minibus route 352, was removed on 30 November when the route was subsumed into the 152.

Left: **Titans poured into Croydon during November 1991, sweeping away most of Croydon's long-standing B20 DMS complement. DMS 2364 (OJD 364R) sidestepped the onslaught of Ts, as seen when passing Streatham garage on 20 January 1992, but it was to be Metrobuses that cleared out this particular bus that 14 March. The second 59 to see DMSs had only had a Croydon allocation since 1 September 1990 and would lose it with the next round of changes that would also see Streatham garage prematurely closed.**
Malc McDonald

The 189 departed Brixton on 4 September for a new year at London General's Stockwell with VCs. Sutton began re-equipping concertedly with Metrobuses during October, taking examples displaced from conversions to minibus in north-west London, but from 8 October a new twist developed when the first Titans arrived at Brixton; Titans because of enormous upheaval at LBL's doomed London Forest subsidiary, whose staff had attempted to strike to defend themselves against stark new working conditions a la Norbiton but had paid the price by having their contracts reassigned elsewhere – mostly to the newly-renamed Capital Citybus. In the same month two Ts appeared at Croydon, taking up service on non-tendered routes 59, 68, 130, 166, 194, 194A, 255, 366 and X30. In November the trickle became a flood when Ash Grove and Walthamstow closed on the 23rd, making available nearly 200 Titans to halve the remaining DMS complement overnight. The last four DMSs at Brixton were DMSs 2316, 2492, 2497 and 2514, and they were gone on 5 December. 180 DMSs were sold in 1991, including DMS 2456 for preservation, leaving just 87 left; from London General 50 continued at Sutton and just the one at Merton (DMS 2406), and from South London there remained twelve at Croydon and 24 at Thornton Heath.

Left: **DMS 2441 (OJD 441R) was withdrawn from Croydon when the garage's first Titans arrived in November, but in April was carrying on as normal, albeit with an interesting local interpretation of the front-mounted instruction as to whom to pay.**
Haydn Davies

DECLINING YEARS

1992-93

Merton's nearly 21-year spell with the DMS ceased on 4 January 1992 when DMS 2406 was withdrawn after working AL165 on the 155; it had been the sole survivor there for two months. As garages in north and west London continued to lose their Ms for minibuses of varying sizes and suitability, the Metrobuses released were directed to Sutton and only 33 DMSs were still working from there by March, and since 18/19 January all without Suttonbus logos, which were unceremoniously removed that weekend to banish the memory of this operation to history. As if in protest, DMS 2343 caught fire at Putney Bridge Station on 8 February while on the 93 and was burnt out – the fourth Fleetline from this garage to meet a fiery end! With the programme of 14 March it was intended that all DMSs be removed from South London, Thornton Heath's going as planned with the loss on tender of the 194B within LBL to Selkent (as 198) and the removal of its allocation on the 59, which was relegated to a Brixton-operated peak-hour shuttle from Farringdon Street only as far south as its home garage so that the 109 could be strengthened again. As well as its own allocation on the 59, Croydon simultaneously lost the 166 and 194 to Selkent and the 194A and 366 were withdrawn. The wholesale replacement of Croydon's short-lived Titans was achieved with the entire stock of Ms from Streatham, which was closed after just five years, but even that left just seven DMSs (2375, 2411, 2438, 2445, 2480 and 2494 plus D 2633) clinging on at Croydon. Only DMSs 2375, 2445, 2480 and D 2633 were indigenous, the others coming from Thornton Heath on transfer, and their remaining pitch was the 130 with occasional forays to the 68 and X30. To keep them functioning, DMSs 2425, 2432 and 2435 were stripped during the summer.

Capital Citybus's last DMSs in service by February 1992 were 211 and 227, formerly known as DMs 1069 and 1154; the honour of being the last in this popular fleet, whose original parent company had done so much to rehabilitate the reputation of the DMS almost single-handedly, fell to 211, which was sold in July. Grey-Green could still put its remaining ex-South Yorkshire lookalikes into the field from a

Above: **DMSs lingered at Merton for some time after the changes of 25 May 1991 were supposed to have seen them all off, due to the production of blinds featuring Merton's new routes. DMS 2406 (OJD 406R) managed to squeak into 1992, giving Merton the medal for operating the DMS for the longest period of time – a spell of 20 years, 11 months and 19 days. It is seen at Stockwell on 8 August 1991.** *Malc McDonald*

Right: **Stripped of both its Suttonbus and London General logos, Sutton's DMS 2448 (OJD 448R) looks suitably life-expired, climbing Anerley Road towards Crystal Palace on 20 January 1992. It would not see the month out.** *Malc McDonald*

234 — THE LONDON DMS

Left: **Thornton Heath's 194B route was scheduled to pass under tender on 14 March 1992 to Bromley as a Selkent operation with Titans, while the 109 was to take its place, also with Ts. Therefore DMSs were withdrawn from Thornton Heath after that date; here for posterity on 6 March is DMS 2500 (THX 500S), its foglights plated over and with red entrance doors.** *Tony Wilson*

Below: **Heavy withdrawals began to rip into Sutton's numbers in earnest as 1992 rolled along, Metrobuses being redeployed to the garage by the uncomfortable expedient of converting their northwest London-area routes to minibuses of varying suitability. DMS 2304 (THX 3045) was a late stayer at Sutton, coming off only in April 1992, six months short of its ten-year anniversary at that garage, and not the only one there to rack up such unlikely stability. In July 1991 it is seen coming into Putney Bridge Station's approach road at the end of a morning peak journey on the 93.** *Haydn Davies*

new garage at Ripple Road, Barking from March 1992, while enough new buses had now arrived at London Buslines and at Metrobus to relegate their DMSs to reserve use only, though with no hint of withdrawal. London Buslines' holdouts were all now in the new company livery and had long since lost their engine shrouds.

Sutton was whittled down during the spring, most of its survivors being taken out by a surge of Ms displaced in April and May when revised weight limits on Hammersmith Bridge forced the conversion to Darts of routes 72 and 33, in that order. Among the withdrawals at this time was DMS 2476, which was converted into a trainer – not so unusual, as this was the intermediate fate of many B20 DMSs before sale, but this time it received a smart dedicated livery with a yellow front and roof and a reclassification to DMT, with ten more similarly treated for London General by the autumn, their blind boxes removed. But of Sutton's service DMSs, only D 2646 remained; its last day in service was Thursday 19 June when it performed A6 on the 93.

Right: **The extensive changes of 14 March 1992, chief among which was the closure of Streatham garage after just five years, saw Croydon's sixty-strong Titan fleet replaced in its entirety by an equivalent number of Metrobuses - but even then, its DMSs managed to stay put. Just seven of them survived, and the final months of one of them was particularly unusual. The craze for re-registering modern buses with the marks of outgoing Routemasters, reflecting their sudden jump in value, never spread to DMSs, though very large numbers of Ms, Ls and a full third of the VC class, ended up wearing them. However, July 1992 saw D 2633 (new as THX 633S) detached from Croydon's final seven and given WLT 916 to reflect its new role as a private-hire vehicle. It is seen thus at West Croydon. It didn't last long with this mark, taking on DGJ 415S in April 1993 so that WLT 916 could go on to Olympian L 16.** *Bill Young*

Now only Croydon was left, but a need was identified for its DMSs to officially remain as cover for vehicles away for maintenance, which theoretically stayed their execution till the end of 1992. Of the seven left, DMSs 2375 and 2411 were withdrawn in May and DMS 2445 in the second half of June, while DMS 2480 went on loan to Merton in June to become positively the last of its type to work on the Wimbledon tennis service, an operation which had seen the DMS at its best in latter years. The diversion to private-hire use of D 2633 in July (under the registration WLT 916, the first ever and only re-registration of a DMS with a Routemaster mark) and the withdrawal of DMSs 2480 and 2494 in October left DMS 2438 as the last Fleetline in LBL service, to accompany the official conversion date of 28 November 1992. Incredibly, it would not be

Right: **After the withdrawal of D 2646 from Sutton, only one DMS-operating garage was left, and that was Croydon, which had seen over 450 of them pass through its doors at one time or another since 6 January 1973. As the summer of 1992 drew on, Croydon's DMS numbers depleted gradually as isolated examples were picked off one after the other, until this shot of June at East Croydon where DMS 2480 (THX 480S) could count itself just one of three. DMSs 2480 and 2494 were withdrawn in October, leaving only one – DMS 2438.** *Rick Godfrey*

THE LONDON DMS

Left: Who would have thought that a DMS could manage a thirty-mile journey, fully loaded, through London's mean and congested streets, without disgracing itself as per the stereotype that never quite faded? For the ceremonial 'last day', DMS 2438 (OJD 438R) had to be on its best behaviour, and it pulled it off to some style - again, not a trait you'd associate with the DMS. The quiet Saturday morning of 2 January 1993 sees the last of the 'Londoners' with the Kennington Road to itself and thus able to open up like it (and many of its ilk) had rarely had the chance to do. *Malc McDonald*

dislodged, surviving to the end of the year and on into 1993. Fittingly, it was selected to perform a special tour on 2 January to commemorate the DMSs' 22nd anniversary of entering service, something which didn't look at all likely at one point. Under the special route number 459, this service began from Chipstead Valley at 09.00 and followed historical DMS-family routes 166, 109, 133, 45, 259 and 283 to Hammond Street, an epic 34-mile, 3¾-hour journey which went off without any of the hitches stereotypical of the DMS – and even after returning via the same route it was put back into service, usually on the 130 but featuring once or twice on the 68 as well. Finally the game was up, occasioned by the imminent expiry of its FFD, and on 20 January DMS 2438 worked TC104 on the 130, its last duty.

Left: At what was once the very northernmost edge of red London Transport bus territory and only recently abandoned, Flamstead End is where DMS 2438 (OJD 438R) is seen on the ceremonial last day of the DMS, 2 January 1993. *Rick Godfrey*

CHAPTER EIGHT

AFTERWARDS

Enough material exists on DMSs post-London to fill a book twice the size of this one, and indeed there are such volumes, the purchase of the Nigel Eadon-Clarke Colourscene trilogy on subsequent disposals and international tour operators being highly recommended. For the purposes of this book, the immediate adventures of buses in LBL-subsidiary and LRT contractor ownership are covered briefly as their roles began to wind down during the 1990s, and finally preservation, which is intended to immortalise in place any kind of bus in a specific time period, is tackled.

In as much as schools services 'count', their previous restricted nature having been almost forcibly altered by officialdom to mainstream status despite the enduring likelihood that non-pupil passengers and enthusiast photographers would avoid them, they enter this story obliquely in that the likes of London Buslines and Metrobus continued to use their DMS survivors on them into the mid-1990s. Even LBL joined in on the act, the private-hire arm of East London picking up D 2600 during July 1992 for use as fit; not only was it rostered alongside two coach-seated Titans on school routes 345 and 449 when it wasn't engaged upon Lakeside express service 723X, but when needs really pressed it was stuck out on the 129 and 174, two normal North Street routes, in January and February 1993, appearing a couple of times each!

Below: LBL's subsidiaries carried the private-hire ethos of the mid-1980s to new heights. East London's arm was particularly successful, close as it was to a host of East Anglia resorts, and until it could muster enough money to buy coaches, made do with existing DMSs and Titans. It's definitely strange seeing this blind box configuration again as D 2600 (THX 600S) passes along North Street in Romford, over a decade after DMSs and Routemasters alike had left the area. *Tony Wilson*

Right: Metrobus's DMS stocks dwindled as newer (and new) buses replaced them from frontline service but still managed to attain almost a decade in renewed service. OJD 211R, formerly DMS 2211, is carrying the less attractive blind set printed later and including the 'by agreement' route 358 in August 1992; after its withdrawal the following February, just two DMSs remained, holding out until the end of 1995. *Haydn Davies*

The ex-South Yorkshire 'DMSs' had also quietly achieved a normal lifespan at Grey-Green; four of them (503, 519, 525 and 526) survived into 1993 and eked out their days on the 173 and 179, plus the schools augmentation of the 20 and 235, even as ex-Newport Metrobuses arrived to replace them. 503 was sold in April and the other three wouldn't outlast the conversion of the 173 to Dart; 526 was the last in service, doing both the morning and afternoon peak on the 235 on 24 September. Metrobus, though officially withdrawing the DMS from service in January 1993 after the sale of several members at the end of the previous year, kept hold of ex-DMSs 2198 and 2243, which continued to turn up on the 61 and 261 (particularly on Saturdays when the 261 needed an extra vehicle) if there was absolutely nothing else available. The latter was sold on 27 March 1995 and the last, DMS 2198, on 22 December on the second try after an earlier sale in August fell through. London Buslines, therefore, could claim the prize for keeping the last DMSs in 'regular' service. Their numbers dwindling gradually, four were replaced in September 1993 by four new Olympians, leaving the final pair, 1007 and 1041, to land on school route 389, which commenced a three-year contract with London Buslines on 7 September 1993 and remained through its renumbering to 698 on 13 April 1994 and for the two school years after that. Quite against type, London Buslines had thus wrung eleven years out of their Fleetlines, on top of the ten since they'd been new, and, having run the first DMSs on a tendered route, they ran the last. The 698 was awarded for 1996-97 to CentreWest from 12 October, and on the day before, Friday 11 October 1996, 1007 and 1041, of which 1007 had been there since the beginning, were finally taken out of service. They were the very last DMSs in London service of any kind.

Left: On 22 July 1996 London Buslines' unprepossessing 1007 (GHV 7N) finds itself working the 698 through Hayes for one last school year. Although the foglights are long gone and it carries neither fleetnames nor fleetnumbers, it is perhaps a good indicator of what condition the standard DMSs might have been in if circumstances had allowed them to reach a full lifespan in the manner of their predecessors. And even after that it remained in the capital with the Big Bus Company, albeit re-registered KLL 898N. *Mike Harris*

AFTERWARDS

Above: The prospective bus driver in London General's catchment area during the mid-1990s could find his first stab at the job behind the wheel of a DMS, or, to give them the dedicated classification adopted by London General for this role, DMT. To go with the usual fitting of an instructor's seat slap bang in the middle of the aisle, a rather smart colour scheme was adopted with a full yellow front. Eleven were operated between 1992 and 1997, and on the outskirts of Hampton Court on 5 May 1995 we see Merton's DMT 2347 (OJD 347R). *Geoff Rixon*

Not that tendering grew that much easier in the post-DMS years than it had been in 1985; a disastrous state of affairs surrounding route 60 at the start of 1999 forced LBSL, as the procurers of bus services in London were by then known, to scramble into action just about anything on four wheels that could be made available following the eleventh-hour collapse of the route's intended contractor. Just one of the dozens of varied buses to fill in was DMS 2333, by then owned by Nostalgiabus, and making a return to a route it would have operated regularly when based at Croydon.

Similarly, as the role for service buses dwindled, so too did the possibility for training work. South London's and those still at Leaside Buses were replaced by Ts in 1992 and Ms 1-5 took over the role at Metroline towards the end

Right: Just about anything that could be thrown at the 60 during its winter of agony appeared; even a DMS. Nostalgiabus had DMS 2333 (THX 333S) as part of its attractively-liveried fleet and slotted it in perfectly well during this central Croydon view of early 1999. *Author's collection*

240

Left: **The Leaside Buses subsidiary's private-hire fleet carved out a solid reputation which was eventually spun off into a company of its own. One of its stalwarts was DMS 2168 (OJD 168R), which had landed in that part of town in September 1987 after training drivers in south-East London. On the occasion of the North Weald bus rally on 27 June 1993, it was piloted there from Enfield Town by the photographer.**
Malc McDonald

of that year. The attractively-liveried London General DMTs, which had replaced earlier, Leyland-engined examples as trainers, were concentrated at Putney and lasted into the privatised era before being replaced in 1997 by the next generation of London buses to come out of service, which in this sector was Ms.

Private-hire work was a useful stopgap between withdrawal and sale and rather more glamorous in scope than training; of the LBL subsidiaries, Selkent (open-top Ds 948 and 1102) London Northern (DMS 2168 and open-top D 2556), South London (D 2633), East London (D 2600) and Leaside Buses (DMSs 681, 1868 and 2168 for Islington schools contracts plus open-top DMS 2291) all used DMSs. The vehicles of the last three mentioned were occasionally pressed into service, one such notable occasion in 1993 taking Leaside's examples to the 38 and 73 as part of a extensive rail replacement service in central London to fill in for services from Charing Cross and Waterloo East stations. DMS 681 of this outfit gained a substantially revised 'face' when it was fitted with a Metrobus-style full-width blind box to work private-hire duties out of Stamford Hill and then, from 13 May 1995, Enfield. As the big-group parents of the newly privatised LBL subsidiaries developed their own ideas about private-hire work, they invariably stood down their DMSs; (Stagecoach)

Left: **Open-topping a bus can prolong its career for many years, which was the case for DMS 2291 (THX 291S), driven under the low bridge at Finsbury Park on 13 August 1987; it had been one of the few B20s used as a trainer. On 13 August 1993, the last day of a set of extensive rail augmentations, it was deputised to help out on the 38 and is seen coming round Hyde Park Corner into Piccadilly. The full blinds do it credit.**
Tony Wilson

AFTERWARDS

Selkent's two open-toppers were withdrawn at the end of 1994, as was D 2556 in 1995 (by MTL London Northern) and the (Cowie) Leaside DMSs in June 1997. Leaside's DMS 2291, on the other hand, gained immortality by being hired by Arsenal to transport its squad around north London on the occasion of two separate triumphs; the league in 1989 and the League Cup and FA Cup in 1993. But when the club constructed a museum at Highbury that year and wanted to mount the front half of the bus as an exhibit, DMS 2291 was not available, so the equally famous former Chocolate Box, D 2629, was acquired and mocked up instead, complete with weight-saving wooden chassis. As the chant goes, 'same old Arsenal, always cheating!'. Arsenal, the FA Cup and the DMS have an indelible association, it seems, as they won the Cup again in 2014 and this time took out DMS 1304 (Red Route Buses) for the parade held on 18 May.

As for preservation, the poor reputation of the DMS with London Transport and its passengers and accompanying unpopularity with enthusiasts, who justifiably blamed the type for seeing off so many RTs, had naturally led to there being far fewer in preservation than your comparable Routemaster or RT. However, after some years of successful subsequent service with operators nationwide, the DMS has been somewhat rehabilitated, and those enthusiasts who grew up with them, for good or ill, have now aged into the financial bracket which can just about cope with the care, feeding and garaging of an expensive, obsolete PSV like the ones they remember travelling on to school, and examples have crept onto the rally field, unobtrusively at first. Those that had faith in the type from the beginning, like the owner of DMS 132, have gone on to inspire future preservationists keen to take the risk, most notably the purchaser of Ogle-refitted DMS 2456, who was 15 at the time. At the turn of the century operators of specifically preserved vehicles made their charges pay for their upkeep by certifying them to Class 5 or Class 6 status and using them on running days, a more versatile and exciting kind of public appearance than the traditional static rally had become. Blue Triangle's DM 1052 was a perfect example – although the recalcitrance of the DVLA in passing buses not fitted with its incredibly restrictive specifications has since forced this vehicle to don the unattractive and thoroughly incorrect post-2001 style of reflective numberplate that no DMS ever wore!

Below: **The Carshalton running day of 15 April 2007 was perhaps the day the preserved DMS found its calling, and indeed inaugurated a new way of enjoying classic buses away from the traditional fixed milieu of a museum where entrants are discouraged from touching the exhibits. The 154 was a long-time DMS route, operating them for nineteen years out of Sutton and/or Croydon, and it's immortalised at Wallington, Shotfield by Blue Triangle's DM 1052 (GHV 52N).** *Author*

Above: Ensignbus's DM 2646 (THX 646S) looks nothing short of spectacular in the loving recreation of the Shillibeer livery for which it is best remembered. On 30 September 2007 it was one of the special guests on the two Routemaster Heritage Routes, and in mid-afternoon is caught setting off from Tower Hill. *Author*

Below: It actually wasn't until the middle of the 2000s that the DMS really established itself on the preservation circuit. A more recent entry is DMS 1426 (MLH 426L), which spent five years of its seven-year service career at Catford and then became a trainer, before an unexpected revival at Norbiton in 1987. It is seen at North Weald on 1 July 2012. *Author*

Quite probably the best of this breed is DM 2646, which was acquired by Ensign in 2004 and magnificently restored to its Shillibeer colours in time for the 2007 season, even gaining back a Leyland engine for the cause. This and DM 1052 performed an exceptionally rare permitted outing of the DMS to London stage service when on 29 September 2007 they participated in one of the regular galas on the Heritage Routes 9(H) and 15(H) that were normally home to the only remaining RMs. DM 1052 was last seen on a running day over the 24 on 25 November 2012 to celebrate the route's centenary.

DMS 1304 from Red Route Buses, meanwhile, straddles the divide between working and preservation, and is often to be found hired by political groups of varying extremity to convey their members to demos in central London. DMS 33, a long-time open-topper with Ensignbus under blue and silver and operating today in red and silver, is known there as 333 for similar work. These buses alone among the working-preserved DMSs just skate within the critical piece of emissions legislation that prohibits post-1973 vehicles from entering Greater London on more than a specific number of days without the payment of an extortionate charge.

Completed by the end of the first decade of the 21st century were DMSs 1426 and 1868, the latter now counting itself in the safekeeping of

AFTERWARDS

Right: **For 2011 the London Bus Museum was obliged to move its spring event to Dunsfold airfield, otherwise the home of BBC's** *Top Gear,* **and the weather just happened to be perfect, showcasing DMS 1868 (GHM 868N) to the very best of its looks following the completion of its full restoration.** *Author*

Below: **DM 999 (GHV 999N) led an unremarkable life, commencing at Muswell Hill in January 1975 and operating subsequently out of Croydon, during which time it was converted to a D. It has plied the rally circuit for some years, and on 16 July 2006 is seen at Alton.** *Author*

the Bromley Bus Preservation Group, which offers safety in numbers alongside a growing number of buses from varying eras and ownerships, not to mention the opportunity to run on recreations of historic routes on town-based special occasions as long as no fares are charged. This organisation has DMS 1455 as an auxiliary vehicle, though its heavily-modified state precludes a complete restoration to original condition. In various degrees of completion at the time of writing are DMSs 115, 550, 1911, 2127 (open-top) and 2216 and DMs 1002 and 1051, while DM 999 represents the Croydon DM era and DMS 2357, amazingly, is the only B20 DMS yet in original condition and brings the white-top livery back for us to remember, though modified DMS 2456 survives, DMSs 2257, 2375 and 2394 are on the cards for full restoration

244   THE LONDON DMS

Left: **B20 DMS 2357 (OJD 357R)** is a work in progress when espied here at the 2009 iteration of Cobham bus rally; the sheer amount of work necessary is evident, with almost every major body panel needing replacement. The bus started its career at Bexleyheath and, following overhaul, served at Thornton Heath, Brixton and finally Merton, coming out of service in July 1991, but it is immortalised here with Palmers Green blinds. *Author*

and Ensignbus's DM 2646, most recently seen on strike relief in London on two occasions in each of 2014 and 2015 and on cover for construction at London Bridge in January 2015, combines the B20 DM experience with its days as a Shillibeer. One preserved B20 which is no more, however, wasn't what it seemed during its years on the rally field; D 2633, reregistered again from WLT 916 to DGJ 415S before sale in July 1993, was further reregistered to become the first of its type to adopt the registration and identity of another, seeing out its years under THX 509S. DMS 2172, its body destroyed by fire early in its career, was stripped to chassis level at Clapham in 1982 and shortened as a testbed for engineering students, and after a long spell at Paddington Technical College is in the ownership of the LBPG at Brooklands Museum.

Left: Seen at Wisley airfield on 4 April 2004, preserved DM 1051 (GHV 51N), combines the attractive 1933-inspired livery with the much less becoming numberplates with the 51mm-wide characters specified from 1 September 2001; DM 1052 subsequently received these and the effect marred its looks so completely that it was decided to use an older picture of that bus in its full authentic glory! *Author*

Above: All that remains of DMS 2172 (OJD 172R) is the front panel and two-thirds of the chassis. Cut down like this for engineering training after a fire at Catford garage, this rig was later acquired by Cobham Bus Museum and displayed to the fascination of guests, as on 4 April 2004. On the off-chance it is taken out on the road, it has had a pair of indicator units from the rear of a Routemaster added. *Author*

Right: The numeric first of each class is, in most cases a shoo-in for preservation after its service career is done, and in the case of DMS 1 (EGP 1J), its innings merited that award somewhat more than could be said for many hundreds of its newer brethren. Even so, it has been overshadowed in its museum life by the more popular RT and Routemaster families, and only in recent years has it seen much on-road exposure. One of the first occasions it went on the road following its donation to the LT Museum was the occasion of the Netley Country Park rally on 8 July 1984. *Tony Wilson*

Below: And here is DMS 1 (EGP 1J) on display in Regent Street on 22 June 2014, during one of the events associated with TfL's Year of the Bus that year. Even though all the exhibits found themselves pointed away from the sun at that time of day, it afforded a view of the rear quarters. *Author*

Finally, DMS 1, which was withdrawn from LT service in 1982 after an almost reasonable eleven years (omitting the year or so it spent in works while they figured out first whether, and then how, to overhaul it), was donated to the London Transport Museum to accompany that body's move from Syon Park to Covent Garden, but there was no room at the latter and it remained out of sight in reserve, rarely being brought out. A change of policy in 2007, however, when the Museum was refitted for the second time since its construction, brought DMS 1 to prominence as an example of OMO (or OPO, if you like), standing alongside RM 1737. However, the enduring lack of room at Covent Garden has since relegated it again to Acton.

And then there is Supercar – the delightfully Heath Robinson affair fashioned out of three public transport conveyances and bearing the front and allover identity of DMS 1515. In 2008 it was purchased by the London Bus Company, the heir to Blue Triangle, and used as an adjunct to the Epping-Ongar Railway.

Right: **No conveyance is more cheerfully outlandish than Supercar, the remarkable pastiche of three forms of public transport created just for an advert but ultimately cemented in the hearts of enthusiasts everywhere. The third of it still licensed as DMS 1515 (MLH 515L) was new in September 1973 for the 91 at Turnham Green, and lasted but a single Certificate of Fitness, spending its last eight months at Elmers End after Ms took over the 91. A decade of training work followed, most of it at Sutton and Merton, before sale in January of 1991. The other two portions comprise a unit of 1973 Tube stock from the Piccadilly Line and a Class 321 Networker cab from Network South East. None of its sections can carry passengers any more, but that's no hindrance.** *Author*

Below: **Supercar's equally improbable rear view at the last North Weald rally on 21 June 2015.** *Author*

AFTERWARDS

247

CONCLUSION

Below: **The story of the DMS is as much a chronicle of the dizzying social and technological change going on in the background as it is about the buses themselves. When this shot of Alperton's DMS 288 (JGF 288K) was taken on 25 March 1972 there was just London Transport, and that was unlikely to change, whatever the flavour of local or national government.** *John Laker*

It's hard to assign blame as such for the debacle that was the first decade of DMS operation, but with twenty years since the DMS went out of service to chew it over, neither the manufacturer nor the operator really comes out of it entirely innocent. As what became British Leyland had gradually swallowed up manufacturer after manufacturer during the 1950s and 1960s to become practically the sole bus-building concern left in the whole country, it was in a uniquely powerful position. Yet the bigger they come, the harder they fall, and fall they did in the end. You could almost say that British Leyland and London Transport deserved one another, and by the 1970s, their core functions hobbled by hidebound practices and union recalcitrance, both were running at such a loss that they had to be propped up repeatedly by central Government.

There was a third factor, of course; politicians. As local and national government elbowed aside professional busmen as arbiters of how to fund and run London's bus services, near-constant and increasingly extreme political changes characterised the period of GLC rule between 1970 and 1986 when one militant left-wing officeholder replaced an equally reactionary right-wing counterpart, only for the process to be reversed every four years during which each incumbent would attempt to undo the policies of its predecessor and then run out of time to implement its own policies, leading to a stagnation which did neither London Transport nor its long-suffering passengers any good. Which party was in charge was absolutely critical as to how much money LT would get, and whether or not it would have to increase its fares just to break even (as was eventually made mandatory by a thoroughly fed-up Government) and not fall apart through sheer neglect. The DMS bore the brunt of this, perhaps to a greater degree than its failed single-deck Merlin and Swift counterparts, and their premature withdrawal was as wasteful to the public purse as was probably buying them in the first place.

The brutal solution eventually adopted was also politically motivated, and that was essentially to throw the baby out with the bathwater. The three-term Conservative government of the 1980s harnessed market forces to drive 'London Transport' out of business altogether, first separating its ownership from the state and then splitting up its operations to sell off, thus taking care of industrial relations and employee overheads alike. Without the regular volume orders from both London Transport and the regional operators that had been subjected to deregulation at the same time, and without New Bus Grant to pay for them, Leyland crumbled and quickly disappeared from the scene. And yet, under this straitened regime, the DMS found its feet, both with London Buses Ltd, which powered half of its survivors with new engines, and with five new independent operators, as long as they took the risk that the DMSs were as unreliable as folk legend said (which was very true at first).

It's taken a long, long time for the DMS to take its legitimate place in the pantheon of London Transport bus types through the medium of active preservation, after so many years of outright opprobrium from enthusiasts, but perhaps it's a reflection of the fact that the vehicles of today bear little similarity to those to LT's standards, with the corresponding drop in interest, as much as it is to the inevitable softening of opinions caused by the passage of time. This particular author, who encountered no operational difficulties with Daimler Fleetlines during the period he travelled on them, and who was fond of his familiar buses, has thus attempted to give the much-maligned DMS as fair a hearing as is possible.

Above: **By the time this picture of Sutton's D 2589 (THX 589S) was taken in July 1991, the centre was crumbling. What the passengers obstinately still referred to as 'London Transport' was now London Buses Ltd, but operating under twelve local identities, some of which had sub-sectors of their own that vied for prominence as a competitive mentality shook up the whole concept of buses as a service. At this point the marketing-driven Suttonbus brand had actually been sidelined by a later reincarnation of a London General identity. Under the skin, there was a new Iveco engine, which gave the DMS the performance it should have had in the first place and prolonged the lives of 200 of them into giving the class a 20-year career as a whole, while inside the cab was a new computerised Wayfarer ticket machine.**
Haydn Davies

CONCLUSION

APPENDICES

Appendix 1a: London Transport Fleetnumbers, Registrations, Engines, Chassis and Body Codes

Order Year	Stock Number	Registration	Chassis code	Bodywork	Engine	LT Code	Delivered
1970	DMS 1-17	EGP 1-17J	CRG6LXB	PRV H44/24D	Gardner 6LXB	1DM1	09.70-10.70
1971	DMS 18-117	EGP 18-117J	CRG6LXB	PRV H44/24D	Gardner 6LXB	1DM1/1	10.70-03.71
1971	DMS 118-131	EGP 118-131J	CRG6LXB	PRV H44/24D	Gardner 6LXB	2/1DM1	06.71
1971	DMS 132	EGP 132J	CRL6-30	PRV H44/24D	Leyland O.680	1/2DM1	07.71
1971	DMS 133-136	EGP 133-136J	CRG6LXB	PRV H44/24D	Gardner 6LXB	2/1DM1	06.71-07.71
1971	DMS 137-167	JGF 137-167K	CRG6LXB	PRV H44/24D	Gardner 6LXB	2/1DM1	07.71-08.71
1971	DMS 168-367	JGF 168-367K	CRG6LXB	PRV H44/24D	Gardner 6LXB	2/1DM1/2	08.71-03.72
1972-74	DMS 368-414	JGF 368-414K	CRG6LXB	PRV H44/24D	Gardner 6LXB	3/1DM3	04.72-06.72
1972-74	DMS 415-494	MLK 415-494L	CRG6LXB	PRV H44/24D	Gardner 6LXB	3/1DM3	06.72-11.72
1972-74	DMS 495-587	MLK 495-587L	CRL6	PRV H44/24D	Leyland O.680	2DM3	10.72-03.73
1972-74	DMS 588-599	MLK 588-599L	CRL6	PRV H44/24D	Leyland O.680	2/2DM3	03.73
1972-74	DMS 600-607	MLK 600-607L	CRL6	PRV H44/24D	Leyland O.680	2/2DM3/1	03.73
1972-74	DMS 608-611	MLK 608-611L	CRG6LXB	PRV H44/24D	Gardner 6LXB	4/1DM3/1	03.73-04.73
1972-74	DMS 612-616	MLK 612-616L	CRL6	PRV H44/24D	Leyland O.680	2/2DM3/1	04.73
1972-74	DMS 617-619	MLK 617-619L	CRG6LXB	PRV H44/24D	Gardner 6LXB	4/1DM3/1	04.73
1972-74	DMS 620-636	MLK 620-636L	CRL6	PRV H44/24D	Leyland O.680	2/2DM3/1	04.73-05.73
1972-74	DMS 637-639	MLK 637-639L	CRG6LXB	PRV H44/24D	Gardner 6LXB	4/1DM3/1	05.73
1972-74	DMS 640-654	MLK 640-654L	CRL6	PRV H44/24D	Leyland O.680	2/2DM3/1	05.73
1972-74	DMS 655	MLK 655L	CRG6LXB	PRV H44/24D	Gardner 6LXB	4/1DM3/1	05.73
1972-74	DMS 656-658	MLK 656-658L	CRL6	PRV H44/24D	Leyland O.680	2/2DM3/1	05.73
1972-74	DMS 659-660	MLK 659-660L	CRG6LXB	PRV H44/24D	Gardner 6LXB	4/1DM3/1	07.73
1972-74	DMS 661-695	MLK 661-695L	CRL6	PRV H44/24D	Leyland O.680	2/2DM3/1	06.73-07.73
1972-74	DMS 696-853	TGX 696-853M	CRL6	PRV H44/24D	Leyland O.680	2/2DM3/1	07.73-04.74
1972-74	DMS 854	TGX 854M	CRL6 (B20)	PRV H44/24D	Leyland O.680	3DM3/5	04.74
1972-74	DMS 855-900	TGX 855-900M	CRL6	PRV H44/24D	Leyland O.680	2/2DM3/1	05.74-07.74
1972-74	DMS 901-917	SMU 901-917N	CRL6	PRV H44/24D	Leyland O.680	2/2DM3/1	07.74-08.74
1972-74	DM 918-947	SMU 918-947N	CRL6	PRV H44/27D	Leyland O.680	2/2DM3/3	08.74-09.74
1972-74	DM 948-999	GHV 948-999N	CRL6	PRV H44/27D	Leyland O.680	2/2DM3/3	09.74-12.74
1972-74	DM 1000	GHV 500N	CRL6	PRV H44/27D	Leyland O.680	2/2DM3/3	12.74
1972-74	DM 1001-1124	GHV 1-124N	CRL6	PRV H44/27D	Leyland O.680	2/2DM3/3	11.74-07.75
1972-74	DM 1125-1141	KUC 125-141P	CRL6	PRV H44/27D	Leyland O.680	2/2DM3/3	07.75-08.75
1972-74	DM 1142-1144	KUC 142-144P	CRL6	PRV H44/27D	Leyland O.680	3/2DM3/3	08.75
1972-74	DM 1145	KUC 145P	CRL6	PRV H44/27D	Leyland O.680	2/2DM3/3	08.75
1972-74	DM 1146-1184	KUC 146-184P	CRL6	PRV H44/27D	Leyland O.680	3/2DM3/3	08.75-01.76
1972-74	DM 1185	KUC 185P	CRL6	PRV H44/27D	Leyland O.680	2/2DM3/3	10.75
1972-74	DM 1186-1217	KUC 186-217P	CRL6	PRV H44/27D	Leyland O.680	3/2DM3/3	11.75-03.76
1972-74	DM 1218-1247	KUC 218-247P	CRL6	MCW H44/27D	Leyland O.680	3/2DM4/3	01.76-04.76
1972-74	DMS 1248-1249	JGU 248-249K	CRG6LXB	MCW H44/24D	Gardner 6LXB	3/1DM4	06.72-07.72
1972-74	DMS 1250	JGU 250K	CRL6	MCW H44/24D	Leyland O.680	2DM4	07.72
1972-74	DMS 1251-1297	JGU 251-297K	CRG6LXB	MCW H44/24D	Gardner 6LXB	3/1DM4	06.72-07.72
1972-74	DMS 1298-1371	MLH 298-371L	CRG6LXB	MCW H44/24D	Gardner 6LXB	3/1DM4	07.72-12.72
1972-74	DMS 1372-1427	MLH 372-427L	CRL6	MCW H44/24D	Leyland O.680	2DM4	11.72-04.73
1972-74	DMS 1428-1451	MLH 428-451L	CRL6	MCW H44/24D	Leyland O.680	2/2DM4/1	04.73-05.73
1972-74	DMS 1452-1467	MLH 452-467L	CRG6LXB	MCW H44/24D	Gardner 6LXB	4/1DM4/1	05.73-06.73

Order Year	Stock Number	Registration	Chassis code	Bodywork	Engine	LT Code	Delivered
1972-74	DMS 1468-1499	MLH 468-499L	CRL6	MCW H44/24D	Leyland O.680	2/2DM4	06.73-09.73
1972-74	DMS 1500-1702	THM 500-702M	CRL6	MCW H44/24D	Leyland O.680	2/2DM4/1	08.73-07.74
1972-74	DM 1703-1720	THM 703-720M	CRL6	MCW H44/27D	Leyland O.680	2/2DM4/3	08.74-10.74
1972-74	DM 1721-1739	SMU 721-739N	CRL6	MCW H44/27D	Leyland O.680	2/2DM4/3	10.74
1972-74	DM 1740-1832	GHM 740-832N	CRL6	MCW H44/27D	Leyland O.680	2/2DM4/3	10.74-03.75
1972-74	DMS 1833-1897	GHM 833-897N	CRL6	MCW H44/24D	Leyland O.680	2/2DM4/1	03.75-08.75
1972-74	DMS 1898-1906	KUC 898-906P	CRL6	MCW H44/24D	Leyland O.680	2/2DM4/1	08.75-09.75
1972-74	DMS 1907-1967	KUC 907-967P	CRL6	MCW H44/24D	Leyland O.680	3/2DM4/1	09.75-12.75
1975-76	DMS 1968-1999	KUC 968-999P	FE30ALR	MCW H44/24D	Leyland O.680	3/2DM7	04.76-06.76
1975-76	DMS 2000	KJD 500P	FE30ALR	MCW H44/24D	Leyland O.680	3/2DM7	06.76
1975-76	DMS 2001-2024	KJD 1-24P	FE30ALR	MCW H44/24D	Leyland O.680	3/2DM7	06.76-09.76
1975-76	DMS 2025-2037	OUC 25-37R	FE30ALR	MCW H44/24D	Leyland O.680	3/2DM7	09.76-10.76
1975-76	DMS 2038-2057	OUC 38-57R	FE30AGR	MCW H44/24D	Gardner 6LXB	4/1DM7	10.76-11.76
1975-76	DMS 2058-2122	KJD 58-122P	FE30ALR	PRV H44/24D	Leyland O.680	3/2DM5	02.76-06.76
1975-76	DMS 2123-2127	OJD 123-127R	FE30ALR	PRV H44/24D	Leyland O.680	3/2DM5	08.76
1975-76	DMS 2128-2166	OJD 128-166R	FE30AGR	PRV H44/24D	Gardner 6LXB	4/1DM5	08.76-01.77
1975-76	DMS 2167-2246	OJD 167-246R	FE30AGR	MCW H44/24D	Gardner 6LXB	4/1DM7	11.76-06.77
1975-76	DMS 2247-2267	OJD 247-267R	FE30ALR Sp*	MCW H44/24D	Leyland O.680	3DM8	07.77-08.77
1975-76	DMS 2268-2346	THX 268-346S	FE30ALR Sp	MCW H44/24D	Leyland O.680	3DM8	08.77-02.78
1975-76	DMS 2347-2472	OJD 347-472R	FE30ALR Sp	PRV H44/24D	Leyland O.680	3DM6	02.77-08.77
1975-76	DMS 2473-2526	THX 473-526S	FE30ALR Sp	PRV H44/24D	Leyland O.680	3DM6	08.77-11.77
1975-76	DM 2527-2646	THX 527-646S	FE30ALR Sp	PRV H44/27D	Leyland O.680	3DM6/1	11.77-08.78

* Special

LT body numbers are D1-2646 in fleetnumber order; no bodies were exchanged.
DMSs 864, 1968, 2059, 2120 and DM 1199 were subsequently fitted with Rolls-Royce engines.

Appendix 1b: Park Royal body numbers

DMS 1-117	B57488-57604
DMS 118-367	B57780-58029
DMS 368-403	B58455-58490
DMS 404-415	B58492, B58491, B58493, B58494, B58496, B58498, B5849, B58497, B58501, B58499, B58500
DMS 415-917	B58502-59004
DM 918-1217	B59005-59304
DMS 2058-2166	B60837-60945
DMS 2347-2526	B60946-61125
DM 2527-2646	B61126-61245

MCW bodies were un-numbered.

Appendix 1c: Bexleybus fleetnumbers, 1988-1990

77-90	DMS 1492, 1580, 1610, 1649, 1656, 1657, 1669-1671, 1679, 1683, 1686, 1687, 2021
91-100	DMS 2063, 2064, 2068, 2074, 2108-2110, 2112, 2118, 2121
101-103	D 1146, 1160, 1195
104-107	DMS 2125, 2143, 2156, 2166

Appendix 2: Re-registrations in London Transport Ownership

D 2633   WLT 916 (07.92), DGJ 415S (04.93)

Appendix 3a: Date of Delivery

Month	Qty	Body	Numbers
09.70	1	PRV:	DMS 1
10.70	19	PRV:	DMS 2-10, 16-25
11.70	24	PRV:	DMS 26-48, 50
12.70	27	PRV:	DMS 11, 13, 15, 49, 51-72, 74
01.71	31	PRV:	DMS 12, 14, 73, 75-102
02.71	13	PRV:	DMS 103-115
03.71	2	PRV:	DMS 116, 117
06.71	15	PRV:	DMS 118-131, 133
07.71	16	PRV:	DMS 132, 134-148
08.71	27	PRV:	DMS 149-175
09.71	32	PRV:	DMS 176-207
10.71	29	PRV:	DMS 208-236
11.71	28	PRV:	DMS 237-264
12.71	31	PRV:	DMS 265-295
01.72	28	PRV:	DMS 296-323
02.72	27	PRV:	DMS 324-350
03.72	17	PRV:	DMS 351-367
	1	MCW:	DMS 1250
04.72	22	PRV:	DMS 368-389
05.72	19	PRV:	DMS 390-407, 410
06.72	21	PRV:	DMS 408, 409, 411-429
	17	MCW:	DMS 1248, 1253-1268
07.72	8	PRV:	DMS 430-437
	50	MCW:	DMS 1249, 1251, 1252, 1269-1311, 1313-1316
08.72	21	PRV:	DMS 438-458
	7	MCW:	DMS 1312, 1317-1322
09.72	16	PRV:	DMS 459-474
	6	MCW:	DMS 1323-1325, 1328-1330
10.72	20	PRV:	DMS 475-493, 495
	18	MCW:	DMS 1326, 1327, 1331-1345, 1347
11.72	23	PRV:	DMS 494, 496-517
	28	MCW:	DMS 1346, 1348-1370, 1373-1375, 1377
12.72	20	PRV:	DMS 518-537
	6	MCW:	DMS 1371, 1372, 1376, 1378, 1379, 1382
01.73	25	PRV:	DMS 538-562
	15	MCW:	DMS 1380, 1381, 1383-1395
02.73	22	PRV:	DMS 563-584
	13	MCW:	DMS 1396-1405, 1407, 1408, 1411
03.73	25	PRV:	DMS 585-609
	18	MCW:	DMS 1406, 1409, 1410, 1412-1425, 1427
04.73	23	PRV:	DMS 610-632
	18	MCW:	DMS 1426, 1428-1434, 1436-1438, 1442-1446, 1448, 1450
05.73	26	PRV:	DMS 633-658
	15	MCW:	DMS 1435, 1439-1441, 1447, 1449, 1451, 1452, 1454, 1456, 1457, 1459-1461, 1463
06.73	23	PRV:	DMS 661-680, 682-684
	11	MCW:	DMS 1453, 1455, 1458, 1462, 1464, 1468-1471, 1474, 1475
07.73	26	PRV:	DMS 659, 660, 681, 685-707
	22	MCW:	DMS 1472, 1473, 1476-1487, 1489-1496
08.73	22	PRV:	DMS 708-729
	15	MCW:	DMS 1465-1467, 1488, 1497, 1499-1504, 1508, 1510-1512
09.73	24	PRV:	DMS 730-753
	27	MCW:	DMS 1498, 1505-1507, 1509, 1513-1534
10.73	17	PRV:	DMS 754-770
	26	MCW:	DMS 1535-1560
11.73	23	PRV:	DMS 771-793
	25	MCW:	DMS 1561-1581, 1583-1586
12.73	13	PRV:	DMS 794-806
	17	MCW:	DMS 1582, 1587-1602
01.74	12	PRV:	DMS 807-818
	15	MCW:	DMS 1603-1617
02.74	8	PRV:	DMS 819-826
	3	MCW:	DMS 1618-1620

Month	Qty	Body	Numbers
03.74	13	PRV:	DMS 827-839
	19	MCW:	DMS 1631-1649
04.74	22	PRV:	DMS 840-861
	19	MCW:	DMS 1650-1668
05.74	23	PRV:	DMS 862-884
	8	MCW:	DMS 1669-1672, 1674, 1675, 1678, 1682
07.74	29	PRV:	DMS 885-913
	26	MCW:	DMS 1673-1676, 1677, 1679, 1680, 1683-1700, 1702
08.74	4	PRV:	DMS 914-917
	20	PRV:	DM 918-937
	3	MCW:	DM 1703-1705
09.74	16	PRV:	DM 938, 939, 941-954
	1	MCW:	DMS 1701
	14	MCW:	DM 1706-1719
10.74	27	PRV:	DM 940, 955-978, 980, 981
	1	MCW:	DMS 1681
	23	MCW:	DM 1720-1740, 1742, 1746
11.74	21	PRV:	DM 979, 982-998, 1001, 1005, 1006
	22	MCW:	DM 1741, 1747-1767
12.74	28	PRV:	DM 999, 1000, 1002-1004, 1007-1011, 1013-1030
	28	MCW:	DM 1768-1789, 1791-1796
01.75	21	PRV:	DM 1012, 1031-1048, 1050, 1051
	12	MCW:	DM 1790, 1797-1807
02.75	16	PRV:	DM 1049, 1052-1066
	17	MCW:	DM 1808-1812, 1814-1823, 1826, 1828
03.75	17	PRV:	DM 1067-1083
	7	MCW:	DM 1813, 1824, 1825, 1829-1832
	1	MCW:	DMS 1834
04.75	16	PRV:	DM 1084-1099
	1	MCW:	DM 1827
	17	MCW:	DMS 1833, 1835-1847, 1849, 1850, 1852
05.75	2	PRV:	DM 1100, 1101
	12	MCW:	DMS 1848, 1851, 1853-1857, 1859-1862, 1866
06.75	14	PRV:	DM 1102-1115
	12	MCW:	DMS 1858, 1863-1865, 1867-1873, 1875
07.75	14	PRV:	DM 1116-1129
	15	MCW:	DMS 1874, 1876-1879, 1881-1887, 1889-1891
08.75	17	PRV:	DM 1130-1138, 1140-1147
	14	MCW:	DMS 1880, 1888, 1892-1900, 1902-1904
09.75	12	PRV:	DM 1148, 1149, 1151-1159, 1161
	21	MCW:	DMS 1901, 1905-1922, 1924, 1925
10.75	23	PRV:	DM 1139, 1150, 1160, 1162-1170, 1172, 1176-1185
	23	MCW:	DMS 1923, 1926-1946, 1948
11.75	19	PRV:	DM 1173, 1174, 1186-1201, 1203
	18	MCW:	DMS 1947, 1949-1963, 1965, 1967
12.75	6	PRV:	DM 1175, 1202, 1204-1206, 1213
	2	MCW:	DMS 1964, 1966
01.76	3	PRV:	DM 1171, 1207, 1209
	11	MCW:	DM 1218-1224, 1226, 1227, 1229, 1230
02.76	2	PRV:	DM 1208, 1210
	16	PRV:	DMS 2058-2073
	11	MCW:	DM 1225, 1228, 1231-1239
03.76	6	PRV:	DM 1211, 1212, 1214-1217
	1	PRV:	DMS 2074
	6	MCW:	DM 1240-1245
04.76	24	PRV:	DMS 2076-2084, 2087-2100, 2102
	2	MCW:	DM 1246, 1247
	8	MCW:	DMS 1968-1973, 1975, 1978
05.76	18	PRV:	DMS 2075, 2085, 2086, 2101, 2103-2116
	15	MCW:	DMS 1974, 1976, 1977, 1979-1984, 1987-1992
06.76	6	PRV:	DMS 2117-2122
	16	MCW:	DMS 1986, 1993-2002, 2004-2007, 2009
07.76	6	MCW:	DMS 1985, 2003, 2008, 2010, 2011, 2020
08.76	6	PRV:	DMS 2123-2128
	10	MCW:	DMS 2012-2019, 2021, 2023

Month	Qty	Body	Numbers
09.76	24	PRV:	DMS 2129-2146, 2148-2153
	13	MCW:	DMS 2022, 2024-2034, 2036
10.76	13	PRV:	DMS 2147, 2154-2165
	20	MCW:	DMS 2035, 2038-2056
11.76	21	MCW:	DMS 2057, 2167-2172, 2174-2184, 2186, 2188, 2189
12.76	11	MCW:	DMS 2173, 2185, 2187, 2190, 2191, 2193-2198
01.77	32	PRV:	DMS 2166, 2348-2353, 2356, 2357, 2359, 2360, 2362, 2363, 2365, 2367, 2369, 2370, 2372-2375, 2377-2387
	6	MCW:	DMS 2192, 2199-2203
02.77	9	PRV:	DMS 2347, 2354, 2355, 2364, 2368, 2371, 2376, 2389, 2390
	14	MCW:	DMS 2204-2217
03.77	26	PRV:	DMS 2358, 2361, 2388, 2391-2413
	5	MCW:	DMS 2218-2222
04.77	10	PRV:	DMS 2416-2423, 2425, 2427
	4	MCW:	DMS 2223-2225, 2227
05.77	23	PRV:	DMS 2366, 2414, 2424, 2426, 2428-2446
	14	MCW:	DMS 2228-2239, 2241, 2242
06.77	10	PRV:	DMS 2415, 2447-2453, 2455, 2456
	10	MCW:	DMS 2226, 2240, 2243-2246, 2249, 2251, 2252, 2254
07.77	15	PRV:	DMS 2454, 2457-2470
	13	MCW:	DMS 2247, 2248, 2250, 2253, 2255-2263
08.77	11	PRV:	DMS 2471-2476, 2478-2482
	13	MCW:	DMS 2264-2276
09.77	9	PRV:	DMS 2477, 2483-2490
	15	MCW:	DMS 2277-2289, 2291, 2294
10.77	21	PRV:	DMS 2491-2499, 2502, 2507, 2511-2513, 2515-2520, 2522
	8	MCW:	DMS 2290, 2292, 2293, 2295, 2297, 2299, 2300, 2308
11.77	14	PRV:	DMS 2500, 2501, 2503-2506, 2508, 2510, 2514, 2521, 2523-2526
	9	PRV:	DM 2527-2532, 2535-2537
	6	MCW:	DMS 2301, 2302, 2306, 2309, 2311, 2312
12.77	1	PRV:	DMS 2509
	9	PRV:	DM 2534, 2538-2545
	10	MCW:	DMS 2303, 2305, 2310, 2316-2319, 2321-2323
01.78	16	PRV:	DM 2533, 2546-2560
	18	MCW:	DMS 2296, 2298, 2304, 2307, 2313-2315, 2320, 2324-2333
02.78	17	PRV:	DM 2561-2577
	13	MCW:	DMS 2334-2346
03.78	16	PRV:	DM 2578-2593
04.78	22	PRV:	DM 2594-2615
05.78	6	PRV:	DM 2616-2621
06.78	13	PRV:	DM 2622-2634
07.78	11	PRV:	DM 2635-2645
08.78	1	PRV:	DM 2646

Appendix 3b: Date of Entry into Service and Initial Allocation
NB Not all DMSs entered service at the garage at which they were initially licensed.

Month	Into Service and First Garage
01.71	DMS 1-5, 7-10, 16, 20-22, 24-28, 32, 33, 36-43, 45, 51, 72 (**S**), DMS 17-19, 23, 29-31, 34, 35, 44, 46-49, 52, 57 (**BN**), DMS 4, 68-71 (**AL**), DMS 53-56, 58-67 (**HT**)
02.71	DMS 73 (**S**)
03.71	DMS 11, 50, 74, 75, 77-87, 89-95 (**W**), DMS 99 (**BN**)
04.71	DMS 76 (**S**), DMS 13-15, 100-103 (**PR**), DMS 104, 105, 107-111, 116 (**WH**)
07.71	DMS 12, 113-115, 118, 125-131 (**WD**), DMS 106, 117, 119-124, 134 (**BN**), DMS 112 (**WH**), DMS 136 (**HT**)
08.71	DMS 137, 144, 145 (**W**), DMS 138 (**WD**), DMS 139 (**BN**), DMS 143 (**HT**)
09.71	DMS 140-142, 146, 147, 149-157 (**FW**), DMS 135 (**V**)
10.71	DMS 158-176 (**WL**)
11.71	DMS 88 (**S**), DMS 177-201 (**BX**)
12.71	DMS 6 (**S**), DMS 202-207, 226-231 (**SF**), DMS 208-225, 232-238 (**TH**), DMS 249 (**WL**)
01.72	DMS 239, 241, 244, 246, 251-266, 268, 283 (**TL**), DMS 242, 243, 245, 247, 248, 282 (**AW**), DMS 250, 267, 269-281 (**NX**), DMS 284 (**WL**), DMS 293, 294 (**W**), DMS 295 (**TH**), DMS 296 (**BN**), DMS 297 (**SF**), DMS 298 (**WD**), DMS 299 (**FW**)
02.72	DMS 148, 285-287, 290-292, 300-307 (**AF**), DMS 288, 289, 308-313 (**ON**), DMS 314 (**WD**), DMS 315 (**FW**), DMS 328-331 (**NX**)
05.72	DMS 316-327, 333-342 (**PM**)
06.72	DMS 96-98 (**S**), DMS 344-347, 366, 368-388 (**WD**), DMS 343, 354-363 (**CF**), DMS 348-353, 364, 365 (**BK**)
07.72	DMS 389-398 (**FY**), DMS 399-410 (**B**), DMS 411-414, 1248, 1250, 1252, 1255, 1261, 1263-1265, 1267, 1268 (**TB**)
08.72	DMS 415-420 (**NB**), DMS 1251, 1253, 1254, 1256-1260, 1262, 1266, 1269-1276 (**A**), DMS 1249, 1277-1285 (**AR**), DMS 1286-1296 (**H**)
09.72	DMS 133 (**V**), DMS 421-442, 444-448 (**E**), DMS 461, 462 (**B**)
10.72	DMS 443, 449-460, 468-475, 478 (**T**), DMS 463-467, 1313-1317 (**WH**), DMS 1297-1303 (**GM**), DMS 1304-1312 (**CT**), DMS 1318-1331, 1333 (**BW**)
11.72	DMS 132 (**TH**), DMS 476, 477, 479-484, 486-489 (**NS**), DMS 485 (**BX**), DMS 492 (**SF**), DMS 1334, 1336-1341 (**RD**)
12.72	DMS 503 (**NX**), DMS 1345, 1346 (**E**), DMS 1349-1351 (**FW**), DMS 1352 (**AF**)
01.73	DMS 490-508, 539-545 (**TC**), DMS 509-529 (**ED**), DMS 530-538 (**W**), DMS 1343-1346, 1361-1372 (**FW**), DMS 1347, 1348, 1352-1360 (**UX**), DMS 1374, 1375 (**AW**)
02.73	DMS 547 (**E**), DMS 548 (**S**), DMS 549 (**A**), DMS 552 (**WD**), DMS 1373, 1376-1390 (**TC**)
03.73	DMS 546, 550, 551, 553 (**BK**), DMS 554, 555, 566 (**AR**), DMS 556-558 (**SW**), DMS 559, 568, 1391-1397 (**TC**), DMS 560-564 (**AF**), DMS 565, 567, 1405, 1407, 1408, 1411 (**AR**), DMS 566, 569-571, 573 (**FY**), DMS 572 (**AW**), DMS 574, 576 (**WN**), DMS 575 (**PR**), DMS 577-579 (**B**), DMS 1335 (**BX**), DMS 1342 (**UX**), DMS 1398-1404 (**EM**), DMS 1406, 1409, 1410, 1412-1419 (**WN**)
04.73	DMS 367 (**TC**), DMS 580, 581 (**FY**), DMS 582 (**AR**), DMS 583 (**A**), DMS 584, 1422 (**W**), DMS 585 (**FW**), DMS 586-594, 597, 598, 614 (**SW**), DMS 1424 (**S**)
05.73	DMS 595, 1428-1434, 1436, 1437 (**WL**), DMS 596, 636, 637, 640-644, 1438, 1442, 1444-1446, 1448, 1450 (**TL**), DMS 599-601, 605-607, 612 (**A**), DMS 602-604, 647 (**NX**), DMS 608-611, 617-619, 638, 639 (**NB**), DMS 613, 615, 620-635 (**AL**), DMS 645 (**S**), DMS 646 (**W**), DMS 1420 (**ED**), DMS 1421, 1423, 1425-1427 (**TH**)
06.73	DMS 648, 649, 652, 654, 656-658, 661-664, 1463, 1464, 1468 (**RD**), DMS 650, 651 (**FW**), DMS 653 (**AW**), DMS 665, 666 (**SW**), DMS 1435, 1439-1441, 1443, 1447, 1449, 1451-1453 (**U**), DMS 1454-1458 (**WH**), DMS 1459 (**V**), DMS 1460 (**TL**), DMS 1461 (**NX**), DMS 1462 (**BK**)
07.73	DMS 667-680, 682, 683 (**EW**), DMS 691, 694 (**FW**), DMS 1469 (**TL**), DMS 1470, 1480 (**BX**), DMS 1471 (**WH**), DMS 1473 (**AL**), DMS 1477 (**NS**), DMS 1479, 1482 (**WD**), DMS 1481 (**E**)
08.73	DMS 684, 1489 (**CT**), DMS 685 (**WH**), DMS 1332, 1476 (**V**), DMS 1472 (**AW**), DMS 1474, 1475 (**FW**), DMS 1478 (**FY**), DMS 1483 (**U**), DMS 1484 (**BN**), DMS 1485 (**HT**), DMS 1486 (**WL**), DMS 1487 (**T**), DMS 1496 (**BX**), DMS 1497 (**NX**)
09.73	DMS 659, 660, 681, 686-690, 692, 693, 695, 1488, 1490-1495 (**BK**), DMS 696-710 (**SW**), DMS 711, 712 (**NX**), DMS 1466 (**U**), DMS 1467 (**CT**), DMS 1498 (**NS**), DMS 1499 (**AR**)
10.73	DMS 240 (**WH**), DMS 713-718 (**ON**), DMS 719-726, 729, 734 (**HW**), DMS 1465 (**H**), DMS 1501 (**PR**), DMS 1505 (**NX**), DMS 1507-1509 (**AL**)
11.73	DMS 1503, 1504, 1506, 1510-1523, 1525, 1526 (**V**), DMS 1527, 1528 (**S**), DMS 1535, 1536 (**AW**), DMS 1537 (**NX**), DMS 1538 (**NB**), DMS 1539 (**AF**), DMS 1540, 1542 (**TL**), DMS 1541 (**PM**), DMS 1543 (**ON**), DMS 1544, 1545 (**FY**), DMS 1546 (**WL**)
12.73	DMS 737, 739-741, 743, 744, 1502, 1524, 1529-1534 (**ED**), DMS 745-784 (**W**), DMS 785-790, 1567-1572 (**MH**), DMS 1547 (**SF**), DMS 1548-1566 (**PB**)
01.74	DMS 727, 728, 730-733, 735, 738 (**A**), DMS 736, 791-800 (**WW**), DMS 742 (**WN**), DMS 801-804 (**CT**), DMS 1500 (**W**), DMS 1573-1583 (**TC**), DMS 1584-1593 (**PR**), DMS 1594 (**BX**)
02.74	DMS 655 (**TH**), DMS 805-817 (**EM**), DMS 1595-1610 (**SF**), DMS 1611-1615 (**EM**), DMS 1616-1622, 1624, 1626, 1628 (**BK**)
03.74	DMS 818-825, 1398 (**EM**), DMS 1623 (**W**), DMS 1625 (**BW**), DMS 1627 (**RD**), DMS 1629, 1630, 1634 (**WN**), DMS 1631 (**U**), DMS 1633, 1635 (**E**)
04.74	DMS 826-831 (**SW**), DMS 835 (**EM**), DMS 1636, 1638 (**BK**)
05.74	DMS 832, 834, 838, 840-853, 861-863, 865, 866-868, 870-872, 1640-1642, 1648-1653, 1659 (**AL**), DMS 833, 836, 837, 839, 855, 856, 859, 1654 (**SW**), DMS 860 (**T**), DMS 1637, 1639 (**BK**), DMS 1643, 1644 (**BX**), DMS 1645 (**NX**), DMS 1646 (**PM**), DMS 1647 (**BN**), DMS 1655 (**E**), DMS 1657 (**CT**), DMS 1664 (**UX**)
06.74	DMS 857, 858, 1661, 1662 (**ON**), DMS 1666, 1667, 1678 (**WL**), DMS 1668 (**BK**), DMS 1658, 1669, 1670 (**H**), DMS 1672-1674 (**B**), DMS 1675 (**CF**), DMS 1682 (**NS**)
07.74	DMS 1656, 1660 (**HT**), DMS 1663, 1671 (**W**)
08.74	DMS 1632 (**TL**), DMS 1652 (**BX**), DMS 1676 (**E**), DMS 1685 (**HT**)

Month	Into Service and First Garage
09.74	DMS 879, 887-889, 891-893, 895, 896, 898-906, 908, 913 (**WN**)
	DM 918-939, 941-947, 1703-1705, 1708 (**W**)
10.74	DMS 869, 873-878, 880-886, 890, 894, 897, 907, 909, 910, 912, 914-917 (**WN**), DMS 1665, 1686, 1690, 1691 (**PM**),
	DMS 1679, 1684, 1696, 1700 (**NX**), DMS 1680, 1683, 1687-1689, 1693-1695, 1697-1700 (**SW**)
	DM 940, 948-954, 1713 (**W**), DM 955, 957-959, 961-963, 966, 1706, 1712, 1715, 1721 (**MH**),
	DM 956, 960, 964, 1707, 1709-1711, 1714, 1716-1720, 1722-1725 (**PB**), DM 1728 (**SF**)
11.74	DMS 864 (**V**), DMS 1692 (**AM**), DMS 1681 (**AW**), DMS 1702 (**NX**)
	DM 965, 967-974, 976, 978, 979, 981-987 (**EM**), DM 975, 980, 990, 1727, 1729-1732, 1734 (**SF**), DM 1726 (**PB**)
12.74	DM 988, 989, 1735, 1736, 1738, 1739 (**SF**), DM 1745, 1752 (**W**)
01.75	DM 977, 991, 996, 997, 999, 1000, 1002, 1003, 1005-1011, 1013-1025, 1027 (**MH**),
	DM 992-995, 998, 1001, 1004, 1028, 1733, 1737, 1740-1744, 1746-1751, 1753-1775 (**HT**), DM 1026 (**EM**)
02.75	DM 1012, 1029-1039, 1776-1782, 1784-1791 (**WL**)
03.75	DM 1040-1050, 1792-1804, 1806-1808 (**TC**), DM 1051-1053, 1055-1066, 1783, 1805, 1809, 1811, 1812, 1814-1817 (**BN**),
	DM 1067-1070 (**SW**)
04.75	DM 1071-1075, 1810, 1813, 1818, 1819 (**SW**), DM 1083, 1088, 1090 (**W**), DM 1821 (**PB**), DM 1822-1824 (**MH**)
05.75	DM 1826, 1829 (**PB**)
	DMS 1851-1853 (**GM**)
06.75	DM 1054, 1089, 1091, 1098, 1102, 1106, 1111, 1112 (**HT**), DM 1080-1082, 1084-1087 (**AL**), DM 1092, 1095, 1101, 1827 (**W**),
	DM 1094 (**SF**), DM 1096, 1107-1109 (**WL**), DM 1097, 1099, 1100 (**MH**), DM 1104 (**BN**)
	DMS 1833-1847, 1849, 1850, 1854 (**WW**), DMS 1848, 1855, 1857 (**WN**), DMS 1856 (**BX**), DMS 1858 (**TB**), DMS 1859 (**TL**),
	DMS 1860, 1863 (**SF**), DMS 1861 (**AL**), DMS 1862 (**A**), DMS 1864 (**TC**), DMS 1865, 1866 (**TH**), DMS 1867 (**NX**),
	DMS 1868, 1869 (**HW**)
07.75	DM 1103, 1113, 1114 (**WL**), DM 1110 (**HT**), DM 1115 (**EM**)
	DMS 1870, 1871, 1876, 1890 (**BK**), DMS 1872 (**RD**), DMS 1873 (**BK**), DMS 1874 (**TC**), DMS 1875 (**ED**), DMS 1877 (**TB**),
	DMS 1878, 1879 (**NB**), DMS 1881 (**BX**), DMS 1882, 1887 (**AR**), DMS 1884 (**TH**), DMS 1885 (**AL**), DMS 1886 (**A**)
08.75	DM 1076-1079, 1116, 1118, 1120-1124, 1130, 1131 (**SW**), DM 1119, 1133, 1134 (**WL**), DM 1126, 1129 (**EM**), DM 1127, 1128 (**W**),
	DM 1132, 1820 (**HT**)
	DMS 1880, 1888, 1895 (**PB**), DMS 1883, 1891, 1892, 1894, 1899, 1900 (**WN**), DMS 1889 (**NS**)
09.75	DM 1138 (**SF**), DM 1140 (**BN**), DM 1825, 1828, 1830 (**W**), DM 1831, 1832 (**EM**)
	DMS 1893, 1896, 1897, 1911, 1913 (**PB**), DMS 1898 (**AR**), DMS 1901, 1902 (**WN**), DMS 1904 (**PR**), DMS 1905 (**EM**),
	DMS 1906, 1909 (**WD**), DMS 1907 (**WH**), DMS 1910 (**NS**), DMS 1912 (**RD**)
10.75	DM 1093 (**SF**), DM 1125, 1144, 1145 (**EM**), DM 1142 (**MH**),
	DM 1117, 1135, 1137, 1141, 1143, 1146-1151, 1153-1159, 1161, 1162, 1170, 1177 (**CF**)
11.75	DM 1152 (**HT**)
	DMS 1927, 1928, 1936, 1937 (**U**), DMS 1903, 1908 (**A**), DMS 1914 (**WL**), DMS 1915 (**TB**), DMS 1916-1918 (**FW**), DMS 1919 (**TC**),
	DMS 1921, 1924 (**BK**), DMS 1922, 1926 (**B**), DMS 1925, 1930 (**E**), DMS 1929 (**WW**), DMS 1931, 1933 (**T**), DMS 1932 (**WL**),
	DMS 1934 (**SW**)
12.75	DM 1105, 1136, 1139, 1160, 1163, 1165, 1166, 1168, 1169, 1172, 1174, 1201 (**HT**), DM 1173, 1176, 1178-1189, 1191-1194, 1200 (**WN**)
	DMS 1920, 1923, 1935, 1938-1963, 1965 (**HL**)
01.76	DM 1175, 1204, 1205 (**W**)
	DMS 1964, 1966, 1967 (**W**)
02.76	DM 1164, 1196, 1203, 1206 (**HT**), DM 1167, 1171, 1190, 1195, 1197, 1198, 1202, 1207-1210, 1213, 1218-1224, 1226-1237, 1239 (**HL**)
03.76	DM 1211, 1212, 1214, 1216, 1217, 1225, 1238, 1240-1242, 1244, 1245 (**UX**)
	DMS 2058, 2060-2064, 2066-2072 (**HT**)
04.76	DM 1199 (**HL**), DM 1215, 1243, 1246, 1247 (**SW**)
05.76	DMS 1969 (**U**), DMS 1971, 1972 (**HW**), DMS 1970, 1973, 1974, 2094, 2096, 2098 (**SE**), DMS 1975, 1977 (**UX**), DMS 1980, 2102 (**ED**),
	DMS 2059 (**V**), DMS 2073-2082, 2084, 2087, 2089-2091, 2093 (**NS**), DMS 2088 (**CF**), DMS 2092 (**SW**), DMS 2097 (**BK**),
	DMS 2100 (**U**), DMS 2101 (**TH**)
06.76	DMS 1968, 2085, 2107, 2110 (**TL**), DMS 1976, 1978, 1981, 1982, 2103 (**AL**), DMS 1979, 2083 (**PR**), DMS 1984 (**TB**),
	DMS 1988, 1990 (**BK**), DMS 1989 (**ED**), DMS 1992, 2112 (**WW**), DMS 2095 (**AR**), DMS 2099 (**SF**), DMS 2104, 2109 (**BW**),
	DMS 2105 (**CT**), DMS 2106 (**S**)
07.76	DMS 1983, 2003 (**PR**), DMS 1985, 1995-1997, 2004, 2113, 2119, 2122 (**TL**), DMS 1986 (**WW**), DMS 1993, 2118 (**BW**),
	DMS 1994, 2116 (**E**), DMS 1998 (**WH**), DMS 1999 (**EM**), DMS 2000 (**WH**), DMS 2001, 2002 (**WL**), DMS 1987, 2065 (**NX**),
	DMS 2108, 2111 (**Q**)
08.76	DMS 2005 (**CT**), DMS 2007 (**TH**), DMS 2006, 2008-2010, 2121 (**AK**), DMS 2114 (**PR**), DMS 2120 (**FW**)
09.76	DMS 1991, 2011-2014, 2115, 2117 (**L**), DMS 2015, 2024 (**WN**), DMS 2017 (**S**), DMS 2018, 2028 (**WD**), DMS 2019, 2031 (**WL**),
	DMS 2021 (**ED**), DMS 2025 (**BX**), DMS 2027 (**AF**), DMS 2029 (**WW**), DMS 2030 (**CT**), DMS 2032 (**V**), DMS 2124 (**W**),
	DMS 2125 (**AL**)
10.76	DMS 2016, 2023 (**AP**), DMS 2020, 2026 (**A**), DMS 2033 (**TL**), DMS 2035, 2037, 2038, 2154-2157 (**SW**), DMS 2036 (**PB**),
	DMS 2086 (**CF**), DMS 2123 (**WN**), DMS 2126 (**RD**), DMS 2127 (**AF**), DMS 2128, 2132, 2134-2138 (**E**), DMS 2129, 2130 (**EM**),
	DMS 2131 (**BX**), DMS 2133 (**WL**), DMS 2141, 2150 (**TH**)
11.76	DMS 2034, 2039, 2142-2145, 2148, 2149 (**NS**), DMS 2041 (**ED**), DMS 2042 (**A**), DMS 2044 (**TH**), DMS 2045, 2049 (**HW**),
	DMS 2046 (**TL**), DMS 2047 (**TC**), DMS 2048, 2050 (**EW**), DMS 2051 (**SP**), DMS 2140 (**TB**), DMS 2146 (**AL**), DMS 2147 (**AM**),
	DMS 2159, 2160 (**WD**)

Month	Into Service and First Garage
12.76	DMS 2040 (**FW**), DMS 2052 (**ON**), DMS 2053, 2181 (**S**), DMS 2054 (**A**), DMS 2055 (**SE**), DMS 2056, 2165 (**TL**), DMS 2057, 2174, 2182, 2183 (**WD**), DMS 2139 (**TH**), DMS 2152 (**UX**), DMS 2153 (**SP**), DMS 2158, 2164 (**RD**), DMS 2163 (**W**), DMS 2168 (**TB**), DMS 2171 (**BN**), DMS 2172, 2175 (**ED**), DMS 2173 (**TC**), DMS 2176 (**PR**), DMS 2177, 2178, 2180 (**T**), DMS 2179 (**WW**), DMS 2184, 2185 (**AF**)
01.77	DMS 2043, 2188 (**BW**), DMS 2186, 2187, 2189 (**A**), DMS 2190 (**WD**), DMS 2191 (**FY**), DMS 2193, 2194, 2196 (**EM**), DMS 2195 (**AP**)
02.77	DMS 2151, 2167, 2169 (**TL**), DMS 2170 (**W**), DMS 2192, 2199-2202 (**AL**)
03.77	DMS 2022, 2209, 2214, 2218 (**WN**), DMS 2161, 2162 (**W**), DMS 2197, 2198 (**WW**), DMS 2203-2207 (**SW**), DMS 2348, 2350-2352, 2357, 2359, 2362, 2363, 2365, 2367, 2370, 2374, 2375, 2378, 2379 (**BX**)
04.77	DMS 2208 (**EM**), DMS 2211 (**BW**), DMS 2212 (**WN**), DMS 2213 (**PR**), DMS 2215 (**ON**), DMS 2216 (**WD**), DMS 2219 (**AF**), DMS 2220 (**SW**), DMS 2221 (**FW**), DMS 2347, 2354-2356, 2360, 2361, 2364, 2368, 2369, 2372, 2373, 2376, 2380, 2381, 2384-2386, 2390, 2393-2395, 2398 (**BX**)
05.77	DMS 2210 (**BW**), DMS 2223 (**WW**), DMS 2225 (**HW**), DMS 2349, 2353, 2358, 2371, 2383, 2387, 2389, 2392, 2397, 2400-2404, 2408, 2413 (**BX**), DMS 2377, 2382, 2388, 2406, 2407, 2409, 2410, 2412, 2432 (**E**)
06.77	DMS 2222, 2228, 2230-2232, 2431, 2433 (**AL**), DMS 2417, 2420, 2422, 2435, 2437, 2439 (**E**)
07.77	DMS 2224 (**FW**), DMS 2226, 2229, 2233, 2239 (**NS**), DMS 2227 (**B**), DMS 2234 (**HW**), DMS 2235-2237 (**BK**), DMS 2240, 2242 (**SP**), DMS 2238, 2241, 2245 (**AP**), DMS 2243 (**WW**), DMS 2391 (**BX**), DMS 2366, 2399, 2405, 2411, 2414, 2418, 2421, 2425, 2426, 2428, 2429, 2438 (**E**)
08.77	DMS 2166 (**PR**), DMS 2244 (**WW**), DMS 2217, 2246-2251, 2254-2260, 2264 (**S**), DMS 2415, 2416, 2419, 2423, 2424, 2430, 2434, 2436, 2440-2443, 2446, 2447, 2449, 2455 (**E**)
09.77	DMS 2252, 2253, 2261-2263, 2266-2269, 2272, 2273, 2278, 2280 (**S**), DMS 2471 (**E**), DMS 2444, 2445, 2448, 2450-2454, 2457, 2459, 2461-2463 (**AD**), DMS 2475, 2476, 2480-2482 (**SW**)
10.77	DMS 2265, 2270, 2271 (**S**), DMS 2478, 2479 (**SW**), DMS 2458, 2460, 2465, 2466 (**E**), DMS 854, 2488 (**CF**)
11.77	DMS 2274-2277, 2284, 2285 (**S**), DMS 2282, 2283 (**RD**), DMS 2287, 2291, 2292 (**BN**), DMS 2456, 2464, 2467-2469, 2472, 2473, 2477, 2483, 2486, 2489, 2496 (**SW**), DMS 2484 (**AD**), DMS 2485, 2490, 2493, 2494, 2498, 2520 (**E**)
12.77	DMS 2286, 2288, 2290, 2293-2295, 2297, 2299, 2300, 2302, 2303, 2305, 2321, 2323 (**BN**), DMS 2487, 2495, 2497, 2507, 2511 (**E**), DMS 2491, 2505, 2517, 2521, 2523 (**W**) DM 2530, 2532, 2537, 2539 (**W**)
01.78	DMS 2296, 2298, 2306, 2308, 2310, 2312-2314, 2316, 2324, 2326-2332 (**WD**), DMS 2279, 2281, 2301, 2304, 2311, 2317-2319 (**BN**), DMS 2470, 2474, 2499-2504, 2506, 2508-2510, 2512-2516, 2518, 2519, 2522-2526 (**W**) DM 2527, 2534 (**W**)
02.78	DMS 2307, 2309, 2315, 2320, 2325, 2333 (**WD**) DM 2546 (**CF**), DM 2528, 2529, 2531, 2533, 2535, 2536, 2538, 2540-2545, 2547-2550, 2552, 2554, 2556, 2557, 2559, 2562 (**BN**),
03.78	DMS 2281, 2289, 2322, 2334-2341, 2344, 2345 (**WD**), DMS 2427 (**E**), DM 2560, 2575, 2576 (**SW**) DM 2551, 2553, 2555, 2558, 2561, 2563-2566, 2568-2574, 2578-2581, 2584-2586, 2588 (**BN**)
04.78	DMS 2343 (**WD**), DMS 2492 (**W**), DM 2583, 2587, 2589, 2590, 2592, 2594 (**BN**), DM 2567, 2577, 2582, 2593, 2595-2597, 2600-2610 (**W**)
05.78	DM 2591 (**SW**)
06.78	DMS 2346 (**WD**), DM 2598, 2619-2626, 2629 (**W**), DM 2611-2616, 2618 (**AL**)
07.78	DMS 2342 (**WD**), DM 2599, 2617, 2627, 2628, 2630, 2632 (**W**)
08.78	DM 2631, 2633-2645 (**SW**)
10.78	DM 2646 (**BN**)

APPENDICES

Appendix 4: Sales by London Transport

Month	Qty	Buses Sold
02.79	1	DMS 251
03.79	16	DMS 2, 72, 92, 93, 114, 195, 199, 219, 275, 295, 296, 356, 371, 671, 1353, 1569
04.79	16	DMS 170, 173, 174, 197, 267, 272, 281, 1251, 1252, 1255-1257, 1429, 1433, 1563, 1661
05.79	24	DMS 215, 256, 258, 293, 331, 398, 430, 495, 581, 602, 731, 812, 1249, 1250, 1253, 1254, 1258-1261, 1270, 1271, 1273
06.79	28	DMS 213, 229, 262, 318, 323, 324, 345, 359, 1262-1267, 1269, 1272, 1274-1281, 1285, 1287, 1288, 1612
07.79	34	DMS 196, 239, 241, 282, 298, 314, 341, 362, 366, 512, 1248, 1268, 1284, 1286, 1289-1292, 1294-1300, 1303-1305, 1307, 1309, 1313-1315, 1404
08.79	51	DMS 135, 218, 225, 284, 286, 330, 339, 344, 395, 407, 412, 415-419, 422, 423, 425, 426, 428, 429, 437, 439-442, 444-446, 510, 712, 824, 1301, 1308, 1310-1312, 1316-1324, 1328, 1329, 1335, 1339
09.79	43	DMS 95, 144, 230, 231, 291, 297, 309, 319, 320, 394, 411, 424, 427, 449, 450, 452-454, 456-460, 462, 468, 469, 471-473, 486, 511, 575, 674, 1282, 1293, 1302, 1306, 1325-1327, 1330, 1333, 1906
10.79	33	DMS 285, 328, 346, 421, 435, 451, 463-467, 470, 474, 478, 482, 573, 594, 604, 1334, 1336-1338, 1342, 1343, 1347, 1349, 1359, 1369, 1372, 1384, 1385, 1431, 1531 DM 1757
11.79	66	DMS 132, 240, 360, 375, 391, 432, 443, 455, 475-477, 479-481, 484, 485, 487-489, 491-493, 496, 499-502, 504-506, 509, 546, 562, 689, 1283, 1331, 1340, 1341, 1344-1346, 1348, 1350-1352, 1354-1358, 1360, 1361, 1363, 1365, 1367, 1370, 1371, 1373, 1374, 1377, 1379, 1387, 1390, 1391, 1400, 1459
12.79	46	DMS 367, 369, 370, 374, 376, 386, 483, 490, 494, 497, 498, 507, 508, 513-522, 524-528, 530, 531, 577, 799, 1362, 1364, 1366, 1368, 1375, 1376, 1378, 1381, 1382, 1386, 1388, 1389, 1405, 1408
01.80	31	DMS 420, 503, 523, 529, 532-541, 543, 544, 547, 552, 580, 736, 1380, 1383, 1392-1395, 1398, 1399, 1401, 1410, 1457
02.80	30	DMS 23, 368, 431, 438, 545, 548, 549, 551, 553, 555, 556, 558-561, 563, 564, 566-568, 570, 1397, 1403, 1406, 1407, 1409, 1412, 1415, 1417, 1520
03.80	35	DMS 30, 49, 316, 381, 399, 401, 403, 405, 436, 447, 554, 578, 579, 583, 584, 588, 591, 595, 597, 807, 1402, 1414, 1416, 1418, 1419, 1421, 1423, 1428, 1430, 1432, 1434-1437, 1446
04.80	29	DMS 413, 414, 542, 601, 603, 605-611, 614, 615, 617-619, 622, 651, 752, 1396, 1443, 1451, 1452, 1456, 1458, 1460, 1463, 1674
05.80	18	DMS 574, 623, 626, 627, 634, 635, 637, 638, 640, 641, 643, 1411, 1413, 1448, 1462, 1474, 1513, 1527
06.80	31	DMS 167, 598, 630, 631, 633, 645, 646, 649, 652-654, 656, 657, 663, 665, 667-670, 775, 781, 864, 1465, 1466, 1475, 1478, 1496, 1523, 1534, 1568, 1654
07.80	22	DMS 220, 632, 639, 664, 675, 677, 680, 685, 687, 699, 703, 710, 734, 1468, 1484, 1487, 1489, 1490, 1494, 1503, 1504, 1529
08.80	18	DMS 599, 612, 655, 659, 660, 694, 697, 700, 701, 704, 706, 707, 729, 767, 1501, 1502, 1512, 1516
09.80	21	DMS 672, 679, 695, 702, 708, 716, 718, 722-724, 726, 732, 1491, 1519, 1521, 1524-1526, 1528, 1530, 1533
10.80	40	DMS 644, 686, 725, 727, 728, 730, 733, 735, 739-741, 743-745, 747-751, 753, 757, 758, 1483, 1514, 1539, 1541, 1544, 1545, 1547-1552, 1554, 1556, 1558, 1562, 1566, 1586
11.80	52	DMS 636, 642, 693, 738, 754-756, 759-763, 765, 766, 768-771, 776, 778-780, 784, 796, 797, 1522, 1532, 1540, 1555, 1557, 1559, 1561, 1564, 1567, 1570-1579, 1582-1585, 1587, 1589, 1590, 1592
12.80	21	DMS 698, 772, 782, 783, 785, 786, 789, 794, 795, 805, 1565, 1581, 1588, 1593-1595, 1597-1600, 1605
01.81	11	DMS 788, 791, 798, 800, 803, 1580, 1596, 1601, 1602, 1607, 1609
02.81	21	DMS 56, 764, 773, 774, 777, 790, 792, 801, 802, 834, 1442, 1445, 1560, 1591, 1606, 1610, 1634, 1639, 1679 DM 1708, 1711
03.81	12	DMS 41, 76, 216, 388, 647, 746, 787, 1604 DM 931, 966, 996, 1039
04.81	102	DMS 60, 69, 74, 80, 89, 691, 721, 742, 823, 826, 830-832, 838, 839, 842, 843, 847, 848, 850, 855, 857, 859, 870, 871, 877, 878, 882, 902, 913, 1497, 1535, 1553, 1611, 1629, 1630, 1635, 1636, 1640-1653, 1655, 1656, 1658-1660, 1662, 1664, 1666, 1670, 1671, 1682, 1693, 1696, 1698, 1699, 1919 DM 929, 932, 941, 954, 961, 963, 965, 968, 974, 986, 987, 1002, 1016, 1035, 1054, 1084, 1085, 1087, 1089, 1153, 1716, 1720, 1743, 1745, 1749, 1755, 1758-1760, 1764, 1765, 1767, 1771, 1779
05.81	2	DMS 1637, 1638
06.81	25	DM 919, 933, 934, 936, 971, 1018, 1037, 1051, 1070, 1086, 1094, 1095, 1098, 1145, 1163, 1165, 1181, 1245, 1718, 1733, 1736, 1737, 1740, 1748, 1766
07.81	11	DMS 34, 43, 44, 243, 244, 845, 858, 895, 901, 1689 DM 1832
08.81	13	DMS 361, 874, 875, 1673, 1680, 1681, 1692, 2073 DM 1211, 1212, 1216, 1812, 1822
09.81	31	DMS 116, 793, 825, 827-829, 833, 835, 836, 873, 886, 888, 889, 893, 894, 896-898, 905, 907, 909, 915, 917, 1687, 1971-1974, 1995, 2079, 2094 DM 1036, 1056, 1088, 1096, 1186, 1217, 1742, 1750, 1752, 1772, 1778, 1782, 1785, 1790, 1805, 1817
10.81	18	DMS 17, 65, 78, 100, 109, 880, 881, 883, 884, 890, 900, 906, 911, 916 DM 990, 1744, 1746, 1784
11.81	27	DMS 908, 1657, 1667, 1669, 1683, 2101 DM 940, 956, 992-994, 1001, 1004, 1043, 1065, 1093, 1097, 1158, 1723, 1727, 1729, 1754, 1761, 1763, 1768, 1776, 1788
12.81	16	DMS 269, 572, 1678, 1686, 1690, 1878, 1952, 1955, 1957, 1958, 2062 DM 1728, 1732, 1739, 1801, 1819

Month	Qty	Buses Sold
03.82	16	DMS 321, 856, 1672, 1940, 1947, 1951, 1982, 2061, 2115 DM 943, 1223, 1224, 1229, 1747, 1751, 1769
04.82	1	DMS 1506
05.82	10	DMS 1469, 1543, 2014, 2072, 2129, 2150, 2164, 2197 DM 1226, 1821
06.82	15	DMS 1866, 2066, 2087, 2088, 2090, 2106, 2126, 2128, 2136, 2141, 2163, 2183, 2191 DM 1780, 1816
07.82	9	DMS 1449, 1697, 2055, 2133, 2184 DM 1235, 1781, 1818, 1825
08.82	57	DMS 565, 593, 629, 690, 1424, 1480, 1498, 1603, 1675, 1685, 1688, 1702, 1863, 1938, 1945, 2007, 2018, 2039, 2045, 2053, 2057, 2060, 2069, 2075, 2114, 2132, 2135, 2137, 2138, 2140, 2144, 2147, 2151-2153, 2155, 2160, 2169, 2178, 2179, 2180, 2185, 2192, 2218 DM 927, 946, 1221, 1236, 1239, 1241, 1244, 1714, 1722, 1724, 1800, 1809, 1826
10.82	64	DMS 3, 10, 14, 27, 31, 32, 37, 38, 42, 45, 47, 54, 55, 73, 77, 83, 85-87, 94, 105, 125, 127, 129, 149, 152, 163, 222, 228, 245, 248, 266, 268, 306, 310, 317, 342, 352, 377, 379, 383, 390, 557, 569, 865, 891, 1440, 1441, 2042, 2051, 2119 DM 922, 945, 969, 972, 1141, 1151, 1176, 1180, 1185, 1191, 1712, 1715, 1726
12.82	265	DMS 4-9, 11-13, 15, 16, 18-21, 24-26, 28, 29, 33, 35, 36, 39, 40, 46, 50-53, 57-59, 61-64, 66-68, 70, 71, 75, 81, 82, 84, 88, 90, 91, 96, 97, 98, 99, 102, 103, 104, 106-108, 110-113, 115, 117-124, 126, 128, 130, 131, 133, 137-142, 145, 147, 148, 150, 151, 153-159, 161, 164-166, 171, 172, 175-189, 192, 194, 198, 200, 202-210, 214, 217, 221, 223, 224, 226, 227, 232-238, 242, 246, 247, 249, 250, 252-255, 257, 260, 261, 263-265, 270, 271, 273, 274, 276-280, 283, 287-290, 292, 294, 299-305, 307, 308, 311-313, 315, 322, 325-327, 329, 332, 334-338, 340, 343, 347-351, 353-355, 357, 358, 363-365, 372, 373, 378, 380, 382, 384, 385, 387, 389, 392, 393, 396, 397, 400, 402, 406, 408-410, 434, 448, 592, 892, 1444, 2043, 2044, 2174-2176, 2190, 2206, 2217, 2225, 2226, 2230, 2231, 2242, 2381 DM 925, 947, 975, 977, 978, 983, 991, 1717, 1719, 1725, 1756
01.83	287	DMS 168, 169, 461, 550, 576, 585, 586, 596, 613, 621, 628, 648, 658, 662, 683, 688, 713, 720, 804, 810, 837, 840, 841, 844, 846, 849, 852, 861-863, 866-869, 872, 885, 910, 1438, 1454, 1467, 1476, 1481, 1492, 1495, 1505, 1507, 1509, 1518, 1542, 1608, 1665, 1676, 1677, 1684, 1691, 1694, 1700, 1701, 1856, 1858, 1861, 1883, 1888, 1943, 1966, 2013, 2016, 2025-2028, 2031, 2033, 2050, 2070, 2076, 2077, 2082, 2083, 2085, 2086, 2089, 2091-2093, 2095-2098, 2102, 2104, 2105, 2107, 2113, 2117, 2127, 2130, 2134, 2139, 2142, 2145, 2146, 2148, 2149, 2154, 2157, 2159, 2165, 2171, 2189, 2193, 2195, 2199, 2207, 2233, 2234, 2237, 2240, 2387, 2403, 2407, 2416, 2439, 2449 DM 918, 920, 921, 924, 926, 930, 935, 937-939, 951, 952, 955, 957-959, 960, 962, 964, 970, 973, 976, 980-982, 985, 988, 989, 995, 997, 998, 1003, 1005-1013, 1015, 1017, 1019-1028, 1030, 1032-1034, 1038, 1041, 1046, 1048-1050, 1052, 1053, 1055, 1057-1061, 1066-1069, 1071, 1074-1076, 1079, 1080, 1092, 1099, 1100, 1101, 1103, 1104, 1107-1109, 1112-1117, 1119-1121, 1128-1134, 1136, 1137, 1140, 1148, 1149, 1150, 1152, 1154, 1162, 1170, 1171, 1173, 1175, 1177, 1182-1184, 1187, 1193, 1196, 1198, 1200, 1203, 1207, 1208, 1213, 1218, 1219, 1220, 1225, 1228, 1232-1234, 1237, 1240, 1242, 1243, 1246, 1247, 1706, 1709, 1710, 1713, 1721, 1730, 1731, 1734, 1735, 1753, 1783, 1786, 1797, 1806, 1808, 1814, 1820, 1823
02.83	59	DMS 134, 160, 162, 201, 212, 589, 620, 673, 737, 876, 879, 887, 899, 903, 904, 912, 914, 1422, 1486, 1517, 1663, 1891, 1939, 2040, 2067, 2071, 2081, 2099, 2122, 2131, 2162, 2170, 2194, 2203, 2224, 2228, 2245, 2373, 2433 DM 928, 944, 949, 1014, 1029, 1040, 1044, 1090, 1118, 1126, 1169, 1230, 1231, 1238, 1703, 1796, 1802, 1803, 1815, 1829
03.83	50	DMS 79, 101, 191, 582, 590, 600, 821, 851, 1508, 1695, 1881, 1964, 1999, 2239 DM 942, 950, 953, 967, 979, 999, 1045, 1064, 1072, 1073, 1078, 1081, 1083, 1122, 1124, 1127, 1189, 1190, 1192, 1201, 1202, 1204, 1205, 1705, 1738, 1741, 1770, 1775, 1792, 1793, 1795, 1798, 1811, 1813, 2596, 2630
04.83	14	DMS 259, 571, 1493, 1625, 1631, 2046, 2047, 2059, 2161, 2219, 2511 DM 1042, 1799, 1807
05.83	2	DMS 22, 193
06.83	12	DMS 1538, 1616, 1864, 1921, 2172, 2415 DM 1031, 1227, 1704, 1707, 1762, 1794
07.83	9	DMS 650, 676, 1453, 1461, 1464, 1471, 1472 DM 1167, 1777
08.83	4	DM 1125, 1139, 1161, 1206
09.83	17	DMS 48, 811, 853, 1849, 1880, 1902, 1924, 1935, 1956, 1991, 2011, 2019, 2182, 2188, 2202 DM 984, 1077
10.83	41	DMS 333, 1615, 1840, 1895, 1899, 1905, 1907, 1908, 1910, 1912-1914, 1920, 1926-1928, 1931, 1954, 1959, 1961, 1963, 1976, 1980, 1992, 1994, 2009, 2010, 2020, 2032, 2035-2038, 2041, 2048, 2049, 2227 DM 1138, 1157, 1164, 1197, 1209, 1210, 1214, 1215, 1824 *Returned:* DM 1138, 1157, 1218
11.83	18	DMS 1934, 1948, 1970, 1986, 1988, 2002, 2021 DM 1135, 1138, 1147, 1155, 1157, 1168, 1172, 1178, 1194, 1218, 2536
12.83	25	DMS 146, 682, 813, 820, 1623, 1624, 1853, 1869, 1898, 1903, 1944, 1960, 1969, 1984, 2023, 2029, 2116, 2123, 2124, 2213, 2214, 2216, 2222 DM 1174, 1830
01.84	15	DMS 822, 1836, 1839, 1893, 1915, 1917, 1923, 1941, 1949, 1962, 1997, 2012, 2022 DM 1179, 1222

Month	Qty	Buses Sold
02.84	64	DMS 136, 143, 175, 190, 616, 625, 705, 709, 715, 809, 814-818, 1546, 1617, 1618, 1622, 1627, 1628, 1632, 1633, 1668, 1841, 1848, 1851, 1860, 1865, 1875, 1892, 1897, 1922, 1925, 1929, 1946, 1965, 1975, 1989, 2000, 2005, 2024, 2058, 2065, 2078, 2084, 2111, 2209, 2232, 2236 DM 923, 1000, 1082, 1091, 1105, 1106, 1111, 1123, 1156, 1166, 1773, 1774, 1789, 1791
03.84	11	DMS 587, 624, 1886, 1983, 2201, 2212, 2215, 2221, 2323, 2348, 2378
04.84	2	DMS 211, 2220
05.84	3	DMS 1842, 2246 DM 1063
06.84	2	DMS 1, 1871
07.84	3	DMS 1835, 1877, 2508
08.84	2	DMS 661, 1619
09.84	5	DMS 404, 808, 1614, 2235, 2510
10.84	3	DMS 806, 1455, 2196
01.85	1	DMS 1843
03.85	4	DMS 1427, 1613, 1968, 2120
04.85	4	DMS 854 DM 1047, 1199
05.85	1	DMS 2244
06.85	12	DMS 1536, 1620, 1621, 1838, 1874, 1876, 1894, 2001, 2030 DM 1188, 1810, 1827
07.85	6	DMS 684, 860, 1847, 1854, 1855, 1896
08.85	14	DMS 1844, 1882, 1981, 2052, 2054, 2167, 2173, 2186, 2198, 2200, 2210, 2211, 2243 DM 1831
09.85	10	DMS 1834, 1887, 1911, 1942, 1977, 2056, 2238 DM 1110, 1142, 1143
10.85	10	DMS 1850, 1933, 2034, 2187, 2204, 2208, 2223, 2229, 2241 DM 1144
02.86	1	DMS 2080
02.87	1	DMS 433
10.87	2	DMS 1482, 1499
11.87	4	DMS 1510, 1846, 1978, 2279
12.87	1	DMS 1903 *Re-acquired:* DMS 1492, 1580, 1610, 1649, 1656, 1657, 1669-1671, 1679, 1683, 1686, 1687, 2021
01.88	2	DMS 2100, 2158, 2485, 2507
03.88	1	DMS 2177
06.88	1	DM 1159
09.88	2	DMS 1450, 1996
01.89	1	DMS 1332
09.89	8	DMS 1492, 1580, 1670, 1671, 1686, 1687, 2125 DM 1146
11.89	9	DMS 1425, 1610, 1649, 1656, 1852, 1862, 1953, 1993, 2064
01.90	3	DMS 1901, 1985, 1990
02.90	9	DMS 717, 819, 1477, 1626, 1679, 1683, 1884, 2021, 2156
03.90	6	DMS 1950, 2063, 2068, 2074, 2118 DM 1195
04.90	4	DMS 1837, 2110, 2121, 2166
05.90	5	DMS 692, 1833, 1859, 1885, 1987
07.90	1	D 2552
08.90	1	DMS 1511
09.90	7	DMS 719, 1447, 1873, 1890, 1904, 2143 DM 1160
10.90	11	DMS 711, 714, 1669, 1889, 1900, 2006, 2108, 2112, 2181, 2320 DM 1804
11.90	3	DMS 1930, 2017, 2109
12.90	1	DMS 1500
01.91	3	DMS 1515, 2404, 2475
02.91	23	DMS 2008, 2251, 2274, 2278, 2299, 2318, 2371, 2393, 2408, 2427, 2458, 2482, 2521 D 2529, 2531, 2561, 2573, 2574, 2590, 2611, 2626, 2638, 2644
03.91	8	DMS 2303, 2315, 2322, 2344, 2460, 2483, 2496 D 2579
04.91	15	DMS 666, 2349, 2355, 2356, 2401, 2424, 2430, 2452 D 2535, 2550, 2581, 2617, 2628, 2631, 2645

Month	Qty	Buses Sold
05.91	36	DMS 1857, 1870, 1879, 1909, 1916, 1998, 2003, 2004, 2250, 2252, 2269, 2277, 2287, 2295, 2298, 2306, 2327, 2335, 2361, 2362, 2370, 2377, 2382, 2392, 2398, 2429, 2442, 2443, 2464, 2520 DM 1062, 1828 D 2527, 2544, 2592, 2598
06.91	16	DMS 2248, 2297, 2330, 2352, 2437, 2440 D 2530, 2532, 2558, 2570, 2571, 2575, 2578, 2584, 2585, 2623
07.91	15	DMS 696, 1937, 2263, 2301, 2302, 2313, 2328, 2329, 2339, 2360, 2410, 2461 D 2551, 2577, 2627
08.91	20	DMS 2103, 2292, 2293, 2465, 2468, 2470, 2515, 2516 D 2539, 2555, 2557, 2563, 2564, 2583, 2593, 2594, 2601, 2607, 2619, 2635
09.91	8	DMS 2259, 2272, 2346, 2457, 2472, 2518 D 2543, 2586
10.91	13	DMS 1979, 2270, 2276, 2300, 2357, 2385, 2388, 2390, 2456, 2498 D 2528, 2613, 2618
11.91	9	DMS 2260, 2265, 2280, 2334, 2338, 2400, 2522 D 2620, 2637
12.91	16	DMS 2255, 2262, 2284, 2308, 2312, 2316, 2337, 2342, 2372, 2374, 2409, 2421 D 2599, 2602, 2629, 2634
01.92	6	DMS 1485, 2282 D 2540, 2549, 2565, 2587
02.92	16	DMS 2249, 2268, 2296, 2317, 2332, 2343, 2395, 2406, 2428, 2448, 2466, 2481, 2486 D 2567, 2568, 2604
03.92	9	DMS 1479, 1967, 2271, 2333, 2380, 2386, 2391, 2597 D 2609
04.92	6	DMS 2258, 2341, 2383, 2479 D 2537, 2621
05.92	31	DMS 678, 2205, 2264, 2294, 2307, 2309, 2325, 2326, 2331, 2336, 2353, 2359, 2368, 2369, 2399, 2402, 2418, 2431, 2436, 2459, 2467, 2471, 2517, 2525 D 2572, 2591, 2603, 2606, 2616, 2624, 2632
06.92	44	DMS 2254, 2256, 2273, 2275, 2286, 2288, 2289, 2305, 2310, 2311, 2314, 2340, 2345, 2350, 2358, 2366, 2379, 2412, 2444, 2447, 2451, 2484, 2491, 2492, 2493, 2495, 2503, 2509, 2513, 2519, 2524 D 2533, 2541, 2546, 2548, 2554, 2560, 2566, 2582, 2589, 2614, 2625, 2641, 2642
07.92	11	DMS 2285, 2375, 2376, 2405, 2411, 2434, 2450, 2462, 2500 D 2580, 2615
08.92	43	DMS 1420, 1470, 1932, 2267, 2319, 2354, 2365, 2389, 2394, 2396, 2414, 2417, 2422, 2446, 2455, 2463, 2473, 2477, 2478, 2487, 2488, 2490, 2501, 2504-2506, 2526 D 2538, 2542, 2545, 2547, 2553, 2562, 2569, 2588, 2605, 2608, 2610, 2612, 2636, 2639, 2640, 2643
09.92	9	DMS 1439, 2266, 2364, 2419, 2420, 2474 D 2534, 2576, 2622
10.92	5	DMS 1473, 1918, 2015, 2247, 2324
11.92	5	DMS 1872, 2253, 2261, 2321, 2494
01.93	2	DMS 1936, 2480
02.93	4	DMS 2426, 2512, 2514 D 2646
03.93	8	DMS 1845, 2363, 2423, 2438, 2497, 2502, 2523 DM 1787
05.93	3	DMS 2469 D 2595, 2633
06.93	2	DMS 1537, 2425
07.93	4	DMS 1426, 1488, 1867, 2453
08.93	2	DMS 2454 DM 2559
09.93	4	DMS 2432, 2435, 2441, 2499
10.93	1	D 2600
07.94	1	DMS 1657
12.94	2	DMS 2281, 2445
08.95	3	D 948, 1102, 2556
10.95	1	DMS 2168
11.95	3	DMS* 2283, 2304, 2351
12.95	2	DMS* 2367, 2384
04.97	4	DMS* 2290, 2347, 2413, 2476
05.97	2	DMS* 2397, 2489
06.97	3	DMS 681, 1868, 2257
07.97	1	DMS 2291

* Classified DMT by London General as permanent trainers.

Appendix 5a: London Transport Garages and Routes Allocated DMSs

Garage	Start Date	End Date	Routes (unscheduled in italics, (ii) denotes second route of same number)
A (Sutton)	05.08.72	19.06.92	**Crew DMS:** 93
			DM: 93
			DMS: 80, 80A, 93, 151(ii), 152, 154, 157, 163, 164, 213(i), 213(ii), 213A, 254, 280, 293, 352, *393*, 413, N54, N68, N88
AA (Colliers Wood)	29.09.90	23.02.91	**DMS:** 152, 163, *200*
AC (Willesden)	12.11.78	01.06.80	**DMS:** 226
AD (Palmers Green)	10.09.77	17.11.81	**DMS:** 34, 121, 212(i), 261(i)
AE (Hendon)	04.01.75	15.06.80	**DMS:** 143, 183
AF (Putney)	05.02.72	08.07.83	**DMS:** 85, 85A, 264(i)
AK (Streatham)	29.08.76	27.10.84	**DMS:** 249
	21.07.90	25.05.91	**DMS:** 49, 59(ii), 109, 118, 137, 137A
AL (Merton)	30.01.71	04.01.92	**Crew DMS:** 77, 155
			DMS: 19, 22, 44, 49, 57, 77, 77B, 127, 131, 152, 152A, 155, 156(ii), 157, 163, 164, 181, 189, 200, 219, 249, 264(ii), 270(ii), 280, 293, 344, 355, M1
AM (Plumstead)	10.11.74	26.04.80	**DMS:** 99, 122A
AP (Seven Kings)	09.10.76	15.08.80	**DMS:** 129, 139, 148, 150
AR (Tottenham)	12.08.72	28.06.82	**DMS:** 67, 106, 259, 279A
AW (Abbey Wood)	08.01.72	30.01.81	**DMS:** 177, 178, 198, 272
B (Battersea)	15.07.72	27.05.83	**DMS:** 19A, 39, 39A
BK (Barking)	13.05.72	31.07.80	**Crew DMS:** N95, N98
			DMS: 23, 145, 148, 156(i), 169, 169C, 192(i), 179, 199, 291
BN (Brixton)	02.01.71	06.03.86	**DM:** 57A, 59(i), 109, 133
			Crew DMS: *109*, 133, 137, 159
			DMS: 50, 95, 109, 133, 137, 137A, 159, 189, 250
	28.04.86	05.12.91	**Crew DMS:** *137, 159*
			DMS: 50, 59(ii), 109, 118, 133, 137A, 159, 250, N69
BW (Bow)	28.10.72	03.09.82	**DMS:** 10
BX (Bexleyheath)	06.11.71	20.07.83	**DMS:** 89, 96, 99, 122A, 132, 269
	16.01.88	23.02.89	**DMS:** 96, 99, 178, 229, 269, 272, 401, 469, 472, *492*
CF (Chalk Farm)	13.05.72	27.10.84	**DM:** 3, 24
			DMS: 46
CT (Clapton)	28.10.72	21.09.82	**DMS:** 22A, 277
E (Enfield)	09.09.72	22.03.82	**DMS:** 107, 107A, 121, 135, 191, 217, 217B, 231
ED (Elmers End)	06.01.73	25.10.86	**DMS:** 54, 75, 194, 194A, 194B, *289*
EM (Edmonton)	10.03.73	24.06.82	**Crew DMS:** 149
			DM: 149, 283(i)
			DMS: 191, 259, 279A, W8
EW (Edgware)	14.07.72	08.12.80	**DMS:** 142, 186, 286, 292
FW (Fulwell)	04.09.71	16.06.79	**DMS:** 90B, 267, 270(i), 281, 285
FY (Finchley)	15.07.72	20.11.80	**DMS:** 125, 221, 263, 296(ii)
GM (Victoria)	28.10.72	04.08.84	**DM:** 2, 2B, RLST (OMO)
			Crew DMS: *2, 2B*
			DMS: 10, 10A, N2, N11
H (Hackney)	12.08.72	31.03.79	**DMS:** 106
HL (Hanwell)	28.10.76	23.11.81	**DM:** 207
			DMS: E1, E2
HT (Holloway)*	16.01.71	21.03.85	**DM:** 4, 17, 29, 45, 104, 168A, 172, 214, 253, N92, N93
Known as Highgate until 04.09.71			**DMS:** 104, 143, 168A, 214, 239, 263, 271, *C11*
HW (Southall)	27.07.74	19.12.79	**DMS:** 92, 120, 195, 232, 232A, 273, 274, 282
L (Loughton)	25.04.76	19.03.82	**DMS:** 20, 20A, 167
MH (Muswell Hill)	01.12.73	03.09.82	**DM:** 43, 102, 134
			DMS: 244, W7
NB (Norbiton)	05.08.72	27.09.79	**DMS:** 131, 213(i), 213(ii), 213A, 285
	27.06.87	29.09.90	**DMS:** *65*, 71, 85, *200*, 213(ii)
NS (North Street)	18.11.72	20.07.80	**DMS:** 66, 66B, 103, 139, 175, 247B, 294
NX (New Cross)	08.01.72	14.03.84	**DM:** 53, 141, N82, ISB
			DMS: 70, 151(i), 177, 184, 188, 192
ON (Alperton)	05.02.72	13.07.80	**Crew DMS:** 18
			DMS: 79, 79A, 83, 92, 182, 297
PB (Potters Bar)	30.08.75	03.09.82	**DM:** 134
			DMS: 84, 242, 284, 298, 299
PM (Peckham)	13.05.72	23.02.80	**DMS:** 78, N85, N86
PR (Poplar)	17.04.71	03.08.82	**DMS:** 5, 56, 173, 277, N84

Garage	Start Date	End Date	Routes (unscheduled in italics, (ii) denotes second route of same number)
Q (Camberwell)	23.02.75	30.09.82	**DM:** *3*, *35*, 40, *68*, 159, 172
			DMS: 42, 188
RD (Hornchurch)	18.11.72	25.10.79	**DMS:** 165, 246, 252
S (Shepherd's Bush)	02.01.71	03.12.83	**DMS:** 72, 220, 283(ii)
SE (Stonebridge Park)	23.05.76	15.08.81	**DM:** 18, 266
			DMS: 112
SF (Stamford Hill)	04.12.71	22.06.82	**Crew DMS:** 149
			DM: 149, 253
			DMS: 67, N83
SP (Sidcup)	05.12.76	23.12.82	**Crew DMS:** *21*
			DMS: 21A, 51, 228, 229
SW (Stockwell)	14.04.73	24.05.91	**DM:** 168, N68, N81, N87, RLST
			Crew DMS: *2*, *2B*, 77, 77A, *88*
			DMS: 37, 44, 77, 77A, 88, 155, 156(ii), 170, 181, 181A, 189, 196, RLST
T (Leyton)	28.10.72	30.01.81	**DMS:** 55, 262, N96
TB (Bromley)	15.07.72	21.10.79	**DMS:** 61, 126, 138
TC (Croydon)	06.01.73	20.01.93	**DM:** 59(i), 130, 130A, 130B
			Crew DMS: *60*, 190
			DMS: *12B*, 50, 59(ii), 60, 68, 109, 127, 127A, 130, 130A, 130B, 154, 166, 190, 194, 194A, 197, 197B, 233, 233A, 234, 234B, 255, 264(ii), *312*, 366, C1, C2, C3, C4, C5, X30
TH (Thornton Heath)	04.12.71	14.03.92	**DM:** *68*, 109, 130
			Crew DMS: 2B, *68*
			DMS: *50*, 59(ii), 60, 64, 109, 115, 154, 157, 194B, 197A, *250*, 264(ii), *312*, 389(i), N69, N78
TL (Catford)	08.01.72	13.02.84	**DMS:** 54, 75, 108B, 124, 124A, 160, 160A, 185
U (Upton Park)	16.06.73	04.06.82	**DM:** 101
			DMS: 5, 23, 147, 162, 173, 238
UX (Uxbridge)	06.01.73	10.09.81	**DM:** 207
			DMS: 222, 223, 224, 224B
V (Turnham Green)	18.09.71	19.12.79	**DMS:** 91, 267, N97
W (Cricklewood)	13.03.71	31.07.80	**Crew DMS:** 16, N94
			DM: 16, 16A, N94
			DMS: 32, 245, 245A, 616
WD (Wandsworth)	24.07.71	20.03.84	**DM:** *28*, 168, N68, N88
			Crew DMS: *28*, N68, N88
			DMS: 44, 168, 168B, 170, 220, 295, 295A, 296(i)
WH (West Ham)	17.04.71	03.09.82	**DM:** 262
			DMS: 5, 58, 238, 241, 262, S1
WL (Walworth)	16.10.71	18.10.82	**DM:** 12, 45
			DMS: 184, 185
WN (Wood Green)	24.03.73	17.06.82	**DM:** 29, 123, 141
			DMS: 144, 221, 298, W1, W2, W3, W4
WW (Walthamstow)	05.01.74	21.01.82	**DMS:** 34, 97, 97A, 123, 144, 158, 212(ii), 275, 276, W21
X (Westbourne Park)	15.08.81	19.09.83	**DM:** 7, 18, *18A*, *28*, 52, *52A*

Appendix 5b: Independent Companies' Garages Allocated DMSs, 1986-1996

ENSIGNBUS (ENSIGN CITYBUS, CAPITAL CITYBUS)

PT (Purfleet)	21.06.86	07.92	62, 62A, *86B*, 145, 165, 246, 248, 252, 347, 348, 365, 446, 550, N99
DM (Dagenham)	02.12.89	07.92	62, 62A, *86B*, 145, 165, 248, 252, 348, 365, 550, N99

CITYRAMA

C (Battersea)	22.03.86	27.10.89	196, 200

SAMPSON'S

— (Hoddesdon)	24.05.86	01.07.88	217B, 317

LONDON BUSLINES

— (Lampton)	13.07.85	03.88	81, *92*, 195
— (Isleworth)	03.88	08.10.90	81, *90*, *92*, 195
— (Southall)	09.10.90	11.10.96	*81*, *90*, *92*, 389(ii), 698

GREY-GREEN

— (Dagenham)	28.03.87	03.92	20, *103*, 125, 173, *179*, 235, *298*, *313*
DX (Barking)	03.92	25.09.93	20, *103*, 173, *179*, 235, *313*

METROBUS

MB (Orpington)	16.08.86	12.95	61, *261*(ii), 353, *354*, *357*, *358*, 36

Above: Metrobus's simple but effective livery of blue and yellow was already well known in the area targeted by the company and became even more familiar in the decade after 16 August 1986, when thirteen former DMSs began a new era for the 61. Seen at Ensigns' yard as preparation progresses (which included a conversion to 'RCL' blind format) are ex-DMSs 1960 (KUC 960P) and 2173 (OJD 173R). *R. C. Riley*

Appendix 6: Independent Companies' DMS Acquisitions for LRT Tendered Routes, 1986-1988

LONDON BUSLINES

DMS No	Reg No	Fleet No	In	Out	Notes
DM 928	SMU 928N	---	07.85	07.87	Destroyed in garage fire 26.07.87
DM 962	GHV 962N	1062 (12.90)	05.86	10.93	
DM 1007	GHV 7N	1007 (12.90)	07.85	10.96	
DM 1019	GHV 19N	---	07.85	07.87	Destroyed in garage fire 26.07.87
DM 1026	GHV 26N	---	05.86	07.87	Destroyed in garage fire 26.07.87
DM 1033	GHV 33N	1033 (12.90)	07.85	06.91	
DM 1036	GHV 36N	---	05.86	07.87	Telecom ad 10.86
DM 1040	GHV 40N	1040 (12.90)	07.85	10.93	
DM 1041	GHV 41N	1041 (12.90)	05.86	10.96	Hitachi ad 10.87-08.89
DM 1064	GHV 64N	---	07.85	05.89	
DM 1078	GHV 78N	1078 (12.90)	07.85	06.91	
DM 1083	GHV 83N	1083 (12.90)	07.85	10.93	
DM 1088	GHV 88N	---	07.85	11.87	
DMS 1869	GHM 869N	1069 (12.90)	05.86	08.93	
DMS 1882	GHM 882N	1082 (12.90)	05.86	08.93	

Loans:
DMS 2000 from Ensign 11.86
Various DMSs from Ensign, 02.03-06.87, including all-over ad 325 (Hitachi) and 589 (Hitachi) and 'Culture Bus' examples (1043, 1476)

CITYRAMA

DMS No	Reg No	Fleet No	In	Out	Notes
DMS 863	TGX 863M	63	06.87	10.89	
DM 935	SMU 935N	35 (01.87)	03.86	10.89	
DM 937	SMU 937N	37 (01.87)	03.86	10.89	
DM 952	GHV 952N	52 (01.87)	03.86	10.89	
DM 958	GHV 958N	58 (01.87)	03.86	10.89	
DM 985	GHV 985N	85 (01.87)	03.86	10.89	
DM 1017	GHV 17N	17 (01.87)	03.86	10.89	
DM 1773	GHM 773N	73 (01.87)	03.86	10.89	
DM 1811	GHM 811N	81 (01.87)	05.86	10.89	
DM 1813	GHM 813N	13 (01.87)	03.86	10.89	
DM 1831	GHM 831N	31 (01.87)	03.86	10.89	
DMS 1836	GHM 836N	36 (01.87)	03.86	10.89	
DMS 1892	GHM 892N	92 (01.87)	03.86	10.89	
---	OKW 522R	22	01.87	10.89	
---	SHE 507S	7	01.87	10.89	

Loans:
DM 1166 from Ensign 07.88
DMS 1624 and 1684 from Brakell, 07.88

SAMPSON'S

DMS No	Reg No	Fleet No	In	Out	Notes
DM 930	SMU 930N	---	11.86	07.88	Ad for *Cheshunt and Walton Telegraph & Gazette*
DM 1030	GHV 30N	---	05.86	07.88	To Ensignbus as 238
DM 1119	GHV 119N	---	05.86	07.88	To Ensignbus as 239
DM 1120	GHV 120N	---	05.86	07.88	
DM 1122	GHV 122N	---	05.86	07.88	
DM 1762	GHM 762N	---	05.86	07.88	To Ensignbus as 252
DM 1794	GHM 794N	---	05.86	07.88	To Ensignbus as 235
DMS 1881	GHM 881N	---	05.86	07.88	

Loans:
DMS 2216 from Davian Coaches, 01-02.87
DM 1003 and 1023 from private owners, 06.87

APPENDICES

ENSIGNBUS / ENSIGN CITYBUS / CAPITAL CITYBUS

DMS No	Reg No	Fleet No	Acquired	Service	Withdr	Disposal	Notes
DMS 415	MLK 415L	228	04.88	04.88	12.89	11.90	
DMS 620	MLK 620L	231	09.88	09.88	11.90	04.91	
DMS 820	TGX 820M	251	09.88	09.88	12.88	12.88	
		240 (06.89)	05.89	08.89	03.92	03.92	
DM 926	SMU 926N	237	09.88	09.88	01.91	04.91	
DM 964	GHV 964N	B 254	01.87	01.87	06.91	06.91	
		B 225 (06.87)					
		225 (04.88)					
DM 1008	GHV 8N	208	09.88	09.88	01.91	04.91	
DM 1015	GHV 15N	255	09.88	09.88	03.92	03.92	
		205 (01.91)					
DM 1020	GHV 20N	B 210	06.86	06.86	01.91	06.91	
		210 (04.88)					
DM 1030	GHV 30N	238	09.88	09.88	06.91	06.91	Ex-Sampson's
DM 1043	GHV 43N	B 223	12.85	01.87	03.92	03.92	
		223 (04.88)					
DM 1048	GHV 48N	B 252	01.87	01.87	10.87	10.87	
		B 228 (06.87)					
DM 1059	GHV 59N	B 249	01.87	01.87	10.87	10.87	
		B 229 (06.87)					
DM 1069	GHV 69N	B 211	11.84	06.86	04.92	04.92	John Bull ad 05.89; Yellow/silver 03.91
		211 (04.88)					
DM 1074	GHV 74N	B 212	06.86	06.86	10.89	06.90	
		212 (04.88)					
DM 1079	GHV 79N	B 229	11.87	11.87	06.91	09.91	
		229 (04.88)					
DM 1092	GHV 92N	B 222	10.85	01.87	01.91	06.91	
		222 (04.88)					
DM 1101	GHV 101N	B 213	04.86	06.86	01.91	04.91	
		213 (04.88)					
DM 1106	GHV 106N	206	09.88	09.88	09.90	11.91	
DM 1114	GHV 114N	B 214	05.86	06.86		10.87	
DM 1118	GHV 118N	B 215	06.86	06.86	03.92	03.92	
		215 (04.88)					
DM 1119	GHV 119N	239	09.88	09.88	04.92	04.92	Ex-Sampson's
DM 1133	KUC 133P	B 248	01.87	01.87	01.91	07.91	
		B 233 (06.87)					
		233 (04.88)					
DM 1142	KUC 142P	B 232	11.87	11.87	01.91	06.91	
		232 (04.88)					
DM 1154	KUC 154P	B 251	12.86	01.87	03.92	03.92	
		B 227 (06.87)					
		227 (04.88)					
DM 1166	KUC 166P	B 250	01.87	01.87	10.90	12.90	
		B 226 (06.87)					
		226 (04.88)					
DM 1170	KUC 170P	B 253	01.87	01.87	01.91	05.91	
		B 230 (06.87)					
		230 (04.88)					
DMS 1371	MLH 371L	251	07.89	08.89	02.90	05.90	
DMS 1424	MLH 424L	B 209	04.84	06.86		04.87	
DMS 1476	MLH 476L	236	08.88	09.88	10.89	05.90	
DMS 1684	THM 684M	234	06.88	06.88	06.91	07.91	
DM 1709	THM 709M	B 224	06.85	01.87	10.89	02.90	
		224 (04.88)					
DM 1738	SMU 738N	B 218	06.83	04.87	10.90	01.91	
		218 (04.88)					
DM 1762	GHM 762N	252	09.88	09.88	03.90	01.91	Ex-Sampson's
DM 1793	GHM 793N	B 216	03.86	06.86	04.92	04.92	
		216 (04.88)					
DM 1794	GHM 794N	235	09.88	09.88	06.91	06.91	Ex-Sampson's
DMS 1856	GHM 856N	256	04.89	08.89	08.90	04.91	
DMS 1949	KUC 949P	209	04.89	08.89	04.91	04.91	

DMS No	Reg No	Fleet No	Acquired	Service	Withdr	Disposal	Notes
DMS 2000	KJD 500P	B 217 217 (04.88)	10.85	06.86	05.89	05.90	Written off in accident
DMS 2204	OJD 204R	B 214 214 (04.88)	12.87	12.87	02.92	05.93	
DMS 2219	OJD 219R	G 109 109 (04.88)		07.87		04.92	Full rear blinds PFH Phones ad 06.90 Yellow livery 08.91
DMS 2229	OJD 229R	B 219 219 (04.88)	03.88	03.88	06.91	06.91	

Also available:
DMS 104 (304, open-top); **DMS 158** (358; open-top used on 550, 1989); **DMS 165** (365, open-top); **DMS 287** (387; open-top); **DMS 325** (G 220, 220; Trocadero ad); **DMS 353** (B 219, G 221, R 221, 221; Evan Evans tour ad; re-registered GVV 205 10.89); **DMS 589** (A 208, 208; Hitachi ad); **DMS 887** (306; open-top); **DMS 1444** (B 203, G 220, 220; London Dungeon ad); **DMS 1469** (B 221, B 219; Hitachi ad); **DMS 1680** (101; Rock Tours ad); **DMS 1682** (A 102, 102; Pritt-stick ad); **DM 1720** (A 103, 103; full rear blinds); **DMS 1941** (A 104, 104; Fuji ad; IBM ad); **DMS 2240** (105; London Pride livery 1989); **DMS 2407** (A 107, G 107; London Pride livery 1989; sole B20 but re-engined with Gardner unit)

Numerous other DMSs were owned by Ensign, in closed- and open-top format, single- and dual-door, for tours and private hire work outside the scope of this volume.

METROBUS

DMS No	Reg No	Fleet No	In	Out	Notes
DMS 1898	KUC 898P	---	08.86	07.92	
DMS 1922	KUC 922P	---	08.86	02.93	unserviceable by 03.91
DMS 1960	KUC 960P	---	08.86	06.92	Plain upper-deck front windows 1989
DMS 1977	KUC 977P	---	08.86	09.92	
DMS 2052	OUC 52R	---	08.86	11.92	
DMS 2054	OUC 54R	---	08.86	02.91	
DMS 2056	OUC 56R	---	08.86	11.92	
DMS 2167	OJD 167R	---	08.86	02.93	
DMS 2173	OJD 173R	---	08.86	02.91	Plain upper-deck front windows 1989
DMS 2198	OJD 198R	---	08.86	12.95	
DMS 2200	OJD 200R	---	08.86	02.93	
DMS 2211	OJD 211R	---	08.86	02.93	
DMS 2243	OJD 243R	---	08.86	03.95	Saunders Abbott ad 03.88-03.91

Loans
DMS 1469 (Hitachi ad) from Ensign, 16.09-08.10.86
DM 1709 (Royal Wedding ad) from Ensign, 09-10.10.86

GREY-GREEN

SYPTE No	Reg No	Fleet No	In	Out	Notes
1501	OKW 501R	501 (10.87)	02.87	<03.93	
1502	OKW 502R	502 (10.87)	02.87	<03.93	
1503	OKW 503R	503 (10.87)	02.87	04.93	
1506	OKW 506R	506 (10.87)	02.87	01.91	
1519	OKW 519R	519 (10.87)	02.87	09.93	
1523	OKW 523R	523 (10.87)	02.87	<03.93	
1525	OKW 525R	525 (10.87)	02.87	08.93	
1526	OKW 526R	526 (10.87)	02.87	09.93	
1527	OKW 527R	527 (10.87)	02.87	03.90	Damaged by fire
1528	OKW 528R	528 (10.87)	02.87	03.91	Accident-damaged 03.91

FRONTRUNNER SOUTH-EAST

Loans
Grey-Green DMS-lookalikes among vehicles driven by Grey-Green drivers on 252, 03.09.88-05.11.88

SCANCOACHES

Loans
DMS 1941 and others from Ensign, 07.87

Appendix 7a: Summary of DMSs Overhauled by Aldenham Works, 1977-1982

Standard DMS / Park Royal (Gardner engines)
DMS 1, 3-22, 24-29, 31-48, 50-68, 70, 71, 73-76, 78-91, 94, 96-113, 115-117, 119-131, 133, 134, 136-143, 145-166, 168, 169, 171, 172, 175-194, 198, 200-212, 214, 216, 217, 220-224, 226, 227, 228, 232-238, 242, 243, 245-250, 252-255, 257, 259-261, 263-266, 268-271, 273, 274, 276-280, 283, 288, 294, 299, 305-308, 310-312, 315, 317, 321, 322, 325-327, 329, 332-338, 340, 342, 347-350, 352-355, 357, 358, 361, 363-365, 372, 373, 377, 378, 380, 382-385, 387-390, 392, 393, 396, 397, 400, 402, 406, 410

Standard DMS / Park Royal (Leyland engines)
DMS 576, 585, 586, 589, 596, 613, 648, 705, 737, 804, 806, 808-811, 813-822

Standard DMS / MCW (Gardner engines)
DMS 1449

Standard DMS / MCW (Leyland engines)
DMS 1537, 1538, 1542, 1543, 1546, 1608, 1613-1628, 1631-1633, 1833-1855, 1857, 1859, 1860, 1862, 1864, 1865, 1867-1887, 1889-1905, 1907-1918, 1920-1934, 1936, 1937, 1939, 1941-1944, 1946, 1948-1950, 1953, 1954, 1959, 1960, 1962, 1963, 1965, 1968-1970, 1975-1994, 1996-1999, 2002, 2003, 2005, 2006, 2008, 2010, 2012, 2015, 2017, 2020, 2021

Standard DM / MCW (Leyland engine)
DM 1787

B20 DMS / MCW
DMS 2247, 2249, 2251, 2252, 2255, 2259, 2261-2265, 2267, 2269, 2270, 2272, 2274, 2276, 2278, 2280, 2282, 2283, 2288-2294, 2296, 2297, 2300, 2302-2304, 2311, 2312, 2314, 2317, 2318, 2320, 2322, 2323, 2325-2328, 2330-2332, 2337-2339, 2341-2346

B20 DMS / Park Royal
DMS 2348, 2349, 2351, 2353, 2356-2359, 2362, 2363, 2366-2368, 2370, 2371, 2374-2377, 2379, 2382-2384, 2386, 2388, 2390, 2393-2397, 2399, 2400, 2402, 2405, 2406, 2409-2415, 2417-2431, 2434-2438, 2440-2443, 2445-2448, 2450-2455, 2457-2463, 2465, 2466, 2471-2473, 2475-2479, 2481, 2484, 2485, 2487, 2490, 2493-2495, 2497-2509, 2512, 2514-2522, 2524, 2525

B20 'DM' / Park Royal
D 2538, 2545, 2547, 2577, 2593, 2611, 2628

Right: **Even though this DMS in Aldenham on 24 April 1980 is unidentifiable, there were only four it could have been, as overhauls of the type were on hiatus at the time; accordingly, it's surrounded by Routemasters.** *John Laker*

Appendix 7b: DMSs Overhauled by Aldenham Works by date into works and outshopping

Date		
04.76	In:	DMS 1
12.76	In:	DMS 118
03.77	Out:	DMS 1
07.77	In:	DMS 3
08.77	In:	DMS 4, 16
09.77	In:	DMS 5, 18, 21
10.77	In:	DMS 20
	Out:	DMS 118
11.77	In:	DMS 6, 7, 19, 33
12.77	In:	DMS 24, 29, 34, 39
01.78	In:	DMS 10, 25-27, 31, 32, 35, 38, 41
02.78	In:	DMS 42, 44, 54, 55, 57, 59, 77, 80, 82
	Out:	DMS 3, 5
03.78	In:	DMS 8, 17, 43, 45, 47, 48, 52, 53, 56, 60, 63, 96-98
	Out:	DMS 4, 16, 20, 21, 33
04.78	In:	DMS 11, 22, 28, 36, 51, 76, 91, 100-105, 107, 108, 110, 111
	Out:	DMS 6, 7, 18, 19, 26, 29, 31, 39
05.78	In:	DMS 14, 64-66, 68, 73, 74, 78, 79, 81, 87, 89, 90, 94, 99, 109, 113, 115
	Out:	DMS 17, 25, 32, 34, 35, 41-44, 47, 57, 59, 60, 67
06.78	In:	DMS 9, 12, 13, 15, 37, 40, 46, 50, 58, 61, 62, 70, 71, 75, 83-86, 88, 106, 112, 116, 117, 119-121, 124, 126, 1449
	Out:	DMS 8, 10, 24, 36, 38, 45, 52-56, 80, 82, 97, 101, 103, 107
07.78	In:	DMS 122, 125, 127-129, 131, 160
	Out:	DMS 11, 14, 22, 27, 28, 48, 51, 63-65, 73, 74, 76, 90, 94, 96, 98, 99, 100, 105, 108, 110, 111, 115
08.78	In:	DMS 123, 137, 142, 143, 147, 149-158, 163
	Out:	DMS 50, 58, 68, 78, 79, 81, 87, 91, 102, 109, 113
09.78	In:	DMS 133, 134, 136, 138-140, 145, 146, 148, 159, 161, 162, 164-166, 168, 171, 172, 177-179, 181
	Out:	DMS 9, 13, 15, 37, 40, 41, 61, 62, 66, 70, 75, 83, 84, 86, 89, 104, 116, 117
10.78	In:	DMS 67, 169, 175, 176, 180, 183-188, 193, 202
	Out:	DMS 12, 46, 71, 85, 88, 106, 112, 119-122, 124-129, 131, 149-151, 154, 160
11.78	In:	DMS 182, 189-192, 194, 198, 200, 201, 203-212, 214, 217, 221
	Out:	DMS 123, 133, 137, 139, 142, 143, 145-148, 152, 153, 155-159, 161, 163, 168, 1449
12.78	In:	DMS 216, 220, 223, 224, 227, 228, 232-238, 273
	Out:	DMS 134, 136, 138, 140, 162, 164-166, 171, 172, 175, 179, 181, 183, 184, 186, 187
01.79	In:	DMS 242, 243, 245, 249, 250, 253, 257, 264, 268-271, 274, 276-278, 305
	Out:	DMS 67, 169, 176-178, 180, 185, 188, 189, 190, 193, 198, 200-204, 206, 207
02.79	In:	DMS 141, 222, 226, 252, 254, 255, 259-261, 263, 265, 266, 279, 280, 283, 299, 310, 312, 317, 333, 334, 336
	Out:	DMS 182, 191, 192, 194, 205, 208-212, 214, 216, 228
03.79	In:	DMS 130, 246, 288, 294, 306-308, 311, 315, 326, 327, 329, 335, 337, 338, 342
	Out:	DMS 217, 220, 221, 226, 227, 232, 234-238, 243, 245, 269
04.79	In:	DMS 247, 248, 321, 322, 332, 340, 349, 350, 352-354, 357, 364, 379
	Out:	DMS 222-224, 233, 242, 249, 250, 253, 265, 268, 270, 271, 273, 274, 276-280, 305
05.79	In:	DMS 347, 355, 358, 361, 365
	Out:	DMS 141, 252, 254, 255, 257, 259-261, 263, 264, 266, 283, 294, 299, 307, 308, 310, 312, 326, 333, 334, 336, 337
06.79	Out:	DMS 130, 248, 306, 311, 315, 317, 329, 335, 338
07.79	In:	DMS 378, 385, 392, 402
	Out:	DMS 246, 247, 288, 325, 327, 340, 342, 349, 350, 352
08.79	In:	DMS 348, 380, 382-384, 406
	Out:	DMS 321, 322, 332, 353, 358, 361, 364, 365
09.79	In:	DMS 363, 387, 389, 390, 396, 397, 400
	Out:	DMS 347, 354, 355, 357, 378, 385, 392
10.79	In:	DMS 372, 373, 377, 388, 393, 585, 586, 596
	Out:	DMS 384, 402, 406
11.79	In:	DMS 410
	Out:	DMS 348, 363, 380, 382, 383, 389, 390
12.79	Out:	DMS 387, 388, 393, 396
01.80	Out:	DMS 373, 377, 397, 400
02.80	In:	DMS 576
	Out:	DMS 372
03.80	In:	DMS 589
	Out:	DMS 596
04.80	In:	DMS 648
	Out:	DMS 410, 585, 586, 589
05.80	Out:	DMS 576
07.80	In:	DMS 613
08.80	Out:	DMS 648
09.80	In:	DMS 705, 737, 1537, 1538, 1542
10.80	In:	DMS 1543, 1546
	Out:	DMS 613
12.80	In:	DMS 804, 806, 1608, 1614

01.81	In:	DMS 808-811, 813-819, 822, 1613, 1615-1626, 1632, 1633, 1833
02.81	In:	DMS 820, 821, 1627, 1628, 1631, 1837, 1841, 1843, 1877, 1878, 1881
	Out:	DMS 705, 737, 1537, 1538, 1542, 1543, 1546
03.81	In:	DMS 1840, 1847, 1871, 1885, 1900, 1920, 1924
	Out:	DMS 804, 806, 808-811, 814, 817, 1608, 1613-1617, 1620, 1621, 1624
04.81	In:	DMS 1834, 1836, 1848, 1850-1852, 1854, 1860, 1864, 1865, 1867, 1868, 1870, 1872-1876, 1879, 1882-1884, 1887
	Out:	DMS 813, 815, 818, 1618, 1619, 1622, 1623, 1625, 1626, 1881
05.81	In:	DMS 1838, 1886, 1889, 1892, 1904, 1907, 1908, 1911, 2351
	Out:	DMS 819, 1632, 1833, 1837, 1841, 1843, 1847, 1877, 1878
06.81	In:	DMS 1910, 1918, 1970, 1975, 1979, 1981, 1985, 1991
	Out:	DMS 820, 822, 1627, 1628, 1631, 1633, 1871, 1924
07.81	In:	DMS 1862, 1969, 1983, 1986, 1992, 1993, 2366
	Out:	DMS 816, 821, 1836, 1840, 1848, 1850, 1854, 1860, 1865, 1867, 1868, 1870, 1875, 1879, 1882-1885, 1900, 1920
08.81	In:	DMS 1835, 1839, 1842, 1844, 1869, 1880, 1890, 1891, 1893, 1894, 1898, 1903, 1905, 1909, 1915, 1921, 1923, 1925, 1927, 1934, 1941, 1942, 1949, 1953, 1962, 1963, 1997
	Out:	DMS 1838, 1851, 1852, 1864, 1872-1874, 1886, 1887, 1889, 1892, 1904, 1907, 1908, 1911, 1979, 1981, 1991, 2351
09.81	In:	DMS 1845, 1846, 1853, 1895, 1896, 1902, 1912-1914, 1917, 1928-1933, 1937, 1939, 1944, 1946, 1965, 1968, 2445, 2448
	Out:	DMS 1834, 1876, 1909, 1910, 1970, 1992, 1993
10.81	In:	DMS 1849, 1897, 1899, 1916, 1926, 1978, 1980, 1984, 2010, 2377, 2388, 2399, 2420, 2438, 2450, 2451, 2453-2455, 2459, 2462, 2465, 2498
	Out:	DMS 1839, 1842, 1862, 1869, 1880, 1890, 1891, 1903, 1905, 1918, 1921, 1923, 1925, 1927, 1934, 1941, 1942, 1949, 1953, 1962, 1963, 1969, 1975, 1983, 1985, 1986, 1997, 2366
11.81	In:	DMS 1857, 1901, 1936, 1943, 1950, 1954, 1976, 1988-1990, 1994, 1996, 1998, 1999, 2001, 2003, 2005, 2006, 2009, 2012, 2015, 2020, 2021, 2479, 2509
12.81	In:	DMS 1855, 1859, 1922, 1948, 1959, 1960, 1977, 1987, 2002, 2008, 2017
		DM 1787
	Out:	DMS 1835, 1849, 1895, 1897, 1899, 1902, 1914, 1916, 1926, 1932, 1937, 1946, 1965, 2010, 2377, 2450, 2498
01.82	In:	DMS 2247, 2312, 2322, 2326, 2328, 2362, 2382, 2411, 2413, 2417-2419, 2421, 2422, 2424, 2427, 2429-2431, 2436, 2440-2442, 2447, 2461, 2475, 2494, 2520, 2522
	Out:	DMS 1978, 2448, 2454
02.82	In:	DMS 2261, 2278, 2314, 2320, 2325, 2331, 2349, 2356, 2376, 2378, 2383, 2386, 2395, 2423, 2443, 2446, 2452, 2458, 2460, 2463, 2466, 2471, 2506, 2512, 2515, 2517, 2519, 2524, 2525
	In:	D 2538, 2577, 2611, 2628
	Out:	DMS 1901, 1943, 1950, 1954, 1980, 1984, 1988, 1989, 1994, 2003, 2005, 2006, 2017, 2021, 2388, 2399, 2445, 2451, 2453, 2465, 2509
		DM 1787
03.82	In:	DMS 2272, 2287, 2323, 2330, 2353, 2379, 2400, 2405, 2406, 2409, 2414, 2415, 2425, 2435, 2481, 2484, 2485, 2487, 2490, 2493, 2497, 2507
	Out:	DMS 1855, 1922, 1936, 1948, 1959, 1960, 1976, 1987, 1990, 1996, 1998, 1999, 2012, 2015, 2417, 2418, 2522
04.82	In:	DMS 2252, 2264, 2269, 2276, 2291, 2311, 2327, 2332, 2337, 2338, 2345, 2357, 2370, 2390, 2402, 2426, 2473, 2476, 2477, 2495, 2500, 2502, 2514
		D 2545
	Out:	DMS 1977, 2002, 2008, 2020, 2322, 2326, 2328, 2362, 2382, 2411, 2413, 2419, 2420, 2421, 2422, 2424, 2427, 2429, 2430, 2431, 2436, 2438, 2440, 2441, 2447, 2455, 2459, 2461, 2462, 2494, 2520, 2524
05.82	In:	DMS 2263, 2265, 2270, 2288, 2292, 2297, 2339, 2341, 2359, 2363, 2393, 2394, 2410, 2412, 2437, 2478, 2499, 2504, 2521
	Out:	DMS 1857, 1859, 2247, 2261, 2278, 2312, 2314, 2331, 2376, 2383, 2386, 2395, 2423, 2442, 2443, 2446, 2458, 2463, 2475, 2479, 2512, 2515, 2517, 2525
		D 2538, 2577, 2628
06.82	In:	DMS 2249, 2251, 2282, 2283, 2290, 2300, 2303, 2346, 2348, 2367, 2396, 2428, 2434, 2457, 2472, 2501, 2505, 2508, 2516
	Out:	DMS 2320, 2325, 2330, 2349, 2356, 2400, 2435, 2452, 2460, 2466, 2471, 2481, 2487, 2507, 2514
		D 2611
07.82	In:	DMS 2255, 2259, 2262, 2267, 2274, 2280, 2289, 2293, 2294, 2296, 2302, 2304, 2317, 2318, 2342, 2344, 2358, 2368, 2371, 2374, 2375, 2384, 2397, 2503, 2518
		D 2547, 2593
	Out:	DMS 2252, 2264, 2269, 2272, 2276, 2291, 2292, 2323, 2327, 2332, 2337, 2338, 2345, 2357, 2370, 2379, 2390, 2393, 2402, 2405, 2406, 2409, 2414, 2415, 2425, 2426, 2473, 2476, 2477, 2484, 2485, 2490, 2493, 2497, 2500, 2502, 2504, 2506, 2519
		D 2545
08.82	In:	DMS 2343
	Out:	DMS 2263, 2270, 2288, 2297, 2311, 2363, 2394, 2412, 2437, 2478, 2495
09.82	Out:	DMS 2251, 2265, 2282, 2283, 2290, 2294, 2300, 2303, 2339, 2341, 2346, 2348, 2353, 2359, 2367, 2368, 2396, 2410, 2428, 2457, 2472, 2499, 2501, 2505, 2508, 2516, 2521
10.82	Out:	DMS 2249, 2259, 2280, 2293, 2302, 2304, 2342, 2343, 2344, 2358, 2375, 2434, 2518
		D 2547
11.82	Out:	DMS 2255, 2262, 2267, 2274, 2289, 2296, 2318, 2371, 2374, 2384, 2397, 2503
		D 2593
12.82	Out:	DMS 2317

Appendix 7c: DMSs Overhauled by Contractors, February-June 1985

Midland Red:
DMS 2250, 2277, 2295, 2298, 2401
D 2535, 2537, 2612, 2632, 2636, 2645

British Leyland, Nottingham:
DMS 2258, 2335
D 2562, 2584, 2585

BEL, Aldenham:
DMS 2248, 2253, 2464
D 2583, 2640, 2643

Appendix 7d: DMSs Recertified at Aldenham, 1979

Park Royal
DMS 23, 30, 49, 287, 289, 290, 292, 302-304, 313, 343, 351, 434, 438, 461

Appendix 7e: DMSs Recertified at Aldenham, April 1980-February 1981

Park Royal
DMS 408, 409, 550, 557, 565, 569, 571, 572, 576, 582, 587, 590, 593, 616, 620, 621, 624, 625, 629, 684, 688, 690, 709, 713, 715, 853

MCW
DMS 1424, 1440, 1444, 1454, 1467, 1469, 1476, 1480, 1492, 1495, 1498, 1505-1509, 1518

Appendix 7f: DMSs Recertified at Wandle garages, May 1985-February 1986

DMS 2256, 2268, 2271, 2273, 2279, 2284-2286, 2299, 2301, 2305, 2307-2310, 2313, 2315, 2316, 2319, 2321, 2324, 2329, 2340, 2347, 2364, 2389, 2404, 2421, 2467, 2469, 2483, 2486, 2489, 2496
D 2527, 2529, 2531, 2534, 2539, 2540, 2542, 2546, 2548, 2549, 2552, 2554-2558, 2561, 2563-2566, 2570, 2576, 2579, 2581, 2591, 2595, 2613, 2617, 2621, 2627, 2633-2635, 2637-2639, 2644
(of which Ds 2531, 2561, 2570, 2581 and 2617 done wholly at Clapham and D 2529 subcontracted to ECW)

Appendix 8: DM to D conversions

DM 923, 925, 927, 939, 945, 946, 950, 957-959, 975, 979, 980, 985, 988-991, 997, 999, 1000, 1003, 1005-1008, 1010, 1011, 1013-1015, 1017, 1019-1024, 1027, 1031-1034, 1040, 1046-1050, 1055, 1058, 1062-1064, 1066, 1069, 1071, 1076, 1102, 1105, 1106, 1110, 1111, 1113-1119, 1125, 1129-1135, 1137, 1138, 1140-1144, 1146-1152, 1154-1162, 1164, 1166-1168, 1170-1180, 1182, 1184, 1186-1188, 1190-1192, 1194-1201, 1203-1207, 1209-1234, 1237-1243, 1245, 1247, 1706, 1710, 1725-1730, 1732, 1734, 1738, 1739, 1753, 1770, 1772-1775, 1781, 1783, 1784, 1786, 1787, 1789, 1804, 1805, 1808-1812, 1814-1816, 1819-1831, 2527-2558, 2560-2595, 2597-2629, 2631-2646
Under LT, Ds were formally reclassified DM upon withdrawal.

Summary of DM-to-D conversions

DM 918-1217 (PRV);   146 of 300 (49%)
DM 1218-1247 (MCW);   26 of 30 (87%)
DM 1703-1832 (MCW):   47 of 130 (36%)
DM 2527-2646 (PRV B20): 117 of 120 (97.5%)

Summary: 219 of 460 (48%) standards
            117 of 120 (97.5%) B20s
Total: 336 of 580 (58%) all DMs

Appendix 9: B20 DMSs fitted with Iveco engines, 1987-1989

DMS 2249, 2254-2258, 2260, 2261, 2264, 2265, 2267, 2268, 2270, 2271, 2273, 2275, 2280-2286, 2288-2290, 2293, 2294, 2296, 2300, 2302, 2304, 2307-2312, 2314, 2316, 2319, 2325, 2331-2337, 2340-2343, 2345-2347, 2351, 2353, 2354, 2356, 2358, 2359, 2363, 2364, 2366-2369, 2374-2376, 2379, 2383, 2384, 2386, 2388, 2391, 2394, 2397, 2399, 2400, 2402, 2405, 2406, 2409, 2411, 2413, 2414, 2417, 2418, 2420, 2421, 2423, 2425, 2426, 2428, 2431, 2432, 2434-2436, 2438, 2441, 2444, 2445, 2448, 2450, 2451, 2455, 2456, 2459, 2462, 2465-2467, 2469, 2471, 2473, 2476, 2477, 2479-2481, 2484, 2487, 2489, 2491-2495, 2497, 2500-2502, 2512-2514, 2518, 2519, 2522-2526
D 2528, 2533, 2537, 2538, 2541, 2543, 2546-2548, 2552-2554, 2560, 2562, 2566-2569, 2572, 2582, 2588, 2589, 2591, 2597, 2599, 2602-2610, 2612, 2614-2616, 2620-2622, 2624, 2625, 2629, 2632-2634, 2636, 2637, 2639-2643, 2645, 2646

Total: 201

BIBLIOGRAPHY

Books
The London Bus Review of ... (1973-1992), LOTS 1974-1994
Reshaping London's Buses, Barry Arnold & Mike Harris, Capital Transport 1982.
London Transport Buses, Lawrie Bowles, Capital Transport 1977-1984.
London Bus Handbook, Lawrie Bowles, Capital Transport 1985, 1986.
London Bus Handbook, part 1: London Buses Ltd, Nicholas King, Capital Transport 1987-1996.
London Bus Handbook, part 2: Independents, Nicholas King, Capital Transport 1987-1993.
London Transport Scrapbook for ... (1976-1980), Capital Transport 1977-1981.
The London Bus Diary 1991/92, R. J. Waterhouse, TPC 1992.
The DMS Handbook, James Adlam and Keith Hamer, Capital Transport 1994.
Londoners in Exile: the DMS Worldwide, G. R. Mills and J. Burnett, Roadliner 1984.
A Generation without Wires; part 1 – North-East, Les Stitson, LOTS 1986.
Daimler Fleetline, Gavin Booth, Ian Allan 2010.
London's Night Buses – volume 1 1913-1983, Philip Wallis, Capital Transport 2011.
London's Night Buses – volume 2 1984-2013, Philip Wallis, Capital Transport 2013.
London Buses in the 1960s, Ken Glazier, Capital Transport 1998.
London Transport in the 1970s, Michael H. C. Baker, Ian Allan 2007.
London Transport in the 1980s, Michael H. C. Baker, Ian Allan 2008.
DMS ColourScene 1979-1984, Nigel Eadon-Clarke, DTS 2001.
DMS ColourScene – Hong Kong, Nigel Eadon-Clarke, DTS 2002.
DMS ColourScene volume 3, Nigel Eadon-Clarke, DTS 2004.
London's DMS Dispersal, Keith Jenkinson, Autobus Review Publications 2005. (two volumes)
London's DMS Garage Allocations 1971-1993, Stuart Robbs, Stuart Robbs Publications 2010.

Magazines, Supplements, Articles and Periodicals
The London Bus (TLB), LOTS, monthly
TLB Extra, LOTS, for the years 1970-1984
London Bus Magazine (LBM), LOTS, quarterly, particularly
   'The Good, the Bad and the Dodgy' by Keith Hamer,
      LBM85 (Summer 1993), LBM87 (Winter 1993/94) and LBM149 (Autumn 2009)
BUSES magazine, Ian Allan, monthly
SUP-44A London Bus Disposals – Where are they Now? March 2008, LOTS 2008.
Fleet History LT9; The Vehicles of London Transport and its Predecessors; Modern Classes (RM Class to date), The PSV Circle 2005.

Websites and Groups
Bus Lists on the Web (www.buslistsontheweb.co.uk)
Ian's Bus Stop – DMS (www.countrybus.org/DMS/DMS1.htm)
The Old Bus Garage (www.self-preservation-society.co.uk/jotter/history/other.shtml#dms)
The R. J. Waterhouse Website – DMSs (www.users.globalnet.co.uk/~cign/rjwsite/index/dms.htm)
London Bus Routes by Ian Armstrong (www.londonbuses.co.uk)
Daimler Fleetline Wikipedia entry (http://en.wikipedia.org/wiki/Daimler/Fleetline)